INTERNATIONAL ECONOMIC INSTITUTIONS

To C. v. M.

INTERNATIONAL ECONOMIC INSTITUTIONS

SIXTH EDITION

M.A.G. van MEERHAEGHE

KLUWER ACADEMIC PUBLISHERS

DORDRECHT / BOSTON / LONDON

Distributors

for the United States and Canada: Kluwer Academic Publishers, P.O. Box 358, Accord Station, Hingham 02018-0358, USA
for the UK and Ireland: Kluwer Academic Publishers, MTP Press Limited, Falcon House, Queen Square, Lancaster LA1 1RN, UK
for all other countries: Kluwer Academic Publishers Group, Distribution Center, P.O. Box 332, 3300 AH Dordrecht, The Netherlands

Library of Congress Cataloging-in-Publication Data

Meerhaeghe, Marcel Alfons Gilbert van, 1921–
    [Internationale economische betrekkingen en instellingen.
English]
    International economic institutions / M.A.G. van Meerhaeghe. --
6th rev. ed.
        p.   cm.
    Translation of: Internationale economische betrekkingen en
instellingen.
    Includes bibliographical references and index.
    ISBN 0-7923-1347-X (alk. paper)
    1. International economic relations. 2. International economic
integration. 3. International agencies.   I. Title.
HF1359.M44   1991
337--dc20   91-23616

ISBN 0-7923-1347-X

Book Information

First published 1964 as *Internationale Economische Betrekkingen en Instellingen*. English language edition first published as *International Economic Institutions* by the Longman Group Ltd 1966. Revised impression 1968. Second edition 1971. Extensively revised and enlarged edition published by Martinus Nijhoff Publishers 1980. Fourth edition 1985. Fifth edition 1987. Sixth edition 1992.

printed on acid free paper

Copyright

*In relations among sovereign nations, morality is
an emotion without a cutting edge.*
HARRY G. JOHNSON

Contents

vii

PART 2: EUROPEAN ORGANIZATIONS

CHAPTER 6. BENELUX   207

List of figures

List of tables

From the Preface to the Third Edition

What made me write this book was a feeling that students of international economics needed to fill out their knowledge of the theory with work on the practice of the major international economic organizations, many of which are having a growing influence on the national economies of their members. There was no single volume given over to a concise treatment of these organizations. The annual reports of the international organizations themselves can be consulted, of course, but as a rule these are not noted for being brief and to the point (the items of importance have to be fished out of a sea of useless detail), nor do they go in for criticism of their own activities.

In selecting the organizations to be dealt with in the book I was guided by the influence they exert. I have left out those whose activities consist mainly in the drafting of recommendations to which, however meritorious they may be, little or no attention is paid. Some of them are included in the Introduction, which provides a summary of a number of institutions not discussed separately in the body of the work. There are, however, two exceptions: the Organization for Economic Cooperation and Development (OECD) as the organization replacing the Organization for European Economic Cooperation (OEEC), and the United Nations Conference on Trade and Development (UNCTAD) whose meetings have succeeded in drawing much attention of the press.

Part 1 covers the international organizations in the strict sense — the International Monetary Fund, the International Bank for Reconstruction and Development, the General Agreement on Tariffs and Trade, the commodity agreements and UNCTAD. Part 2 describes the European organizations (since it is only in Europe that regional groupings have achieved anything significant), with Benelux and the Organization for European Economic Cooperation (and the Organization for Economic Cooperation and Development) coming first, chiefly because of their historical importance: the emergence of organizations such as the Council for Mutual Economic Assistance (Comecon), the European Economic Community and the European Free Trade Association would be less than clear otherwise.

Preface

The text has again been brought up to date and extensively revised, especially the EC chapter. The chapter on the OECD has been transferred to Part One. The brought-up-to-date chapter on the CMEA has been maintained, but at the time of writing its abolition was still not decided. A new treaty on central and eastern European cooperation was not yet approved.

My thanks are due to the persons listed below, who were kind enough to comment on the draft of certain chapters of part of chapters: my former students Mr Marc Quintyn of the International Monetary Fund and Luc Everaert of the World Bank, who — in addition — prepared information needed to bring the chapters concerned up to date, Dr Horst Bockelmann, economic adviser of the Bank for International Settlements. Mr J. Schotte of the Benelux secretariat, Mr Lars Erik P. Nordgaard of the EFTA Brussels Office. Of course, this does not necessarily imply that they share the conclusions of the chapters involved. Numerous international and national civil servants and libraries kindly answered my questions. I want to thank especially Mr Jozef van den Broeck, head Information Office Belgium of the Commission of the European Communities, and Mr A. Carchon, conseiller d'Ambassade Belgium and the library of the Belgian central bank.

I am very grateful to my wife, who has helped me at every stage of the preparation of this edition. She also undertook the compilation of the list of articles and the indexes.

M.A.G. v. M.

Preface

Abbreviations

ACM	Arab Common Market
ACP	African, Caribbean and Pacific (countries)
AfDB	African Development Bank
ALADI	*Asociación Latinoamericana de Integración*
ALALC	*Asociación Latinoamericana de Libre Comercio*
AsDB	Asian Development Bank
ASEAN	Association of South-East Asian Nations
BENELUX	Belgium-Netherlands-Luxemburg Economic Union
BIS	Bank for International Settlements
BLEU	Belgium-Luxemburg Economic Union
BRITE	Basic Research in Industrial Technologies for Europe
CABEI	Central American Bank for Economic Integration
CARICOM	Caribbean Community
CARIFTA	Caribbean Free Trade Association
CEAO	*Communauté Economique de l'Afrique Occidentale*
CGIAR	Consultative Group on International Agricultural Research
CMEA	Council for Mutual Economic Assistance
COCOM	Coordinating Committee of the Consultative Group
COMECON	see CMEA
DAC	Development Assistance Committee
EAEC	European Atomic Energy Community
EAGGF	European Agricultural Guidance and Guarantee Fund
EC	Economic Communities
ECA	Economic Commission for Africa
ECAFE	Economic Commission for Asia and the Far East
ECE	Economic Commission for Europe
ECLAC	Economic Commission for Latin America and the Caribbean
ECOSOC	Economic and Social Council

ECOWAS	Economic Community of the West-African States
ECSC	European Coal and Steel Community
ECU	European Currency Unit
ESCWA	Economic and Social Commission for Western Asia
EEA	European Economic Area
EEC	European Economic Community
EFTA	European Free Trade Association
EIB	European Investment Bank
EMA	European Monetary Agreement
EMCF	European Monetary Cooperation Fund
EMUA	European Monetary Unit of Account
ENEA	European Nuclear Energy Agency
EPA	European Productivity Agency
EPTA	Expanded Programme of Technical Assistance
EPU	European Payments Union
ESCAP	Economic and Social Commission for Asia and the Pacific
ESPRIT	European Strategic Programme for Research and Development in Information Technologies
EUA	European Unit of Account
Euratom	European Atomic Energy Community
FAO	Food and Agriculture Organization
GAB	General Arrangements to Borrow
GATT	General Agreement on Tariffs and Trade
GDP	Gross Domestic Product
GNP	Gross National Product
GSP	Generalized System of Preferences
IAEA	International Atomic Energy Agency
IBEC	International Bank for Economic Cooperation
IBRD	International Bank for Reconstruction and Development
ICAO	International Civil Aviation Organization
ICSID	International Centre for the Settlement of Investment Disputes
IDA	International Development Association
IDB	Inter-American Development Bank
IEA	International Energy Agency
IFC	International Finance Corporation
IIB	International Investment Bank
ILO	International Labour Organization
IMCO	Inter-Governmental Maritime Consultative Organization
IMF	International Monetary Fund
ITO	International Trade Organization
ITU	International Telecommunication Union

LAFTA	Latin American Free-Trade Association
LAIA	Latin American Integration Association
MCA	Monetary Compensatory Amount
MCCA	*Mercado Común Centroamericano*
MIGA	Multilateral Investment Guarantee Agency
MRU	Mano River Union
NATO	North Atlantic Treaty Organization
NEA	Nuclear Energy Agency
OECD	Organization for Economic Cooperation and Development
OECS	Organization of Eastern Caribbean States
OEEC	Organization for European Economic Cooperation
OPEC	Oil Producing and Exporting Countries
RACE	Research and Development in Advanced Communication Technologies for Europe
SDR	Special Drawing Right
SELA	Latin American Economic System (*Sistema Económica Latinoamericana*
SPRINT	Strategic Programme for Innovation and Technology Transfers
UDEAC	*Union Douanière et Economique de l'Afrique Centrale*
UDEAO	*Union Douanière des Etats de l'Afrique Occidentale*
UN	United Nations
UNCDF	United Nations Capital Development Fund
UNCTAD	United Nations Conference on Trade and Development
UNDP	United Nations Development Programme
UNESCO	United Nations Educational, Scientific and Cultural Organization
UNESOB	United Nations Economic and Social Office in Beirut
UNIDO	United Nations Industrial Development Organization
UNSF	United Nations Special Fund
UPU	Universal Postal Union
VAT	Value Added Tax
WHO	World Health Organization
WIPO	World Intellectual Property Organization
WMO	World Meteorological Organization

Introduction

Der Worte sind genug gewechselt, lasst mich auch endlich Taten sehn.

J. W. GOETHE

Since the International Monetary Fund (IMF) and the International Bank for Reconstruction and Development (IBRD), which are analysed in Part 1, are specialized agencies linked by special agreements with the United Nations, a few words about the UN and two of the other specialized agencies, the Food and Agriculture Organization and the International Labour Organization, are called for. This is followed by a short account of the Bank for International Settlements, which is also referred to in connection with the IMF and the IBRD. The rest of this introduction is devoted to some non-European attempts at economic integration (which have not yet been very successful) and to the regional development banks.

1. THE UNITED NATIONS (UN)

The United Nations comprises 159 countries (December 1990) which have accepted the Charter of the United Nations, which was signed at San Francisco on 26 June 1945 by fifty-one states and came into force on 24 October 1945. The aims of the organization include the maintenance of peace and security, the promotion of better standards of living and the encouragement of economic and social progress for all nations by means of international cooperation.

The principal organs of the UN are:

The General Assembly
The Security Council
The Economic and Social Council (ECOSOC)
The Trusteeship Council
The International Court of Justice
The Secretariat.

1

The General Assembly meets each year from September till December, and special sessions may also be convened. It is entitled to make recommendations on all matters relating to the United Nations Charter and to deliberate on the powers and functions of the other organs, which submit regular reports to it. The members of ECOSOC are elected by the General Assembly.

The Secretariat is headed by a secretary-general, this post having been held successively by T. Lie (Norway, 1946—52), D. Hammarskjöld (Sweden, 1953—61), U Thant (Burma, 1961—71), K. Waldheim (Austria, 1972—81) and J. Perez de Cuellar (Peru, 1981—). Its departments include one for economic and social affairs.

A. *The Economic and Social Council (ECOSOC)*

ECOSOC drafts studies and reports on, and makes the preparations for the sessions of the General Assembly in respect of, international economic and social problems. If need be, it calls international conferences, gives advice and assistance to the Security Council and, with the consent of the General Assembly, provides services for the member states.

The Council consists of fifty-four members, eighteen of whom are elected annually for a period of three years by the General Assembly. It meets as often as necessary, usually twice a year (once in New York and once in Geneva). Decisions are taken by a simple majority, each member having one vote. The Council is mainly a central policy-making and coordinating organ. The Council coordinates the activities of the specialized agencies and negotiates the agreements defining their relations with the UN.

In addition to the functional commissions — on statistics, population, social and similar matters — five regional economic commissions have been set up within the framework of ECOSOC.

1. The Economic Commission for Europe (ECE), with headquarters in Geneva, was set up in 1947. ECE, unlike many European organizations, also numbers the Eastern European countries among its members, although they withheld cooperation from 1949 until 1953. It thus constitutes a forum for discussion of East—West economic problems.
2. The Economic Commission for Asia and the Far East (ECAFE), whose headquarters are in Bangkok, was also established in 1947. As a result of a reorganization in 1974, the ESCAP (Economic and Social Commission for Asia and the Pacific) replaced ECAFE.
3. The Economic Commission for Latin America and the Caribbean (ECLAC) with its headquarters in Santiago (Chile), was set up in 1948.
4. The Economic Commission for Africa (ECA), with its headquarters in Addis Ababa, was established in 1958.
5. The Economic Commission for Western Asia (ECWA), with headquarters in Beirut (Lebanon), was set up in 1973 to provide a wider scope of

facilities for those countries previously served by the UN Economic and Social Office in Beirut (UNESOB). In 1985 the name of the Commission was changed into the Economic and Social Commission for Western Asia (ESCWA) with headquarters in Baghdad (Iraq).

B. *Development Assistance*

1. *The United Nations Development Programme (UNDP)*

A programme of technical assistance to the less-developed countries was launched in 1948 and the Expanded Programme of Technical Assistance (EPTA) in 1949. A proposal was advanced in 1952 to set up a Special United Nations Fund for Economic Development. This eventually resulted in a General Assembly resolution in 1958 to establish a United Nations Special Fund (UNSF) with effect from 1 January 1959; its object is to help less-developed especially the least developed countries to utilize large-scale capital resources more effectively by supplying technical surveys and manpower assistance. It was not set up in order to provide capital.

On 22 November 1965 EPTA and UNSF, which had made available about 2 billions dollars' worth of aid, were amalgamated to form the United Nations Development Programme; each of them retained its special characteristics.

2. *The United Nations Capital Development Fund (UNCDF)*

In December 1966 the United Nations Capital Development Fund was set up to assist less-developed countries by providing grants and long-term loans at very low interest. Since it began its operations its resources amounted to 414 million dollars. As its functions overlap those of IDA, the developed countries are not willing to make available significant resources.

2. THE SPECIALIZED AGENCIES

The specialized agencies, which are linked to the UN by special agreements laying down cooperation procedures, include the International Labour Organization, the Food and Agriculture Organization, the United Nations Educational, Scientific and Cultural Organization (UNESCO, 4 November 1946), the International Civil Aviation Organization (ICAO, 4 April 1947), the International Bank of Reconstruction and Development, the International Monetary Fund, the International Telecommunication Union (ITU, 17 May 1865), the Universal Postal Union (UPU, 1 July 1875; a new constitution came into force on 1 January 1990), the World Health Organization (WHO, 7 April 1948), the International Finance Corporation, the International

Development Association, the World Meteorological Organization (WMO, 23 March 1950), the International Maritime Organization (IMO, 22 May 1982; formerly the Inter-Governmental Maritime Consultative Organization IMCO, 17 March 1958), the World Intellectual Property Organization (WIPO, 17 December 1974) and the United Nations Industrial Development Organization (UNIDO). ECOSOC is responsible for coordinating their activities. The International Atomic Energy Agency (IAEA), set up in 1957 under the auspices of the United Nations in order to encourage peaceful uses of atomic energy (*inter alia* by promoting the exchange of scientific and technical information, in particular in favour of the less-developed countries), is not a specialized agency.

Since the IMF and the IBRD, as well as the IFC and the IDA, are dealt with in Chapters 1 and 2, a brief word will now be said about the better-known of the other specialized agencies, the FAO, the ILO and the UNIDO.

A.   *The Food and Agriculture Organization (FAO)*

The FAO was established in Quebec on 16 October 1945. Its headquarters, which had initially been in Washington, were transferred to Rome in 1951. Regional offices operate at Accra, Bangkok, Santiago (Chile) and Washington D.C. There are also offices in Geneva (in cooperation with ECE) and in Vienna (jointly with IAEA).

With a view to improving the production and distribution of agricultural commodities and food, the Organization was entrusted with the task of collecting and studying the appropriate facts and figures and of promoting better credit facilities, international commodity agreements and technical assistance. The FAO's activities have been concentrated on the last-named field. The Organization combats malnutrition and hunger, and coordinates programmes on every aspect of food and agriculture, including forestry and fisheries.

The World Food Programme (1963) is a joint effort by the UN and the FAO to use supplies of food as an instrument of economic and social development and also for relief purposes. A World Food Council established as a result of the World Food Conference of 1974, is an organ of the United Nations.

A General Conference determines the FAO's policy, approves the budget (569 million dollars for 1991) and elects the director-general. A Council, in which forty-nine countries are represented, acts as an interim governing body. The director-general heads a staff of approximately 8 000 (including the staff engaged in field projects).

B. *The International Labour Organization (ILO)*

The ILO was founded as far back as 1919, with its headquarters in Geneva. In 1946 it became a specialized agency of the United Nations. Its objectives are vague and general. Neither it nor the FAO has the power to do more than make recommendations. A peculiar feature of the ILO is that the national delegations include, in addition to two government representatives, one employers' and one workers' delegate. The tripartite representation has been breaking down since the war, however: in many new states the social structure does not permit representation along these lines.

The ILO's supreme deliberative body, the International Labour Conference, elects the Governing Body of the organization, i.e., the Executive Council which is also composed of government, employers' and workers' members. The International Labour Office is the organization's secretariat; its staff of over 3 000 is headed by M. Hansenne (Belgium). The budget for 90—91 amounts to 330 million dollars.

Since 1975, the Council has consisted of 56 members, elected for a three-year term. Of these, 14 represent the employers, 14 represent the workers and 28 represent governments.

The ILO's activities consist chiefly in the collection, study and publication of statistical and other material concerning labour questions, the drafting of international social legislation and the provision of technical assistance.

In the field of integration of social legislation, only meagre results have been achieved. Owing to the divergent economic and social structures of the member states, few of them have ratified the conventions adopted by the International Labour Conference. ILO technical assistance, however, is appreciated by the less-developed countries.

In 1961 an International Institute of Labour Studies was founded in Geneva and in 1965 an International Centre for Advanced Technical and Vocational Training was established in Turin.

The ILO tries to bring employment considerations to the fore in the activities of all agencies within the UN-system, and for this purpose launched the World Employment Programme. The aim of the programme is to assist decision-makers in less-developed countries in identifying and putting into effect specific employment-promoting policies.

C. *The United Nations Industrial Development Organization (UNIDO)*

In December 1965 the General Assembly adopted a resolution calling for the establishment of a United Nations Organization for Industrial Development (UNOID). A further resolution in November 1966 formally created the renamed United Nations Industrial Development Organization to promote the industrialization of the less-developed countries. In 1965 it took over the activity of the Centre for Industrial Development, which had been set up in

1961 within the Secretariat's Department of Economic and Social Affairs to coordinate the industrial development activities of the various UN bodies and agencies. UNIDO whose headquarters are in Vienna is governed by the Industrial Development Board, which consists of 53 members elected by the General Assembly. UNIDO became a specialized agency in 1986.

One of the many proposals put forward by the Secretariat at UNIDO III (1980) relates to a global fund for the stimulation of industry within the framework of a massive transfer of resources. The developed countries rejected the proposals. UNIDO IV (1984) recommended more industrial cooperation among less-developed countries.

The regular budget totals 157 million dollars for the biennium 1990-91 (administrative and research activities). In 1989 UNIDO's technical assistance amounted to 134 million dollars.

3. THE BANK FOR INTERNATIONAL SETTLEMENTS (BIS)

The Bank for International Settlements was established in Basle in 1930 pursuant to an international Convention between Switzerland and the governments of Belgium, France, Germany, the United Kingdom and Italy. The Convention was signed following the negotiations on the problem of reparations owed by Germany after World War I and the adoption of the Young Plan at The Hague Conference on 20 January 1930. The Bank began operations on 17 May 1930. It played no role in the discussions leading to the Bretton Woods agreements.

The objectives of the Bank, as stated in Article 3 of its Statutes, are to promote cooperation between central banks, to provide additional facilities for international financial operations, and to act as Trustee or Agent in regard to international financial settlements which are entrusted to it under the agreements concluded with the parties concerned. In addition to its extensive trusteeship and agency functions, which started with the execution of the Young Plan and are described below, the first two of these spheres of activity have become increasingly important, particularly since World War II.

At present the central banks of all European countries (except the USSR and Albania) and of Canada, Japan, South Africa and Australia are members of the Bank.

When the Bank's initial capital was issued, the subscribing central banks and financial institutions were given the option of subscribing for the shares of their respective national issues themselves or arranging for their subscription in their own countries. As a result, part of the Belgian and French issues and the whole of the United States issue are not held by the central banks to which they were originally allocated (some 16 per cent of the issued share capital is held by private shareholders). While all shares carry equal rights with respect to the annual dividend, the private shareholders have no right of voting or representation at the general meeting, since the latter rights are reserved, by the Bank's Statutes, for the central banks of the countries concerned.

The authorized capital of the Bank is 1 500 million gold francs (roughly 2 912 million dollars) divided into 600 000 shares of 2 500 gold francs each; 473 125 shares in issue, all paid up to the extent of one-quarter of their nominal value (625 gold francs). The founder central banks of Belgium, France, Germany, Italy and the United Kingdom have always held a majority of the votes, and the Statutes of the Bank permit these banks, together with the monetary authorities of the United States, to subscribe up to 55 per cent of any further issue of shares. All the unissued shares may be subscribed or acquired only by central banks, and in extending invitations to subscribe for these shares the Statutes of the Bank require the Board to give consideration to the desirability of associating with the Bank the largest possible number of central banks that make a substantial contribution to international monetary cooperation and to the Bank's activities.

Apart from the general meeting, the organs of the BIS are a Board of Directors (which meets not less than ten times a year) and the management (consisting of the President of the Bank, the general manager and the managers). The functions of Chairman of the Board and President of the Bank are currently exercised by one person, B. Dennis (Sweden). The general manager heads a staff of about 400.

The BIS carries out a wide range of banking operations, which derive mainly from its ability to assist central banks in managing and investing some of their monetary reserves. Presently some eighty central banks have deposits with the BIS.

The BIS received deposits in gold and currencies (38 673 million gold francs on 31 March 1990) of which approximately 97 per cent comes from central banks. About 80 per cent of the deposits are under three-months deposits. These time deposits and the Bank's own resources are used to make short-term investments, e.g., by buying Treasury bills, and to grant credits to central banks.

The deposits of central banks are generally made on the prevailing market terms. Moreover, like all BIS operations, they must be in conformity with the monetary policy of the central banks of the countries concerned.

In its gold and currency operations, the BIS avoids speculative positions. All operations are offset by corresponding spot or forward transactions. Some operations may not be undertaken by the Bank, e.g., the issue of bank notes, the making of advances to governments, the acquisition of a predominant interest in any business concern and the acceptance of bills of exchange.

The BIS played an important role in working out the Basle Agreements of 1961 on cooperation on foreign-exchange markets and is one of the participants in the network of swap arrangements between the US authorities and other central banks. (A swap is a spot sale offset by a forward purchase.)

After an agreement of the G 10 governors in December 1974 a Basle Committee on Banking Supervision was set up, the secretariat of which is provided by the Bank. The Committee discusses the problems concerned, coordinates the sharing of supervisionary responsibilities among national authorities and seeks to enhance standards of supervision, notably in relation to solvency.

Apart from its banking activities the BIS serves as a central bankers' club. Information is exchanged on the international monetary situation, at the meetings of the Board and at other informal meetings. The monetary authorities of the United States, Canada and Japan, though not represented on the Board, regularly take part in these informal meetings. Subjects discussed include the trend of the gold, foreign exchange and eurocurrency markets and international debt problems. The growth of the eurocurrency market has given rise to regular consultation between central banks, since this market is to a large extent outside their control.

The Bank participates as an observer in the meetings of the Interim Committee of the IMF, which studies the reform of the international monetary system. On 21 January 1974 the IMF allowed the BIS to accept, hold and use SDR.

The BIS acts as Secretariat to the Committee of the Governors of the central banks of the member states of the EEC, as well as to its sub-committees and groups of experts (e.g., Committee of Deputy Governors of the central banks, study group for the technical problems raised by monetary integration).

With regard to its functions as agent or trustee, the Bank was appointed the agent of the governments concerned with reparations under the Young Plan of 1930. These functions ceased many years ago, but the Bank remains the trustee of the 1924 Dawes Loan and of the 1930 Young Loan. It is also trustee for the assented bonds of the 1930 Austrian Government International Loan. Between 1948 and 1958, intra-European payments in the OEEC were carried out through the intermediary of the BIS. The BIS is also the depositary in connection with certain ECSC loans granted between 1954 and 1961. Since 1958 the Bank has been the agent for the OECD in respect of the European Monetary Agreement terminated on 31 December 1972. The BIS is now the OECD's agent in the application of the exchange guarantee agreement concluded by 18 European central banks on 1 January 1973. Since 1 June 1973 the Bank has been the agent of the European Monetary Cooperation Fund, set up on 6 April 1973 by the member states of the EEC. Since 1 October 1986 the BIS acts as the clearing agent for the association of commercial banks formed in relation to the private ECU clearing system.

Finally, it collects and centralizes statistical information on monetary reserves for the Group of Ten (see Chapter 1) and Switzerland. Its studies on the eurodollar market, published in the Bank's *Annual Report*, are authoritative.

4. REGIONAL INTEGRATION

A. *Latin America*

1. *The Asociación Latinoamericana de Integración (ALADI)*

Though several proposals for regional cooperation between the Latin American countries had already been made in the early 1950s, it was not until the Economic Conference of the Organization of American States was held in Buenos Aires in August-September 1957 that the first governmental discussions took place. On 18 February 1960, the Montevideo Treaty establishing the Asociación Latinoamericana de Libre Comercio (ALALC), or Latin American Free-Trade Association (LAFTA), was signed by Argentina, Brazil, Chile, Mexico, Paraguay, Peru and Uruguay. The Treaty came into effect on 2 June 1961. Colombia and Ecuador became members in 1961, Venezuela in 1966 and Bolivia in 1967. An agreement on multilateral clearing was signed in Mexico City in September 1965. In 1969 the LAFTA countries and the Dominican Republic signed a multilateral credit agreement (the Agreement of Santo Domingo); its facilities were extended in September 1981.

The LAFTA Treaty provided for the gradual removal of restrictions on trade flows between member countries over a period not to exceed twelve years.

Actually, trade liberalization came to an end in the mid-sixties; in 1967 it proved impossible to agree on a list of products in order to liberalize a second 25 per cent of trade between members: some states were, for example, opposed to the inclusion of wheat and petroleum, which they thought would favour Argentina and Venezuela respectively. Governments had to take into account the opposition of domestic producers to major tariff reductions on competing imports.

More progress has been made in the field of industrial complementary agreements, more than twenty of which have been concluded. These agreements involve specialization in particular products and are designed to facilitate the reduction of duties and the establishment of a common external tariff.

The Water Transport Agreement of 30 September 1966 came into force in May 1974. It reserves the right to transport general cargo and refrigerated cargo in trade between the member states to the national vessels of these states. Bulk transport of petroleum and its derivatives is excluded from the agreement.

The absence of progress in the field of trade is mainly due to the wide differences in levels of prosperity. It was recognized from the outset that a special dispensation was needed for the poorest of the member countries (Paraguay, Ecuador). Subsequently, however, other countries — Chile, Colombia, Peru and Uruguay — began to fear the growing competition from the industrially more advanced LAFTA countries — Argentina, Brazil and Mexico. In fact, it has been alleged that LAFTA is "an exercise in Mexican imperialism".

In March 1981 the LAFTA was replaced by the Asociación Latinoamericana de Integración (ALADI) or the Latin American Integration Association (LAIA) whose short-term objective is the establishment of an economic preference area. The long-term aim is the establishment of a Latin American common market. On 4 May 1983 already Brazil announced its withdrawal and its intention to rely in the future on bilateral trade agreements.

In 1987 Argentina and Brazil concluded an integration agreement. It was extended to Chile and Uruguay in 1990. The four countries agreed to establish a common market from 1995. Membership is open to other ALADI countries.

A manifestation of the centrifugal forces at work is the Andean Group Agreement (the Cartagena agreement), concluded on 26 May 1969 by the five Andean countries (Bolivia, Chile, Ecuador, Colombia, Peru). It aims at making this group a more powerful partner *vis-à-vis* the larger countries in LAFTA. Venezuela joined the Group in 1973 but Chile left in 1976.

Trade liberalization and the introduction of a common external tariff for numerous industrial products are tied to agreements allocating industries by country. By the end of 1981 such agreements had been concluded only for the metalworking, automobile and petrochemical industries but have so far only been implemented partly.

2. *The Mercado Común Centroamericano (MCCA)*

A Central American Economic Cooperation Committee was set up as a subsidiary of ECLA in 1952. As a result of its efforts a Multilateral Treaty of Free Trade and Central American Economic Integration was concluded between Costa Rica, El Salvador, Guatemala, Honduras and Nicaragua at Tegucigalpa on 10 June 1958.

The 1958 treaty was superseded by a broader General Treaty on Central American Economic Integration signed in Managua on 13 December 1960 by El Salvador, Guatemala, Honduras and Nicaragua, together with an Agreement establishing the Central American Bank for Economic Integration (CABEI). Costa Rica joined on 23 September 1963. The Treaty aimed at creating a customs union.

The Central American Central Banks System (SBCC) was created on 25 February 1964. It is responsible for coordinating the monetary policies of the member countries and laying the foundations of a Central American Monetary Union.

By mid-1969 the Central American Common Market (MCCA) provided for by the Managua Treaty had become a reality. At that time, tariff duties on 95 per cent of the tariff items applicable to intrazonal trade had been abolished. A common external tariff covered about 97 per cent tariff items. The Secretariat of the MCCA is in Guatemala City.

As a result of the conflict between El Salvador and Honduras, trade between these two countries has been discontinued from July 1969 till October 1980. Honduras withdrew from the MCCA in January 1971.

Some member countries fear that industrial growth may result in industrial concentration in the two more advanced countries (Guatemala and El Salvador), especially as foreign capital — the inflow of which has increased considerably since the establishment of the MCCA — is in most cases employed to buy out existing firms. Coordination of agricultural development programmes has proved to be impossible.

The MCCA collapsed in the eighties. Several initiatives have been taken to establish a free-trade association (the last one in August 1990 to establish an association in 1992.)

3. *The Caribbean Community (CARICOM)*

In 1958 a Federation of the West Indies was established, comprising ten island territories in the Caribbean which at that time were all under British sovereignty. In 1962 the federation came to an end — mainly because of the unwillingness of the larger islands (Jamaica, and Trinidad and Tobago, who became independent members of the Commonwealth) to give financial support to the smaller and more backward islands and to free the movement of labour within the area.

On 15 December 1965 an agreement setting up the Caribbean Free Trade Association (CARIFTA) was signed by Antigua, Barbados and British Guiana (the latter gaining independence as Guyana in 1966). It provided for a limited trade liberalization scheme and was originally intended to come into force on 1 September 1966. However, Guiana did not ratify the agreement until 30 December 1966, and in October 1967 negotiations started with a view to enlarging CARIFTA and its establishment on May 1 1968. A new agreement was signed by Antigua, Barbados, Guyana and Trinidad and Tobago on 30 April 1968; Dominica, Grenada, St. Kitts-Nevis with Anguilla, St. Lucia and St. Vincent signed on 1 July, Jamaica and Montserrat a month later, Belize in May 1971.

With a view to converting CARIFTA into a customs union the Treaty of Chaguaramas establishing the Caribbean Community (CARICOM) was signed on 4 July 1973. It came into force on 1 August 1973 for Barbados, Guyana, Jamaica and Trinidad and Tobago and on 1 May 1974 for the six less-developed members (Grenada, Dominica, St. Vincent and St. Lucia, Belize and Montserrat, the two latter having the status of colonies). Antigua and St. Kitts-Nevis with Anguilla joined in 1974; the Bahamas in 1983.

Trade in products originating in the community had immediately to be liberalized, with the exception of the products included in the Reserve List.

Quantitative restrictions and other non-tariff barriers had to be eliminated. A common external tariff would enter into force on 1 August 1973, but in August 1990 the same decision was taken: now the common tariff would be implemented as from 1 January 1991 (only for the larger members).

A Caribbean Development Bank (Caribank) came into operation on 26 January 1970 and a Caribbean Investment Corporation on 28 August 1973 in order to promote industrial development.

Although attempts of the Eastern Caribbean countries (Antigua, Dominica, Grenada, Montserrat, St. Kitts-Nevis with Anguilla, St. Lucia, St. Vincent) at closer cooperation and even at political unity date back to 1962, it was only on 11 July 1968 that the Agreement establishing the East Caribbean Common Market was signed. In 1972 agreement was reached on the common external tariff and in 1981 the Organization of Eastern Caribbean States (OECS) was established.

4. *The Latin American Economic System (SELA)*

Whereas membership of the ECLA and the IDB is not exclusively Latin American, the Latin American Economic System consists of Latin American States only. The agreement was signed on 18 October 1975 and entered into force on 16 June 1976. SELA has been set up as a permanent advisory organ for cooperation and for coordination of the positions of the member states in international organizations and in their relations with other states and with groups of states. It is also responsible for promoting "the integral, self-sustaining and independent development of the region". In order to attain these objectives, SELA will, for example, create Latin American multinational enterprises and encourage the processing of raw materials in the region. The Latin American Council, in which each member country has one representative, is the supreme organ. In addition, there are action committees and the Permanent Secretariat, which has its headquarters in Caracas.

B. *Asia*

The Association of South-East Asian Nations (ASEAN)

A declaration setting out the aims of ASEAN, which provides for a fairly limited degree of economic cooperation, was signed by Indonesia, Malaysia, the Philippines, Singapore and Thailand on 8 August 1967. Its main objective was to resist Vietnamese aggression. A Permanent Secretariat has been set up in Djakarta. Papua New Guinea was granted an observer status in 1981. Brunei became the sixth member state on 1 January 1984.

On 27 November 1975 the ASEAN countries decided to lower gradually their mutual trade restrictions, the target being the establishement of a free trade area. On 24 February 1976 the Treaty of Amity and Concord in South-East Asia was concluded. It provides *inter alia* for preferential supply of basic commodities in the event of a shortage, reduction in mutual tariffs and certain common industrial projects (with preferential tariffs). The different levels of protection of the member states give rise to difficulties (Indonesia has the highest tariff, while Singapore has practically no trade barriers).

On 18 January 1977 the Philippines and Singapore decided to decrease tariffs on all products in their mutual trade by 10 per cent. On 23 February 1977 a similar agreement was signed by all the member countries. This Preferential Trade Agreement went into effect on 1 January 1978. The initial tariff cut was later raised to 25 and 50 per cent. In 1988 the number of preferences exceeded 14 000 items, but they account for less than 5 per cent of intra-ASEAN trade.

So far industrial cooperation did not prove a success. Mainly on the initiative of the private ASEAN Automotive Federation, a Complementation Scheme for the automobile industry has been adopted in 1981 which assigns the production of each motor vehicle part to one member country only.

C. *Africa and the Middle East*

1. *The West African Economic Community (CEAO)*

In June 1959 seven independent states — Dahomey, Ivory Coast, Mali, Mauritania, Niger, Senegal and Upper Volta (later renamed Burkina Faso) — in what had been French West Africa concluded a customs union in order to preserve the economic relations which existed prior to independence. Disagreements soon arose, however, and the treaty was in fact only implemented between Senegal and Mauritania.

A new convention establishing a Customs Union of the West African States (*Union Douanière des Etats de l'Afrique Occidentale* — UDEAO) was signed in March 1966 and became operative in December 1966; this too, however, was not implemented.

In May 1973 a treaty establishing the West African Economic Community (*Communauté Economique de l'Afrique Occidentale* — CEAO) was signed by the Ivory Coast, Mali, Mauritania, Niger, Senegal and Upper Volta. It came into effect on January 1974. The CEAO established a Community Development Fund on 1 January 1976. Benin and Togo assist as observers. The headquarters are at Ouagadougou (Burkina Faso).

2. *The Mano River Union (MRU)*

On 3 October 1973 Liberia and Sierra Leone signed the Mano River Declaration, which provided for the establishment of a customs union, to be introduced on 1 January 1977. Balance-of-payments difficulties in Sierra Leone caused postponement of the scheme. The liberalization programme finally entered into force on 1 May 1981. Guinea joined in 1980. The headquarters are at Freetown (Sierra Leone).

3. *The Economic Community of the West African States (ECOWAS)*

The treaty establishing the Economic Community of the West African States was signed on 28 May 1975 by the Mano River and CEAO countries and by Benin, Gambia, Ghana, Guinea, Guinea-Bissau, Nigeria and Togo. Cape Verde became a member of the Community shortly afterwards. Membership of ECOWAS does not preclude participation in organizations of a more limited geographical scope. ECOWAS aimed at establishing a customs union within a period of 15 years from the entry into force of the agreement, but only in June 1989 it decided to remove non-tariff barriers to intra-community trade over a four-year period. In addition, tariffs on 25 industrial products will be gradually phased out (the speed varying according to the level of industrialization of member countries). The headquarters are at Lagos.

4. *The Central African Customs and Economic Union (UDEAC)*

In June 1959 an Equatorial Customs Union (*Union Douanière Equatoriale* — UDE) was established between four territories of the Federation of French Equatorial Africa which were to become independent a year later (Congo, Gabon, the Central African Republic and Chad). Cameroon joined the UDE as an associate member in June 1961.

In 1964 the member countries decided to broaden the scope of cooperation between them in the fields of infrastructure and industrialization. On 8 December 1964 they signed a treaty creating the Central African Customs and Economic Union (*Union Douanière de l'Afrique Centrale* — UDEAC), which came into force on 1 January 1966. This treaty provides for the unification of investment codes and maintains the uniform tax arrangements and the Solidarity Fund introduced by the UDE treaty. So far integration projects have not made much progress.

Under the single-tax system, exporting countries levy a production tax on exports to the regional market; it is generally lower than the import duty on the same products. Importing member countries do not levy any tax or duty on such imports but receive a proportion of the proceeds of the single tax from the exporting country. This procedure compensates importing countries for the loss of customs revenue on imports from other member countries.

However, the two landlocked member countries, the Central African Republic and Chad, soon became dissatisfied with the distribution of benefits in the Union, since new industrial projects were located in the other partner countries. Their withdrawal from UDEAC came into effect on 1 January 1969. Meanwhile, on 2 April 1968, they had signed an agreement with Zaïre setting up a United States of Central Africa, subsequently renamed the Union of Central African States, for the purpose of gradually establishing a common market. By December 1968, however, the Central African Republic had already decided to leave the Union of Central African States and to rejoin UDEAC.

In 1983 an Economic Community of Central African States (*Communauté Economique des Etats de l'Afrique Centrale* — CEEAC) was established, but so far without results.

5. *Arab Economic Cooperation*

Since the creation of the League of Arab States in 1945, several attempts have been made to establish an Arab Common Market. Finally, on 6 June 1962, an Agreement for Economic Unity between the Arab League States was signed; it became effective in 1964 when Iraq, Jordan, Kuwait, Syria and the United Arab Republic ratified it. On 13 August 1964 these countries also signed an agreement to establish an Arab Common Market as from 1 January 1965, but Kuwait's National Assembly voted against implementation of the agreement in July 1965. In 1977 Libya joined the ACM. Egypt's membership was suspended. Mauritania became member of the Common Market in 1980.

Arab unity dreams disappeared with president Gamal Nasser. At the end of the eighties regional groupings were set up. In February 1989 five North African countries established the Arab Maghreb Union (AMU), but so far, little has been achieved. At the same time four other Arab countries (Egypt, Iraq, Jordan, North Yemen) created an Arab Cooperation Council, with headquarters in Baghdad.

5. REGIONAL DEVELOPMENT BANKS

Although there are a large number of regional development banks, we shall only deal with the three largest: Inter-American Development Bank, the Asian Development Bank and the African Development Bank, which cover nearly the whole of America, Asia and Africa; many developed countries participate in the activities of these banks. Among the other important development banks are the Caribbean Development Bank and the Arab Fund for Economic and Social Development.

A. *The Inter-American Development Bank (IDB)*

The proposals for the establishment of a regional development bank put forward by a number of Latin American countries after World War II failed at first to receive the support of the United States, which feared duplication of existing institutions such as the IBRD. Finally, the United States promised to become a member of the Inter-American Development Bank (IDB), which was established on 1 January 1960 and started operations on 1 October 1960. The IDB's headquarters are in Washington, DC.

During 1976 the IDB broadened its membership for the first time to include countries from outside the Western Hemisphere. As at 31 December 1989 no less than 17 of the 44 members were non-regional member countries, notably Japan, Germany, Spain, France, Italy and the United Kingdom. On 31 December 1989 the authorized capital amounted to 34.5 billion dollars. The Seventh general increase, which went into effect 17 January 1990, increased it to 61 billion dollars.

The capital of the Fund for Special Operations amounts to 8 458 million dollars (initially 150 million). Contributions to special funds carry no voting rights and the funds are used to make loans on softer financial terms. The IDB also administers other funds totalling 1 130 million dollars, consisting of resources transferred to the Bank by the United States (under the Alliance for Progress), Venezuela and other countries; 19.9 billion dollars have been borrowed on international capital markets.

In 1964 the IDB set up an Institute for Latin American Integration (INTAL), with its headquarters in Buenos Aires, to carry out studies and research. In 1985 an Inter-American Investment Corporation was established in order to promote private investment (it is similar to the IFC: see Chapter 2).

The Bank has already granted loans totalling 41.5 million dollars. Of this total 28 per cent has gone to energy, 22 per cent to agriculture and fisheries, 13 per cent to industry and mining. Brazil has received 16 per cent of the cumulative total of loans, Mexico 12 per cent and Argentina 10 per cent. In 1989 technical cooperation amounted to 60 million dollars, which brought the cumulative total to 724 million dollars.

B.   *The Asian Development Bank (AsDB)*

Proposals for the establishment of an Asian regional bank were being made in the early 1960s, but it was not until the United States decided to contribute to the resources of the bank that any progress was made. The Agreement establishing the Asian Development Bank came into force on 22 August 1966. The headquarters were established in Manila (Philippines). The Bank started operations on 19 December 1966. At present there are thirty-two regional and fifteen non-Asian member countries.

As at 31 December 1989 the available resources were 12.2 billion dollars. As regards the voting power, 64.5 per cent is held by the regional members (12.4 per cent by Japan) and 35.5 per cent by the other members (12.4 per cent by the United States).

Special funds which grant aid on concessional terms were established in

1968 (e.g., the Technical assistance special fund), in 1974 (the Asian development fund) and in 1988 (Japan Special Fund).

The first AsDB loan was made in January 1968. By the end of 1989 a total of 25 598 million dollars had been released for 906 projects. The Bank also provides technical assistance to improve the members' capacity to make effective use of external project financing.

C. *The African Development Bank (AfDB)*

An agreement establishing the African Development Bank came into force on 10 September 1964, and headquarters were set up in Abidjan (Ivory Coast). At the end of 1988 there were 50 regional and 25 non-African numbers (since 1979 membership is not limited to African countries). On 31 December 1989 the paid up capital was 1980 million dollars, and the outstanding debt 3 035 million dollars.

An African Development Fund — established in 1972 by AfDB states and thirteen industrial countries (participating members) — provides finance on concessional terms. The AfDB as a group and the participating countries as a group have each 1 000 votes. The resources amount to 3 440 million dollars.

At the end of 1988 the cumulative transfers of resources to regional member countries amounted to 3 422 million dollars, those of concessionary resources to 1 954 million.

6. CONCLUSION

Through the multiplication of international institutions one begins to doubt the longer the more their efficiency. This not only goes for these organizations themselves but also for the coordinating organization, the UNO. Coordination is unexisting. Continuously, new funds or organizations with about the same assignments as the existing ones are founded.

When there is no coordination within the UNO itself, how can one expect to find coordination between the activities of the Specialized Agencies. Neither the General Assembly nor ECOSOC, nor the Secretariat, which nevertheless consists of about 20 000 persons, (the agencies under the UN umbrella over 50 000 persons) think this problem is of any importance whatsoever. Even former UNO employees point out the defective operation of the UNO administration. So M. Hill speaks of "the jungle" of United Nations and agency regional and subregional structures. The UNO are aware of this situation ... but obviously they acquiesce in it. Development assistance has gradually become the most important function of the entire UN system. There is, however, an urgent need for a thorough review of the elaborate administrative structure of the UN's development activities. As the Jackson report (see Bibliography) puts it, the UN "machine as a whole" is "becoming slower and more unwieldy, like some prehistoric monster". But it takes until 20 December 1977 before the UNO agreed upon directives for internal reorganization. In the meanwhile the prehistoric monster remains very much alive.

The UNO is in essence an organization in which "words" reign supreme. The organization produces tons of paper, but yields no results. The international political and economic problems remain unsolved. Resolutions are of little or no importance. As an Ambassador of the United States stated: The UNO is a "shadow world of rhetoric".

How could it come this far? Many member countries are not livable. They rose from the partition of former colonial imperia. Still, no efforts are made by these countries to change the inherited arbitrary borders and thus unite themselves in livable entities (by which one could take into account economic, social and ethnological circumstances). Because every single one of these small states disposes of one vote, the less-developed countries are able to make the UNO adopt whatever kind of resolution and to obstruct or even render impossible any discussion.

It is easily understandable that big and middle sized countries do not automatically agree upon the opinions of the General Assembly, where countries which represent less than 10 per cent of the total population of the participating countries and which contribute to 2 per cent of the budget, can take decisions by a two-thirds majority. A ponderation of the votes could remedy this lack of sense of reality.

This automatic majority leads to unilateral and little representative resolutions. About 85 per cent of the 159 members of the UNO is very little concerned with "the respect of the human rights and the basic freedoms", one of the principal goals of the organization.

The politicization of the UNO contributes to her minimal efficiency (and this is also the case in most of the specialized agencies). How can one take protest against South Africa seriously when it emanates from dictatorial regimes who often oppress important minorities of other races, from about fifty states who "... sont en guerre entre eux ou pratiquent chez eux le génocide entre tribus, ou entretiennent des camps d'entraînement pour terroristes, façon bien particulière d'affirmer sa foi dans les droits humains fondamentaux, la dignité et la valeur de la personne humaine" (Gaxotte). All the same, condemnations by a majority of dictatorial regimes may rejoice an immediate and large publicity in the press. Therefore one must not be surprised to witness at UNO meetings "vitriolic attacks on the West in general, and the United States, specifically".

And the cost of this gigantic talk-organization (about 6 billion dollars a year) keeps on rising. The cost of one page of the minutes surpasses the average national income of the least developed countries. A session of the General Assembly alone needs 230 million pages of documentation. The Commission for the Human Rights, for example, meets for several weeks without yielding any result.

The United States, who account for 25 per cent of the budget, protest the longer the more against these wastes and unjustified expenditures. Thus the UNO paid secretly 432 000 dollars to give publicity to their own activities. In no way the UNO turned out to be the inspiror of these articles (often written by UNO employees). The recruitment of UNO officials has little to do with competence. The connection (or "special" relation) with ministers of Foreign Affairs is decisive. They would even sell functions. The union of UNO-personnel protested against these bargains ... but the secretary-general claims not to have found significant proof. And still: "Letting politics outweigh competence, integrity and efficiency in the choice of high officials is a sure road to demoralization and inefficiency" (T. Meron). Because of his large and vague authorities, a powerful action of the secretary-general could prevent many abuses. But the only concern of the secretary-general is re-election and this implies that he has to be on good terms with everybody and on no account takes initiatives (the golden rule of bureaucracy). That's why S. Goodspeed in 1967 wrote, and it still holds today: "Leadership is lacking both from the Assembly and from ECOSOC. To a certain extent it has had to be furnished by the Secretariat, a most unlikely source".

Like the League of Nations, the UNO turned out to be a failure. Switzerland is not a member of the UNO and isn't less happy with it. World organizations may contribute to world peace, but in fact peace depends upon the attitude of the countries which occupy a dominant position. Analogous to the Pax Romana, one can speak of a Pax Britannica during the second half of the 19th century and in a way of a Pax Americana from 1945 until about 1965. The same dominant powers apply double standards. Why war against Iraq, when many similar aggressions were and are not 'punished'? The end of the cold war and the American economic and other 'rewards' to the 'allies' are an explanation, but it is still a discrimination.

BIBLIOGRAPHY

A. *General Works on International Institutions*

D. Wallace, Jr. and H. Escobar, *The future of international economic organizations* (New York, Praeger, 1977); G. Schiavione, *International organizations: a dictionary and directory* (2nd ed., London, MacMillan, 1986); A. Weber, *Geschichte der internationalen Wirtschaftsorganisationen* (Wiesbaden, Franz Steiner, 1983).
   See also *The Europe Year Book. A world survey* (published since 1926), especially Volume I, which deals with international organizations.

B. *The UN*

In addition to the annual *World economic survey* (published since 1948), mention should be made of the publications by the Regional Commissions, the *Economic survey of Latin America* (since 1949; not issued in 1959, 1960 and 1961) and the *Economic Bulletin for*

Latin America (since 1956, twice annually); the *Economic survey of Africa* (since 1961, published at intervals) and the *Economic Bulletin for Africa* (since 1961, twice annually); the *Economic survey of Asia and the Far East* (since 1948; in 1952 issued as No. 3 of the *Economic Bulletin for Asia and the Far East*) and the *Economic Bulletin for Asia and the Far East* (since 1948, quarterly); the *Economic survey of Europe* (since 1948; in 1953 published as a supplement to the *Economic Bulletin for Europe*) and the *Economic Bulletin for Europe* (since 1948, issued twice annually).

An appraisal of UN development aid is provided by *A study of the capacity of the United Nations development system* (New York, UN, 1969) (the Jackson report) and by *A United Nations structure for global economic cooperation* (New York, UN, 1975).

See also E. Luard, *International agencies, the emerging framework of interdependence* (London, MacMillan, 1977); M. Hill, *The United Nations system. Coordinating its economic and social work* (Cambridge, Cambridge University Press, 1978); R.I. Meltzer, Restructuring the United Nations system: institutional reform efforts in the context of North-South relations, *International Organization*, Autumn 1978 and *ABC of the United Nations* (New York, UN, 1981); F. Huhle, Internationale Institutionen. Hemmschuh oder Förderer weltwirtschaftlicher Integration?, *IFO-studien*, 1984, No. 1.

On regional integration: *Multilateral development finance institutions of developing countries and the promotion of economic co-operation and integration. Report by the UNCTAD scretariat* (United Nations, New York 1984); *Current problems of economic integration. The problems of promoting and financing integration projects* (UNCTAD, New York, 1986); *Intégration économique entre pays en développement: coopération commerciale, coopération monétaire et financière, et examen de l'évolution récente au sein des principaux groupements de coopération et d'intégration économiques de pays en développement. Rapport du secrétariat de la CNUCED* (UNCTAD, New York, 15 Dec. 1990).

On the BIS: P. Van den Bergh, The Bank for International Settlements, *Revue de la Banque*, 1989, No. 7.

The extracts quoted are from: M. Hill, *op. cit.*; S.S. Goodspeed, *The nature and function of international organization* (New York, Oxford University Press, 1967); P. Gaxotte, l'O.N.U. a 32 ans et 148 membres, *Le Figaro*, 13—14 May 1978; D.A. Kay, A comment, *International Organization*, Summer 1976; T. Meron, Staff of the United Nations Secretariat: Problems and directions, *American Journal of International Law*, 1976.

PART 1

World Organizations

1. The International Monetary Fund

Any "reforms" that would make the IMF "demo-
cratic" and "universal" and its support "automatic"
would make it inefficient and ineffective and would
lead to its eventual demise as a useful instrument
of world economic development. It should not be
turned into a satellite or replica of the United
Nations.

G. HABERLER

This chapter is devoted to the origins of the IMF and to its principal provisions and operation. A brief appraisal is followed by a few suggestions for
further reading.

1. ORIGINS

Owing to the war's ravages in the majority of European and some Asian
countries, the restoration of international trade after World War II called for
considerable capital transfers from North America to the rest of the world.
The Unites States did not wish to sidestep the task of financing reconstruction, but wanted to avoid a repetition of the situation which had arisen after
World War I, when the settlement of debts had proved a source of monetary
difficulties.

A. *Plans*

Discussions on these problems had already been opened during the war,
leading to the simultaneous publication on 7 April 1943 of a British and an
American plan for the establishment of an international monetary institution.

The British plan, *Proposals for an International Clearing Union*, was
drawn up by J. M. Keynes in collaboration with British Treasury experts. It

23

provided for the founding of an international bank which would be able to grant credits to the member countries to the extent of 75 per cent of their average imports and exports during the period 1936—39. These credits would be expressed in a new currency unit, the *bancor*, the gold value of which would be adjusted at regular intervals to the requirements of monetary circulation (in order to avoid disturbances due to fluctuation in gold production). The national currencies would be determined in *bancors*; any modification would require the consent of the International Clearing Union.

This project was advantageous to Britain, which, with its considerable foreign trade, would have obtained a high *bancor* quota (5.4 billion dollars, as against 4.1 billion for the United States) and by means of purchases in North America, without restrictions on consumption for its own population, would have been able to hasten its industrial recovery. The plan was unacceptable to the United States, since the considerable flow of European orders immediately after the war would have given rise to inflationary pressure.

The plan put forward by the American government, *Preliminary draft outline of a proposal for a "United and Associated Nations Stabilization Fund"*, was prepared by a team headed by H. D. White, an Assistant to the Secretary of the Treasury, H. Morgenthau, and thus came to be known as the White plan. It was based on the establishment of a fund of at least 5 billion dollars to which the member states would transfer a part of their exchange reserves; this fund would serve to grant credit, within certain limits to the signatories (in the Keynes plan there was no capital, but creation of book money instead). Unlike Keynes, White further opted for an international currency unit with a fixed gold parity, the *unitas*. The two plans revealed a fundamental difference of approach: In Britain's view, the Fund should act as an automatic body whose management should display a minimum of discretion; the United States, however, considered that the Fund's objective could be realized in the most effective way be conducting its operations with a certain degree of discretion.

After the publication of a French and a Canadian plan and consultation of several countries (including the Soviet Union), Britain and the United States arrived at an agreement that was published on 21 April 1944. It was discussed with other countries in June 1944 in Atlantic City, New Jersey, and finally submitted to the UN Monetary and Financial Conference, which met at Bretton Woods, New Hampshire, from 1 to 22 July 1944 and decided to set up two institutions, the International Monetary Fund and the International Bank for Reconstruction and Development.

The Fund and the Bank both came officially into existence on 27 December 1945, after a sufficient number of countries together representing a certain part of the capital (80 per cent for the Fund, and 65 for the Bank) had approved the Articles of Agreement of the two agencies. The World Bank opened for business on 25 June 1946, but the Fund started financial operations only in March 1947. In the subsequent years many plans have been drafted for the reform of the international monetary system. The best-known of these is the Triffin Plan. To a certain extent, R. Triffin wishes to return to the Keynes Plan by converting the IMF into an international central bank. E. M. Bernstein, a former IMF official, has also put forward numerous proposals, several of which, moreover, have been implemented.

B. *Groups*

The Group of Ten (the United States, Canada, the United Kingdom, Germany, France, Italy, Belgium, the Netherlands, Japan and Sweden; Switzerland was an observer) was established in 1962 when some countries were prepared to grant aid to the United Kingdom. Afterwards these countries regularly held talks on the international monetary situation. Important decisions are often made by the Group of Ten, G10 (e.g. the Smithsonian Agreement of 15 December 1971). Since 1975 there are annual summits of heads of state or government. Participants are the members of the Group of Five, G5 (France, Germany, Japan, the United Kingdom and the United States) and Italy, since the second summit also Canada (often referred to at G7). G5, G7 and G10 may meet at ministerial level. The United States, Japan and Germany constitute The Group of Three, which discusses generally international monetary problems.

The Group of Twenty-Four was established by a decision of the Group of 77 (of the United Nations Conference on Trade and Development) at a meeting in Caracas in April 1972. It includes a geographically representative cross section of less-developed countries and seeks to ensure that the interests of these countries are taken into account in the reform of the international monetary system. But the members of the Organization of Economic Cooperation and Development (the developed countries) are also called the Group of Twenty-Four.

C. *Amendments*

In July 1966 the Ministers and Governors of the Group of Ten agreed that "at some point in the future, existing types of reserves may have to be supplemented by the deliberate creation of additional reserve assets". All but one considered that it would be prudent to begin preparing immediately for such a contingency.

Agreement was finally reached on an outline plan for deliberate reserve creation — "the result of an intensive and even microscopic examination of many alternative possibilities". On 28 July 1969 the first amendment to the Articles of Agreement entered into force, establishing a new facility based on special drawing rights (SDR) and making certain changes in Fund rules and practices.

In September 1972 the Fund requested the Committee of Twenty (which represented the member-countries of the IMF, including the Group of Ten countries) to formulate proposals for the reform of the international monetary system. The report of the Committee (abolished in 1974) has been worked out by the Interim Committee (established at the annual meeting of 1974), which has the same task as the Committee of Twenty. Agreement on some points was reached at Kingston (Jamaica) in January 1976.

At the 1974 annual meeting, a Joint Ministerial Committee of the Board of Governors of the World Bank and the Fund on the Transfer of Real Resources to Developing Countries (Development Committee) was established. This Committee advises the Board of Governors of the World Bank and the Fund on the transfer of resources to less-developed countries. It pays special attention to the problems of the least developed countries and of the less-developed countries most seriously affected by balance-of-payments difficulties.

A second amendment came into force on 1 April 1978, introducing fundamental changes in the Articles of Agreement: they relate to the exchange arrangements, the reduced role of gold in the Fund and the aim of making the SDR the most important reserve asset.

In May 1990, the Interim Committee agreed that it was necessary to strengthen and enhance the instruments available to the Fund to prevent and deter overdue obligations, which had become a real problem in the 1980s. Subsequently, the Board of Governors adopted a resolution (effective 28 June 1990) approving a proposal for a Third Amendment of the Fund's Articles. It would add new provisions suspending (by a 70 percent majority of the Executive Board's total voting power) voting and certain related rights of those members who persist in their failure to fulfill any of the obligations under the Articles, after having been declared ineligible to use the general resources of the Fund. The Third Amendment is not yet effective.

2. OBJECTIVES

These were defined in six points (Article 1), the first two of which (promotion of international monetary cooperation and expansion of international trade) are rather in the nature of general directives. The Fund's real task consists mainly in the objective laid down in point 6, namely, to shorten the duration and to reduce the degree of disequilibrium in members' balances of payments. In direct relation to this, endeavours are made:

a) to give confidence to member states by placing the general resources of the Fund, subject to adequate safeguards, temporarily at their disposal; in this way, they are afforded the opportunity of eliminating disequilibria without taking measures that are harmful to national or international prosperity (point 5);

b) to promote exchange stability, and maintain orderly exchange arrangements and to avoid competitive exchange depreciation (point 3).

Originally, it was desired to avoid a return to the repeated devaluations and depreciations by means of which the leading countries had tried in the 1930s to outdo each other in the field of trade. But the Fund did not succeed in attaining this objective.

With regard to the promotion of multilateral trade, point 4 also prescribes cooperation in the establishment of a multilateral payments system in respect of current transactions and in the removal of exchange restrictions that hamper the growth of world trade.

3. ORGANIZATION

A. *Members*

Thirty of the forty-five countries represented at the Bretton Woods talks accepted membership before 30 December 1945. The USSR refused to sign the Articles of Agreements. Poland, Czechoslovakia and Cuba withdrew from the Fund on 14 March 1950, 31 December 1954 and 2 April 1964 respectively, but Poland again became a member (1986) as well as Czechoslovakia (1990).

Membership negotiations are under way with Switzerland (that country would have a director: see below), the USSR and Albania. Cuba and North Korea are the most important non-members.

As a result of the admission to membership of many Asian and African territories that have become independent, the number of member countries has greatly increased (from 58 in 1956 to 155 in 1991).

Membership of the Fund gives the right to participation in the Special Drawing Rights (SDR) Department (Introductory Article ii, and Article 17,*1*).

Any country can withdraw from the Fund by giving notice to Fund headquarters (Article 26,*1*). If a member country does not meet its commitments, it may be denied the right to draw on the Fund's resources; if, after a reasonable period has elapsed, it remains in default, it will be requested to withdraw from the Fund (Article 26,*2a* and *b*). In 1954 Czechoslovakia was obliged to resign in this way.

B. *Capital*

The quota — or share in the capital — of the original members was laid down in the Articles of Agreement. In subscribing to these quotas, each original member country had to pay a quantity of gold that was equivalent to the smaller of the following amounts: 25 per cent of its quota; 10 per cent of its net official holdings in gold or dollars at the time when the Fund notified the members of the commencement of its operations. The difference between the quota and the sum paid in gold was met in the country's own currency.

The quota for the countries that acceded subsequently and the proportion of the quota that had to be paid in gold was fixed at the time of their admission.

At intervals of not more than five years, the Board of Governors can, as a result of a general review, propose a general change in the quotas. A member's quota may also be adjusted at any time, at the request of the country concerned (Article 3,*2a*). Article 3,*2b* enables the Fund to propose at any time a proportional increase in quotas of those members that were members on 31 August 1975 equivalent to the profits on sales of gold transferred from the special disbursement account to the general resources account (see 4E1d: Article 5,*12c* and *f*). No quota may be changed without the consent of the country concerned (Article 3,*2d*).

At the end of two five-year periods, no changes (1951) or only changes in the small quotas (notably those of some Central American countries: 1956) had been decided upon; according to resolutions adopted on 2 February and 6 April 1959, the majority of quotas was raised by 50 per cent, and for certain countries the increase was even greater. Within the framework of the fourth quinquennial review (1965), there was a general increase by 25 per cent, of all quotas plus special increases for some member countries whose quotas were considered to be out of line with their economic importance. Overall increases were again approved in 1970 and 1976 (fifth and sixth general reviews) of respectively 35 and 33.6 per cent. In 1976 the aggregate quota of the oil exporting countries as a group was doubled (to 9.88 per cent of the total) and the collective share of the other less-developed countries kept constant at 20.9 per cent of the total.

On 11 December 1978 the Board of Governors agreed (seventh review) to increase all quotas by 50 per cent (with special increase for some less-developed countries).

On 31 March 1983 the Board of Governors adopted a resolution authorizing an increase of 47.5 per cent in quotas, with larger increases for eleven members, mostly oil-exporting less-developed countries (eighth review). The resolution came into force on 30 November 1983, when members having not less than 70 per cent of quotas on 28 February 1983, had consented to the increase.

The new quotas for individual members were arrived at by distributing 40 per cent of the overall increase in proportion to existing quotas and 60 per cent selectively to reflect changes in members' relative positions in the world economy.

On 28 June 1990 the Board of Governors adopted a resolution for an increase in the total of Fund quotas by 50 per cent. This increase of

45 082.15 million SDR will bring the size of the Fund to 135 214.7 million SDR. It was decided that 60 per cent of the overall increase would be distributed to all members in proportion to their present individual quotas so as to maintain the balance between different groups of countries. The remainder would be distributed according to the members' new relative economic positions. Moreover, Japan's quota will be further increased to the level of Germany's new quota and the United Kingdom and France agreed to establish equality of their quotas. However, to bring the new quotas (Table 1) into effect, some conditions must be met. First, members not having less than 85 per cent of the total present quotas, must notify the Fund of their consent to the increase before 31 December 1991 and pay the increase within the time period prescribed by the Executive Board's resolution. Furthermore, no increase in quota shall become effective until the effective date of the proposed Third Amendment of the Articles of Agreement.

Apart from the general increases, several individual adjustments were made, e.g., for France in 1947, Australia in 1960, Germany in 1966, the People's Republic of China in 1980 and Saudi Arabia in 1981.

Before the second amendment 25 per cent of all increases in quotas had to be settled in gold. Facilities (e.g. settlement in five annual payments) were granted in 1959, 1965 and 1970 solely to countries with limited gold reserves.

Since the second amendment 25 per cent of the increase in the quotas is not longer payable in gold but in SDR (Article 3,*3a*). The quotas also are expressed in SDR (Article 3,*1*). The Board of Governors may decide, by a 70 per cent majority of total voting power, on the same basis for all members, that this payment can be made in whole or in part, in the currencies of other member-countries (with their approval) or in the member's own currency.

Payments may be made in gold instead of SDR or currency at a price agreed on the basis of the market price, provided the Fund allows it by an eighty-five per cent majority of the total voting power (Article 5,*12d*). When 'majority' is used below, it refers, unless stated otherwise, to majority of the total voting power.

In so far as it has no need of the resources in question, the Fund agrees to the substitution of the national currencies in the general resources account (which includes the subscriptions) by cash certificates or similar obligations (issued by the member country or the institution with which it has deposited its subscriptions, in most cases the central bank); these securities are not negotiable and bear no interest (Article 3,*4*).

C. *Administration*

1. *The Board of Governors*

The IMF is headed by a Board of Governors. Each country appoints a governor and an alternate who serve until a new appointment is made. The Board examines the operation of the Fund. The Board may also be convened at the request of at least fifteen governors, or by a number of governors who together represent one-quarter of the total votes, at the request of the Executive Board or by the Council (Article 12,*2c* and Schedule D, *5a*); the Board can even vote by mail (Article 12,*2f*). It approves the annual report and the accounts (the latter are verified beforehand by an auditor), elects its chairman (from among the governors) and every two years the Executive Directors other than the appointed executive directors.

Table 1. Current and proposed highest Fund quotas, 31 December 1990, in million SDR.

Country	Current quota	Proposed quota
United States	17 918.3	26 526.8
Japan	4 223.3	8 241.5
Germany	5 403.7	8 241.5
France	4 482.8	7 414.6
United Kingdom	6 194.0	7 414.6
Saudi Arabia	3 203.4	5 130.6
Italy	2 909.1	4 590.7
Canada	2 941.0	4 320.3
Netherlands	2 264.8	3 444.2
China	2 390.9	3 385.2
Belgium	2 080.4	3 102.3
India	2 207.7	3 055.5
Australia	1 619.2	2 333.2
Brazil	1 461.3	2 170.8
Venezuela	1 371.5	1 951.3
Spain	1 286.0	1 935.4
Mexico	1 165.5	1 753.3

Source: IMF.

Powers relating to important institutional matters are directly conferred on the Board and are exclusively decided upon by the Board. Other powers are subject to delegation (Article 12,*2b* and Schedule D,*3a*) to the Council, to the Executive Board or to both. In order to avoid inconsistency of measures taken by different organs in the event the Council is created, the Council cannot take action pursuant to powers delegated by the Board of Governors conflicting with any action of the Board of Governors (or, in the case of the Executive Board, with any action of the Council) (Schedule D,*3c*).

Each governor has the same basic number of votes, i.e. 250, augmented by one vote for each part of his country's quota equal to 100 000 SDR (Article 12,*5a*), thus benefiting the countries with a small quota. Decisions are adopted by simple majority of the votes cast (Article 12,*5c*), but in certain cases more votes are required (e.g., an eighty-five per cent majority for changing the number of directors). In practice, most decisions are taken unanimously after a consensus has been reached.

When a vote has to be taken on the waiver of the conditions under which currency can be purchased (Article 5,4: see 4A1a) or on loss of eligibility to use the Fund's resources (Article 5,5: see 4A1a), each member's votes are adjusted by the addition of one extra vote for each 400 000 SDR of net sales of its currency from the general resources up to the date of the vote or, as the case may be, subtraction of one vote for each 400 000 SDR of net purchases of the currencies of other member countries (or of SDR provided instead of these currencies; see below: Article 5,3*f*) up to the date of the vote, in so far as these net purchases and sales were deemed not to be greater than the quota of the country concerned (Article 12,5*b*).

2. *The Council*

By an eighty-five per cent majority the Board of Governors may establish the Council in the form of a permanent organ of the Fund with decision-making authority (Article 12,*1*), in order to continue the activity of the Interim Committee.

The Council, if established, will be charged with the general functions of supervision and adaptation of the international monetary system, including the continuing operation of the adjustment process and developments in global liquidity; and in this connection, review of developments in the transfer of real resources to less-developed countries (Schedule D,*2a*).

3. *The Executive Board*

Within the limits of the powers conferred upon it by the Board of Governors, the Executive Board is responsible for conducting the business of the Fund (Article 12,*3*). In a few cases powers are directly conferred on it. There are now twenty-two directors, six of whom are appointed and sixteen elected. Each of the six countries with the largest quotas (United States, United Kingdom, Western Germany, France, Japan and Saudi Arabia) appoints one director: the others are elected by the remaining countries. In order to ensure a desirable balance in the composition of the Executive Board the number of elected directors may be changed.

Elections are held every two years. Each governor votes for only one candidate (Schedule E,*2*). In the elections of the directors, both geographical and political factors play an important role. The countries of Latin America elect three directors; those of the Nordic Countries (Denmark, Finland, Iceland, Norway and Sweden) jointly elect one director as do the groups of countries of English-speaking and French-speaking Africa and those of South-East Asia.

Each appointed director has as many votes in the Executive Board as the country he represents, and the elected director can cast as many votes as the number which counted towards his election but in a single block (Article 12,*3i*). The directors meet whenever this is necessary. Member countries which were unable to appoint directors can send a representative to the meetings at which items affecting them come up for discussion (Article 12,*3j*).

4. *The Managing Director*

The Executive Board appoints the managing director, who shall not be a governor or director and who is responsible for the day-to-day management of the Fund (Article 12,*4*). The managing director is chairman of the Executive Board but is not entitled to vote, except in case of a tie. He is assisted by a staff (1907 on 31 January 1991) whom he is empowered to appoint (Article 12,*4b*). Taking into account the qualifications required, the staff has to be recruited on a broad geographical basis (Article 12,*4d*). Both the managing director and the staff may receive directives from the Fund only (Article 12,*4c*).

At the first meeting of the Executive Board (6 May 1946), C. Gutt of Belgium was appointed managing director. In 1951 he was succeeded by Sweden's I. Rooth, who in turn gave way in 1956 to his fellow countryman P. Jacobsson. Upon the latter's death in 1963, P. P. Schweitzer (France) was appointed managing director; he was succeeded by H. J. Witteveen (Netherlands) in 1973, by J. de Larosière (France) in 1978 and by M. Camdessus (France) in 1987.

The headquarters of the Fund are in Washington, DC — on the territory of the country with the largest quota (Article 13,*1*).

4. FUNCTIONS AND OPERATION

A. *Financing of balance-of-payments deficits*

All transactions and operations are conducted through the general department. Transactions relate to exchanges of monetary assets by the Fund for other monetary assets, operations to other uses or receipts of monetary assets by the Fund. Transactions and operations involving SDR are, however, conducted through the SDR department. If the Fund, which may hold SDR in the general resources account (Article 17,*2*), is a party to a transaction of operation in SDR this is conducted through both departments (Article 16,*1* and Introductory Article, *ii* and *iii*). Transactions in SDR refer to exchanges of SDR for other monetary assets, operations in SDR to other uses of SDR. Moreover, the Fund performs some financial or technical services that are not on its account (see 4A1b) and thus are not conducted through the general department (Article 5,*2b*).

1. *Provisions*

a. *The general resources*

A member eligible to use the general resources may, subject to the conditions set forth in the Articles, purchase SDR or the currencies of other members in exchange for its own currency if it represents that it has an unfavourable balance-of-payments of reserve position, or if its reserves develop in an unfavourable way (Article 5,*2a* and *3b*). Prior to the second amendment the purchase could also be paid with gold.

The Articles of Agreement are rather vague as to the use of the general resources: "The Fund shall adopt policies on the use of its general resources, including policies on stand-by or similar arrangements, and may adopt special policies for special balance-of-payments problems" but it must safeguard the temporary use of the resources and ensure that these resources are employed in accordance with the provisions of the Fund (Article 5,*3a*). If the Fund deems that a member is using the general resources in a manner contrary to the purposes of the Fund it requests the country concerned to justify its action. The Fund can restrict, and then deny, use of the general resources (Article 5,*5*).

Members' purchases have to remain within certain limits. Before the second amendment the purchase could not lead to a situation whereby the Fund's holdings of the purchasing member's currency were increased by more than 25 per cent of its quota in a period of twelve months prior to the purchase or exceed 200 per cent of the quota. Now the 200 per cent limit only has been preserved (Article 5,*3b*). This provision can be waived on terms which safeguard the Fund's interests (Article 5,*4*).

A reserve tranche (the former gold tranche) purchase is always allowed: it does not cause the Fund's holdings of the member's currency in the general resources account to exceed 100 per cent of its quota (Article 30,*c*). In defining the reserve tranche the Fund may exclude purchases and holdings relating to compensatory financing of export fluctuations, international buffer stocks and other purchases if the Fund decides so with an eighty-five per cent majority (Article 30,*c*).

The Fund may agree (by a general approval or an approval for specific cases) to provide participants in the SDR department with SDR instead of the currencies of other members (Article 5,*3f*). Similarly the Fund may provide a member with other members' currencies in exchange for SDR and conversely may provide a participant with SDR held in the general resources account in return for other members' currencies (Article 5,*6*). For these two kinds of transactions there is no requirement of need with respect to the balance-of-payments or reserve position. They may not, however, lead to a situation whereby the holdings of a member's currency exceed the amount of the members' quota after excluding the transactions that are not taken into account for the purpose of the definition of the reserve tranche. The members whose currencies are supplied or accepted by the Fund must agree with these transactions.

All currencies can be used but the Fund may select the currencies to be provided, taking into account the balance-of-payments and reserve position of members, exchange market developments and the desirability of promoting over time balanced positions among members. Only in the case of the Fund's having declared holdings of a currency scarce (see 4E1c) it will not be possible to purchase that currency in order to redeem an equivalent amount of its own currency held by another member and offered by the holder for repurchase (Article 5,*3d*).

Each member must ensure that its currency is freely usable or that balances of its currency purchased from the Fund can be exchanged at the time of the purchase for freely usable one (at an exchange rate on the basis of Article 19,*7a*; see 4A1c; Article 5,*3e*) i.e. for a currency that the Fund determines to be used in making payments of international transactions and to be widely traded in the principal exchange markets (Article 30,*f*).

The financing of large-scale and continuous exportation of capital is prohibited (Article 6,*1a*); a member country can be requested to prevent this by the necessary control measures. In a few cases (e.g., in order to stimulate exports of goods), financing of capital transactions of reasonable amount is permitted (Article 6,*1b*). The reserve tranche may be used to meet capital transfers (Article 6,*2*).

b. *Arrangements not on the account of the Fund*

Article 5,*2b* enables the Fund to perform financial and technical services (including the administration of resources contributed by members) which are not on its account (the assets in the accounts of the general department or in the SDR department would not be available to meet obligations or liabilities in the course of these services). Examples of these services are the Trust Fund and the subsidy account (see 4A2b).

c. *Special Drawing Rights*

The Fund is authorized to allocate SDR (to members that are participants in the SDR department) in order to meet the long-term global need (Article 18,*1a*), as and when it arises, to supplement existing reserve assets (Article 15,*1*).

While since 1969 the SDR had been defined as equivalent to 0.888671 g of fine gold, since the second amendment no definition is provided. The method of valuation will be determined by the Fund by a 70 per cent majority; by an 85 per cent for a change in the principle of valuation or a fundamental change in the application of the principle in effect (Article 15,*2*).

Any member accepting the obligations involved is entitled to participate in the SDR department (Article 17,*1*). Non-members, non-participant members, institutions that perform the functions of a central bank for more than one member and (since the second amendment) official entities in general may be prescribed as holders (prescribed holders) by an 85 per cent majority (Article 17,*3i*). As mentioned before (see 4A1*a*) the Fund too is a holder through its general resources account.

Decisions on allocation or cancellation of SDR are taken for consecutive periods of five years. The allocations or cancellations take place at intervals of one year (Article 18,*2a*). The allocation rates are expressed as percentages, uniform for all participants, of quotas on the date of decision; the cancellation rates as percentages of net cumulative allocations of SDR, again on the date of decision (Article 18,*2b*). Exceptions are provided for (Articles 18,*2c* and *3*).

Decisions on allocation and cancellation are made by the Board of Governors (by an 85 per cent majority) on the basis of proposals from the managing director concurred in by the Executive Directors (Article 18,*4a*). In its decisions concerning allocation or cancellation of SDR, the Fund is to seek to avoid economic stagnation and deflation as well as excess demand and inflation in the world (Article 18,*1a*). The first allocation decision, more particularly, had to bear in mind the likelihood of a better working of the adjustment process in the future (Article 18,*1b*).

Participants are able to use SDR to acquire an equivalent amount of currency from participants designated by the Fund or from participants who agree to provide this amount of currency (Article 19,*2a* and *b*). In the first case the SDR are expected to be used only for balance-of-payments or reserve position requirements or in the light of developments in overall reserves and not merely in order to change the composition of reserves (Article 19,*3a*). But the use of SDR will not be challenged on the basis of this expectation; instead, representations may be made, if there is abuse, and the Fund may suspend the right of the participant to use SDR it acquired after the suspension (Article 19,*3b*). The Fund may waive the expectation mentioned above in any transaction which promotes reconstitution obligations (see below) by other participants, prevents or reduces negative balances of the other participants, or offsets the effect of a failure by the other participants to fulfill the expectation of Article 19,*3a* (Article 19,*3c*).

In designating the participants which have to provide currency the Fund will take into account, *inter alia*, their balance-of-payments and gross reserve position (but this does not preclude the possibility that a participant with a strong reserve position will be designated even though it has a moderate balance-of-payments deficit), the reconstitution obligation (see below), the necessity to reduce negative balances in SDR and the desirability of a balanced distribution of SDR holdings among participants (Article 19, *5a(i)* and *(ii)*).

A designated country must provide on demand a freely usable currency but not beyond a point where holdings of SDR in excess of its net cumulative allocation are double that amount, though it may provide — or agree to provide — currency beyond this limit (Article 19,*4a* and *b*).

The Fund may also prescribe — by a 70 per cent majority — operations in which participants are authorized to engage in agreement with other participants on such terms and conditions as the Fund deems appropriate (Article 19,*2c*).

The exchange rates for transactions between participants must as a rule be such that participants using SDR receive the same value whatever currencies might be provided and whichever participants provide those currencies (the equal value principle) (Article 19,*7a*).

Prescribed holders may, under terms and conditions prescribed by the Fund enter into transactions and operations with participants, other prescribed holders and the Fund (Article 17,*2* and *3*, ii and iii). The Fund may also use SDR in operations and transactions with participants (Article 17,*2*).

Participants using their SDR were obliged to reconstitute their holdings in accordance with Schedule G or such rules adopted with a 70 per cent majority (Article 19,*6*). Two principles were laid down:

a) a participant's average net use of its SDR calculated on the basis of the previous five years must not exceed 70 per cent of its average net cumulative allocations over those years;
b) participants must bear in mind the desirability of balancing their holdings of SDR with their other reserves (Article 19,*6*; Schedule G).

On 1 January 1979 the percentage was raised to 85 and on 30 April 1986 the obligation to reconstitute SDR holdings was abolished.

Prior to 30 April 1981 if a participant failed to fulfill its reconstitution obligations, the Fund could suspend the right of the participant to use its SDR (Article 23,*2a*). Since then this rule has been abrogated.

Any participant may decide not to accept any allocation made to it (to "opt out") (Article 18,*2e*) and may terminate its participation at any time (Article 24,*1a*). A participant withdrawing from the Fund will be deemed to have simultaneously terminated its participation in the SDR department (Article 24,*1b*).

2. *Operation*

a. *The general resources*

At the outset, the Fund only helped certain Western European countries to overcome their postwar difficulties. When the European Recovery Programme (or Marshall Plan: see Chapter 5) began to operate in mid-1948, the Fund decided to help Western Europe in exceptional circumstances only. A fairly restrictive policy was also pursued in respect of other countries. There was no question of automatic support. Under these circumstances a call on the Fund by non-European countries was regarded as evidence of weak monetary policy; it even gave rise to speculation.

1. *The "tranche" decisions and stand-by arrangements*

The Executive Board therefore decided on 13 February 1952 that member countries could henceforth acquire IMF resources in every case (apart from exceptional circumstances) until such time as the Fund held an amount of the currency in question equal to the corresponding quota. Subsequently these directives were defined more closely.

Before the second amendment, a member country which had not yet purchased any currency (or settled previous transactions) and had paid 25 per cent in gold upon accession, could immediately take up foreign exchange to the amount of 25 per cent of its quota. As this share corresponded to the gold paid, it was known as the gold tranche. As from the second amendment, it has been renamed the "reserve tranche" and can be less than 25 percent, since the part of a member's quota that must be contributed in reserve assets may be less than 25 per cent (Figure 1).

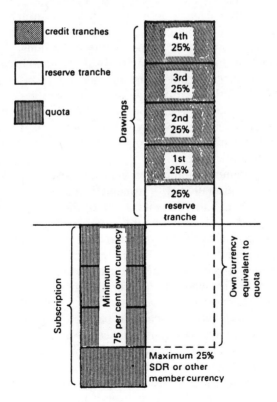

Figure 1. The IMF reserve and credit tranches.

If other countries have purchased the currency of the member concerned, the reserve tranche increases by an equivalent amount. This supplement is sometimes called the super reserve tranche. In the terminology of the Fund the reserve tranche is defined more broadly so as to include the super reserve tranche.

Drawings (that means purchases) raising Fund holdings of a currency about 100 per cent of the quota are made in four credit tranches of 25 per cent. For transactions within the first tranche a broad policy is applied, provided the country concerned makes an effort to restore its balance-of-payments equilibrium. In practice members are given the benefit of the doubt if there exists a divergence of opinion. Subsequently, currency is provided only if this contributes towards monetary stability at an acceptable level and the member presents a comprehensive programme.

Purchases within the first credit tranche can take the form of a direct drawing or can be made under a stand-by arrangement (see below), while drawings within the higher tranches are nearly always made under stand-by or extended arrangements (see 4A2a).

In 1952 a new method was worked out for drawings (in principle) beyond the then gold tranche — the stand-by arrangements, whereby the Fund undertakes to supply currency upon request, up to an agreed amount and within a specified (renewable) period (six months or one year and more recently for longer periods in arrangements concerning the upper credit tranches), without any further review of its position and policies.

Since September 1969 stand-by arrangements have been concluded only for purchases beyond the gold (reserve) tranche. Before a stand-by arrangement is concluded and after discussion with a Fund mission, the member sets out in a letter of intent the policies to be followed and the results to be achieved. The Fund expects the programme to be as specific as possible (formulation in quantitative terms).

Terms and conditions of the arrangements developed gradually. While there is normally consultation with a member from time to time during the period in which this member is making use of the Fund's resources beyond the first credit tranche (whether or not the use results from stand-by arrangement), consultation clauses are incorporated in all stand-by arrangements.

Beyond the first credit tranche there are normally phasing and performance clauses. Phasing clauses imply the progressive release of the amounts under the stand-by arrangements at predetermined intervals, provided the performance criteria are met.

In exceptional cases phasing need not be used in stand-by arrangements that go beyond the first credit tranche when the Fund considers it essential that the full amount of the arrangement be promptly available. In these arrangements, the performance clauses will be so drafted as to require the member to consult the Fund in order to reach understandings, if needed, on new or amended performance criteria even if there is no amount that could still be purchased under the arrangement.

Only objective performance criteria needed to evaluate implementation of the programme will be used. Given the diversity of members' problems and institutions, no general rule as to the number and content of these criteria can be adopted. Common performance criteria have been the extent of credit expansion by the central banks, the extent of reliance on the banking system by the government, the amount of new short- or medium-term foreign borrowing, the minimum level of net foreign reserve and the avoidance of specified restrictive measures in the exchange and trade field.

When a member does not observe the criteria his right to draw is suspended. Consultation with the Fund is necessary in order to determine the circumstances under which new drawings are possible.

A country which concludes a stand-by arrangement does not necessarily have to make use of it, but a small rate of interest (a commitment charge of 0.25 per cent) is calculated on the full amount of the arrangement.

A stand-by arrangement is advisable when it is a question not so much of immediate assistance but rather of serving a precautionary need and having certain amounts available. A first agreement was concluded with Belgium in June 1952. It soon became evident that the stand-by arrangement could also be of great help to members experiencing balance-of-payments difficulties and having both an immediate and a prospective need for financing. Twenty-seven stand-by arrangements became effective in the financial year 1982/83.

The total drawings (Table 2) on 30 April 1990 of 112.2 billion SDR are composed of 27.8 billion SDR reserve and first credit tranches drawings, 42 billion SDR stand-by arrangements, 6.9 billion SDR oil facilities drawings, 17.5 billion SDR compensatory drawings and 17.1 billion SDR extended facility drawings (and 0.6 billion SDR buffer stock drawings).

The consequences of the Fund's more flexible policy since 1952 are not immediately evident from Table 2 because of a favourable economic situation and the operations of the European Payments Union. A similar observation can be made in connection with the Fund's decision in 1961 to relax its policy in respect of cases of balance-of-payments disequilibrium due to capital movements. Short-term capital movements increased sharply after the convertibility of many currencies in 1958.

During the financial years 1969 and 1970 drawings reached record levels as a consequence of payments imbalances of industrial countries and periodic crises in the exchange markets, although the persistent deficit of the US balance of payments provided the world with more and more dollars. Only in 1972 was there a revival of drawings as a consequence of the exchange market crisis in 1971. As from 1975 drawings rose sharply following the marked rise in oil prices. Since 1978 transactions fell again, partly because of the larger amount available in the international money and capital markets. They rose again in 1982 as a consequence of the continued payments imbalances of several countries. The expansion of Fund credit slowed down only in 1985/86 after the recovery in world economic activity and more efficient adjustment policies.

Table 2. IMF transactions 1948—90, in million SDR (financial year ended 30 April[a].)

Year	Purchases	Stand-by arrangements approved	Repurchases
1948	606	—	—
1949	119	—	—
1950	52	—	24
1951	28	—	19
1952	46	—	37
1953	66	55	185
1954	231	63	145
1955	49	40	276
1956	39	48	272
1957	1 114	1 162	75
1958	666	1 044	87
1959	264	1 057	537
1960	166	364	522
1961	577	460	659
1962	2 243	1 633	1 260
1963	580	1 531	807
1964	626	2 160	380
1965	1 897	2 159	517
1966	2 817	575	406
1967	1 061	591	340
1968	1 348	2 352	1 116
1969	2 839	541	1 542
1970	2 996	2 381	1 671
1971	1 167	502	1 657
1972	2 028	314	3 122
1973	1 175	322	540
1974	1 058	1 394	672
1975	5 102	390	518
1976	6 591	1 188	960
1977	4 910	4 680	868
1978	2 503	1 285	4 485
1979	3 720	508	4 859
1980	2 433	2 479	3 776
1981	4 860	5 198	2 853
1982	8 041	3 106	2 010
1983	11 392	5 450	1 555
1984	11 518	4 287	2 018
1985	6 289	3 218	2 730
1986	4 101	2 123	4 289
1987	3 685	4 117	6 169
1988	4 153	1 702	7 935
1989	2 541	2 956	6 258
1990	4 503	3 249	6 042
Total	112 202	66 684	74 195

[a] Totals may not equal sums of items because of rounding.
Source: IMF, *Annual report of the Executive Board for the financial year ended 30 April 1990.*

So far the largest drawings have been made by the United Kingdom (12 518 million SDR). It is followed at a distance (5 000 to 6 000 million SDR) by India, Argentina, the United States and Brazil.

In 1956 the Fund took measures to prevent speculation against the pound after the Suez crisis: the United Kingdom was granted an immediate drawing of 561.5 million dollars and a stand-by arrangement for 738.5 million. Between 1956/57 and 1958/59 France was given assistance totalling 390 million dollars. In 1961 further speculative movements — which in fact were based on the unfavourable competitive position of the United Kingdom — necessitated further recourse to the Fund by that country, namely a drawing of 1 billion dollars and a stand-by credit of 0.5 billion dollars. In 1962 this credit was extended to 1 billion dollars. It was available until 1964, when the United Kingdom drew the amount. In 1965 another drawing of 1.4 billion dollars was granted, and in 1967 a new stand-by arrangement was agreed upon for the same amount. On 19 June 1968 the United Kingdom drew the full amount of this arrangement. On 20 June 1969 the Fund approved another stand-by arrangement of 1 billion dollars over the next twelve months. Already on 4 July, the United Kingdom purchased the equivalent of 0.5 billion dollars.

The remaining amount was purchased before 30 April 1970. Again in support of the pound a gold tranche drawing of SDR 583.6 million was made on 28 July 1972 and a reserve tranche drawing of 700 million SDR and a drawing of 1 billion SDR under the oil facility in January 1976. A stand-by arrangement concluded in December 1975 of 1 billion SDR was fully used in May 1976. On 3 January 1977 a new stand-by arrangement of 3 360 million SDR was approved, of which an amount of 1 640 million was drawn. The arrangement expired on 2 January 1979.

The United States had to cope with balance-of-payments deficits from 1958 onwards. It was obliged to draw 3 552 million dollars within its reserve tranche between 1964 and 1972. On 1 November 1978 the United States announced an anti-inflation programme including a drawing on its reserve position in the Fund amounting to 2 275 million SDR.

Members are required to consult the Fund about the currencies to be used in repurchase. Whereas prior to May 1958 more than 90 per cent of the drawings were made in United States dollars, the situation has since changed considerably, as a result of the convertibility of many currencies. Sales of dollars represented approximately one third of the cumulative total sales on 31 July 1990 (Table 3).

The waiver provisions (Article 5,4) were first used in August 1953, when Turkey was allowed to draw more than 25 per cent of its quota within a single year. Many waivers (almost routinely) have since been granted.

Temporary facilities
In order to help members with balance-of-payments problems caused by the sharp rise in prices of petroleum, the Fund established a temporary facility

Table 3. Cumulative total of sales of most important currencies by the IMF, 31 July 1990, in million SDR.

US dollars	34 890.4
Deutsche marks	10 950.0
Japanese yen	8 152.7
Saudi Arabian riyals	7 948.5
French francs	3 561.7
Netherlands guilders	2 920.0
Italian lire	2 754.1
Pounds sterling	2 631.9
Canadian dollars	2 335.4
Belgian francs	2 316.9

Source: IMF.

on 13 June 1974 for a period ending on 31 December 1975 (in addition to any other assistance).

The last drawings under the oil facility (relating to the balance of payments in 1975) were made in May 1976. Purchases over the whole period (September 1974—May 1976) totalled 6 902 million SDR in 156 transactions. The larger portion (63 per cent) was drawn by developed countries, notably by the United Kingdom and Italy (which accounted for 35 per cent of total drawings), while the remainder was purchased by 45 less-developed countries. All amounts drawn under the oil facility have now been repurchased (repaid).

A supplementary financing facility approved on 29 August 1977 entered into effect on 23 February 1979, the date on which loan agreements for a five-year period between the Fund and lenders were completed for 7 754 million SDR.

The purpose of this new facility was to provide additional assistance, in conjunction with use of the Fund's ordinary resources, to members facing serious payments imbalances that are large in relation to their quotas. It was available only in support of economic programmes under stand-by arrangements reaching into the upper credit tranches or under extended arrangements. The Fund's requirements concerning, for instance, conditionality, phasing and performance were the same as with an upper credit tranche stand-by or extended arrangement but the drawings under the supplementary financing facility normally exceeded one year and could extend up to three years.

In September 1977 the Fund agreed to pay the lenders interest of 7 per cent until 30 June 1978. Since then, the rate of interest was determined every six months on the basis of the US-Government five-year securities.

In total 7.2 billion SDR of the 7.8 billion that had been available, was disbursed. The largest beneficiaries were Turkey and Yugoslavia.

2. *The extended facility*

If the solution to a member's balance-of-payments problem requires a longer period than is provided for credit-tranche resources, drawings under extended arrangements may be made since 13 September 1974; they may take place over periods of up to three (in exceptional circumstances, four) years. An extended facility can, for example, apply in the following situations: (i) in an economy suffering serious payments imbalance relating to structural maladjustments in production and trade and where price and cost distortions have been widespread; or (ii) an economy characterized by slow growth and an inherently weak balance-of-payments position which prevents pursuit of an active development policy. The request for an extended arrangement must be accompanied by a programme stating the policies and measures for each 12-month period in order to meet the objectives of the programme. Purchases are subject to phasing performance clauses relating to the implementation of key policy measures.

Although the extended facility is available to all members, it is more likely to be beneficial for less-developed countries. So far thirty arrangements in favour of these countries have been approved. Of a total of 25 863 million SDR approved, 15 029 million was purchased on 30 April 1989 (Brazil: 2 843 million; India: 2 596 million; Mexico: 2 287 million).

3. *The enlarged access*

The enlarged access policy replaces the supplementary financing policy. It was made possible by new borrowing agreements, the first of which was a medium-term agreement for 8 billion SDR concluded with the Saudi Arabia Monetary Agency on 7 May 1981, which was followed by short-term agreements totalling 1.3 billion SDR with the Bank for International Settlements, 18 central banks or official agencies of Fund members, and Switzerland.

On 30 April 1990 7 209 million SDR credit was outstanding under this policy.

The enlarged access policy is used to increase the resources available under stand-by and extended arrangements for programmes that need substantial Fund support. Access limits are the same as under stand-by and extended arrangements (Table 4).

4. *Financing for debt and debt-service reduction*

In 1989 the Fund decided to provide support for debt and debt-service reduction operations in conjunction with appropriate flows of new funds from the private sector. This support has to be linked to medium-term adjustment programmes with a strong element of structural reform adopted in the context of stand-by or extended arrangements. The board considers requests on a case-by-case basis (e.g., its own liquidity position, the strength of the countries' policy).

The Fund approved arrangements with several countries, three of which

Table 4. Potential cumulative disbursements under arrangements and facilities, in per cent of member quotas.[a]

Under stand-by and extended arrangements[b, c]	
Annual	90—110
Three-year	270—330
Cumulative	400—440
Special facilities[c]	
Compensatory and contingency financing facility (CCFF)	
— *Compensatory financing*	40
— *Contingency financing*[d]	40
— *Optional tranche*[e]	25
— *Excess cereal import costs*	17
— *Combined*[f]	122
Buffer stock financing facility	45
Under SAF and ESAF arrangements	
Structural adjustment facility[g]	
— *First year*	20
— *Second year*	30
— *Third year*	20
— *Cumulative*	70
Enhanced structural adjustment facility[h]	
— *Cumulative*	250

[a] Under exceptional circumstances, the amounts disbursed may exceed the following limits.
[b] Excludes drawings on available reserve tranches.
[c] These arrangements and facilities are financed directly with Fund resources.
[d] Contingency financing generally may not exceed 70 per cent of access made under the associated arrangement, with a cumulative sub-limit of 35 per cent of quota on account of deviations in interest rates.
[e] May be applied to supplement the amounts for compensatory financing, contingency financing, or excess in cereal import costs.
[f] Where a member has a satisfactory balance of payments position — except for the effect of an export shortfall or an excess in cereal costs — a limit of 83 per cent of quota applies to either the export or cereal element, with a combined limit of 105 per cent of quota.
[g] This facility is financed with the 2.7 billion SDR in reflows from the Trust Fund.
[h] This facility is being financed with SAF resources and with special loan and grant contributions.
Source: IMF.

(Costa Rica, Mexico and the Philippines) concluded agreements on financial packages with their commercial bank creditors.

5. *Special facilities*

The Fund's financial assistance is available to all its members on a non-discriminatory basis, but the Fund has recognized that primary producing countries, most of which are less-developed countries, may need additional financial support. Accordingly, there are two special financial facilities designed to help primary producing countries, known as the compensatory financing and the buffer stock facilities.

a. *Compensatory and contingency financing facility.* In February 1963 the Fund stated that it was prepared to grant special assistance to primary producing countries when a balance-of-payments deficit occurs as a result of fluctuations in export earnings from primary commodities. A drawing implies two conditions: the shortfall has to be temporary and out of the member's control; the member must cooperate in order to solve its balance-of-payments problem.

Initially, the compensatory facility was not used frequently, as a result of the upturn in prices of many commodities in 1963—65. Subsequently the conditions governing the grant of such assistance were eased.

In 1979 compensatory financing was broadened to include tourist receipts and worker remittances in calculating the export shortfall, and in 1981 a further extension allowed compensation for countries faced with an excessive rise in the cost of specific cerial imports.

The compensatory and contingency financing facility was established in August 1988 and serves two purposes. The compensatory element provides resources to cover export shortfalls or excessive cerial import costs arising from events beyond members' control. The contingency element provides Fund-supported arrangements to maintain the momentum of adjustment when faced with a broad range of unforeseen, adverse external shocks (e.g., declines in export prices or increases in import prices).

On 30 April 1990 the compensatory and contingency financing credits amounted to 3 823 million SDR.

b. *Buffer stock financing.* In June 1969 the Executive Directors established a new facility for members having a balance-of-payments need in relation to the financing of buffer stocks under international commodity agreements that meet appropriate criteria (e.g. they must be consistent with the temporary use of Fund resources).

The Fund has assisted members under the fourth, fifth and sixth Tin Agreements, the 1979 International Sugar Agreement and the 1979 International Natural Rubber Agreement. In April 1990 it decided that the facility may be used for financing members' contributions to the 1987 International Natural Rubber Agreement.

b. *Other resources for low-income members*

In addition to its general resources the Fund has generated other resources to provide low-income members with assistance on concessional terms. Such assistance was first provided through the Trust Fund and through other Fund administered accounts. Now it is provided through loans under the structural adjustment facility (SAF) and under the enhanced structural adjustment facility (ESAF).

On 5 May 1976 the Executive Directors decided to establish a Trust Fund in order to provide additional aid on concessionary terms to the 61 eligible less-developed countries with balance-of-payments problems. The Trust Fund is financed by profits from gold sales by the IMF, by voluntary national contributions and by incomes from investments and loans.

Under an agreement reached in the Interim Committee (August 1975), one third (50 million ounces) of the gold holdings of the IMF had to be sold, half of it at the former official price (42.2 dollars) to all members in proportion to their quota on 31 August 1975 (restitution operation) and the other half for the benefit of the less-developed countries that were members on that date. The latter part had to be sold in public auctions by the Fund as Trustee on behalf of the Trust Fund.

The major part of the Trust's resources derived from the profits from the gold auctions, after deduction of a share of profits that equals the share of less-developed member quotas in the IMF on 31 August 1975. This amount was transferred directly to each less-developed country in proportion to its quota. The profits of the gold sales totalled 4.64 billion dollars of which 1.3 billion dollars was distributed to 104 less-developed countries. The amount available for Trust Fund loans was 3.7 billion dollars or 3 billion SDR, including income from investments and from loans made. The Trust Fund disbursed 2 991 million SDR. The Fund was terminated on 30 April 1981.

The subsidy account was established on 1 August 1975 to assist the Fund's most seriously affected members to meet the cost of using the 1975 oil facility. It was financed by contributions from 24 (mostly developed) member-countries and Switzerland totalling 160.3 million SDR. In addition 26.5 million SDR was earned on the investments of the contributions pending their disbursement.

The final payments were made in August 1983 and the account terminated. During the financial years 1976/84 payments totalled 186.8 million SDR. They have reduced the cost of using the 1975 oil facility to less than 3 per cent. The most important beneficiaries have been the Philippines (41.5 million), Pakistan (30.3 million) and India (28.7 million).

In order to reduce to low-income less-developed members the cost of using the supplementary financing facility, a supplementary financing facility subsidy account was established on 17 December 1980. The resources of the account are derived from repayments of Trust Fund loans, donations, borrowings and investment income. The rate of subsidy may not exceed three per cent per annum. As of 30 April 1986 subsidy payments totalling 307 million SDR were made.

1. *The structural adjustment facility (SAF)*
In March 1986 the Fund established this facility to provide balance-of-

payments assistance on concessional terms to low-income less-developed countries that agree to undertake medium-term structural adjustment programmes in order to overcome their balance-of-payments problems. The facility is to be funded with about 2.7 billion SDR in Trust Fund reflows expected to become available in 1985—91. Similar to the case of the Trust Fund, eligibility for SAF arrangements has been based on a per capita income criterion. On this basis 62 members are eligible to use the SAF. On 30 April 1989 32 SAF arrangements have been approved for a total amount of 1983 million SDR.

The member concerned develops and updates, with the assistance of the Fund and the World Bank, a medium-term policy framework for a three-year period. Detailed annual programmes are formulated prior to disbursement of annual loans.

2. *The enhanced structural adjustment facility (ESAF)*

It was recognized from the beginning that the resources available under the SAF might prove insufficient to support strong and comprehensive adjustment programmes necessary in the poorest countries. Therefore, in December 1987 the Executive Board established the ESAF to provide additional assistance to low-income countries undertaking structural adjustment programmes.

Objectives, eligibility and basic programme features parallel those of the SAF. Differences relate to provisions for access, monitoring and funding.

The facility is funded in part from SAF resources and in part from contributions (loans and grants) from aid agencies of members. Total concessional resources available for lending from the ESAF Trust were 5.1 billion SDR on 30 June 1990, in addition to the SAF resources. On 30 April 1990 a total amount of 1370 million SDR was approved in arrangements with 11 countries.

c. *Special Drawing Rights*

The first amendment to the Articles of Agreement made it possible to bring the SDR department (at that time the Special Drawing Account) into operation on 6 August 1969. A first allocation was made on 1 January 1970 (3 414 million SDR), a second on 1 January 1971 (2 949 million), a third (2 952 million) on 1 January 1972, a fourth (4 032.7 million) on 1 January 1979, a fifth (4 003.3 million) on 1 January 1980 and a sixth (4 052.5 million) on 1 January 1981. The SDR issues amount to 21.4 billion.

Up to 30 July 1990, a total of 181 billion SDR has been used in a wide variety of transactions and operations.

Since many currencies started floating in the seventies the Fund was obliged to introduce a new method of valuation of the SDR in order to stabilize its value. Since 1969 and until the second amendment, the SDR has been defined as equivalent to 0.888671 g of fine gold. As from 1 July 1974 one SDR was made equal to the sum of specified amounts of 16 currencies weighted on the basis of their share in world trade in 1968—72. (The currencies of those members with a share of world's total exports of goods and services exceeding one per cent were chosen for that purpose).

Since 1 January 1981, the number of currencies has been reduced to the currencies of the five countries with the largest shares of world exports of goods and services. The percentage weights assigned to these currencies as modified on 1 January 1986, are 42 for the US dollar, 19 for the Deutsche mark, 15 for the Japanese yen, and 12 each for the French franc and the pound sterling (Table 5).

The interest earned on excess SDR holdings (and paid on holdings below total SDR allocation) is determined weekly by reference to a combined market interest rate (weighted average on interest rates on specified short-terms domestic obligations in the money markets of the five currencies used for the valuation of the SDR). For the week beginning 24 April 1989 the rate was 8.05 per cent a year.

Table 5. SDR valuation (31 July 1990).

Currency	Currency amount (1)	Exchange rate (2)	US dollar equivalent (3)
Deutsche mark	0.5270	1.59600	0.330201
French franc	1.0200	5.35000	0.190654
Japanese yen	33.4000	146.92000	0.227335
Pound sterling	0.0893	1.85270	0.165446
US dollar	0.4520	1.00000	0.452000
			1.365636

SDR 1   = US$ 1.365640
US$1.00 = SDR 0.732260

Column 1: The currency components of the basket.
Column 2: Exchange rates in terms of currency units per US dollar, except for the pound sterling, which is expressed in US dollars per pound.
Column 3: The US dollar equivalents of the currency amounts in Column 1 at the exchange rates in Column 2 — that is, Column 1 divided by Column 2, except for the pound sterling, for which the amounts in the two columns are multiplied.
Source: IMF.

B. *Exchange-rate stability*

1. *Provisions*

Before the second amendment which has changed fundamentally the provisions concerning the exchange arrangements, each member was obliged to establish a par value which had to be expressed in gold or US dollars and could change that par value only with a view to correcting a "fundamental disequilibrium". The IMF had to be consulted beforehand; it ascertained whether the proposed change in the par value, together with any previous changes (since the accession of the country in question), exceeded the original rate by 10 per cent. If this was not so, the Fund raised no objection; if the 10 per cent limit was exceeded, it had to make known its decision within a certain time limit. Should the proposed change not have been greater than 20 per cent, the Fund declared its attitude, if so requested, within seventy-two hours. If it was higher than 20 per cent, the Fund was entitled to a longer period of reflection.

In the case of spot exchange transactions, deviations from parity exceeding 1 per cent were prohibited; in the case of other transactions, the margin could not be greater than the Fund deemed reasonable (former Article 4,*3*). Gold transactions were allowed only on the basis of the parity determined by the Fund (and within the prescribed margins).

Countries which, within the limits prescribed by the Fund, freely bought and sold gold for the settlement of international transactions were considered to fulfill the obligation under the former Article 4,*3*. This provision was included at the insistence of the United States, which thus did not have to purchase other currencies at their par value.

According to the new Article 4 the essential purpose of the international monetary system is to provide a framework which facilitates the exchange of goods, services, and capital and sustains sound economic growth; in addition, the principal objective is the development of the conditions necessary for financial and economic stability. Members must collaborate with the Fund and with other members in order to assure orderly exchange arrangements and to promote a stable system of exchange rates. This implies obligations with respect to domestic and external economic and financial policies. Each member should avoid manipulating exchange rates or the international monetary system in order to prevent effective balance-of-payments adjustments or to gain an unfair competitive advantage. Members must follow exchange policies compatible with these undertakings (Article 4,*1*).

Members may apply the exchange arrangements of their choice but have to notify the Fund of their decision. Any changes in the exchange arrangements must be communicated promptly (Article 4,*2a*).

Two types of arrangements are mentioned in Article 4,*2b*: (a) the maintenance by a member of a value for its currency in terms of the SDR or another denominator, other than gold, selected by the member, or (b) cooperative arrangements by which members maintain the value of their currencies in relation to the value of the currency or currencies of other members.

The Fund can, by an 85 per cent majority recommend general exchange arrangements that accord with the development of the international monetary system but without limiting each member's freedom to choose another exchange arrangement consistent with Article 4,*1* (Article 4,*2c*). The Fund may, for example, determine that international economic conditions permit the introduction of a widespread system of exchange arrangements based on stable but adjustable par values. The Fund will make the determination on the basis of the underlying stability of the world economy and notify members that the provisions of Schedule C apply (Article 4,*4*). According to Schedule C, *1* members may (but are not obliged to) establish a par value in terms of the SDR, or in terms of another common denominator (but gold or a currency are excluded) as is prescribed by the Fund.

A member wishing to establish a par value can at any time propose a par value to the Fund.

The margins for spot exchange transactions between currencies with par values will not be more than 4 1/2 per cent on either side of parity. By an 85 per cent majority the Fund may establish a different margin (Schedule C, *5*).

In order to oversee the effective operation of the international monetary system and the compliance by each member of its obligations concerning the exchange arrangement, the Fund will exercise strict surveillance over the exchange rate policies of the members and give guidance with respect to these policies. Each member will provide the Fund with the information necessary for such surveillance and, if so requested by the Fund, enter into consultation with the Fund on the member's exchange rate policies (Article 4,*3*).

2. *Operation*

The par values established when the Fund started operations were agreed despite the fact that evaluation was difficult in the circumstances, and the exchange rate between the dollar and the pound soon gave rise to difficulties. This was found advisable in order not to delay operations.

The artificial exchange rate between the dollar and the non-convertible pound sterling, for example, meant that exports from the other West European countries to Britain were stimulated and those to the United States inhibited. In the countries concerned, therefore, there was a sterling surplus and a dollar deficit. In order to remedy this situation, France established a free market for sterling and dollars in January 1948. French exporters to Britain were obliged to convert the proceeds of their sales into the national currency at the official rate, while exporters to the United States enjoyed more favourable terms. Hence, exports to Britain were curbed and those to the United States were encouraged. Similarly, it was advantageous for exporters of certain British goods to the United States to arrange for them first of all to pass in transit through France, since dollars fetched more pounds on the French market than in London. The Fund protested against this system, and as the French government did not abandon it, the Fund deprived France on 16 October 1948 of the right to draw any further on IMF resources. (This ban was extended until 15 October 1954).

Italy applied a similar system and — as in the case of France — justified it by the overvaluation of sterling in relation to the dollar, but in November 1948 concluded an agreement with Britain terminating it.

The devaluation of sterling by 30.5 per cent on 18 September 1949 served to eliminate the difficulties but was the signal for a whole series of devaluations. Between 18 and 21 September, the Fund gave decision on thirteen applications to change par values (Australia, Belgium, Denmark, Egypt, Iceland, the Netherlands, Norway and South Africa being among the countries concerned). At the same time exchange rates were modified by countries for which no par value had yet been agreed or which were not member states (e.g., Austria).

The Fund did not have the time needed to make a thorough investigation of every case. This was also due to the fact that the Fund had taken no initiative in the matter and tended rather to play a passive role. (No provision was made, on the other hand, for granting assistance.) Nevertheless, most of the par values of the major industrial countries established in 1949 were maintained for nearly twenty years.

The Fund did not approve the new par value of the French franc until 27 December 1958. Among the changes subsequent to 1949 were three revaluations, the German and Dutch currencies being revised upward by 5 per cent in March 1961 and the German currency again by 9.3 per cent in October 1969. When the United Kingdom devalued by 14.3 per cent on 18 November 1967, a number of other countries followed suit, including Ireland, Israel and Spain. New Zealand devalued by 20 per cent, Denmark by 8 per cent, Hong Kong by 5.7 per cent and Iceland by 24.6 per cent. The Fund accepted those adjustments as introducing a better balance among the world's currencies without competitive exchange depreciation.

On 12 November 1968 Iceland devalued by a further 35.2 per cent and on 10 August 1969 France by 11.1 per cent. Turkey devalued by 40 per cent on 9 August 1970, Ecuador by 28 per cent on 17 August 1970 and Yugoslavia by 16.7 per cent on 23 January 1971, while Austria revalued by 5.05 per cent on 9 May 1971.

With regard to the exchange margins of 1 per cent on either side of parity, the Fund has had to resign itself to the fact that this margin was often wider. In a communication sent to the member countries in December 1947, the Fund legitimized these floating currency practices by regarding them as multiple currency practices, which it could permit on a temporary basis.

Temporary fluctuating rates have sometimes been tolerated and even recommended in order to facilitate the determination of a suitable fixed parity.

On 20 March 1981 the Fund defined its policy regarding multiple currency practices. Are considered as such and require the prior approval of the Fund:

a) official action that gives rise "to a spread of more than 2 per cent between buying and selling rates for spot exchange transactions" (an exchange spread arising without official action or representing additional costs and exchange risks is not considered a multiple currency practice);

b) official action that creates a broken cross rate (the exchange rate between two currencies is inconsistent with their exchange rates in terms of a third currency). This is considered to be the case when the cross rate differential exceeds 1 per cent for more than one week.

Approval of multiple currency practices will be granted for periods of approximately one year, provided the practices are temporary and do not give the member concerned an unfair comparative advantage.

It is difficult to judge how far the IMF provisions have been complied with because some countries, while having an agreed par value, have not carried on all, or even any, of their transactions at parity exchange rates, and other countries, without agreed par values, have maintained fixed (unitary) exchange rates for many years. Since 1954 Fund members have adhered increasingly to the par value system, and by 1969 those so doing accounted for over 90 per cent of world trade.

The continuing weakness of the United States balance of payments and the resulting lack of confidence in the United States dollar gave rise to substantial speculative capital movements. Western Germany and the Netherlands let their currencies float on 9 May 1971 while the Belgium-Luxemburg Economic Union changed the regulations on its dual exchange market in order that the free market rate could henceforth make a premium (and not only a discount as before) in relation to the official market rate (the dual market was abolished in 1990).

On 15 August 1971 the United States suspended convertibility of the dollar into gold and other reserve assets, thus removing one of the foundation stones of the international monetary system. Other countries now allowed their currencies to float and France introduced a dual-exchange market.

Speculation against the United States dollar continued and on 18 December 1971 the Club of Ten — not the Fund — reached an agreement on a realignment of the major currencies: a devaluation (in terms of gold and SDR) of the dollar by 7.89 per cent, the Swedish krona and the Italian lire by 1 per cent, a revaluation of the Benelux currencies by 2.76 per cent, the German mark by 4.61 per cent and the yen by 7.66 per cent. The Canadian dollar continued to float. On the same day the Fund raised the margins of fluctuations for the exchange rates against the intervention currencies from 1 to 2.25 per cent either side of the parity, as indicated by par values or central rates. Members not wishing to maintain their exchange rates on the basis of par values (without opting for floating exchange rates) could henceforth communicate a central rate to the Fund. These rates take effect unless the Fund finds them unsatisfactory. They could be expressed (at that time) in gold, SDR or in another member's currency.

The widening of margins has meant that the exchange rates of a currency against another currency (other than the intervention currency) may at a given moment fluctuate within margins of 4.5 per cent either side of parity. If, at a certain moment, the dollar in Belgium reaches the upper limit (+2.25 per cent) and at the same moment in France reaches the lower limit (−2.25 per cent), the deviation of the exchange rate between the Belgian and the French franc against parity is equal to 4.5 per cent. If subsequently the dollar in Belgium reaches its lower limit and in France its upper limit, the fluctuation in time equals 9 per cent.

Toward the EMS

The potential fluctuations of 9 per cent made some members fear that capital movements would be encouraged. Hence the decisions of the European Economic Community (EEC) countries on 21 March 1972 (effective 24 April 1972) not to allow margins of fluctuations between member countries currencies exceeding 2.25 per cent on either side of the mutual parity (the so-called "snake" countries; the width of the snake can, of course, be less than 2.25 per cent). According to an earlier agreement of 21 August 1971 the Benelux currencies fluctuated even within smaller margins (0.75 per cent on either side of the mutual parity: the Benelux worm thus moved within the snake).

On 1 May 1972 the United Kingdom, Ireland and Denmark and on 23 May Norway, joined the EEC countries but on 23 June the United Kingdom and Ireland had to suspend their participation and let their currency float. Denmark followed suit on 27 June but rejoined on 10 October.

After a temporary stabilization of exchange markets in the second half of 1972 new difficulties arose at the end of 1972: short-term interest rates increased more in Europe than in the United States, preventing the return of funds to that country. Another destabilizing factor was the use of the dollar as a vehicle currency for the outflow of funds from Italy, largely to Switzerland. Italy established a dual exchange market in January 1973 and the Swiss franc started floating.

Another devaluation of the dollar (by 10 per cent) followed on 13 February 1973 (raising the official price of one ounce fine gold to 42.2 dollars) but intervention in support of the new dollar exchange rate was still necessary. The yen and the lira became floating currencies. On 12 March the EEC countries decided no longer to intervene in order to keep the dollar within the margins agreed in December 1971. At the same time the German mark was revalued by 3 per cent (the Austrian schilling by 2.25 per cent). The snake agreement was maintained. The dollar became a floating currency in relation to most EEC countries.

After a new speculative attack against the dollar and the tensions caused within the snake the German mark was revalued by 5.5 per cent on 29 June

1973 and the Dutch and Norwegian currencies were revalued on 17 September and 16 November respectively.

The sharp rise in oil prices had important consequences. France was obliged to let its currency float from 21 January 1974 until 10 July 1975 and again from 15 March 1976. The French and Italian dual-rate exchange markets were abolished on 21 and 22 March 1974 respectively. The Benelux arrangement came to an end on 15 March 1976.

On 29 April 1977 the Fund adopted principles for the guidance of member's exchange rate policies: (a) manipulation of exchange rates or of the international monetary system aimed at preventing effective balance-of-payments adjustment or gaining an unfair competitive advantage must be avoided; (b) intervention on the exchange market is obligatory if necessary to counter disorderly conditions (characterized *inter alia* by disruptive short-term movements in the exchange rate); (c) interests of other members should be taken into account when those interventions are made.

During the seventies, especially from 1970 to 1973, a wide variety of exchange practices has developed. This contrasts with the last three complete years of the operation of the par value system (1968 to 1970), when only Canada changed from a fixed peg to a floating arrangement. (The DM also floated briefly in 1969 before returning to a par value.)

At the end of 1978 the EEC decided to create a European Monetary System (which came into force on 13 March 1979). For each currency a central rate expressed in European Currency Units (ECU), has been established. Fluctuation margins are maintained to 2.25 per cent around these exchange rates. EEC countries with a floating currency may opt for margins up to 6 per cent on the implementation of the EMS (Italy did so till 1990), but these margins should be gradually reduced. Intervention in currencies of participating countries is compulsory when the intervention points defined by the fluctuation margins are reached.

Since the snake agreement (1972) the Deutsche mark was revalued eight times, the Dutch guilder six times, the Belgian franc three times, the Danish crown two times. Devaluations were more frequent: six times in Denmark, five times in Italy, four times in France and Norway, three times in Sweden, once in Belgium.

After the formation of the EMS (1979) twelve realignments took place (the last but one on 11 January 1987); the last on 5 January 1990 to take account of Italy's decision to place the lira within the 2.25 band.

Spain and the United Kingdom entered the EMS exchange rate mechanism in June 1989 and October 1990, respectively (both with margins of fluctuations of 6 per cent).

In the early eighties a steep rise of the dollar in the exchange markets was observed. In late February 1985 only the dollar began to depreciate relative to most other major currencies: it lasted till 1988.

Exchange-rate arrangements

On 30 September 1990 it was possible to distinguish the following categories of countries in the field of exchange-rate arrangements. Classification is often misleading, however. Floating currencies may be managed in such a way that the result is little different from pegging.

a) 25 countries whose currency is pegged to the dollar, including Afghanistan, Ethiopia, Iraq, Syrian Arab Republic, Yemen;
b) 14 African countries pegging their currency to the French franc;
c) 5 countries pegging their currency to another currency (South African Rand, Indian Rupee, Australian dollar);
d) 7 countries pegging their currency to the SDR, including Iran, and Libya;
e) 37 countries pegging their currency to other composites, including Algeria, Austria, Finland, Hungary, Israel, Jordan, Malaysia, Morocco, Norway, Poland, Romania, Sweden, Thailand;
f) 4 countries whose currency shows a limited flexibility vis-à-vis the dollar, including Saudi Arabia;
g) 9 countries forming the European Monetary System: Belgium, Denmark, France, Germany, Ireland, Italy, Luxemburg, Netherlands, Spain;
h) 3 countries with a more flexible currency, adjusted according to a set of indicators: Chile, Colombia, Madagascar;
i) 23 countries with more flexible (managed floating) currencies, including China, Egypt, Greece, India, Indonesia, Mexico, Pakistan, Portugal, Turkey, Yugoslavia;
j) 26 countries with independently floating currencies, including Argentina, Australia, Bolivia, Brazil, Canada, Japan, New Zealand, Philippines, South Africa, United Kingdom, United States, Uruguay, Venezuela and Zaïre.

C. *Currency convertibility*

1. *Provisions*

The provisions for the encouragement of multilateral trade (Article 8) were inserted in the Articles of Agreement under pressure from the United States, which regard the restoration of multilateral trade as the main purpose of the Fund. Without the Fund's approval, the introduction or maintenance of restrictions on current international transactions is prohibited; discriminatory measures *vis-à-vis* the currencies of certain member countries or multiple currency practices are also ruled out (Article 8,*2* and *3*). Though controls necessary to regulate international capital movements are allowed, these controls must not restrict payments for current transactions or unduly delay transfers of funds in settlement of commitments (Article 6,*3*). These commitments also relate to current transactions. It is seen from Article 30,*d*, that "payments for current transactions" comprise not only current transactions but also "transfer payments" such as donations, gifts and inheritances. Discrimination against "scarce" currencies is possible (see below).

In the period immediately after World War II, the majority of countries were unable to fulfill these provisions without jeopardizing their balance-of-payments equilibrium. For this reason, the restrictions on payments and transfers (referred to in Article 8) could provisionally be maintained (Article 14,*2*). After the second amendment the provisions of Article 14 relating to ". . . restrictions . . . that were in effect on the date on which it became a member" have, however, been maintained. Even though a member is availing itself of Article 14,*2*, it may not introduce *new restrictions* on current payments without the approval of the Fund under Article 8. The Fund has to report each year on the restrictions still in force and if it finds that a member maintains restrictions inconsistent with the purposes of the Fund, the member may be declared ineligible to use the general resources of the Fund (Article 14,*3*). Members have to declare whether they wish to avail themselves of the transitional arrangements of Article 14,*2* or whether they are prepared to accept the obligations laid down in Article 8.

With a view to the implementation of currency convertibility, each member is, subject to certain conditions, obliged to purchase amounts of its currency held by another member for SDR (prior to the second amendment: gold) or that member's currency if the latter so requests and furnishes evidence that this currency has recently been acquired as a result of current transactions or that it is required in order to pay for operations of the same type (Article 8,*4*). As such evidence is difficult to provide, this clause has had little practical effect.

The IMF articles do not contain a definition of a 'convertible currency'. This concept was always ambiguous. A new concept, the 'freely usable currency', is adopted by the Second Amendment.

2. *Operation*

Initially, only the United States, Mexico, Panama and El Salvador (in 1946) and Guatemala (in 1947) accepted the obligations set out in Article 8. The other members invoked Article 14.

To a certain extent under pressure from the United States, the United Kingdom made an effort in 1947 to restore convertibility of sterling. After the United States had granted a loan of 3 750 million and Canada a loan of 1 250 million dollars, the Bank of England declared the pound convertible on 15 July 1947. Many creditors, however, converted their sterling claims into dollars, so that the Bank's exchange reserves rapidly dwindled. Convertibility had to be suspended on 20 August 1947. The failure of this experiment made the other countries extremely cautious.

The transition period therefore had to be extended. Moreover, many states were unwilling to forgo the possibility of imposing restrictions until such time as their competitors proceeded to do so. After 1947 there were only a few additions to the number of countries with fully convertible currencies (Honduras in 1950, Canada in 1952, the Dominican Republic and Haiti in 1953). Nevertheless, the expansion of multilateral trade was encouraged by the European Payments Union (EPU: see Chapter 6).

On 27 December 1958 limited external convertibility of the currencies of thirteen members of the EPU was introduced. Greece followed suit in May 1959. Non-residents of these countries became entitled to convert their current earnings into gold or dollars. Fifteen other countries which did not belong to the EPU also introduced external convertibility, i.e., Australia, Burma, Ceylon, Ghana, India, Iraq, Jordan, Libya, Malaya, Morocco, New Zealand, Pakistan, South Africa, Sudan and Tunisia.

On 15 February 1961 ten countries (Belgium, France, Ireland, Italy, Luxemburg, the Netherlands, Peru, Sweden, the United Kingdom and Western Germany) ceased to avail themselves of Article 14. In other words, they too restored full convertibility. In the succeeding years many countries followed suit. On 30 April 1990 sixty-eight member countries had a convertible currency. As most of them are developed countries, almost 70 per cent of world trade is thus conducted on a multilateral basis.

As required by Article 14,*3* the Fund publishes annual reports in which all restrictions on international payments maintained by member countries are recorded. Since March 1952 the possibility of withdrawing these restrictions has been examined each year with the countries concerned. The Fund and GATT engaged in close consultation with regard to the balance-of-payments need for imposing restrictions. Although they are pursuing two different aspects (restrictions on payments and restrictions on trade) of the same aim, they have managed "to settle down to a reasonable working basis" (B. Tew).

D. *Promotion of international cooperation*

1. *Provisions*

General directives on the furthering of international cooperation in the monetary and commercial field are contained in several of the Articles of Agreement (Article 1, *i* and Article 4,*1*). Member countries are repeatedly exhorted to take account of the possible comments of other participating countries. Any country that takes steps to diminish the demand for currency which has been declared scarce (see below) has to bear in mind the objections of other member countries when applying such measures (Article 7,*4*). Provision is also made for negotiations in the event of the restrictions under Article 14 conflicting with agreements previously concluded between certain states (Article 8,*6*).

The Fund itself cooperates with all international organizations having similar responsibilities (Article 10). Finally, it can ask member countries for such information as it deems necessary for its operations (Article 8,5).

2. *Operation*

Apart from the consultations the Fund regularly has with other international and regional organizations (especially with the World Bank) and with the countries that take advantage of Article 14 or accept the obligations of Article 8 (these consultations are now effected on the basis of the new Article 4), mention should also be made of the training and technical services provided by the Fund. Staff members or outside experts are assigned, in teams or individually, to countries requesting assistance in the preparation and carrying-out of monetary, exchange or fiscal policies, the drafting of banking legislation or the development of financial statistics. The Fiscal Affairs Department, the Central Banking Department and the Bureau of Statistics, in collaboration with other departments, play an important part in this work.

The IMF Institute, set up in 1964, was given the task of centralizing and expanding the Fund's training programme. Its major task has been to conduct regular courses on financial analysis and policy for officials from central banks and Finance Ministries of member countries. Courses on balance-of-payments methodology and public finance are also provided. The courses are given in English and French, in Spanish (since 1966) and in Arabic (since 1985). The number of officials trained since the programme's inception totals some 7 300 from mostly less-developed countries.

E. *Conservation (and increase) of resources*

1. *Provisions*

In the event of a depreciation or appreciation of a currency, the SDR value of the currency held by the Fund (in the general resources account) has to be maintained (Articles 5,*11a*). This provision does not apply to computations relating to exchange rates and margins for exchange transactions (Article 4 and Schedule C) since the common denominator must not be the SDR (Article 5,*11b*).

The other provisions with respect to conservation of the Fund's resources are aimed, on the one hand, at obliging member states gradually to repurchase the national currency for SDR or the currencies of other members specified by the Fund (Article 5,7 and Schedule B), and, on the other, at avoiding a deficit in a given currency. In addition, charges and remunerations as well as gold sales influence the resources of the Fund.

a. *Charges and remunerations*

The Fund levies a service charge on the purchase by a member of SDR or the currency of another member in the General Resources Account in exchange for its own currency, provided that the Fund may levy a lower service charge on reserve tranche purchases than on other purchases. The service charge on reserve tranche purchases shall not exceed 0.50 per cent. The Fund may also levy a charge for stand-by or similar arrangements. The Fund may decide that the charge for an arrangement shall be offset against the service charge levied on purchases under the arrangement. Finally, the Fund levies periodic charges on its average daily holdings of a member's currency resulting from purchases from the Fund and from certain other transactions that increase these holdings (Article 5,*8a* and *b*).

Whenever the Fund's holdings of a member's currency (after exclusion of currency holdings on which the member is obliged to pay charges to the Fund) are below a percentage equal to the sum of 75 per cent of the quota prior to the second amendment plus the amounts of any subsequent quota increases (and minus similar amounts relating to quota decreases), as a percentage of the new quota, a remuneration is paid by the Fund (in principle in SDR). For countries joining the Fund after the second amendment the percentage will be calculated on the basis of the percentages of quotas of the other members on the date on which that country becomes a member (Article 5,*9*).

b. *Repurchases*

When its balance-of-payments and reserve position improves, a member is normally expected to repurchase the Fund's holdings that result from a purchase and are subject to charges. If, according to the Fund, the member has not respected this obligation, the Fund may, after consultation with the member, represent to the member that it should repurchase, whereupon the member will be obliged to make the repurchase (Article 5,*7b*).

The member which has used resources in the credit tranches, compensatory financing and buffer stocks is obliged to repurchase not later than five years from the date of a purchase.

Countries settling previous purchases reacquire their own currencies from the Fund. Members are not obliged to buy back the entire amount themselves; if other members acquire the same currency from the Fund, the amount of these purchases is subtracted.

The Fund can prescribe that repurchases may be made in instalments beginning three years, and ending five years, after the purchase. A member must discharge this obligation even if its balance-of-payments and reserve position has not improved. By an eighty-five per cent majority, the periods for repurchase may be changed uniformly for all members (Article 5,*7c* and *d*).

The Fund may supplement the policies on the selection of currencies to be sold (Article 5,*3d*; see 4A1a) by selling those holdings of a member's currency that have not been repurchased in accordance with the member's obligation. The sale is without prejudice to other actions of the Fund (e.g., higher charges on the holdings that should have been repurchased and a declaration of ineligibility (see below) to use the Fund's general resources (Article 5,*7h*).

Repurchases must be made with SDR or with the currencies of other members specified by the Fund. The Fund's holdings of the currency of a member that is used in repurchase may not be increased by repurchase above the level at which they would be subject to charges. As already seen (4A2a), the Fund has to develop policies on the currencies to be used in repurchase (Article 5,*7i*).

Under Article 5,*7j*, the issuer of a currency that has been specified by the Fund for use in a repurchase and is not a freely usable currency must guarantee the repurchasing member the necessary amounts of the currency in exchange for a freely usable currency it has selected (at a rate of exchange consistent with Article 19,*7a*), if the repurchasing member wishes to do so at the time of the repurchase.

c. *Replenishment and scarce currency*

In order to replenish its holdings of any member's currency in the general resources account needed in connection with its transactions, the Fund may propose to this member that, in accordance with conditions to be agreed upon, it should lend the Fund an amount of its currency (or grant consent for such a loan to be obtained from an institution either within or outside the country's territory). However, there is no obligation to do so (Article 7,*1i*). As from the second amendment the criterion for replenishment is not the "scarcity" (in the traditional sense) of the currency, but the Fund's need to obtain additional amounts of a currency for use in present or prospective transactions.

The Fund can also (Article 7,*1ii*) require the member, if it is a participant, to sell its currency to the Fund for SDR held in the general resources account, subject to the provision of Article 19,*4* and *5* (see above).

If the Fund observes a general shortage in a given currency, it brings this to the notice of the member countries and examines the underlying causes. A representative of the country concerned participates in the preparation of the Fund's report (Article 7,*2*), in which it is ascertained whether this country is in default (e.g., by the maintenance of import restrictions). The Fund may take such steps as may be needed to remedy this situation. If the demand for the currency concerned remains so high that the Fund runs the risk of no longer being able to supply it, it declares this currency "scarce" (Article 7,*3a*). After consultation with the Fund, all member countries are authorized temporarily to introduce strictly necessary restrictions on exchange transactions with the country whose currency has become scarce (Article 7,*3b*).

d. *Gold sales*

Pursuant to the amended Articles the Fund has to complete the sale of up to twenty-five million ounces of gold, at the former official price, to those countries that were members on 31 August 1975 and up to another twenty-five million ounces at a price based on prices in the market (see 4A2b).

In selling gold the Fund must:

a) promote better international surveillance of international liquidity;
b) make the SDR the principal reserve asset in the international monetary system;
c) avoid management of the price, or establishment of a fixed price, in the gold market.

Members undertake (Article 8,7) to collaborate with the Fund and with other members in order to ensure that their policies with respect to reserve assets will be consistent with the objectives set out in (a) and (b) above (Article 5,*12a*).

The Fund may sell gold for the currency of any member after consulting the member for whose currency the gold is sold, provided that the Fund's holding of member's currency held in the general resources account will not be increased by the sale above the level at which they would be subject to charges (Article 5,*12b*). The Fund may accept payments from a member in gold instead of SDR or currency in any operations or transactions under this Agreement. Payments to the Fund under this provision shall be at a price agreed for each operation or transaction on the basis of prices in the market (Article 5,*12d*).

The balance of gold held after the disposition of the fifty million ounces referred to above can be sold by the Fund at the former official price. When the Fund does so, an amount of the proceeds equivalent at the time of sale to one SDR per 0.888671 g of fine gold will be placed in the general resources account and, except as the Fund may decide otherwise under Article 5,*12*, any excess will be held in the special disbursement account (Article 5,*12f*).

The special disbursement account is established in the general department, but the assets are kept separate from the other assets of the general department. Pending use of the assets held in the special disbursement account, the Fund may invest them in income-producing and marketable obligations of members or of international financial organizations. No investment can be made without the approval of the member whose currency is used to make the investment. The obligations must be denominated in SDR or in the currency used to make the investment (Article 5,*12h*).

The special disbursement account may be terminated by a seventy per cent majority. The assets held in the special disbursement account may be used at any time: (a) to make transfers to the general resources account for immediate use, e.g., balance-of-payments assistance on special terms to less-developed members in difficult circumstances (Article 5,*12f*); (b) for distribution to those less-developed countries that were members on August 31, 1975, in proportion to their quotas on that date (Article 5,*12f*).

The Fund may decide, by an eighty-five per cent majority to transfer a part of the excess referred to in Article 5,*12f* above to the investment account (Article 5,*12g*) which it is authorized to establish in the general department by a majority of the votes cast (Article 12,*6f(i)*). Other assets of this account can consist of currencies transformed from the general resources account for immediate investment, the income from investment and the proceeds of matured or liquidated investments (Article 12,*6f(ii)*).

The Fund may invest a member's currency held in the investment account in marketable obligations of that member or in marketable obligations of international financial organization. No investments may be made without the approval of the member whose currency is used to make the investment. The Fund will invest only in obligations denominated in SDR or in the currency used for investment (Article 12,*6f(iii)*).

2. *Operation*

a. *Charges and remunerations*

The scale of "continuing" charges laid down in the original Articles of Agreement remained in effect until 1 May 1963, when minor changes were introduced. Since 27 July 1969 no service charge has been payable in respect of reserve tranche purchases. A service charge of 0.5 per cent is payable on purchases other than reserve tranche purchases. There is also a charge of 0.25 per cent a year, akin to a commitment fee, payable at the beginning of each 12-month period on the undrawn balance of a stand-by or extended arrangement. A member subsequently making a purchase under the arrangement receives a refund of the charges attributable to the purchase. In addition, charges on balances in excess of 100 per cent of quota on transactions effected since 1 July 1974 are subject to a schedule, in which charges increased on the basis of time. With effect from 1 May 1981 a single rate of charge was introduced (Table 6). The rate is determined at the beginning of each financial year and is "based on the estimated income and expense of the Fund and taking into account a target amount of net income".

b. *Repurchases*

In 1952 the Executive Board decided that repayments would normally have to be made within three to five years. This decision is now embodied in the

Table 6. Fund charges on transactions on 31 January 1991 (per cent a year).[a]

Credit tranches, compensatory financing facility, buffer stock financing facility, and extended fund facility	Service charge Periodic charge	0.5 8.78
Supplementary financing facility	Service charge Periodic charge	0.5 Rate of interest paid by the Fund plus 0.325 per cent
Enlarged access policy	Serivce charge Periodic charge	0.5 Net cost of borrowing by the Fund plus 0.2 per cent

[a] Except for service charge, which is payable once on a transaction and is stated as a percentage of the amount of the transaction.
Souce: IMF.

new provisions. For drawings under stand-by arrangements in practice a maximum of three years is laid down.

On 22 March 1978 the Executive Board decided under the new Article 5,7c that the repurchase must be made in equal quarterly instalments (during the period beginning three years and ending five years after the date of the purchase).

A member that has outstanding purchases under the decision on the stabilization of prices of primary products is expected to make a repurchase at an earlier date when, and to the extent that, the international buffer stock for the financing of which the purchase was effected makes distributions in currency to the member.

Although any convertible or other currency deemed convertible for the purpose of repurchase was normally acceptable for repurchases, the Fund had, before the second amendment, adopted policies on the currencies to be used in repurchase; however, at that time there was no explicit basis for these policies in the Articles.

In the same way that drawings are best concentrated, as far as possible, on the currencies of countries with a strong balance of payments, repurchases are best made in the currencies of countries with a weak balance of payments. A list of the countries concerned is used by the Fund as a guide when advising members what currencies to use in drawings and repurchases.

Repurchases of all types since the inception of the Fund have amounted to the equivalent of 68 153 million SDR on 30 April 1989, approximately 30 per cent in dollars. Owing to the fact that fewer dollars were drawn, repurchases exceeded drawings to such an extent that as from February 1964 the dollars holdings of the Fund were often higher than 90 per cent of the United States quota. Up to 1969, and again from 1972 to 1974, the Fund could no longer accept repurchases in dollars.

c. *Replenishment and scarce currency*

One of the methods by which the Fund increases its resources consists in raising members' quotas. It also purchased members' currencies for gold. It did this on several occasions up to 1971.

In 1956, 1959 and 1960 the Fund sold 800 million dollars' worth of gold to the United States in order to acquire income-earning United States government securities. The gold value of these investments (terminated in 1971) was guaranteed by the United States government. The Fund borrowed the equivalent of 250 million dollars in Italian lire in August 1966 (the financial terms being similar to those applied under the General Arrangements to Borrow: see below). Japan acquired this claim from Italy in 1970 and the Fund repaid it in 1971.

On 23 December 1969 the IMF agreed to purchase South Africa's current gold production at 35 dollars an ounce over a period of five years, even if the free market price was lower. Gold stocks in existence at that date could also be gradually disposed of at the same price. South Africa could not, however, sell any gold to other monetary authorities. This agreement has been terminated in December 1973 (South Africa's gold sales amounted to the equivalent of 777 million SDR on 31 December 1971; no sales have taken place since 1971).

The Fund has not yet applied Article 7,*3*. Drawings on the dollar have in fact been restricted, but this currency was not declared scarce, even though it *was* scarce until 1951—52. To a certain extent this would have been superfluous, since most countries were availing themselves of Article 14.

The General Arrangements to Borrow (GAB)
International cooperation has increased support for the key currencies to overcome the difficulties they have experienced. In this connection, mention should be made of the General Arrangements to Borrow.

Owing to the large-scale short-term capital movements that occurred in the second half of 1960 as a result of lack of confidence in the dollar and sterling, it was feared that the Fund's resources might sometimes prove inadequate to protect these two currencies against speculation. On the strength of the former Article 7,*2* (new Article 7,*1*), therefore, the Fund embarked on negotiations with the Group of Ten which culminated in the agreement of 5 January 1962 concerning the lending of foreign exchange by certain member countries. The GAB came into effect on 24 October 1962 for a four-year period (6.2 billion dollars). A four-year extension from October 1966 was approved in 1965. The agreement was further extended each time for a period of five years.

Here the Fund acts as an intermediary. When one of the parties to the agreement makes a call on the Fund, the latter ascertains whether it needs supplementary resources for this purpose and if so requests the other countries to lend it a certain amount in their own currencies. Taking into account the present and future trend in their balances of payments, these countries then decide whether they can accept the proposal of the Fund's managing director.

On 24 February 1983 the Executive Directors approved the revision and enlargement of the GAB increasing the credit commitments from 6.4 billion SDR to 17 billion SDR (Table 7). The revised GAB became effective for a five-year period on 26 December 1983 when the participants had notified the Fund that they concur in the enlarged commitments. The Swiss National Bank adhered to the amended arrangements in April 1984.

A credit arrangement with Saudi Arabia relating to 1.5 billion SDR (and extended ever since) is separate but associated with the revised GAB. In the future, the GAB would be available not only for drawings by participants but also for purchases from the Fund for conditional financing for all its members, including members that are nonparticipants to the GAB, if the Fund commands inadequate resources to finance exceptional balance-of-payments difficulties of a size and character that would threaten the stability of the international monetary system. The Fund pays interest to the GAB countries at the rate at which it pays interest on holdings of SDR (see 4A2c).

Table 7. GAB credit commitments of Group of 10 countries and Switzerland.

Country	Million SDR	Shares in per cent
United States	4 250.0	25.00
Germany, Federal Republic of	2 380.0	14.00
Japan	2 125.0	12.50
France	1 700.0	10.00
United Kingdom	1 700.0	10.00
Italy	1 105.0	6.50
Canada	892.5	5.25
Netherlands	850.0	5.00
Belgium	595.0	3.50
Sweden	382.5	2.25
Switzerland	1 020.0	6.00
Total	17 000.0	100.00

Source: *IMF Survey*, March 1983.

Loans have in any case to be repaid through the Fund within three to five years. Upon request, the Fund attends to this before the borrowing country effects repayment.

Of the drawings of 1, 1.4 and 1.4 billion dollars by the United Kingdom in December 1964, May 1965 and June 1968, part was able to be made by means of these GAB (405, 525 and 476 million dollars respectively). On the first two occasions, Switzerland made available under its parallel arrangement amounts of 80 million dollars and 40 million dollars respectively. Also in June 1968 the Fund borrowed 265 million dollars in connection with the purchase of 745 million dollars by France. In June 1969 the Fund borrowed 200 million dollars and in September 1969 another 190.5 million dollars in connection with purchases by the United Kingdom and France respectively. A further 30 million dollars was borrowed in February 1970 in relation to a further purchase by France.

By August 1971 all indebtedness had been repaid by the Fund. No further borrowings took place until 1976. In order to finance the purchases under the stand-by arrangements for the United Kingdom and Italy, the Fund borrowed in January and May 1977 the equivalent of 582.9 million SDR under the GAB in connection with two of the purchases by the United Kingdom and 82.5 million SDR under the GAB in May 1977 for a purchase by Italy. In 1978/79 the equivalent of 777.3 million SDR was borrowed in connection with the purchase of the US under the reserve tranche.

d. *Gold sales*

The sale of one sixth of gold holdings for the benefit of the less-developed countries has already been dealt with (see Trust Fund). Direct sales of gold for distribution to members at the former official price of 35 SDR an ounce were made under a four-year programme. By the end of the programme in May 1980 25 million ounces of fine gold, equivalent to 874.3 million SDR was sold. At 30 June 1990 the Fund held 3 217 tons of gold.

e. *Income and reserves*

The Fund determines annually the proportion of its net income to be placed to the general or the special reserve and the proportion to be distributed.

In 1956, faced with a continuous excess of the Fund's expenditure over income, the Fund initiated an investment programme. Part of its gold was sold and the proceeds invested in United States Government securities in order to make good the erosion of capital that had resulted from an accumulation of administrative deficits.

After the elimination of the deficit the income from investment was placed in a reserve against possible future deficits, namely the special reserve. While the general reserve can be distributed to members, the special reserve cannot. Total reserves at 30 June 1990 amounted to 1 397 million SDR (of which 1 031 million were in the special reserve).

The greater part of the "operational" income, 1 940 million SDR in 1989/90, is derived from charges on balances of members' currencies held by the Fund in excess of their various quotas and from interest on holdings of SDR in the general resources account.

At 30 April 1990 the holdings on which the Fund levied charges amounted to 22 098 million SDR, the creditor position on which the Fund

paid remuneration to 15 486 million SDR. The operational expense was
1 256 million, the administrative expense 189 million, the net income of the
general resources account 86 million.

f. *Inter-central bank cooperation*

Although they were adopted outside the framework of the Fund, attention is
called to some monetary arrangements because of the influence they can
have on Fund operations.

In March 1961, at the Bank for International Settlements, the governors
of the central banks of Belgium, France, Germany, Italy, the Netherlands,
Sweden and the United Kingdom agreed to cooperate on foreign exchange
markets to assist currencies in difficulty as a consequence of speculation.
They have to hold each other's currencies to a greater extent than previously
and provide each other with short-term loans of currencies required for the
purpose of helping to finance sudden flights of capital.

APPRAISAL

Since its foundation the Fund has supplied foreign exchange amounting to no
less than 112 billion SDR. And we must not omit to mention the technical
assistance provided during the annual consultations with all member countries, within the IMF Institute, and assistance in the form of other advice
offered by the staff or experts recruited from governments and central banks.

Yet the Fund's policy has not been a success, partly because of the
indulgent attitude adopted towards credit requests and partly because
attention has been focused increasingly on aid to less-developed countries.
Nor has the Fund ever taken serious initiatives in the field of international
monetary arrangements: it always resigned itself to the existing situation. In
fact, its *raison d'être* disappeared in 1971 along with fixed exchange rates.

Credit granted too easily

As was stressed in the Fund's annual report for 1964, balance-of-payments
equilibria can normally be restored within a reasonably short time, and
without prolonged unemployment and stagnation in deficit countries or
undue inflationary pressures on surplus countries, by means of appropriate
economic policies. In other words, a smoothly operating international monetary system requires a sound economic, and more particularly monetary,
policy on the part of the various countries.

Even if the Fund has no jurisdiction in the internal policies of the member
states it should be firmer in making its assistance conditional on the countries

concerned pursuing sound economic policies and should withdraw such assistance if its directives are not followed — a principle that has not been applied often enough in the past, especially in the case of the United Kingdom, the United States and many less-developed countries. The United States, for example, could not be persuaded to devalue the dollar at the right time and to a substantial degree.

"The main long-run obstacle to the resurrection of an international monetary system ... is likely to be the vacuum created by the present concentration of the International Monetary Fund on courting political popularity with bailing-out credit, to the exclusion of any one far-sighted provision of international monetary leadership" (H. G. Johnson).

In addition, the role of the Fund does not imply aiding the private banks which have made reckless loans.

Undue preference to the less-developed countries

Although the Fund was not set up as an institution for assistance to less-developed countries (this is indeed incompatible with the non-discriminatory rules) its "reforms" constitute attempts to give as much assistance as possible to the less-developed countries. Although the many new facilities have no inbuilt legal discriminatory provision, in fact they are intended to benefit the less-developed countries. The wisdom of this can be questioned.

It is said of some less-developed countries, quite rightly, that "despite long-term Fund collaboration" they have made "little progress toward achieving the agreed objectives. The internal and external imbalances in these countries have not improved significantly, substantial inflation has persisted, and reliance on restrictive practices has continued" (S. Mookerjee). Corruption and inefficiency, even at the highest political and administrative levels, are the rule in many less-developed countries. As H. G. Johnson puts it, the Fund "has increasingly transformed the traditional concept of lending for a short term and at penalty rates only in the case of a liquidity crisis into the quite different concept of lending at subsidized rates to countries short of real resources — and itself into an agency for robbing the rich in order to give to the poor".

One of the consequences of the Fund's policy is the inflation of so many facilities in favour of the less-developed countries (Oil Facility, Trust Fund, Subsidy Account, Buffer Stock Facility, Supplementary Finance Facility, SAF and ESAF); this has contributed to making the rules of the Fund rather a hotchpotch. There is no longer a sharp distinction between the rules of the Fund and the Bank. If its members think that the Fund has primarily to provide aid to the less-developed countries, why not merge with the World Bank? The political and other problems that this raises — for instance, the managing director of the Fund is currently a European and the president of the Bank an American — are surely not insoluble (cf. appraisal IBRD).

The international monetary reserves

The international monetary reserves are influenced by many fortuitous and uncorrelated factors such as the deficits in the reserve-currency countries and the willingness of monetary authorities to hold these currencies. We must not forget that the international monetary reserves are not needed to finance trade but to finance balance-of-payments deficits. Only when balance-of-payments difficulties give rise to trade restrictions is there a correlation between reserves and trade.

There is general agreement that "There is no way of measuring the 'need' [for international monetary reserves] by scientifically tested rules and formulas. After all, one cannot foretell either which countries will suffer deficits of certain magnitudes or the propensities of the politicians in power" (F. Machlup).

The control of international liquidity "remains one of the most difficult problems, and one where we have not made any progress. Indeed, the situation has even deteriorated since I came to the Fund" (H. Witteveen, 1978). After all, the value of foreign exchange transactions in the main money centers is at least fifty times higher than the value of world trade in goods and services (about 3 500 billion dollars). And the resources of the central banks of the Group of Ten are comparatively insignificant (325 billion dollars). Despite what the authors of the Bretton Woods agreement had expected, "it has proved impossible (or, at least, inexpedient) to devise effective controls over short-term capital movements, which have returned to plague the stability of the system" (H. G. Johnson). This is also related to the fact that the Fund has no supervision over major financial agreements. As it is, the Fund has no say in the General Arrangements to Borrow, nor in the swap arrangements, although IMF decisions may be influenced by the latter. It is worth noting that the Fund has had no control over the operations of the European Monetary Agreement either. In fact, the important decisions are taken by the Group of Seven.

The ideal course would be to convert the Fund into an international central bank with supranational powers (provided the management was independent), but in the present circumstances this is impracticable.

The Federal Reserve System *de facto* fulfills the role of central bank of the world, while neither the other countries nor the IMF have much say in matters. Only the United States can ignore a persistent balance-of-payments deficit: they just pay in dollars that are accepted by each country (as long as there is confidence in the dollar). The net international investment position of the United States fell from 106 billion dollars net assets in 1980 to approximately 700 billion net foreign liabilities in 1990. No wonder that world inflation has been stimulated. In this respect the governments of the United States have shown little sense of responsibility.

In the dollar reserve system the other countries and the IMF should have some degree of control over American economic policy. Since many central banks have converted balances of unreliable currencies into German marks, Swiss francs and even Japanese yen, the share of the German mark in the total of the official reserve currencies rose from 2 per cent in 1970 to 21 per cent in 1990.

Countries which have little enthusiasm for giving the United States such a dominant role have hopes of creating a European reserve currency unit, but this will not be practicable without a minimum of economic policy coordination and of political unity, which is hardly likely to be àchieved in the near future. Meanwhile Germany and Japan could also provide money to the world.

SDR

In spite of the Fund's decision to express all its published statistics in SDR, the SDR is a unit of account which is not often used in practice (and is not even stable, while its value is determined on the basis of five currencies).

Nevertheless, the proposal to make the SDR the principal reserve asset of the international monetary system would be attractive if the IMF were well administered. This, however, is not the case. The allocation of SDR took place when the world was overwhelmed with dollars; thus the creation of SDR gave a further stimulus to international inflation. And once again it was decided to allocate further SDR (not for quantitative reasons but in order to keep the idea of SDR alive!). Under the existing circumstances the SDR is "une sorte de prime au déficit, créée au détriment des pays qui vivent selon leurs moyens" (C. de Ribet-Petersen). Many countries use their SDR (allocated to finance deficits resulting from unsound economic policies) and then leave things as they were.

BIBILOGRAPHY

A. *IMF publications*

In addition to the *Annual report of the Executive Board*, the *Summary proceedings, Annual meeting of the Board of Governors*, the *Annual report on exchange arrangements and exchange restrictions*, the Fund publishes the following reviews: *International Financial News Survey* (weekly up to 28 July 1972), *IMF Survey* (fortnightly, since 14 August 1972); *International Financial Statistics* and *Balance of Payments Statistics* (monthly and yearbook issue); *Government Finance Statistics Yearbook; Direction of Trade Statistics* (monthly; jointly with the IBRD); *World Economic Outlook* (twice a year); *Staff Papers* (four issues a year) and *Finance and Development* (quarterly; jointly with IBRD, designed to explain the operation of the two organizations) regularly publish interesting articles about the IMF.

See also *Selected decisions of the International Monetary Fund and selected documents* (12th ed., 1986). Papers of a *Pamphlet Series*, written by IMF officials, appear at irregular intervals, notably: M. Ainley, *The General Arrangements to Borrow* (1984); *Technical assistance and training services of the International Monetary Fund* (1985); *Selected publications of*

Sir Joseph Gold on the International Monetary Fund and monetary law, Heidelberg, Recht und Wirtschaft, 1990.

Since 1981 the Fund also releases *Occasional Papers*, e.g.: B. Vibe Christensen, *Switzerland's role as an international financial center* (July 1986); *Fund-supported programs, fiscal policy, and income distributions* (Sept. 1986); P. S. Heller, *Aging and social expenditure in the major industrial countries, 1980—2025* (Sept. 1986).

See also, *The International Monetary Fund, 1945—1965. Twenty years on international monetary cooperation* (1969) — Vol. 1: J. K. Horsefield, *Chronicle*; Vol. 2: M. G. De Vries et al., *Analysis*; Vol. 3: *Documents* (reproducing most of the documents referred to in the first two volumes); M. G. De Vries, *The International Monetary Fund, 1966—71, The system under stress* (1976): 2 volumes; trace in detail the steps which have led to the Fund's main policy decisions (Vol. 2 reproducing documents); M. G. De Vries, *The International Monetary Fund, 1972—1978. Cooperation on trial* (1986): 3 volumes (Vol. 3 is a compilation of documents); M. G. De Vries, *The IMF in a changing world, 1945—85* (1986), paperback containing updated articles; *Problems of international money, 1972—85* (ed. M. Posner, 1986), papers of a seminar.

B. *Other publications*

At irregular intervals bibliographies on the abundant literature concerning the Fund and the international monetary system are published in the *Staff Papers*, the last by A. Salda, relates to 1984 (in the December 1985-issue).

J. Williamson, *The lending policies of the International Monetary Fund* (Institute for International Economics, Washington, 1982); L. T. Katseli, Devaluation: a critical appraisal of the IMF's policy prescriptions, *American Economic Review*, May 1983; R. Vaubel, The moral hazard of IMF lending, *The World Economy*, September 1983; G. Biron, J. Mont, G. Noppen, Le DTS, *Revue de la Banque*, 1985, No. 8.

C. F. Bergsten & J. Williamson, *The multiple reserve currency system and international monetary reform* (Institute for International Economics, Washington, 1982); J. Williamson, *The exchange rate system* (Institute for International Economics, rev. ed., Washington, 1985); id. (ed.), *IMF conditionality* (Institute for International Economics, Washington, 1983); B. Tew, *The evolution of the international monetary system, 1945—85* (3rd ed., London, Hutchinson, 1985). C. D. Finch, *The IMF. The record and the prospect*, Princeton, NJ, International Finance Section, 1989; Committee on Banking and Urban Affairs, *Role of the International Monetary Fund* (Hearing before the Subcommittee on International Development Finance, Trade and Monetary Policy, H.R., 101st Congress, 2nd session, March 1, 1990), Washington, U.S. Government Printing Office, 1990.

The extracts quoted are from: B. Tew, *The International Monetary Fund: its present role and future prospects* (Princeton, Princeton University Press, 1961); C. de Ribet-Petersen, Les droits de tirage spéciaux, *Economie Appliquée*, 1971, No. 3; H. G. Johnson, On living without an international monetary system, *Euromoney*, April 1975; id. World inflation and the international monetary system, *Three Banks Review*, Sept. 1975; F. Machlup, The need for monetary reserves, *Banca Nazionale del Lavoro Quarterly Review*, Sept. 1966; S. Mookerjee, Policies on the use of the Fund resources, *IMF Staff Papers*, Nov. 1966; A conversation with Mr. Witteveen, *Finance and Development*, Sept. 1978.

2. The World Bank Group

> *It will be the duty of the Bank, by wise and prudent lending, to promote a policy of expansion of the world's economy in the sense in which this term is the exact opposite of inflation.*
>
> JOHN MAYNARD KEYNES

On the same pattern as that used for the IMF, this chapter deals first with the principal provisions concerning the International Bank for Reconstruction and Development, and with its functions and significance. Its origins have already been outlined in the previous chapter. We then go on to discuss the Bank's two affiliates — the International Development Association and the International Finance Corporation.

THE INTERNATIONAL BANK FOR RECONSTRUCTION AND DEVELOPMENT

1. OBJECTIVES

Although in the drafting of its objectives a great deal of importance was attached to the need for reconstruction in countries ravaged by the war (Articles 1,*i—v* and 3,*1*) and for the promotion of international trade expansion and balance-of-payments equilibrium (Article 1,*iii*), the Bank's main aims may be said to be:

1. Making or guaranteeing loans for development projects in less-developed countries, either from its own capital or with borrowed funds (Article 1,*ii*). Article 1,*ii* refers also to the encouragement of capital formation in the less-developed countries by guarantees and participations in private investments, but, in fact, the Bank has not acted as a guarantor or a participant in such investments.
2. The provision of technical assistance to the less-developed countries, which in most cases have no experts available in the field of investment

73

projects; the Bank has therefore been constrained — although the Articles of Agreement do not explicitly refer to it — to engage in technical assistance to an increasing extent.

2. ORGANIZATION

A. *Members and capital*

Only IMF countries can join the Bank (Article 2,*1*; but see Article 6,*3* below). A distinction is made between original and other member countries; the latter's share in the capital is determined subsequent to their accession.

The number of member states has therefore grown in parallel with membership of the Fund. As at 1 January 1990 the Bank had 153 member countries. Cuba resigned from the Bank in November 1960, and in 1964 also withdrew from the IMF.

Initially, the Articles of Agreement specified an authorized capital of 10 billion dollars (Article 2,*2a*), with provision for increasing it (Article 2,*2b*). As a result of the Soviet Union's refusal to join (her subscription was fixed at 1.2 billion dollars), shares could be allotted to new member countries without increasing the capital, especially as most of the new members were countries with limited resources. The accession of Western Germany and Japan in 1953 could have caused the maximum to be exceeded, but their shares were kept at a low level.

On 15 September 1959 the capital was increased to 21 billion dollars (210 000 shares of 100 000 dollars). The subscriptions of all member states were doubled; a few countries whose quota was considered to be too small by comparison with their economic importance (e.g. Western Germany and Japan) were given the opportunity to subscribe jointly to 10 000 shares. In order to enable other countries to be accepted or to make possible special increases, the capital was raised many times (in 1963, 1965, 1970, 1977, 1980, 1981, 1984 and 1988).

Since the change in the valuation method of the SDR on 1 July 1974, its value diverges from the dollar value. Since 1978 the Bank expresses the value of its capital stock on the basis of the SDR. The capital was raised successively to 34 billion SDR (1977), to 70.5 billion SDR (1980), to 71 650 million SDR (1981) and to 78 650 million SDR (1984). As of 27 April 1988 the capital was increased to 102.6 billion SDR, representing 1 420 000 shares of 100 000 dollars each.

On 30 June 1990 the subscribed capital amounted to 94 623 million SDR, the paid-in capital to 5 679 million SDR. The largest shareholders are from the ranks of the developed countries (Table 8).

Twenty per cent of each quota can be called up (as is necessary for the Bank's activity) — 2 per cent in gold or dollars, 18 per cent in national currency (Articles 2,*5i* and *7i*). This was what was done when the Bank was

Table 8. Subscriptions to capital stock of principal IBRD countries, 30 June 1990.

Country	Amount (million SDR)	Per cent of total
United States	14 810	15.65
Japan	8 545	9.03
Germany	6 598	6.97
United Kingdom	6 324	6.68
France	5 033	5.32
Netherlands	3 235	3.42
China	3 187	3.37
India	2 888	3.05
Canada	2 874	3.04
Italy	2 291	2.42
Saudi Arabia	2 291	2.42
Belgium	2 277	2.41
Total	94 623	100.00

Source: IBRD, *Annual report*, 1990.

set up; the doubling of member countries' subscriptions in 1959 without an increase in the paid-in portion meant in practice that 1 per cent became payable in gold or dollars and 9 per cent in national currency. The countries whose share was more than doubled had to pay 10 per cent of the additional increase. Subsequently 10 per cent had to be subscribed.

The balance serves as security for the Bank's obligations. Calls of up to 80 per cent of each quota may be made for specific purposes (according to the choice of each member state, in gold, dollars or in the currency which the Bank requires), i.e. to provide guarantees or to fulfill commitments arising out of the borrowing of funds on the capital markets of the member countries or the underwriting of capital provided by private investors (Article 2,*5ii* and Article 4,*1a, ii* and *iii*). The 1959 and subsequent capital increases were intended mainly to augment the Bank's borrowing capacity on capital markets and consequently its lending, and not so much to obtain fresh funds from member countries. As soon as new resources are required, 20 per cent of the (supplementary) capital can be called.

The provisions concerning withdrawal and exclusion of member states (Article 6,*1* and *2*) are similar to those of the Fund. Countries which are no longer Fund members have to relinquish their membership of the Bank unless the Bank agrees by three-quarters of the voting power to allow it to remain a member (Article 6,*3*). Poland withdrew from the Bank on 14 March 1950 and Czechoslovakia — which failed to pay its full subscription — ceased to be a member (Article 6,*2*) on 31 December 1954. The accounts were settled in accordance with accurately determined terms and conditions (Article 6,*4*). Poland and Czechoslovakia rejoined the Bank on 27 June 1986 and 20 September 1990, respectively.

B. *Administration*

The Bank is administered along similar lines to the Fund. The Board of Governors meets once a year in September to approve the annual report and accounts (which have previously been examined by an auditor), to elect the directors and to take decisions on matters falling exclusively within its jurisdiction (Article 5,*2*). With respect to extraordinary meetings, the same rules apply as for the Board of Governors of the IMF (up to the present, none has been held).

The Executive Directors (Article 5,*4*) now number twenty-two, five of whom are appointed by the five largest shareholders and seventeen elected. The Executive Directors elect the president of the Bank (Article 5,*5*); his terms of reference are the same as those of the managing director of the Fund.

The first president, E. Meyer, was elected on 4 June 1946, but remained in office only until 18 December of that year. In February 1947, J. J. McCloy of the United States accepted the post. On 1 July 1949 he was succeeded by his compatriot E. R. Black. Since 1 January 1963, G. D. Woods, since 1 April 1968, R. S. McNamara, since 1 July 1981, A. W. Clausen, since 1 July 1986 B. B. Conable and since 1 July 1991 L. Preston have held the office of president.

The Bank's headquarters are also in Washington. Its staff numbered 6 394 on 30 June 1990, nearly four times bigger than IMF's staff. All dealings with the member countries are through the Treasuries, central banks or similar agencies (Article 3,*2*).

3. FUNCTIONS AND OPERATION

A. *Acquisition of resources*

1. *Provisions*

At present, 1 per cent in gold and 9 per cent in the national currency are callable from each member country. In addition, the Bank obtains funds by selling securities issued or guaranteed by it or in which it has invested part of its resources (Article 4,*8i*); the consent of the country where the sale takes place is required. Lastly, the Bank can borrow currency direct from each member state, provided the country concerned agrees (Article 4,*8iii*). Unused funds can be applied by the Bank to repurchasing bonds issued or guaranteed by it or in which it has interests, with the consent of the country where the purchase is made (Article 4,*8i*). Investments in other securities can be made only from a special reserve, which can serve wholly or in part for this purpose, subject to a three-quarters majority decision by the Executive

Directors (Article 4,*8iv*). The Bank's resources are likewise increased when it sells claims or when its previous loans are repaid.

During the first ten years of its operations, the Bank could charge a commission of not less than 1 per cent and not more than 1.5 per cent on the outstanding portion of all loans made by the Bank out of borrowed funds and on all guaranteed loans. All commissions are set aside as a special reserve (Article 4,*4, 5* and *6*). Thereafter it had discretion to reduce or to increase the rate of commission (taking account of the experience of the ten-year period and the volume of the special reserve) (Article 4,*4a* and *5a*). In fact the minimum level has been applied up to the present. The Bank also applies a commitment charge of 0.75 per cent (on the undisbursed portion of a loan) to offset the cost of holding funds at the disposal of the borrower.

The Bank's funds are partially protected against devaluation and depreciation. The Bank asks any country whose currency has been devalued (or in which the domestic purchasing power has declined) to make a payment in its own currency in order to cover the Bank's loss in respect of subscriptions to the capital and of repayments on loans (Article 2,*9a*). If these loans have not been provided from the Bank's capital but with funds which were obtained from such sources as interest and commission, the guarantee does not apply. Similar provisions apply in the case of a revaluation (Article 2,*9b*). The amounts in national currencies which are not required by the Bank remain deposited with the central bank or similar institution of the country concerned (Article 5,*11*). Always provided that the Bank has no immediate need of the currency in question, a member state may pay the contributions it owes in the form of Treasury certificates which are non-negotiable and interest-free, affording the possibility of conversion at any time into an asset of the Bank with the central bank or a similar institution of the country concerned (Article 5,*12*).

2. *Operation*

a. *Capital subscriptions*

After the establishment of the Bank, most of the member states, an important exception being the United States, paid the greater part of their subscriptions in national currency in the form of Treasury certificates. Subsequently the Bank urged them at regular intervals to repurchase the certificates for national currency, but these requests met with little success at the outset. The production facilities of the Western European countries were faced with an enormous pent-up demand. In these circumstances, these countries did not think it advisable to increase the Bank's purchasing capacity. In 1949 the sellers' market for many products changed into a buyers' market, and numerous industrial countries were then prepared to provide national currencies.

In the course of the years that followed, the majority of the developed countries gradually paid up a larger proportion of their subscriptions in national currency, so that by 30 June 1990 Treasury certificates represented only 1 594 million dollars.

On 16 March 1973 the Bank decided that all members establishing central rates for their currencies had to maintain the value of currency holdings (Article 2,9) on the basis of those rates. On 30 June 1990 a total of 0.5 million dollars was payable by the Bank and one million dollars receivable.

In cases where amounts of devalued currencies have been acquired from net earnings in these currencies, the Bank has a loss (e.g., 23 million dollars after the devaluation of sterling and other currencies in November 1967).

b. *Sale of bonds*

The Bank has acquired the bulk of its funds by issuing bonds, Initially, it came up against difficulties in this respect, since the member countries did not regard favourably the emergence of a competitor for their own loans. Because of the sharp growth in the Bank's lending operations, new borrowings by the Bank in the five fiscal years 1986—90 aggregated 51 768 million dollars, compared with 44 815 million in 1981—85 and 22 426 million in the preceding five years. The borrowings of the bank consist of placements with central banks and governments and public offerings through the investment market.

Of the outstanding debt at 30 June 1990 5.3 billion dollars are short-term borrowings (exclusively in US dollars, average costs 8.24 per cent) and 81.219 billion dollars are medium- and long-term borrowings (average cost: 7.86 per cent; currency composition: US dollars 24.6 per cent, yen 27.3 per cent, DM 18.1 per cent and Swiss Francs 9.9 per cent.

c. *Repayment of loans*

As most of the loans originally had a term of at least twenty-five years, and as repayment usually started after a seven-year period of grace, very few reimbursements were received in the Bank's early years. In 1975/76, however, repayment conditions were changed so as to ensure that loans outstanding and disbursed would not rise above the imposed limit (Article 3,3).

Cumulative repayments at 30 June 1990 amounted to 43 393 million dollars.

d. *Sale of claims*

As the majority of American financial institutions showed little interest in long-term investments in less-developed countries, the Bank's increasing activity was initially accompanied by reduced opportunities for realizing securities. Gradually, however, the Bank succeeded in finding takers for this paper too. In order to stress the soundness of the loans, it has arranged in most cases for another financial institution (e.g. one or more well-known banks) to participate. The latter then immediately takes over a (usually small) part of the loan. Sometimes "portfolio sales" are made (after the loan contract has been signed and disbursements have been made).

Until 1980 the Bank has sold 2 980 million dollars' worth of its loans. It halted these transactions because of sharply rising interest rates. From September 1985 to June 1986 the Bank carried out a 300 million dollar loan-sales pilot programme in order to determine if it should reactivate its sales of participations in IBRD loans made to or guaranteed by member countries.

e. *Net earnings*

Since 1948 the statement of income and expenses has regularly shown a favourable balance which, with the expansion in transactions, has gradually mounted.

From 1 July 1964 onwards payments into the special reserve of 1 per cent on the new unredeemed loans were suspended. This reserve may only be used to fulfill commitments arising out of the Bank's loans or guarantees. On 30 June 1990 it amounted to as much as 293 million dollars.

In accordance with a resolution of 27 July 1950 the net income has automatically been credited to a supplemental reserve against losses on loans and guarantees from currency devaluations (when Article 2,9 does not apply). In 1976 the supplemental reserve was renamed general reserve.

In fiscal 1964 it was decided to allot part of the reserve to the International Development Association (IDA). Similar decisions were taken in subsequent years, bringing the total transfers to the IDA to 2 641 million dollars. Of this amount 525 million dollars was payable at 30 June 1990. At the same date the general reserve totalled 9 196 million dollars. In fiscal 1990 income from investments was 1 492 million dollars, and income from loans 6 767 million (interest 6 628 million, commitment charges 139 million).

The interest charged depends on the rate which the Bank itself has to pay on its bonds. The rate charged remained at 5.5 per cent until February 1966, when it was raised to 6 per cent. Further increases were made on 1 January 1967 (6.25 per cent), on 1 August 1968 (6.5 per cent), on 1 August 1969 (7 per cent), on 1 August 1970 (7.25 per cent), on 1 January 1975 (8.5 per cent) and on 1 June 1976 (8.85 per cent). Since 1 July 1976 the lending rate has been reviewed quarterly and is set at 0.5 per cent above the weighted average cost of funds borrowed in the preceding 12 months. Since 1 July 1982 the variable-rate system is adjusted semiannually (on 1 January and 1 July). During the first semester of 1990 the rate was 7.75 per cent.

B. *Application of resources*

1. *Provisions*

The resources and facilities of the Bank are available to member states only (Article 3,*1a*). Bank loans and guarantees may not exceed the sum of the capital and the ordinary and special reserves, less any losses which may have occurred (Article 3,*3*). The following supplementary conditions also have to be fulfilled (Article 3,*4*).

a) When the member state on whose territory the project is being executed does not itself act as borrower, the payment of the principal and interest on the loan is guaranteed by the country concerned, its central bank or another institution approved by the Bank. This clause limits the possibility of loans to private institutions. Governments are not over-eager to guarantee loans because they have insufficient control over the enterprises in question and fear they may be accused of favouritism.

b) The borrower must be unable to obtain the necessary funds in any other way on terms which the Bank deems to be reasonable. The intention here is to obviate the Bank's using its limited resources to finance projects for which capital is easily found. When public or private institutions try to abuse their position as lenders in order to impose exaggerated financial, economic or even political conditions, the Bank intervenes so as to exercise a regulatory influence on the international capital market.

c) The proposed interest, other charges and amortization schedule for the loan must be in keeping with the nature of the project. The Bank is thus prevented from investing funds in projects which are insufficiently productive to cover the charges.

d) The country which applies for the loan or guarantee must be in a position to fulfill its obligations. This condition is closely linked with the previous one and is aimed at preventing certain countries from floating foreign loans which are too large in proportion to future exchange earnings. If, for example, a member state is about to contract a relatively excessive number of dollar loans, the Bank will advise this country to include new commitments in other currencies. With increasing progress towards convertibility (cf. the decision of 15 February 1961 by numerous Western European states), it was possible to abandon this bilateral approach and to extend the borrowing capacity of many less-developed countries with the Bank.

e) Except in special circumstances, the loans granted or guaranteed by the Bank are intended for the execution of well-defined reconstruction or development projects.

The Bank may not make its lendings conditional on the proceeds being spent in the territory of a specific member or members (Article 3,*5a*). The proceeds of the loan have to be used exclusively for the execution of the projects for which they were intended. For this purpose, the Bank opens an account in the name of the borrower; only expenditure already incurred in connection with the project can be settled from it (Article 3,*5b* and *c*). Unused funds can be applied by the Bank to repurchasing bonds issued or guaranteed by it or in which it has interests, with the consent of the country where the purchase is made (Article 4,*8i*). Investments in other securities can be made only through the special reserve, which can be used wholly or in part for this purpose, subject to a three-quarters majority decision by the Executive Directors (Article 4,*8iv*). In December 1965 the Articles of Agreement were amended so as to allow the bank to make, participate in or guarantee loans to the International Finance Corporation (see below) up to four times the Corporation's unimpaired subscribed capital and surplus (Article 3,*6*). Transfers to the International Development Association (see below) can be made only from the net income of the Bank.

2. *Operation*

a. *Loans*

Initially, the Bank had to contribute to the recovery of the economies of countries which had been severely affected by the war. Thus, in 1947, loans totalling 497 million dollars were granted to France, the Netherlands, Denmark and Luxembourg (on the basis of the escape clause in Article 3,*4*: "except in special circumstances"). Western Europe needed not only new means of production, but also food, fuel and primary commodities, and imports of these goods could not be financed by loans from the Bank. After the European Recovery Programme came into operation, the Bank directed its main activities to the less-developed territories. On 25 March 1948 two loans were granted for the first time to a less-developed country, i.e., to Chile.

In the period from its establishment until 30 June 1990 the Bank granted 3 176 loans totalling 186 662 million dollars. It disbursed 137 445 million dollars. Annual aid is growing fast: 1 023 million dollars in 1964/65; 1 580 million in 1969/70; 6 989 million in 1978/79 and 13 900 million in 1989/90.

Of the Bank's total cumulative lending operations at 30 June 1990 (Table 9), approximately one-fifth went to each of the two following sectors: energy; agriculture and rural development; about one sixth to transportation; and one tenth to development finance companies. There have been important changes in the Bank's lending policy. From 1948 to 1963 most emphasis was on infrastructure projects. In subsequent years more attention was paid to direct productive activities, such as agriculture, industry and tourism. Over the last decade lending for sectors such as education and water supply has increased, while sectors such as population and nutrition and urban and rural development have been added to the programme.

Table 9. IBRD loans by purpose, cumulative total at 30 June 1990.

Purpose	Amount (million dollars)	Per cent of total
Energy	40 823	21.9
Agriculture and rural development	36 112	19.3
Transportation	28 486	15.3
Development finance corporations	18 897	10.1
Non-project	15 134	8.1
Industry	13 482	7.2
Water supply and sewerage	8 378	4.5
Urban development	7 850	4.2
Education	6 635	3.6
Small-scale enterprises	4 526	2.4
Telecommunications	3 189	1.7
Population, health and nutrition	1 702	0.9
Public sector management	980	0.5
Technical assistance	449	0.2
Total	186 662	100.0

Source: IBRD, *Annual report*, 1990.

Initially the Bank did not finance petroleum production but chiefly electrical energy. This situation changed with the quadrupling of oil prices in 1973—74 and the growing balance-of-payments deficits of oil- and energy-importing less-developed countries. More recently there has been a decline in this sector as average annual lending in current dollars dropped to 2 331 million for the period 1988—90. The Bank became the largest external lender in the energy sector. In July 1977 the Executive Directors approved a programme to speed up petroleum production in the less-developed countries. Of the total loans to the energy sector 80 per cent went to power projects.

Particularly since 1964, the Bank has made efforts to increase its lending to agricultural and rural development. The annual average rose from 120 million dollars in the mid-1960s to 2 741 million dollars over the period 1984/86. There has been a preference for programmes aimed at increasing the productivity of the small farmer. Irrigation projects constitute the major lending category (24 per cent of lending). About 19 per cent is directed to agricultural credit and livestock projects (e.g., groundwater development, drainage, pasture improvement, tree-crop planting, livestock purchase, farm machinery, buildings, fencing, on-farm processing, storage facilities). Another 20 per cent goes to loans for area development.

More than half the transportation loans relate to highway projects, almost one quarter to railways and a seventh to ports and waterways.

Loans to development finance companies were initially directed only towards privately controlled companies but later government-owned companies were also being assisted. The purpose is to support public and private medium-scale and smaller-scale industries, with project costs below the range of 5 to 10 million dollars.

Apart from aiding development finance companies the Bank has assisted specific manufacturing enterprises. For example, in 1976/77 it made 45 million available for a cement plant in Morocco; in 1978/79 it lent 250 million to India for the construction of a fertilizer plant; in 1982/83 the Bank helped Brazil to finance its steel expansion (304 million dollars) and in 1985/86 it lent India 302 million for the building of a fertilizer plant and 200 million for the modernization of the cement industry. In 1989/90 200 million went to Hungary, 300 million to Algeria and 400 million to Yugoslavia to support structural adjustment programmes in order to increase the importance of competitive markets.

Nonprojects loans usually furnish foreign exchange in order to finance imports of materials and equipment for existing productive facilities; some loans help towards implementing a general investment programme and a few relate to reconstruction work following a war or a natural disaster (400 million to Mexico after the earthquake of September 1985). The reconstruction loans (497 million dollars) referred to above are included in the cumulative total of nonproject loans. Nonproject lending in the form of structural adjustment loans has gained importance. The Bank stopped lending for tourism in 1986.

More aid is being given to water supply and sewerage (4.5 per cent of total cumulative lending in 1990 against 0.9 per cent in 1970).

In 1962 the Bank began to provide finance for education projects. Emphasis was put on vocational and technical education and training and on secondary education. In the late 1960s projects aimed at achieving qualitative improvements and meeting crucial manpower needs were considered more important. Loans for experimental approaches (e.g., educational television, mobile training units) were granted.

Asia obtains more than one-third of total loans, especially India with 9.8 per cent of total (Table 10) and Indonesia with 7.9 per cent. In Latin America the highest shares go to Brazil, Mexico and Colombia, in Africa to Morocco and Nigeria.

The above-mentioned figures include credits given under three special programmes. On 23 December 1975 an Intermediate Financing Facility, known as the Third Window, became effective. Its objective was to provide assistance on terms intermediate between those of the Bank and the IDA. Accordingly, an Interest Subsidy Fund has been set up. The (voluntary) contributions to the Fund were provided by some Bank members and Switzerland. The Subsidy Fund supplemented interest payments due to the Bank by paying the Bank twice a year an amount equal to 4 per cent per annum of the outstanding principal of loans made on Third Window terms. The remainder was to be paid by the borrower.

Since 1978, however, no Intermediate Financing Facilities have been

Table 10. IBRD loans to principal recipient countries, cumulative total at 30 June 1990.

Country	Amount (million dollars)	Per cent of total
India	18 319	9.8
Brazil	17 982	9.6
Mexico	17 364	9.3
Indonesia	14 829	7.9
Turkey	10 165	5.5
Korea	7 154	3.8
Philippines	6 751	3.6
Colombia	6 534	3.5
Yugoslavia	5 815	3.1
Nigeria	5 594	3.0
China	5 280	2.8
Morocco	5 178	2.8
Argentina	5 121	2.7
Thailand	4 187	2.2
Pakistan	4 175	2.2
Algeria	3 535	1.9
Egypt	03 123	1.7
Total	186 662	100.0

Source: IBRD, *Annual report*, 1990.

granted. From 1975/76 to 1976/77 the assistance totalled 700.4 million dollars.

Another form of Bank assistance is the Structural Adjustment Lending approved in 1980 for nonproject and programme lending. It is designed to support major changes in policies and institutions in order to reduce current-account deficits in the medium term while maintaining the development effort of less-developed countries. Through fiscal 1990 the Bank approved adjustment programmes totalling 14 billion dollars.

A Special Action Programme established for a two-year period was approved in February 1983 of which the Structural Adjustment Lending programme became a part. Its aim is to restore the development efforts of less-developed countries despite adverse external circumstances.

b. *Guarantees*

At Bretton Woods it was envisaged that the Bank would mainly guarantee loans by private investors rather than grant loans itself. In fact, the Bank has made only limited use of its power to attach a guarantee to bonds issued for the financing of investments for development purposes. Guaranteed loans were to compete with the Bank's borrowings and the cost would be higher than direct borrowing from the Bank. The amount of the outstanding debt guaranteed by the Bank has gradually decreased (from 27.4 million dollars in 1949 to 3.1 million in 1966), and it dropped to zero in 1967.

c. *Investments*

Although the Articles of Agreement make no provision for this, part of the available funds (other than those from its special reserve) for which no immediate employment could be found are held primarily in dollars. The short-term assets include government and quasi-government obligations 8 544 million dollars at 30 June 1990) and time deposits and other obligations with commercial banks and financial institutions (8 302 million dollars at 30 June 1990).

C. *Utilization of currencies*

1. *Provisions*

The provisions with respect to the currencies to be used for loans, interest payments and redemption may be divided into three groups.

a) Those of the first group are aimed at giving the member countries a certain amount of control over the national currency which they have paid in. If the currency were to be disbursed arbitrarily by the Bank, it might lead to payments difficulties for the countries concerned. For this reason, the Bank can only use the 9 per cent which was paid by each member state in its own currency, provided that the country in question gives its consent in each case (Article 4,2a). The same condition also applies to the use of the amounts which become available as a result of repayments in national currencies (Article 4,2b). The application of funds acquired in any other way, e.g., by the payment of 1 per cent in gold or dollars by the member countries or by the operations of the Bank (profits, issue of bonds or cash certificates), remains unrestricted (Article 4,2c, d, and e).

b) A second set of provisions relates to the currency in which the loans are made available within the territory of the countries concerned. The Bank supplies the borrowing country with the foreign exchange it needs for the implementation of the project, excluding the currency of the country on whose territory the project is located (Article 4,3a). Departures from the rule may be made in special circumstances and for part of the loan, either by supplying the borrower with local currency, if he cannot acquire it on reasonable conditions (Article 4,3b), or by providing him with gold or foreign exchange (Article 4,3c). This is not done for the purposes of the direct execution of the project, but to finance the increased general foreign-exchange requirements stemming therefrom.

c) The third group of provisions concerns the currency in which the interest and amortization payments have to be made. As a general rule, this is fixed by the Bank (Article 4,*4b*). In the case of a loan that was financed with payments by the member countries, the reimbursements have to be effected in the same currency, unless the state whose currency was provided accepts repayment in another currency (Article 4,*4b i*). If the loan has been provided from other resources, e.g., funds acquired on the market of a member country, the Bank ensures that the total amount of its debts in a given currency does not exceed its claims in that same currency (Article 4,*4b ii*).

2. *Operation*

Immediately after the Bank was set up, the United States authorized unrestricted use of the subscription it had paid. The majority of the other countries did not follow this example (see above), which meant that most of the capital subscribed remained frozen and the Bank had to rely on loans.

The obligation laid down in Article 4,*4b ii* (the debt in a given currency may not exceed the claims in the same currency) is met by requiring repayment in the currency which the Bank has to use in order to obtain the currency needed. If, for example, the loan was expressed in pounds sterling but the Bank had to float a loan on the American market in order to obtain the necessary funds, then repayment must be made in dollars.

As the interest rate in soft-currency countries was generally higher than in hard-currency countries, the loans have been placed mainly on the capital markets of the latter group (the United States, Switzerland, Japan, Belgium, Canada and, from the mid-1950s onwards, Western Germany and the Netherlands).

Repayment therefore had practically always to be made in hard currency, so that borrowing countries could not, on the strength of future soft-currency income (e.g., sterling), obtain a loan in a similar currency. In other words, the industrial countries with soft currencies derived no advantages from the fact that their currency was easier to acquire for many less-developed countries, and they charged the Bank with indirectly favouring "tied" loans (Article 3,*5a*). The Bank therefore urged the soft-currency member countries to expedite payments in their own currency (on their shares) and enable the Bank to use these funds for its transactions. Furthermore, it has — despite a higher rate of interest than, for example, in the United States — floated loans on the markets of European industrial countries. The first of these operations was effected in London in 1951, taking the form of a 5 million-pounds loan with a 3-per-cent issue premium and a 3.5-per-cent interest rate, whereas on the New York market, the Bank's bonds yielded only 3.15 per cent on the basis of Stock Exchange quotations.

With the increasing financial stability of the European countries, it became easier for the Bank to place loans in them, and thus accommodate countries in need of certain European currencies without requiring repayment in dollars.

As regards Article 4,*3* the Bank is concerned to ensure that loans which are larger than the amount necessary to finance the import of the required capital goods do not cause the countries concerned to lose sight of the need for domestic saving. Nevertheless, since 1950 less importance has been attached to the distinction based on the category of expenditure (national or foreign currency) entailed by a project. In cases which have the same priority, however, preference is given to financing a project which involves expenditure of foreign exchange. Expenditure in local currency can only be covered up to 50 per cent.

D. *Technical assistance*

To help backward territories in the preparation of development programmes, the Bank is able to call upon a large number of experts who provide information on the profitability prospects of certain projects, their general repercussions on the economy of the country in question and the most appropriate financing methods.

Before a member state makes a formal application for a loan, the project is analysed by the Bank's experts and, if need be, amendments are proposed. In this way, the Bank is not automatically obliged to turn down certain applications or to risk financing uneconomic schemes.

As it is not always an easy matter for a new state to submit suitable projects, it has been the practice since 1949 to send General Survey Missions to certain countries in order to study development prospects. The members of these missions are appointed in cooperation with other international organizations (including FAO and WHO). Since the mid-1960s General Survey Missions have been replaced by a programme of country-by-country economic reporting with the same objective. Technical assistance is being extended to some oil-exporting countries which do not borrow from the Bank; the Bank is then reimbursed on a cash basis for its services.

In East and West Africa, where the development problems are especially complex, the Bank has established Regional Missions, primarily to assist the governments in those areas to identify and prepare specific projects for submission to the Bank or IDA. The offices of these missions are located in Nairobi and Abidjan respectively. The Bank also maintains a regional mission in Thailand, with its headquarters in Bangkok. A number of resident missions have been opened (e.g., in Ethiopia, Sudan, India, Saudi Arabia).

The Economic Development Institute, set up by the Bank in January 1956 with the support of the Ford and Rockefeller Foundations, sponsors or cosponsors courses and seminars dealing with management of the overall economy or of particular sectors and with project analysis, and management. Most of the Institute's training activities intended for government officials from the less-developed countries are held outside Washington.

Under a Project Preparation Facility (1975) the Bank advances funds to help overcome weakness in borrowers' capacities to complete project preparations and to support the entities responsible for preparing or carrying out their projects.

1. *Coordination of development assistance*

Coordination between multilateral and bilateral donors of assistance and between donors and recipient countries is an important element in the development policy. The first aid coordination group was set up in 1958 in the form of a consortium to help India implement the third five-year plan; in 1960 another one was established to finance part of Pakistan's second five-year plan. In addition to the World Bank and its affiliate, the International Development Association, Canada, France, Japan, the United Kingdom, the United States and Western Germany participated in both consortia, which have met annually since their inception and have served as vehicles for comments on the economic performance and capital requirements of the recipient countries. They have also been instrumental in coordinating external aid and improving the terms on which it is given.

For many other less-developed countries, the Bank has undertaken to organize Consultative Groups of interested capital-exporting countries. Although they do not engage in annual aid pledges, these groups are in other respects intended to serve the same purposes as the consortia (*i.a.* Philippines, Sri Lanka, Bolivia, Bangladesh, Nigeria, Mauritania). The Bank also participates (but does not take the lead) in meetings of two other coordinating groups relating to Indonesia and Turkey.

Over the past decade the Bank has become more involved in cofinancing. Under such an arrangement, funds from the Bank and from other sources finance a particular project. In this way the capital flow to less-developed countries can be increased and more effective use can be made of available assistance. The colenders benefit from the Bank's country-by-country analysis and project appraisal. In 1977/78, for example, over 2 778 million dollars — more than half from official sources, a third as export credits (from public or private sources or both) and the remainder through private financing — was made available to the Bank in 81 projects. As of January 1983 additional cofinancing instruments were introduced: direct financial participation in the late maturities of a syndicated loan; guarantee of the late maturities; acceptance of a contingent participation in the final maturity of a commercial loan. The annual volume of cofinancing increased rapidly in recent years and reached 13 billion dollars in 1988/90. In July 1989 an expanded cofinancing-operations programme was established to support borrowers' access to private capital markets. On 14 June 1990 the Executive Directors authorized the negotiation of the first cofinancing-operations programme operation (a private placement of bonds in the US capital market by the Housing Development Financing Corporation of India).

In May 1971 a Consultative Group on International Agricultural Research (CGIAR) was established under the sponsorship of the Bank, FAO and UNDP to provide financial support to international agricultural research centers. The group provided 225 million dollars in 1989 (of which the Bank contributed 33 million) to the research centers.

2. *The International Centre for the Settlement of Investment Disputes (ICSID)*

Private capital often fails to be attracted to the less-developed countries because it fears dangers other than the normal business risks (e.g., nationalization and restrictions on transfer facilities). As a step in the direction of overcoming this difficulty and encouraging a freer flow of private capital to the less-developed countries, the Bank drafted a Convention on the Settlement of Investment Disputes between States and Nationals of Other States. The Convention, which was sent to member governments in March 1965, came into force on 14 October 1966. By 24 May 1991 94 countries had ratified the Convention.

The Convention provides for the establishment of an International Centre for the Settlement of Investment Disputes (ICSID) as an autonomous institution under the auspices of the Bank. It does not perform the functions of conciliator or arbitrator itself but maintains lists of qualified persons, from which the parties to the disputes are able, if they so desire, to choose conciliators and arbitrators. The Centre provides the necessary procedural facilities. It is supervised by an Administrative Council composed of one representative of each contracting party. The president of the Bank acts as chairman of the Council, which held its inaugural meeting on 2 February 1967.

An increasing number of investment contracts, bilateral treaties and national laws contain provisions for the submission of disputes to the Centre. The first request for arbitration proceedings was registered on 13 January 1972, concerning a dispute between Holiday Inns, Occidental Petroleum Corporation and the Moroccan Government. The dispute has been settled amicably. So far, thirty-one arbitration cases have been brought before the Centre. Ten have been settled amicably, in twelve and award has been rendered and five cases are pending. The Centre has developed several sets of model clauses, each appropriate to specific classes of situation.

On 27 September 1978 the Centre's jurisdiction was extended (Supplementary Mechanism) to conciliation and arbitration concerning investment disputes between a member and a non-member and to the settlement of non-investment disputes.

3. *The Multilateral Investment Guarantee Agency (MIGA)*

In September 1985 the Executive Directors of the Bank approved the establishment of a new international facility, the Multilateral Investment

Guarantee Agency (MIGA). The Convention creating MIGA entered into force on 12 April 1988. MIGA's authorized capital amounts to 1 billion SDR or the equivalent of 1.082 billion dollar. Ten per cent of the subscribed capital is paid in cash, another 10 per cent in non-interest bearing and non-negotiable promissory notes, and the remaining 80 per cent are subject to call if needed to meet MIGA's obligations.

MIGA issues guarantees of investments in less-developed countries against non-commercial risks, including currency inconvertibility, political unrest, expropriation, and breach of contract where the investor is unable to obtain relief within the host country. MIGA also carries out promotional and technical-assistance operations for less-developed member countries. It does not conclude any contract or guarantee before approval by the host government. Initially MIGA will not guarantee amounts exceeding 1.5 times the assets (capital and reserves).

MIGA is expected to finance itself from premiums and other revenues such as returns on investment.

The Bank sees MIGA as a response to the world debt crisis and the decline in capital flows to less-developed countries in the first half of the 1980s. Investors' concerns about political risks in less-developed countries constitute an important barrier to more investment.

Members of MIGA will contribute capital in relation to their allocation of shares in the World Bank's capital. Nevertheless — and less promising — MIGA's voting structure will be based on the principle of equal voting power of capital-exporting and capital-importing countries. At 30 June 1990 61 countries have ratified the convention.

On 25 January 1989 the Agency's Board of Directors approved a standard contract and general conditions of guarantee for MIGA. At the end of 1989 28 preliminary guarantee applications from investors in projects in 50 countries have been registered. The first guarantees have been issued in 1990.

THE INTERNATIONAL DEVELOPMENT ASSOCIATION

1. ORIGINS

In February 1958, having announced a plan along these lines some two years previously, the United States Senator E. S. M. Monroney proposed the creation of an international organization for the granting of loans to less-developed countries at a lower interest rate, for a longer term and on more favourable repayment conditions than those offered by the Bank. According to its sponsor, this scheme would contribute to reducing the growth in the already considerable burden of indebtedness of these territories. At the meeting of the Bank's Board of Governors on 1 October 1959 the executive directors were instructed, on a proposal by the United States, to draft an agreement setting up such an organization. This draft was submitted to the sixty-eight Bank member countries on 1 February 1960, and the Articles of Agreement of the International Development Association (IDA) came into effect on 24 September of that year. IDA began operations on 8 November 1960.

2. OBJECTIVES

The Association was established in order to grant the less-developed countries loans on more flexible terms than those of the Bank (Article 1). The main aim is to ensure that repayments do not have an adverse effect on the balance of payments of the countries in question, more particularly by allowing redemption in soft national currency (soft loans) instead of insisting on hard foreign exchange. The loans are granted for the promotion of economic development and in order to raise productivity and living standards. The IDA does not obstruct, but supplements, the activities of the Bank.

3. ORGANIZATION

A. *Members and capital*

The Bank members listed in a schedule to the IDA Articles of Agreement which agreed to join IDA prior to 31 December 1960 are deemed to be original member states (Article 2,*1a*). Their subscriptions were also fixed beforehand. The sum of these subscriptions — which in general are proportionate to those of the Bank — is 1 billion dollars. A few of the scheduled countries did not become member states (e.g., Uruguay and Venezuela).

Other Bank countries may apply for membership of the IDA; their subscription is then determined by the Association itself (Article 2,*1b*).

The capital (which is variable) consists of two parts — contributions from the developed countries (763.07 million dollars initially) and contributions from the less-developed countries, including Spain and Greece (236.93 million dollars initially).

The industrial countries have to settle the amount of their subscription entirely in gold or convertible currency. The others have to pay only 10 per cent in gold or convertible currency and may contribute the balance in national currency. This obligation can be met without seriously endangering balance-of-payments equilibrium. Not until five years after the establishment of the Association in the case of the original member countries, or after their joining in the case of the others, has the amount to be fully paid up (Article 2,*2c* and *d*). As in the Bank, non-interest-bearing Treasury certificates may also be employed (Article 2,*2e*).

If it considers that the available resources are inadequate, the Association may authorize a general increase in subscription. These subscriptions are called *additional* subscriptions (Article 3,*1a*). Each member country then has to be afforded to the opportunity of subscribing for an amount at which level its relative voting power will be maintained. However, no country is obliged to do so (Article 3,*1c*). Individual increases may always be effected at the request of the country concerned (Article 3,*1a*). As at 30 June 1990, 138 countries were member states of the Association. Cessation of Bank membership automatically means that the country concerned is excluded from the Association (Article 7,*3*).

B. *Administration*

The Association is managed in the same way as the Bank. The president of the latter is also president of the Association. This applies also to the governors and directors, at least in so far as the country which appointed them, or one of the countries which elected them, is also an IDA country (Article 6,*2b* and *4b*). The terms of reference of the Board of Governors and the Executive Directors correspond to those of their Bank equivalents. With regard to the number of votes allotted to each member country, the Articles of Agreement differ somewhat from those of the Bank. Each original member state of the IDA has 500 votes and one additional vote per 5 000 dollars of its initial subscription. The voting rights of other member states and those attaching to additional subscriptions are determined by the Board of Governors. *Supplementary* subscriptions (see below) give no entitlement to supplementary votes (Article 6,*3*). Although Part I countries have provided 95.65 per cent of subscriptions and supplementary reserves they represent 61.52 per cent only of voting power. With respect to relations between the Association and the Bank, the same rules apply as for the IFC before 1965 (no loans from the Bank: Article 6,*6a*).

4. FUNCTIONS AND OPERATION

The provisions relating to the functions and operation of IDA differ considerably from those applying to the Bank and the IFC.

A. *Acquisition of resources*

1. *Provisions*

The Association too may contract loans, grant guarantees and buy and sell securities issued or guaranteed by it (Article 5,*5*), but substantial loans on the capital markets of the developed countries are not feasible, since the Association's income is too small to cover the cost of such operations. Primarily lending resources consist of subscriptions (initial and additional) and supplementary resources (Article 3,*2*).

If the Association does not require a currency, it has to allow the country concerned to convert the amounts paid in or payable in this currency into non-interest-bearing certificates or bonds issued by the government or central bank (Article 2,*2e*). The member countries have to guarantee against exchange risks the 90 per cent of their subscriptions which they may pay in national currency. In case of devaluation, a supplementary amount is paid which ensures that the gold value of the subscription remains the same. In the case of revaluation, a refund is made. In contrast with the similar provisions of the Bank's Articles, this obligation no longer applies if the currency in question has been either spent or sold by the Association for another currency (Article 4,*2*).

2. *Operation*

The Association has at its disposal the entire subscriptions of Part I countries (which at 30 June 1990 totalled 22) and only 10 per cent of the subscriptions of Part II countries. The remainder (paid in the member's own currency) cannot be used without the consent of the member. Kuwait, which became a member state on 13 September 1962, paid its subscription entirely in convertible currency and was included among the Part 1 countries. Many of the Part II countries paid part of their subscription that they could have paid in their own currency in convertible funds and a portion of the non-convertible funds has actually been utilized.

When in September 1963 resources were in danger of becoming inadequate, it was decided to ask the wealthy countries for supplementary subscriptions of 753 million dollars (the "first replenishment", which became effective on 29 June 1964). A second replenishment came into force on 23 July 1969. It provided for 1 200 million dollars (including supplementary contributions of 17.5 million from Canada, Denmark, Finland, the Netherlands and Sweden, and a loan of 12 million from Switzerland) to be paid in three annual instalments of 400 million.

Under the third replenishment (effective as from 22 September 1972) 18 Part I and three Part II countries (Ireland, Spain and Yugoslavia) made 2 511 million dollars available. The resolution on the third replenishment also provided for adjustment of the voting power of all participating members. This was achieved through a provision that a portion of each Part I member's contribution was to be in the form of an additional subscription carrying voting rights. Part II members were given the opportunity to make additional subscriptions to maintain their voting power as a group. Through the fourth replenishment (effective as from 17 January 1975) 24 member states plus Switzerland provided 4 500 million dollars of supplementary resources. In the same way as under the third replenishment an adjustment of the voting power was introduced. The fifth, sixth, seventh and eight replenishments entered into force on 29 November 1977, 24 August 1981, 31 March 1985 and 4 March 1988 respectively and provided resources of 7638, 7790, 9000 and 13840 million dollars. Negotiations for the ninth replenishment were completed on 14 December 1989 and provide resources of 15500 million dollars for the period 1991—93.

On 30 June 1990 the subscriptions and supplementary resources totalled 54628 million dollars.

The Association has entered into agreements to borrow a total of Sw. F 182 million (equivalent to 109.4 million dollars) from the Swiss Confederation. The first loan (Sw. F 52 million, with repayments starting on 1 July 1979) was made in June 1967 and the second loan, amounting to Sw. F 130 million (repayments starting on 8 November 1983) in November 1972. The loans carry no interest. The outstanding balances of Sw. F 181 480 000 were converted into grant contributions pursuant to an agreement which came into force on 1 April 1981.

Since 1964, the Bank has transferred a portion of its net income to the IDA (2641 million dollars at 30 June 1990,) of which 2561 million dollars can be used by that body for general purposes. Of this amount 1714 million has been received and 847 million is receivable.

Nearly a third of subscriptions (27 per cent) are accounted for by the United States. The shares of Japan (19.2 per cent), Germany (11.6 per cent) and the United Kingdom (8.5 per cent) are also important (Table 11).

B. *Application of resources*

1. *Provisions*

The Association provides no funds if finance can be made available by the private sector on reasonable terms or by a bank loan (Article 5, *1c*), or if the country in which the project is located raises an objection (Article 5, *1e*). It has no power to impose conditions stipulating the territory where the goods required have to be purchased (Article 5, *1f*).

The provisions differ on several points from those in the Bank's Articles, namely:

a) The Association provides funds only for the implementation of projects which are clearly priority operations from the point of view of economic development (Article 5, *1b*).
b) The Bank grants loans and guarantees only. The Association may, with the resources it acquires from additional subscriptions or from repayments, interest and other charges on these loans, also apply other financing methods (if the authorization for these additional subscriptions makes provision for such measures). With the same reservation, this is allowed in the case of supplementary funds and the proceeds, such as repayments,

Table 11. Subscriptions and supplementary resources of Part I IDA members, 30 June 1990, in million dollars.

United States	14 765
Japan	10 472
Germany	6 344
United Kingdom	4 640
France	3 217
Canada	2 558
Italy	2 112
Netherlands	1 961
Sweden	1 474
Australia	1 015
Belgium	877
Denmark	633
Kuwait	599
Norway	592
Austria	417
Finland	360
Ireland	62
South Africa	57
New Zealand	56
Luxemburg	28
Iceland	7
United Arab Emirates	6
Total	54 628

Source: IBRD, *Annual report*, 1990.

interest and other charges, stemming from their use (Article 5, *2a*). This enables the IDA to acquire holdings.

c) If the member state in whose territory the project is located does not itself act as borrower, the Bank is obliged to ask for a guarantee from this country, its central bank or a similar body. The Association itself judges whether such a guarantee is necessary (Article 5, *2d*)

d) The Bank must see that the projects are sufficiently profitable for interest payments and redemptions to be made. If the borrower is not in a position to meet his commitments, the Association is allowed, taking into account the financial and economic situation of the party concerned, to alleviate or otherwise amend the conditions of the loan (Article 5, *3*).

The Association may also provide technical assistance at the request of a member (Article 5, *5v*).

2. *Operation*

Notwithstanding the possibilities offered by Article 5, *2d*, all IDA credits are made to governments, who can cede them to national institutions. On 30

June 1990 the funds provided by the IDA, called credits to distinguish them from Bank loans, amounted to 59029 million dollars (Table 12), 40011 million of which was disbursed.

The major beneficiary sector is agriculture and rural development; moreover, commitments have increased sharply over the years — from 17.4 per cent of total cumulative credits at 30 June 1968 to 35.5 per cent at 30 June 1990. This is due to the expansion of development projects in rural areas with per capita incomes of less than 75 dollars per year. Credits for transportation amount to 12.7 per cent of the total (against 34.5 per cent at 30 June 1968). More than half the transportation credits relate to highway projects. Most of credits to industry relate to fertilizers and other chemicals. Like the Bank and the IFC, the IDA grants credits to development finance companies.

Since 1962 the IDA has financed more and more investments for educational purposes. In 1985/86, for example, a 120 million dollars credit was granted to China to help sixty provincial universities and the State Education Commission.

Table 12. IDA credits by purpose, cumulative total at 30 June 1990.

Purpose	Amount (million dollars)	Per cent of total
Agriculture and rural development	20672	35.5
Transportation	7414	12.7
Energy	6041	10.4
Nonproject	5999	10.3
Education	4519	7.8
Urban development	2517	4.3
Water supply and sewerage	2362	4.1
Development finance corporations	2121	3.6
Industry	1918	3.2
Population, health and nutrition	1672	2.9
Telecommunications	1294	2.2
Technical assistance	898	1.5
Small-scale enterprises	582	1.0
Public sector management	302	0.9
Total	58222	100.0

Source: IBRD, *Annual report*, 1990.

The bulk of IDA credits have gone to South Asia (Table 13), and principally to India (29.1 per cent of total cumulative lending at 30 June 1990), Bangladesh (9.0 per cent) and Pakistan (5.6 per cent). These countries together account for 36 per cent of IDA population, excluding China. The IDA's assistance is concentrated on the poorest countries — with an annual per capita gross national product of less than 650 dollars (in 1988 dollars).

Table 13. IDA credits to principal recipient countries, cumulative total on 30 June 1990.

Region	Amount (million dollars)	Per cent of total
India	16 956	29.1
Bangladesh	5 249	9.0
China	3 927	6.7
Pakistan	3 237	5.6
Tanzania	1,769	3.0
Ghana	1 449	2.5
Kenya	1 397	2.4
Sudan	1 337	2.3
Sri Lanka	1 324	2.3
Ethiopia	1 265	2.2
Uganda	1 091	1.9
Zaire	1 061	1.8
Nepal	1 058	1.8

Source: IBRD, *Annual report*, 1990.

The Association's loans are very advantageous. At the beginning of its operations all the credits were for fifty years, repayable in easy stages after ten years of grace and with no interest except for a service charge of 0.75 per cent (on the part paid and unredeemed). After the 10-year period of grace, 1 per cent of the credit had to be repaid annually over the next 10 years, while for the remaining 30 years the corresponding rate was stepped up to three per cent. At present the loans have 30 year maturity with ten years of grace and no service charge. In March 1988, the Board of Directors decided to start reviewing the service charge on an annual basis. As regards the standards of project preparation and evaluation, however, policy is no different from that applied in the IBRD. The favourable conditions granted preclude the selling of claims to private investors, and the IDA has not yet made use of its powers to attach a guarantee to securities transferred by it.

In July 1985 a Special Facility for sub-Saharan Africa began operations. Its mandate is to support financially reform programmes undertaken by African governments. Under its African Facility, IDA committed 1 267 million dollars by June 1990, of which 1 174 million dollars are outstanding. In December 1987 a special programme of assistance was launched to help mobilize and coordinate quick-disbursing aid and concessional debt relief to support adjustment in low-income, debt-distressed, sub-Saharan countries. In the period 1988—89 a total of 2.7 billion dollars was disbursed by donors under the programme. At the end of 1989, total pledges by the industrialized world amounted to 5.8 billion dollars.

C. *Utilization of currencies*

1. *Provisions*

A distinction is made between the developed and the less-developed countries in respect of currency utilization. The amounts paid by the former in
their own currency have to be applied more or less proportionately; the sums
paid in other currencies or gold are more readily accessible (Article 4,*1e*).
The 10 per cent of the subscriptions (in gold or convertible currency) of the
less-developed territories can be used without restriction by the Association.
This is not the case for the remaining 90 per cent; the funds contributed in
national currency may only be used for:

a) the Association's administrative expenses in the country concerned;
b) payment for goods and services produced on the territory of the member
    state and needed by that state for the execution of the projects financed
    by the Association (if this expenditure is compatible with sound monetary
    policy);
c) projects located outside the country, provided they are justified by its
    economic and financial situation and subject to its consent (Article 4,*1a*).

The amounts received by the Association as a result of subscriptions other
than initial subscriptions may be used in accordance with the conditions laid
down at the time they are granted (Article 4,*1b*). The use of currencies
acquired from interest, commission and repayments is subject to the same
restrictions as the principal from which they derive (Article 4,*1c*). All other
currencies received by the Association may be freely used and exchanged
without any restriction by the member whose currency is used or exchanged
(Article 4,*1d*).

2. *Operation*

As the share of the industrial countries amounts to about 96 per cent of the
overall capital, the Association does not suffer unduly from the limited
possibilities of using the national currencies paid by the less-developed
countries.

   In some cases IDA has agreed to finance local expenditures with foreign
currencies, on condition that the amount of the currencies concerned is
relatively small.

THE INTERNATIONAL FINANCE CORPORATION

1. ORIGINS

In every case of a loan to a private enterprise, the Articles of the Bank
require a repayment guarantee by the government concerned. This consider-

ably limits the Bank's range of action. The project for setting up a finance corporation which would remedy this situation dates back to 1951. It formed part of a plan, sponsored by the United States government, for aid to the less-developed countries, which itself had been drawn up in connection with President Truman's Point Four programme. (After President Eisenhower took office, the project was allowed to lapse.) The slowdown in the armaments race in 1953 and the fear that the communist world would now fight the capitalist system mainly in the commercial field led to a change in United States policy. The United States was prepared to cooperate in the establishment of a finance corporation, provided this institution refrained from participating in the capital of the enterprises concerned (subsequently it was to waive this provision; see below). In December 1954 the United Nations instructed the Bank to prepare draft articles for the new corporation; this draft was submitted to the IBRD countries on 11 April 1955. After it had been approved by a sufficient number of countries (thirty-one states which together had subscribed over 75 per cent of the capital), the Articles of the International Finance Corporation (IFC) came into force on 20 July 1956.

2. OBJECTIVES

The International Finance Corporation aims to supplement the Bank's action by encouraging, jointly with private investors, the establishment, improvement and expansion of private enterprises of a productive character in the member states and more especially in the less-developed countries. To this end:

a) it supplies funds to private enterprises, if the necessary private capital is not available on reasonable terms, and without demanding any repayment guarantee from the government concerned (Article 1,*i*);
b) it promotes opportunities for the investment of private capital by bringing together local and foreign investors and an experienced supervisory staff (Article 1,*ii*);
c) it helps to create, in the countries concerned, conditions which are of a nature to attract local and foreign private capital to productive investment (Article 1,*iii*).

3. ORGANIZATION

A. *Members and capital*

Only IBRD member countries may belong to the Corporation. Membership was offered to the fifty-six countries which fulfilled that condition on 30 June 1955; if they subscribed to the required number of shares prior to 31 December 1956, they were automatically accepted as original member states

(Article 2,*1a*). The capital, of 100 million dollars (Article 2,*2a*) consists of 100 000 shares of 1 000 dollars each (Article 2,*2b*).

To facilitate the accession of other countries, a capital increase can be effected without difficulty: a simple majority of votes cast in the Board of Governors is sufficient to raise it by up to 10 per cent (10 000 shares) (Article 2,*2c i*). For a more substantial increase, a three-quarters majority of the total voting power is required (Article 2,*2c ii*). Several IBRD countries did not join the Corporation or subsequently withdrew from it (e.g., Algeria); this meant that the maximum capital was not raised for several years, even after the accession of new members. An increase of 10 million dollars in the authorized capital was made in 1963 and another increase from 110 to 650 million dollars was approved on 2 November 1977. In December 1985 the capital was brought to the amount of 1.3 billion dollars. A new increase was envisaged in 1990.

Subscriptions were initially payable in gold or dollars (Article 2,*3c*). They now have to be paid in dollars or freely convertible currencies (which the IFC has to convert into dollars).

On 30 June 1990 there were 135 member states (114 of which are less-developed countries), and a paid-in capital of 1 072 million dollars. The relative interest of the principal member countries in the Corporation is given in Table 14.

B. *Administration*

The Corporation is managed in much the same way as the Bank. In order to curtail administrative costs, the member states are represented on the Board of Governors of the Corporation by the persons who are members of the Bank's Board. The Bank president is *ex officio* chairman of IFC Board; he appoints the president of IFC (Article 4,*5*). The directors of the Bank fulfil the same function in the Corporation, provided that at least one of the states voting to elect them is a member country of the latter institution (Article 4,*4*). Until October 1961 R. L. Garner, the vice-president of the Bank from 1947 to 1956, was president of the Corporation. Since then, the president of the Bank has also been president of IFC. The executive vice-president (Sir William Ryrie on 30 June 1990), who heads a regular staff of 595, carries out his duties under the president's supervision.

The Corporation, then, has all the features of a subsidiary which has its own administration but which has to follow the Bank's instructions with regard to the more important decisions.

IFC headquarters are in the same place as those of the Bank. Like the Bank, the Corporation may open other offices in the territory of member countries (Article 4,*8*). The Corporation also invests members' currencies with the central bank or a similar body designed by the country in question (Article 4,*9*).

Table 14. Principal IFC members with their paid-in subscriptions to capital stock on 30 June 1990.

Country	Amount (thousand dollars)	Per cent of total
United States	231 429	21.59
Japan	79 794	7.44
Germany	72 861	6.80
United Kingdom	68 400	6.38
France	68 400	6.38
India	45 976	4.28
Canada	45 976	4.28
Italy	41 942	3.91
Netherlands	31 726	2.96
Belgium	27 446	2.56
Australia	26 751	2.50
Brazil	19 885	1.85
Argentina	19 205	1.79
Indonesia	16 131	1.50
Venezuela	15 593	1.45
Saudi Arabia	14 447	1.35

Source: IFC, *Annual report*, 1990.

4. FUNCTIONS AND OPERATION

A. *Acquisition of Resources*

1. *Provisions*

The Corporation's resources are separate from those of the Bank; it was prohibited from contracting loans with the Bank or from supplying it with funds. It was nevertheless possible to make arrangements with the Bank in respect of facilities, transfer of personnel or services and repayment of administrative expenses (Article 4,*6*). In September 1964 a proposal was made that the IFC should be offered the possibility of borrowing from the Bank. This move received general support and came into force on 17 December 1965.

The provisions concerning the acquisition of the necessary funds are less extensive than in the case of the Bank. In the same way as the Bank the Corporation may indeed float loans (Article 3,*6i*) and issue bonds (Article 3,*6iv*).

The Corporation endeavours to transfer its interests to private investors whenever a suitable opportunity arises (Article 3,*3vi*). The Corporation may guarantee securities to which it has subscribed in order to facilitate placing them (Article 3,*6iii*).

The funds received or receivable by the Corporation are not guaranteed against exchange risks; they remain subject to the restrictions, regulations and exchange control of the member countries concerned (Article 3,*5*). The underlying intention here was that the Corporation should not have an advantage over other enterprises.

2. *Operation*

A first loan of 100 million dollars from the Bank was received in October 1966. On 30 June 1990 these loans totalled 1 221 million dollars (of which 909 million were withdrawn and outstanding). Borrowings from other sources amounted to 2 670 million dollars on 30 June 1990 (all of which was withdrawn and outstanding). Net income amounted to 25 million dollars in 1985/86, net assets to 886 million.

IFC has sold part of its cumulative gross commitments to financial institutions or other investors. The initiators of the investments enjoy preference; in any case, contact is established with them in order to prevent participation from being transferred to hostile groups.

On the basis of investments disbursed and outstanding at 30 June 1990, the average return of the equity part of the IFC's portfolio was 17.7 per cent (that on the loan part being 7.3 per cent).

B. *Application of resources*

1. *Provisions*

The Corporation may invest its funds in any enterprise of a productive type that is established on the territory of one of the member countries (Article 3,*1*), provided this country does not raise any objection (Article 3,*3ii*). Participation by the government or official bodies does not necessarily preclude investment by the Corporation (Article 3,*1*).

Originally, the Corporation could not subscribe to shares of private enterprises, but this resulted in such a restriction of transactions that the relevant clause (Article 3,*2*) was amended in 1961. However, the Corporation may not make use of its shareholding to play an influential role in the enterprise in which it has invested funds (Article 3,*3iv*). It has likewise to ensure a reasonable diversification of investments (Article 3,*3vii*); functioning as a holding company, and indirectly managing a number of enterprises, is not permissible.

The Corporation may convert the funds which it does not require for its financing operations into any type of bond whatsoever (Article 3,*6ii*). The Bank does not enjoy so much freedom of action. Only the sums which are transferred to pension funds and similar reserve funds have to be invested by the Corporation, as also by the Bank, in readily negotiable securities.

2. *Operation*

Initially, the Corporation granted loans only (in most cases at five to fifteen years). Applications for small amounts were refused on the ground of unduly high administration costs and those for large amounts were turned down in order to ensure that funds were not prematurely exhausted. The loans granted ranged from 0.1 to 3.5 million dollars.

Since the amendment to the Articles of Agreement in 1961, there has been an upward trend in the acquisition of holdings. On 30 June 1969, as much as 39 per cent of the Corporation's portfolio was in equity but this portion declined gradually until it stood at 19 per cent on 30 June 1978. In April 1978, however, the Board of Directors decided to increase the level of equity financing. However, on 30 June 1990 the corresponding percentage was only 19.1 per cent.

Investment in equities enabled the IFC to provide and mobilize all forms of risk capital and to promote projects itself.

While the IFC commitments averaged approximately 10 million dollars a year over the first five years, they rose to an average of 1 525 million in 1987—90 (2 201 million in 1989/90). Gross cumulative commitments on 30 June 1990 were 8 147 million dollars. This figure does not give an accurate picture of the real influence exercised by the IFC. For every dollar the IFC invests for its own account, other investors will invest approximately four dollars.

On 30 June 1990 the IFC held 495 investments totalling 4 752 million dollars, consisting of 4 068 million loans and 684 million participations.

The growth of the IFC's portfolio has meant that supervision of existing investments has become as important a part of its day-to-day operations as the processing of proposals for new investments. This in turn has been reflected in the continuity of the relationship between the IFC and many of the companies it has helped to finance, e.g., in the number of second and even third commitments of the Corporation. In its equity investments, IFC does not generally vote its share or participate in the day-to-day management of the company, but it asks for special equity features (e.g., preferences or additional reserves), which are needed to make its investments salable to other investors.

The bulk of the IFC's investments have profited construction materials, particularly cement, mining, and iron and steel.

Since the IFC is a shareholder of private development finance companies, it is represented on the boards of many of them and has contributed to the improvement of their operation. The Corporation also aims at establishing, supporting and strengthening institutions contributing to the development of local capital markets.

Without setting any fixed ceiling, the IFC now gives consideration to loan and equity commitments of up to 30—35 million dollars in a single enterprise, whereas previously the highest individual commitment was 6 million dollars. Larger commitments are made when the Corporation is assured of participations by other institutions. The term of the loans is normally seven to twelve years. Amortization is due semi-annually after the expiry of a period of grace and a commitment fee of 1 per cent per year is payable on the undisbursed portion of the loan.

C. *Utilization of currencies*

1. *Provisions*

The provisions concerning the currencies to be used are not very extensive. The Corporation, unlike the Bank, is free to dispose of its capital as it wishes (since this is fully paid up in gold or dollars). No conditions are imposed on the private enterprises to which it grants loans or whose shares it has taken up as regards the use of the funds provided in a given country (Article 3,*3iii*).

2. *Operation*

Before 1961, IFC loans were mainly made in dollars. But as soon as the Corporation was also permitted to acquire holdings, it was prepared to denominate its investments in other currencies. On 30 June 1990 57 per cent of the loans and equity investments were denominated in US dollars, 18.2 per cent in Deutsche mark and 4.5 per cent in Swiss franc.

In every case, the enterprise concerned examines with the Corporation which is the best currency for the sums granted to be paid in.

Appraisal

Since their foundation, the World Bank institutions have committed funds amounting to approximately 260 billion dollars. The Group's contribution towards the total disbursed flow of finance (private, official, bilateral and multilateral) from DAC countries to the less-developed countries was about 15 per cent.

The influence of the Bank, which has accounted for the lion's share of the aid, is more significant than would appear from the figures. For one thing, it has mainly financed investments, which form the basis for further development; for another, its technical assistance has often been indispensable to the implementation of growth programmes.

The same holds true for IDA and IFC. As a general rule, the latter institution, which has become the Group's main instrument for dealing with private enterprises, has always operated with private groups (on average, other investors have provided about four dollars for every dollar invested by the IFC). The comparatively small contribution by the IFC is attributable largely to the fact that it grants no funds which can be provided by the private sector on reasonable terms. Moreover, as one of the IFC's aims is to realize its interests as quickly as possible in order to maintain its scope for action, the projects have to be profitable in the short run and also attractive to private investors. In most cases, private capital is to be found for such investments. The IFC's activities are in some measure determined by those of the IBRD and IDA. Without a minimum economic infrastructure, private investments are frequently out of the question.

Changing priorities

Although a Bank project should "be of high priority to the economic growth of the country" (E. H. Rotberg) concerned this has not been the case for most projects. Policy has gradually become more flexible. Since 1964 projects which a few years previously would have been rejected have been financed on favourable terms.

At the same time the emphasis placed on different sectors has changed. Initially only basic infrastructure was considered important, later more attention was given to (heavy) industry and subsequently to technical assistance. Since the mid-sixties rural development (especially in low-income areas) has been favoured. The share of roads, railways, ports and waterways in total loans fell from 32 per cent in 1968 to 13 per cent in 1989; the share of agriculture and rural development increased from 9 per cent to 36 per cent over the same period.

It is seen from the annual reviews of project performance results that many projects reviewed were changed during implementation and experienced time and cost overruns. Among the reasons for these changes were deficient project preparation and design, weak management, general economic instability and political changes. There is a "continuing downward trend in the major indicators of performance" (*Annual report*, 1986). One wonders, for example, why the Bank is financing such risky and fundamentally uncertain sectors as family planning, training and education. Is no financing to be done by the governments of the less-developed countries? These sectors are important but are better left to the countries concerned.

Sentences such as: "Curriculum reform, designed to introduce subjects more relevant, both to pupil's interests and to countries' particular needs, is central to the Bank's educational strategy", have a pleasant ring but are liable to cause too many conflicts with the countries concerned.

Furthermore, the fact is all too often overlooked that the utilization of more capital requires the fulfilment of certain prior conditions, such as the availability of pre-investment studies. Countries which were able to submit well-prepared high-priority projects have benefited more than those which were not. In other words, there is a lack of those pre-investment studies which are needed to decide rationally whether and how specific development projects should be carried out, and to facilitate the training of the manpower required to implement them successfully.

Till 1980 most of the Bank's loans are project-based. But good projects did not prevent wrong policies. The country's resources released by the Bank loan may be used for a bad project. Hence the change in the Bank's policy since 1980: more importance is given to aid for sectors (sector-adjustment loans) and economic recovery programmes (structural adjustment loans). The Bank should make the granting of loans dependent on policy results as regards essential aspects. In this field there is no cooperation between the Bank and the Fund.

In fact, the relations between the two institutions are deteriorating. Weeks after the collapse of talks between the IMF and Argentina, the Bank announced in September 1988 the approval of a total of 1.25 billion dollars in loans for that country. Political interference (the US administration) seems to be an explanation.

In 1987 the Bank began to treat environment more seriously. Even so its environmental conditions are sometimes ignored once the money is handed over. Other priorities in recent years are the financial sector, the women-in-development initiative and poverty alleviation.

The Bank Group supports the development of market-oriented financial systems through comprehensive financial-sector adjustment loans and credits (commitments totalling 1 695 million dollars relating to such operations were approved from January 1989 through June 1990). The women-in-development initiative focuses on increasing women's productivity and income. Poverty-reducing efforts (in respect of nutrition, primary health care, water and sewerage, and provision of food to those below a threshold consumption level) have become part of country-assistance strategies.

Vain exercise

As too much waste occurs and money is often spent on things which have a low priority, donor countries and other agencies are, in fact, beginning to pay close attention to the economics of aid utilization. Many authors "approve of this, despite the liability of neo-colonialism" (I. M. D. Little and J. M. Clifford).

Even governments which believe in aid to less-developed countries arrive at the bitter conclusion that it is very often a vain exercise. Nor have five- or ten-year plans eliminated the difficulties. Again, it is not very intelligent to impose a growth philosophy upon countries, which prefer — and they have the right — to sacrifice economic growth to religious conviction. A Bank's report on Africa concluded that most African states pursue unstable but always wrong policies (they are complicated by artificial boundaries) and that changing these policies is a necessary condition to progress.

The Bank's administration has succeeded "in consistently suppressing elementary economic principles in favour of nonsense concepts, thoroughly confusing capital and income in order to provide implicit propaganda for more aid for the developing countries and greater resources and power for the Bank in managing the transfers" (H. G. Johnson).

Finally, it should be pointed out that foreign aid is not indispensable to economic growth and that it is even harmful: ". . . the flow of unearned grants generally obstructs the development of qualities, attitudes and efforts which make for material advance and divert attention from these prime determinants of development" (P. T. Bauer).

The role of private capital

The share of the private sector could be stepped up if greater confidence could be inspired among investors (cf. the Convention on the Settlement of Investment Disputes). If private capital is to be drawn into development plans, it needs to be assured of an adequate yield and to be guaranteed reasonable facilities for the transfer of profits. A nationalization policy is unlikely to attract private investments.

Moreover, why should the less-developed countries stimulate private investment? In any case they receive money from foreign national and/or international institutions. Considerations regarding capacity are less important. No wonder considerable amounts of domestic capital are flowing out of the less-developed countries.

Although it is one of the Bank's objectives to promote private foreign investment, most loans granted to development finance companies go to government-owned finance companies (which initially did not receive loans of this kind). The same applies to industrial enterprises. (At first only a few loans were granted to state-owned industrial enterprises.) In my opinion, it is contrary to the Bank's Articles of Agreement to grant loans to centrally planned economies and to countries which carry out nationalizations. (The Bank, however, has not always kept strictly to this principle.) The Bank may only grant loans to countries when private capital is not available on reasonable terms. But private capital is not attracted by countries where the government regulates everything and in such cases it cannot be said that private capital is not available.

The debt crisis

The Bank did not foresee and did not warn for the debt crisis of 1982. It failed to play a leading role in that respect. During the seventies most western banks crowded around the less-developed countries. Caution was not their principal quality. As some shareholders became worried, they spoke a reassuring language ("The exposure of banks to the risk of rescheduling or default on less-developed countries debt is not really great", *Monthly Economic Letter*, Citibank, June 1976). But the foreign debt of less-developed countries kept on growing. The total external debt ran from 852 billion dollars in 1982 to 1 322 billion dollars in 1989 (of which 1 047 billion long-term). The total debt service of less-developed countries amounted to 134 billion in 1982 and 171 billion in 1989 (amortization 74 billion, interest 97 billion).

In most cases a reasonable amortization schedule is drawn up separately for each individual loan, but owing to the large number of loans concluded with several creditors, the possibility of ensuring the servicing of the loan in subsequent years is often seriously jeopardized.

In fact, new loans should only be granted if they do not give rise to excessive repayment obligations. Meanwhile, for many countries the consolidation of short-term commitments seems to be inevitable. It should be possible for the IMF to be more closely associated with discussions on the conclusion of new loans.

The banks are looking for retrieval to the states and the international institutions. They push their governments to quota and subscriptions increases in IMF and Bank. But not the states, nor international economic institutions must bear risks; risk appraisal is the task of the private banks. ". . . countries with excessive debts must like the rest of us follow appropriate adjustments policies, and private sector banks will need to show a matching responsibility" (Sir Geoffrey Howe at the annual IMF meeting 1982).

In 1989—90 the Bank initiated a debt and debt-service reduction programme (the so-called Brady plan) providing official support to severely indebted, middle-income countries for voluntary debt and debt-service reduction by commercial banks as a complement to adjustment measures, new lending by them, investment, and the repatriation of flight capital.

BIBLIOGRAPHY

A. *IBRD publications*

The Bank publishes regulations concerning loans and issues, an *Annual report*, jointly with IDA, and *Summary proceedings* 19—, *Annual report of the Board of Governors*. There are also annual reports of the ICSID and the IFC.

Since 1986 the Bank publishes *The World Bank Research Observer* and *ICSID Review, Foreign Investment Law Journal* and since 1987 *The World Bank Economic Review*. See also *Abstracts of Current Studies* and *Research News*.

Reports are issued periodically on operations in past years or on activities in certain parts of the world (Africa, Asia, America), e.g., *IDA in retrospect: the first two decades of the International Development Association* (New York, Oxford University Press, 1982).

Regularly the Bank assembles some articles about its activities from *Finance and Development* and publishes them separately, e.g., *The World Bank and the world's poorest* (June 1980); E. H. Rotberg, *World Bank: a financial appraisal* (January 1981). Another sort of publications are the *World Bank Staff Working Papers*, covering the whole range of Bank activities. The *Sector Policy Papers* review a specific field, e.g., *Fishery* (December 1982).

Since 1978 statistics concerning world development indicators have been published in annual reports by the World Bank: *World Development Report* and *The World Bank Atlas*.

Also of interest: J. P. Gittinger, *Economic analysis of agricultural projects* (Baltimore, Johns Hopkins University Press, 2nd ed., 1982); G. M. Meier, *Pricing policy for development management* (Baltimore, Johns Hopkins University Press, 1983); W. C. Baum and S. M. Tolbert, *Investing in development. Lessons of World Bank experience* (Oxford, Oxford University Press, 1985). S. Edwards, *Exchange-rate misalignment in developing countries* (Baltimore, Johns Hopkins University Press, 1988).

B. *Other publications*

A. van de Laar, *The World Bank and the poor* (Boston, Martinus Nijhoff, 1980); B. S. Frey and F. Schneider, *Competing models of international lending activity* (Stockholm, Institute for International Economic Studies, February 1983); W. Ascher, New development approaches and the adaptability of international agencies: the case of the World Bank, *International Organization*, Summer 1983.

The extracts quoted are from: B. Ward and P. T. Bauer, *Two views on aid to developing countries* (London, The Institute of Economic Affairs, 1966); H. G. Johnson, book review of E. S. Mason and R. E. Asher, The World Bank since Bretton Woods (Washington, The Brookings Institution, 1974), *Economica,* November 1975; E. H. Rotberg, The World Bank — a financial appraisal: II, *Finance and Development*, December 1976; I. M. D. Little and J. M. Clifford, *International aid* (London, Allen & Unwin, 1965).

3. The General Agreement on Tariffs and Trade

> *The GATT is an institution blessed with an objective that can never be achieved, namely free trade reciprocally negotiated. It is nevertheless uncertain whether it will show the same capacity for survival as the early Christian Church whose object, the perfectibility of mankind, has proved at least equally difficult to achieve.*
>
> EDMUND DELL

The implementation of a multilateral trade and payments system was facilitated by the establishment of the Fund and the Bank. It proved more difficult to reach agreement on the reduction of customs duties and the abolition of quantitative restrictions and discriminations, partly owing to the fact that these matters were more closely bound up with balance-of-payments equilibrium. In order to avoid a recurrence of the protectionism of the 1930s vigorous efforts were necessary to dismantle these various kinds of trade barriers. This chapter is devoted to the action taken in this respect within the framework of the General Agreement on Tariffs and Trade.

1. ORIGINS

One of the aims of the Atlantic Charter (August 1941) and of the Lend-Lease Agreements (February 1942) was a world trading system based on non-discrimination and free exchange of goods and services. This explains why, as far back as 1943—44, discussions on postwar trade problems had already been held between Britain, Canada and the United States, but it was not until 6 December 1945 that the United States submitted a proposal.

This provides for the establishment of an International Trade Organization (ITO) which, as a specialized agency of the United Nations, would aim to achieve the gradual liberalization of trade, to combat monopolies, to expand the demand for commodities and to coordinate the countercyclical policies of the various countries.

111

In exchange for a loan of 3 750 million dollars from the United States, Britain undertook to restore the convertibility of sterling from 15 July 1947 onwards (see Chapter 1,4C), abolish discrimination in foreign trade and cooperate in the establishment of the organization. After ECOSOC had expressed itself in favour of convening a conference, a preparatory committee was appointed and meetings of this committee took place in London from 18 October to 26 November 1946.

No agreement was reached on certain articles (including those relating to indirect forms of protection) of the London Draft Charter. A drafting committee, which included among its members the United States, Canada, the United Kingdom, France and the Benelux countries, was set up for the purpose of seeking another formulation for the points at issue. While this committee was drafting a new text at Lake Success from 20 January to 25 February 1947, the United States expressed a wish to engage in direct negotiations with the members of the committee.

Thus it was that two types of discussion were held simultaneously at Geneva in the spring and summer of 1947. From 10 April to 22 August the preparatory committee continued its work on a draft charter for the ITO, and from 10 April to 30 October bilateral negotiations took place among most of the states represented on the committee, to which other countries, including Brazil, Burma, Ceylon, Pakistan and Southern Rhodesia had now been added. The reciprocal tariff concessions which resulted from these negotiations were embodied in the General Agreement on Tariffs and Trade (GATT), signed on 30 October 1947, containing a provisional codification of trade relations among the signatory countries. By the terms of a protocol of 30 October 1947 the General Agreement was applied, from 1 January 1948, pending the entry into force of the ITO.

The charter for the ITO was discussed by delegates from fifty-six countries at the Havana Conference (21 November 1947—24 March 1948) which drew up the Havana Charter. By mid-1950, this charter had been approved by the parliaments of only two countries, Liberia and Australia. In the United States, it provoked so much criticism that in December 1950 President Truman withdrew the bill which had been laid before Congress. This meant that the establishment of the Organization was rendered impossible for the time being. The escape-clause-mindedness of the less-developed countries, Commonwealth preferences, the creation of COMECON and the OEEC were among the main difficulties preventing the approval of the Charter.

Meanwhile, a significant number of countries had already sought membership of GATT. At Annecy in April 1949, negotiations were opened among the twenty-three countries which were already GATT members and ten other countries (Denmark, the Dominican Republic, Finland, Greece, Haiti, Italy, Liberia, Nicaragua, Sweden and Uruguay). In 1950 the validity of the tariff concession lists was extended for three years (until the end of 1953, but not for Brazil and Nicaragua), the accession of Austria, Peru, Turkey and

Western Germany was settled and further reciprocal concessions were granted.

Initially, the Agreement consisted of three parts. In Part I (Articles 1 and 2) the basic obligations which are to be fulfilled by the contracting parties are laid down — the most-favoured-nation clause and the schedules of tariff concessions. These Articles may be amended only by a unanimous vote.

Part 2 (Articles 3 to 23 inclusive) constitutes a code of fair trade and contains the essential trading rules of the Havana Charter. Part 3 (Articles 24 to 35) deals, *inter alia*, with the conditions of application, membership and withdrawal, amendments to the Agreement and its relation to the Havana Charter.

The contracting parties also undertake to observe to the fullest extent of their executive authority the principles of Chapters 1 to 6 (concerning *inter alia* the objectives, development problems, trade policy, international cartel policy and commodity agreements) and Chapter 9 of the Havana Charter (Article 29,*1*).

The Agreement has been ratified only by Haiti. The other countries waited in vain for ratification by the United States. This was needed because the United States accounts for 20 per cent of world trade and, by the terms of Article 26,*6*, the Agreement requires ratification by as many countries as together account for 85 per cent of international trade. However, this has not prevented the Agreement from being applied: it is at present being implemented under the terms of the Protocol of Provisional Application and of the Protocols of Accession. "Provisional application" of GATT under the terms of the various protocols means that governments are permitted to deviate from Part 2 rules if they cannot follow them without violating domestic legislation which was already in force when they became contracting parties (the "grandfather" clause). There are not many such laws, and the provisions of Part 2 in effect have just as much binding force as those in the other parts of GATT. The few cases of non-observance on account of "existing legislation" might be regarded as exceptions, even though they might not be temporary. The possibility of applying the Agreement without complete observance of Part 2 was endorsed at Annecy (10 October 1949) and Torquay (21 April 1951) and in similar subsequent protocols.

In 1954—55 the text of the General Agreement was revised. Amendments were incorporated in two instruments, the Protocol amending Part 1 and Articles 29 and 30, and the Protocol amending the Preamble and Parts 2 and 3. The first Protocol requires acceptance by all contracting parties. As a result of non-ratification by Uruguay this Protocol was abandoned on 1 January 1968. Meanwhile, the second Protocol had come into force on 28 November 1957. It was agreed that any contracting party which could not apply certain articles of Part 2 should communicate the domestic laws in question to the other parties.

In 1965 a new part (Part 4) was added to the General Agreement. It was implemented *de facto* as from 8 February 1965 and came into force on 27

June 1966. Part 4 relates mainly to the expansion of exports of less-developed countries (Articles 36 to 38).

In 1979 agreement was reached on numerous amendments (see below).

2. OBJECTIVES

The aims of the General Agreement are set forth in the preamble. A distinction has to be made between the general aims, which are also pursued by many other international economic organizations, and the specific tasks. The general aims are the improvement of standards of living, full employment, a large and steadily growing volume of real income and effective demand, the full use of the world's resources and the expansion of production and international trade.

It is the specific task of GATT to contribute to the attainment of these objectives through arrangements directed to the substantial reduction of tariffs and other trade barriers and to the elimination of discrimination.

In Part 4, the contracting parties agree that the attainment of the general aims is particularly urgent where less-developed countries are concerned. Henceforth, in the interest of the less-developed countries, endeavours must also be made to ensure the stabilization of commodity prices, better access to the markets of the developed countries for processed and manufactured products of the less-developed countries, and the diminution of the burdens which these countries assume in the interest of their economic development (Article 36).

3. ORGANIZATION

A. *Members*

The accession of a new member country requires a two-thirds majority vote by the contracting parties (Article 33). In a certain sense, this is inconsistent with the character of the Agreement; as the trade benefits are granted to all GATT members, a state should only be accepted by unanimous vote. However, it was desired to obviate a situation in which the acceptance of an important country might be impeded by member states which supply comparatively little to that country and compete against it on the markets of the other contracting parties.

Moreover, member states which do not assent to the accession of a given country are allowed to refrain from applying the provisions of the Agreement, or of Article 2, *vis-à-vis* this country if the two countries have not entered into tariff negotiations with each other (Article 35,*1*). In other words, membership does not necessarily involve a uniform tariff system with respect to all participating countries. This provision was added on the initiative of India.

A country with a considerable production and export potential (such as Western Germany or Japan) usually has to make substantial concessions in exchange for acceptance as a member state. The majority of countries agree to its accession only if they are certain that increased exports to the new member state will offset a fall in exports to the other GATT countries.

Countries with overseas territories have to state whether the commitments entered into are also valid for these territories (Articles 26,5a and b). If any such territory possesses or acquires full autonomy in the conduct of its external commercial relations, it may be deemed to be a GATT country on the recommendation of the responsible contracting party (Article 26,5c).

As a result of decolonization, the number of member countries has greatly increased in recent years. Membership rose from thirty-seven on 28 November 1957 to one hundred on 31 December 1990. Tunisia has provisionally acceded to the Agreement, and twenty-eight former colonies are applying the GATT until such time as they have finally established their trade policies. Of the central and Eastern European countries, only Czechoslovakia is an original member state. Yugoslavia and Poland became members in 1966 and 1967 respectively. Hungary and Bulgaria have followed GATT activities as observers since 1966 and 1967 respectively. Romania and Hungary became members in 1971 and 1973 respectively. Important countries which are not yet members are the USSR (it acquired observer status on 16 May 1990) and the People's Republic of China (in 1990 the Contracting Parties had not yet decided on China's request to resume its membership).

A few countries (Taiwan, Syria, Lebanon, Liberia) have withdrawn, all in the early years of the GATT.

Japan's request for accession met with a great deal of opposition, since this country was regarded as a dangerous competitor. Not until 11 August 1955 was the required two-thirds majority obtained. Several countries (Australia, Austria, Belgium, Brazil, Cuba, France, Haiti, Luxemburg, the Netherlands, New Zealand, Rhodesia-Nyasaland, South Africa and the United Kingdom) then availed themselves of Article 35. As a result of bilateral agreements, these countries, with the exception of South Africa, subsequently agreed to extend the provisions of GATT to their trade with Japan.

Participation in the trade negotiation rounds is not confined to members of the GATT.

B. *Administration*

Unlike other international agencies, GATT is not an organization in the strict legal sense, though the member countries do act as a body and make collective decisions and judgments which are an important part of the GATT mechanism. As a legal subterfuge, this body is referred to in the text of the General Agreement as the "CONTRACTING PARTIES"; member governments acting individually are mentioned as "contracting parties". So when the GATT speaks of notifying the CONTRACTING PARTIES or of the decisions by the CONTRACTING PARTIES, it means notifying the institution and the institution's collective decision. It does not mean notifying certain other member governments or decisions by certain countries.

The contracting parties' main activity is tariff and trade negotiations, at which the member countries grant each other concessions in the field of trade (or undertake not to increase certain customs duties), and meetings and consultations to resolve trade problems.

At the sessions of the contracting parties, each country has one vote and, except in a few specific cases (accession of other countries, waiving of members' obligations in special circumstances), decisions are taken by a simple majority of the votes cast (Article 25). In practice, GATT decisions are generally arrived at by consensus and not by vote.

Between the annual sessions, which usually last three to four weeks, most of the work of the contracting parties is carried on by the Council of Representatives (established on 4 June 1960) and a number of committees.

Since 1968 the contracting parties have delegated extensive powers to the Council. Committees deal with Budget, Finance and Administration, Tariff Concessions, Trade and Development; the Committee on Trade and Development regularly reviews the implementation of part IV of the Agreement. There are also many Committees established under the Tokyo Round negotiations; they relate to Anti-Dumping Practices, Customs Valuation, Government Procurement, Import Licensing, Subsidies and Countervailing Measures, Technical Barriers to Trade, Civil Aircraft, Dairy Products, Meat. Other bodies include the Textiles Committee.

The establishment of the Trade Review Mechanism was a result of the mid-term review of the Uruguay Round (April 1989). Under this Mechanism the Council is to examine the impact of each member's trade policies and practices on the multilateral trading system. The four largest trading entities are subject to review every two years, the next sixteen largest every four years, and other members every six years. The United States' examination was held on 14 December 1989. During the review speakers expressed strong concern about the use of unilateral measures under Section 301 of the United States Trade Act.

In the early stages, conferences and meetings were serviced by the Secretariat of the Interim Commission for the International Trade Organization; after the *de facto* rejection of the Havana Charter, the Secretariat devoted its entire attention to GATT (from 1952).

The Secretariat was gradually expanded (about 400 employees in 1986); it is headed by a Director-General (until 1965 Executive Secretary), a post held from 1947 to 1968 by E. Wyndham White (United Kingdom), from

1968 to 1980 by O. Long (Switzerland) and since October 1980 by A. Dunkel (Switzerland).

In 1955, at the ninth session of the contracting parties, an attempt was made to create an organization for the administration of GATT, to be known as the Organization for Trade Cooperation (OTC), but its constitution, like that of the ITO, failed to receive parliamentary approval.

An International Trade Centre was established in 1964 in order to help the less-developed countries in their attempts to step up exports. Since 1 January 1968 the Centre has been jointly operated by GATT and UNCTAD. It offers training courses and advice on trade promotion, and carries out market research and research into export-marketing techniques.

The budget estimate for 1990 amounts to 75 million Swiss francs. The highest contribution was by the United States (15.6 per cent), Germany (11.6 per cent), Japan (8.9 per cent) France (7.0 per cent), and the United Kingdom (6.5 per cent), although each member country has one vote only.

4. FUNCTIONS AND OPERATION

A. *Elimination of discrimination*

1. *Provisions*

The main instrument employed in efforts to eliminate discrimination in imports and exports is the most-favoured-nation clause (Article 1). This provision, which figured in most trade agreements in the nineteenth century for the purpose of preventing discrimination in the field of customs duties, acquired a broader significance in GATT. Any advantage, favour, privilege or immunity (not only with regard to customs duties, but also affecting other import and export charges or transfers of payments for imports or exports) which is granted by one of the contracting parties to a product originating in or destined for any other country has to be accorded immediately and unconditionally to like products originating in or destined for the territories of all other member countries (Article 1,*1*). This applies also to transit trade, freedom of which may not be impeded (Article 5).

The most-favoured-nation clause is the best possible method of preventing the largely bilateral nature of GATT negotiations from stamping its imprint on world trade; were this to happen, each country would be inclined to grant greater commercial advantages to its principal customers than to the other member countries.

Special clauses were included so as not to jeopardize traditional trading relations between certain territories.

As regards the countries of the former British and French empires, the former Belgian and Dutch colonies, and territories which, like the Philippines and Puerto Rico, were or still are associated with the United States, for example, preferences with the former metropolitan countries and between themselves may be maintained. The difference between the ordinary or most-favoured-nation rate of duty and the preferential duties may not, however, exceed the limits laid down in the Agreement (and if nothing has been provided for in this connection, they may not be in excess of the margin in operation on 10 April 1947) (Article 1,4). Among the preferences to which this rule applies are those between the Netherlands and the Belgium-Luxemburg Economic Union.

There are three major exceptions to the most-favoured-nation principle — the advantages granted to adjacent states in order to facilitate frontier traffic, and to countries which form a customs union or a free-trade area.

The first exception ordinarily relates to the transport of small quantities (e.g., by frontier workers) and does not in fact jeopardize the most-favoured-nation principle (Article 24,3a).

The other two exceptions have acquired great importance in recent years on account of the tendency towards economic integration. The contracting parties are normally favourably disposed towards customs unions and free-trade areas provided they are designed to facilitate trade between the countries concerned and provided that no barriers are raised to the other contracting parties' trade with these countries (Article 24, 4). The following conditions are therefore laid down:

a) Customs duties and trade regulations may not, after the entry into force of the customs union (or free-trade area), have a more adverse incidence on trade with contracting parties which are not members of the union (area) than the duties and regulations in each of the countries concerned prior to the formation of the union (area) (Article 24,5a and b). The objection has rightly been made that the establishment of a customs union usually leads to a change in trade flows, which means that it is difficult to assess the repercussions of a tariff change. If a contracting party proposes to increase a customs duty (in a way which is inconsistent with the concessions granted), negotiations are held on the matter (Article 24,6).

b) Where only an interim agreement has been concluded between the countries concerned, this has to include a plan for the creation of the customs union or the free-trade area within a reasonable length of time (Article 24,5c). Any contracting party that joins a customs union or free-trade area, or which signs an agreement for the implementation of cooperation of this kind, is obliged to notify the other countries of such action. If the contracting parties as a whole do not consider the agreement to be such as to lead within the prescribed period, to a customs union or free-trade area, they must inform the countries concerned accordingly. There countries have to modify their plans to fit in with the ideas of the other member states or else abandon their plans (Article 24, 7a and b).

Waivers of these fairly strict conditions are permissible (Article 24, *10*); they require a two-thirds majority. Further exceptions to the most-favoured-nation clause are the anti-dumping duties (Article 6: see below), the complaints procedure (Article 23: see below) and the waiver procedures of Article 25 (see below).

2. *Operation*

The parties to GATT have repeatedly had to consider whether economic integration between certain of their number was consistent with the Agreement. Approximately three-quarters of the member countries, indeed, now belong to some regional group or other.

A great many problems arose with the establishment of the European Coal and Steel Community. A supranational authority had not been provided for in the General Agreement. Several countries (notably Denmark, Sweden and Norway, who relied heavily on the Six for imports of coke, iron and scrap iron) feared a revival of the European steel cartel and higher prices. The ECSC promised to take account of the interests of other countries (both consumers and suppliers) and the exemption which had been applied for was finally granted on 10 November 1952. This was done on the basis of Article 25,5 (see below), and not Article 24, since the integration is only partial.

The formation of the EEC gave rise to considerable debate. The fundamental hostility of many non-Community countries has meant that the contracting parties have still not delivered an opinion on the compatibility of the EEC Treaty with the GATT. *De facto*, the existence of the Community has been recognized since the Dillon Round (see below), in which the six EEC countries acted as a unit.

The consequences of the enlargement of the European Community in 1973 were closely examined by the contracting parties. As the new member countries had to adopt the common external tariff and the agricultural policy of the original six, they were obliged to withdraw a number of previously agreed tariff concessions. Negotiations to provide compensation for countries whose trade might be harmed by the increase in duties (Article 24,6) resulted in a lowering of the common external tariff of the Communities on a wide variety of specific products.

A wary attitude has been adopted towards the free-trade area such as EFTA (see Chapter 9), and the Agreement establishing a free-trade area between the United Kingdom and Ireland concluded in December 1965. As was the case with the European Community's trade agreements, no decision has been taken regarding their compliance with GATT provisions.

In the Tokyo Round "Framework Agreement" (see below) preferences for or between less-developed countries are considered as a permanent legal feature of the world trading system (the "enabling clause"). GATT members may give preferential and more favourable treatment only to less-developed countries; in that respect they may ignore the most-favoured-nation clause. In point of fact, the non-reciprocity had already been recognized in 1965 (Article 36).

In October 1984 the contracting parties examined the Australia/New Zealand Closer Economic Relations Trade Agreement (ANZCERT) which came into force on 1 January 1983. It was agreed that the parties to ANZCERT would report to the Council biennially on its operations until free trade is achieved. Free trade was achieved in July 1990, five years ahead of schedule.

The Canada-United States Free-Trade Agreement entered into force on 1 January 1989. The Council agreed in February 1989 to establish a working party, to examine the compatibility with GATT provisions.

B. *Stabilization and reduction of import duties*

1. *Provisions*

The provisions with respect to stabilization and reduction of import duties are contained in Parts 1 and 3 of the Agreement and are thus mandatory.

The member countries recognize that customs duties often constitute serious obstacles to trade. Negotiations to reduce these and similar duties or to bind them at existing levels are of great importance. The contracting parties may therefore sponsor such negotiations from time to time (Articles 28*bis,1*). As low-tariff countries have less to offer in this connection than high-tariff countries, the binding of low duties or of duty-free treatment is in principle recognized as a concession tantamount to the reduction of high duties (Article 28*bis,2*).

These negotiations lead to the compilation of schedules of concessions. Each contracting party guarantees the other parties treatment which is no less favourable than that provided for in the schedules annexed to the Agreement (Article 2,*1a*). For countries which have granted preference to certain other member countries, the schedule consists of two parts — one for the ordinary and one for the preferential duties. Goods originating in a country to which the latter apply may not be subject to customs duties which are higher than those provided for in the appropriate part of the schedule (Article 2,*1c*).

The following cases do not come under the provisions of Article 2:

a) anti-dumping and countervailing duties (Article 2,*2b*);
b) charges equivalent to an internal tax imposed on the like domestic product (even if this is an article that was necessary for the production of the imported product) (Article 2,*2a*);
c) fees and other charges commensurate with the cost of services rendered (Article 2,*2c*).

The usual period of validity for tariff concessions is three years, but a different term may be fixed by a two-thirds majority of votes cast. At the beginning of such a period, each party is entitled to modify or withdraw the concessions granted another GATT country, following negotiation and agreement with this country or any other member state recognized as having a leading interest as a supplier (Article 28,*1*). In this concession, the parties should endeavour to ensure that the reciprocal advantages are not less favourable than those obtaining before the negotiations (Article 28,*2*). If no agreement is reached, the concessions may nevertheless be withdrawn, but any interested contracting party is allowed to withdraw equivalent concessions (Article 28,*3a*). This right also exists for countries not primarily concerned which consider the agreement to be unsatisfactory (Article 28,*3b*). In both cases, the country wishing to discontinue compensatory concessions has to do so within six months of the withdrawal of concessions and has to notify the contracting parties accordingly thirty days beforehand. In this way, an arrangement is still possible.

During a three-year period of validity, the rule is that no tariff concessions are changed except in special circumstances (Article 28,*4*) or if the country concerned has reserved its right to enter into negotiations for the withdrawal or modification of concessions. Provision is also made for consultation in the case of the withholding or withdrawal of concessions granted to a country that ceases being a contracting party to GATT (Article 27).

2. *Operation*

In addition to the annual meetings of the contracting parties, a number of tariff negotiating conferences were held during the first 15 years of GATT's operation, the first of them at Geneva in 1947. In 1949 a conference met at Annecy, in 1950—51 at Torquay, and in 1956 and 1960—62 (the Dillon Round) in Geneva again. Further, there were smaller-scale negotiations preceding the accession of individual countries (such as Japan).

Although it was possible to achieve considerable stabilization of customs duties, these conferences led to gradually diminishing results as far as reductions were concerned. This was ascribable in large measure to the negotiation technique: the bilateral discussions on a product-by-product basis afforded the different interest groups too much opportunity to exert pressure on their respective governments. As a result, negotiations were confined to items giving rise to no major competition problem in any country. What was really needed was a system of multilateral negotiations for uniform reductions of the customs duties of all member states in accordance with certain principles ("linear" or "across-the-board" reductions). France submitted a proposal along these lines as far back as 1951. Since 1 January 1958 the schedules are automatically extended for three-year periods (or such periods as might be chosen by a two-thirds vote of the contracting parties).

The contrast between the smaller and larger countries was also responsible for the course of events. The former are usually free-trade-minded and levy low duties. The latter know that they have little to fear from retaliatory measures by the smaller countries. In the case of concessions to other large countries, they are circumspect about these benefits being automatically extended to all contracting parties. The United States was originally opposed to tariff reductions. The American government was in fact bound by certain legislative provisions, e.g., in respect of the peril point (the rate below which it was believed a further cut would seriously injure domestic producers).

a. *The Kennedy Round*

The establishment of the EEC and the applications to join it made by certain other countries obliged the United States to adopt something of a different attitude. With a view to the maintenance of United States outlets on the European markets, the Trade Expansion Act of 1962 abolished the peril-point principle and authorized the President, for a period of five years (expiring on 30 June 1967), to reduce import duties by 50 per cent and to abolish them entirely when the United States and the EEC together accounted for 80 per cent of total world exports of the products concerned (the dominant supplier clause). The fact that the United Kingdom did not join the EEC (as had been assumed in 1962—63) made this last clause largely inoperative.

In these circumstances the contracting parties were able to decide in May 1963 that a further tariff conference (the Kennedy Round) should be held in 1964. The Kennedy Round began on 4 May 1964. Only the countries which were prepared to make a general across-the-board reduction (the EEC countries and the majority of EFTA countries, the United States and Japan) participated in the initial discussions. Eventually, negotiations were conducted by fifty-three countries accounting for 80 per cent of world trade.

After some protracted bargaining and delays due to difficulties in the EEC (see Chapter 8) an agreement was reached on 16 May 1967 and signed on 30 June 1967. Substantial progress was made compared with previous conferences. The reduction of customs duties decided in respect of industrial products averaged 36 per cent over the next five years. Trade in the 3 600 products concerned was valued at approximately 40 billion dollars (the corresponding figure for the Dillon Round being 5 billion).

Much less was accomplished in the agricultural sector, mainly because the EEC, which was in the process of establishing its common agricultural policy, was unwilling to accept substantial reductions in its level of protection. The EEC also held that negotiations should aim at the gradual reduction of the *total* support to agriculture defined on the basis of the difference between the price of the product in the world market and the price obtained for it by the farmer in a particular country (inclusive of any direct subsidy). In the case of wheat the provisions were incorporated in the International Grains Arrangement of 1967 (Chapter 4).

In addition, a new anti-dumping code was adopted (see below). Other non-tariff barriers were not accorded much attention.

b. *The Tokyo Round*

The seventh trade negotiation round (the Tokyo Round) was opened in Tokyo on 12 September 1973. The declaration of 14 September 1973 stated *inter alia* that the negotiations would include tariffs, non-tariff barriers and other measures which impede or distort international trade in industrial and agricultural products, including tropical products and raw materials; developed countries would not expect reciprocity from less-developed countries, and the particular situation of the least-developed countries would be given special attention.

The negotiations were considered as a composite exercise. This meant that no agreement was reached on any one specific matter (with the exception of the agreement on tropical products) until the entire negotiations had been completed. Although planned to be concluded in 1975, the negotiations did not end until 12 April 1979, when an important package of agreements was concluded, and supplemented by other agreements approved at the annual session on 26—29 November.

The first practical results of the Tokyo Round were the concessions and contributions on tropical products made by Australia, the European Community, Finland, New Zealand, Norway, Sweden and Switzerland as from 1 January 1977 (followed by Canada and Japan on 1 April 1977 and Austria on 1 July 1977). The Community undertook to suspend partially or wholly the most-favoured-nation rates on unroasted coffee, cocoa, and twenty other tariff items. Some member states which apply internal taxes on certain tropical products have undertaken not to increase the level of these taxes in the future.

The average tariff reduction agreed in 1979 is 33 per cent for industrial products; it did come into effect gradually over an eight-year period. The value in 1976 of the trade thus affected exceeded 110 billion dollars. Tariff concessions in respect of agricultural products amounted to approximately 15 billion dollars out of 48 billion dollars (1976). Progress has been made in the harmonization of tariffs. The countries with the highest initial levels have tended to make the largest reductions.

In addition, several major industrialized countries have signed an Agreement on Trade in Civil Aircraft, under which all customs duties and similar charges are eliminated (also on aircraft parts). The agreement entered into force on 1 January 1980 between Canada, the EEC, Japan, Sweden and the United States. The number of signatories has now become twenty-two (in 1984 the agreement was extended to 32 further categories). Further multilateral agreements were reached on a number of non-tariff aspects of trade: they cover subsidies and countervailing duties; technical barriers to trade; government procurement; customs valuation; import licensing procedures;

and a revision of the earlier anti-dumping code. Further agreements were reached on bovine meat and dairy products. All these agreements are dealt with below.

c. *The Uruguay Round*

On 19 September 1986 the Uruguay Round was launched in Punta del Este. The agenda included (for the first time) agriculture, services (banking and insurance), piracy of patents and trademarks, counterfeiting. The emphasis shifted from tariffs to subsidies, market-sharing agreements and the application of safeguards.

At the mid-term review in December 1988 a preliminary agreement was reached on the disputes-settlement procedures, tariffs and services, but the meeting broke down on agriculture. Results on the revision of the Tokyo Round agreements remain provisional pending the final outcome of the Uruguay Round. In December 1990 there was a deadlock and talks were adjourned; they resumed in 1991.

In agriculture the United States backed by 14 farm-exporting nations (the Cairns group), seeks cuts of 90 per cent in export subsidies and 75 per cent in internal supports and border protection over ten years. The EC is willing only to reduce by 30 per cent its farm support over ten years. For other products such as fruit, vegetables and tobacco, it proposes a reduction of 10 per cent. The EC considers the American objectives to be politically unrealistic.

C. *Elimination of quantitative restrictions*

1. *Provisions*

The elimination of quantitative restrictions, which is required under Article 11, *1*, has not been a prior condition for accession to GATT, mainly because of the many exceptions provided for in the General Agreement, namely:

a) Prohibition or restriction of exports is temporarily authorized in order to prevent or relieve critical shortages of foodstuffs or other essential products (Article 11,*2a*). Article 20,*j* sanctions measures in respect of the acquisition or distribution of products in short supply either generally or locally. This provision — which was originally intended as a temporary measure — was retained in the Agreement by a decision of the contracting parties on 20 February 1970.

b) Prohibition or restriction of imports or exports is permitted for the purpose of the application of standards or regulations concerning the classification, grading or marketing of commodities in international trade (Article 11,*2b*).

c) Import restrictions on agricultural and fisheries produce are tolerated when domestic production is itself limited or in surplus (Article 11,*2c*); this provision was inserted at the insistence of the United States.

d) Import restrictions may also be applied in order to safeguard balance-of-payments equilibrium (Articles 12 and 18,*B*). These restrictions may not exceed those necessary: (1) to forestall or to halt a serious decline in monetary reserves (Article 12,*2a i*); (2) to achieve a reasonable rate of increase in monetary reserves which are too low (Articles 12,*2a ii*, and 18, *9*).

Countries which have recourse to quantitative restrictions for balance-of-payments reasons undertake to relax them gradually, as the balance-of-payments position improves (Article 12,*2b*, and 18,*9*). In fixing the quantities to be imported, they:

a) may give priority to the more essential products (Article 12,*3b*);
b) should avoid unnecessary damage to the commercial or economic interests of the other contracting parties (Article 12,*3c i*);
c) should refrain from applying restrictions which would prevent the import of small quantities of certain goods and impair regular channels of trade (Article 12,*3c ii*), or which would prevent the importation of commercial samples or prevent compliance with patent, trademark, copyright or similar procedures (Article 12,*3c iii*).

Balance-of-payments equilibrium without quantitative restrictions is not, however, imposed upon the member states as one of the principal goals of economic policy. There is express recognition of the right to aim first of all at full employment (Article 12,*3d*). Endeavours are, however, made to limit the repercussions of this on international trade: any contracting party applying new restrictions or raising the level of those already existing will immediately afterwards (or if possible beforehand) consult the other member states about its balance-of-payments difficulties, possible corrective measures and their repercussions on the other contracting parties (Article 12,*4a*). The restrictions are discussed annually (or biennially in the case of Article 18) with the countries affected by them (Article 12,*4b*); if they are inconsistent with GATT provisions, modifications are proposed (Article 12,*4c i*). If the country concerned does not comply with the recommendations, then the contracting parties may grant the countries whose trade is adversely affected permission to take counter-measures (Article 12,*4c ii*).

For the purpose of judging exchange rates, monetary reserves and balances of payments, GATT establishes contact with the IMF (Article 15), whose findings it accepts (Article 15,*2*).

Every contracting party has, within a certain time limit, to become a member of the IMF or to enter into a special exchange agreement with the contracting parties (Article 15,*6*). The decisions of the Fund as to whether action by a contracting party in exchange matters complies with the Articles of Agreement of the IMF or with the terms of the special agreement have to be accepted by GATT (Article 15,2).

The non-discrimination rule also applies to quantitative import and export restrictions (Article 13). Trade in a commodity for which quotas have been introduced has to correspond as closely as possible to the probable distribution of trade among the countries in question if there were no restrictions (Article 13,2). The government concerned is obliged to provide the contracting parties with information on the application of the quota arrangements, the values of the licences granted in the course of a recent period and the distribution of these licences among suppliers (Article 13,2a and c). Any contracting party is entitled to request the holding of consultations for a reappraisal of the quota distribution conditions (Article 13,4).

In order to meet the exigencies of non-convertibility, provision has been made for several exceptions to the principle of non-discrimination in the case of quotas (Article 14).

2. *Operation*

Quantitative restrictions have usually been maintained for agricultural or balance-of-payments difficulties. Initially, it was mainly balance-of-payments problems that were invoked (in 1950 by nearly two-thirds of the members). As the financial position improved and more progress was made towards convertibility, the restrictions could have been alleviated. In order to prevent the import of certain products, many countries nevertheless still invoked Article 12 (or Article 18,*B*), although they were no longer experiencing balance-of-payments difficulties. As they stated that they were unable to remove these protective measures immediately, it was decided in 1955 to grant provisional waivers (of a maximum duration of five years) for so-called residual restrictions. Originally, the idea has been to amend GATT accordingly, but in the end this "hard-core waiver" was based on Article 25,5. Only Belgium had recourse to it in order to protect agriculture. After the extensions of the time-limit the hard core waiver expired at the end of 1962.

The strict conditions attaching to the waiver of the residual restrictions prompted other countries to make direct use of Article 25,5 for this purpose. Among those who did so were Luxemburg and the United States (1955), and Western Germany (1959). The United States got a waiver unlimited in scope and time. Although it concerned only certain agricultural products, it gave rise to much criticism.

Each year the contracting parties consider whether the residual restrictions cannot be eliminated; some results have been achieved, especially since 1958.

According to one of the framework (for conduct of international trade) decisions of 28 November 1979 the preference should be given to restrictive import measures which have the least disruptive effect on trade and the simultaneous application of more than one type of trade measure should be avoided. Moreover, developed countries have to take into account the export interests of less-developed countries when resorting to these trade measures.

The majority of the barriers relate to agricultural products. In the case of industrial products, quantitative restrictions are usually justified by claims of dumping or "market disruption" (see below).

Although Article 12 relates to quantitative restrictions, it has also been invoked for the introduction of additional import levies (contrary to Article 2) or surcharges. In this connection too, Article 25,5 has been applied. Thus India was able to put import duties up temporarily by 25 per cent in 1973. In several other cases (e.g., Uruguay) the contracting parties considered surcharges a better method than quantitative restrictions. When Canada (in 1962) and the United Kingdom (in 1964) introduced surcharges, the contracting parties did not grant a waiver, although here too surcharges could be considered less restrictive than quotas. This was also the case with the 10 per cent import surcharge introduced by the United States in August 1971 and maintained until December 1971.

D.   *Combating other forms of protection*

1. *Provisions*

The contracting parties may not apply duties, domestic levies or regulations (with respect to purchase, sale, transport or distribution) to foreign products in order to protect domestic production (Article 3,1). Goods imported from other countries are not subject, either directly or indirectly, to duties or other internal levies which are higher than those applied to similar domestic products (Article 3,2).

Regulations also have to be applied in the same way (Article 3,4,5 and 7). Quota arrangements for cinematographic films, for example, are allowed under certain conditions (Article 4). Stipulations concerning the compulsory use of certain domestic products in the manufacture of some articles are debarred (Article 3,5), but regulations on this subject applying at given dates (1 July 1939, 10 April 1947, or 24 March 1948 — whichever is opted for by a contracting party) may remain in force, provided that any such regulation which is contrary to paragraph 5 is not modified to the detriment of imports and is treated as a customs duty for the purpose of negotiations (Article 3,6).

Articles 7 (on valuation for customs purposes), 8 (on fees and formalities connected with imports and exports), 9 (on marks of origin) and 10 (on the publication and administration of trade regulations) also contain provisions aimed at rendering indirect forms of protection impossible. Article 7, for instance, lays down the way in which the value of imported goods is to be established — in other words, the basis on which *ad valorem* duties are calculated. The tariff is, indeed, often applied on the wholesale price of similar domestic merchandise and not on the value of the imported merchandise, or on purely arbitrary or fictitious values (the Article 7,*2a*).

When drafting GATT rules, account also had to be taken of the fact that in many countries foreign trade in certain products was in the hands of the government, and this could entail — without customs duties or quantitative restrictions — a marked degree of protection. State trading enterprises therefore have to be guided, in their purchases and sales, solely by commercial considerations such as price, quality, availability and transport costs (Article 17,*1*). This, however, does not apply to products which are for the use of the authorities themselves (Article 17,*2*). An exception is also made in the case of products that are to be purchased by the government which are not intended for commercial resale or for use in the production of goods for sale (Article 17,*2*). Subsidies which are granted exclusively to domestic producers are likewise permissible (Article 3,*8b*).

There is little possibility of preventing action by state enterprises favouring domestic producers. For this reason, when the Agreement was reviewed in 1955, the text of Article 17 was supplemented by a recommendation that negotiations should take place among the member countries concerned (Article 17,*3*). This provision opened the way for the inclusion in GATT of states with a collectivist economic system.

As regards subsidies in general, there is no prohibition. The contracting parties are merely obliged to notify the other countries of any subsidies which directly or indirectly increase exports or reduce imports. If the subsidy causes serious harm to another country, the latter may request negotiations with a view to limiting such subsidization (Article 16,*1*).

In the case of export subsidies, a distinction is made depending on whether they are granted for primary commodities or manufactured goods. As regards manufactured goods, the contracting parties have to cease to grant, as from 1 January 1958 or the earliest practicable date thereafter, all subsidies which make the export price lower than the domestic price (Article 16,*4*). In the case of primary products, export subsidies have to be avoided as far as possible. If they are nevertheless granted, this may only be done in order to maintain the share of the country concerned in world trade in the product affected (Article 16,*3*).

Dumping (a product is introduced into the commerce of an importing country at less than its normal value) is condemned if it causes or threatens material injury to an established industry in a member's territory or materially retards the establishment of a domestic industry. Dumping occurs when "the price of the product exported from one country to another is less than the comparable price, in the ordinary course of trade, for the like product when destined for consumption in the exporting country". Where there is no such comparable domestic price, comparison is made with export prices in any third country or with the cost of production in the country of origin plus a reasonable addition for selling cost and profit (Article 6,*1*). Sanctions may be applied in the form of anti-dumping duties (Article 6,*2*).

Dumping can be practiced with or without government aid. In the former case the duty levied to offset or to prevent dumping is called a countervailing duty ("a special duty levied for the purpose of offsetting any bounty or subsidy bestowed, directly or indirectly, upon the manufacture, production or export of any merchandise": Article 6,*3*).

2. *Operation*

Since initially these forms of protection were in most cases of less importance than customs duties and quantitative restrictions, they have not been accorded so much attention by the contracting parties. As with quantitative restrictions, however, their relative importance has increased as a result of the progress made in the reduction of tariffs. The negotiations in respect of non-tariff measures form the distinction between the Tokyo Round and earlier GATT negotiations.

a. *Customs valuation*

In a few cases the interpretation of Article 7 has given rise to disputes. For example, the United States protested against the Canadian law of 12 October 1962 fixing the import value of American potatoes on the basis of prices in the United States during the three previous years. The Canadian government claimed that the calculation of an average was justified by the exceptionally low prices of American potatoes in 1962. The committee appointed by the contracting parties, however, deemed this action to be contrary to Article 7 and Canada was requested to repeal the law in question.

In the Tokyo Round agreement was reached on a Customs Valuation Code. It aims at providing a system conforming to commercial realities. The Code's five valuation methods (ranked in hierarchical order) must be followed by the signatory countries. The first is based on the invoice price, the second and third on the transaction value of identical or similar goods exported to the same country. In the fourth method, the resale method, the resale price of the imported goods is used as a starting point for calculation and in the fifth method costs and profits are used to compute a value. The Code entered into force on 1 January 1981. Special and differential treatment is given to less-developed countries. On 31 December 1989 there were 28 signatories only to the Agreement.

b. *Excise duties*

Several countries have also come up against excise duties in respect of items which are not produced by the importing countries. Although domestic duties of this kind are not expressly prohibited by the Agreement, they nevertheless form a convenient means of restricting imports of certain goods. They are applied in particular to products such as coffee, sugar and tobacco, which account for a substantial proportion of the exports of less-developed countries.

As already said, some member countries of the European Communities have agreed not to increase the level of these taxes in the future.

c. *State trade*

Article 17 does not provide a solution for all problems which occurred in trade with the communist countries, which are unable to offer tariff concessions. Czechoslovakia's membership has given rise to no great difficulties; the obligations between this country and the United States, however, have been suspended since 1951. During the Kennedy Round it was admitted that a planned increase of imports from the contracting parties by state-trading countries must be considered equivalent to a tariff concession. Thus the protocol of accession of Poland provided for an annual increase of at least 7 per cent in the total value of Poland's imports from GATT countries. The Romanian agreement followed the Polish model with minor variations. Hungary's concessions were based solely on its tariff schedule (no annual rate of increase of imports from contracting parties being specified). In late October 1982 the United States suspended application of the most-favoured-nations tariff treatment to Poland, on the ground that the country did not honour its import commitment since 1978.

The 1989 reform movement in Central and Eastern Europe marked GATT's work. During the session of 4—5 December 1989, for example, the United States stated that it would support the granting of observer status to the Soviet Union, Poland requested renegotiation of its terms of accession to take account of its recent efforts to build a more open economy, and Czechoslovakia, noting its similar efforts, asked for the termination of the suspension of GATT obligations between itself and the United States.

In July—August 1990 the Uruguay Round negotiators agreed that in order to ensure the transparency of the activities of state trading enterprises such enterprises must be notified to the GATT, for review by a working party. The agreement (which relates to Article 17) is provisional pending the outcome of the Round. Any party having reason to believe that another party has not met its notification obligation may raise the matter with the state concerned. If no satisfactory results are obtained, a counter-notification may be made to the GATT.

The following definition was adopted: 'Governmental and non-governmental enterprises, including marketing boards, which have been granted exclusive or special rights or privileges, including statutory or constitutional powers, in the exercise of which they influence through their purchases or sales the level or direction of imports or exports.'

d. *Subsidies, anti-dumping and countervailing duties*

The majority of the member countries have gradually eliminated their export subsidies on goods other than primary commodities (Article 16,*4* has been accepted only by developed countries). In 1961 a panel of experts found that the few subsidies which are still applied to industrial products have only a slight influence on world trade. In fact, the export of industrial products is in most countries encouraged by many — often indirect — means.

During the last years, however, many countries have made use of export subsidies (whether directly or by means of government aid to production). Moreover, the provisions of Article 16,*1* on notification and consultation have been ignored. Many less-developed countries think it necessary to subsidize exports of their infant industries. The use of anti-dumping and countervailing duties has increased proportionally with the application of subsidies.

It is often a difficult matter to judge the fairness of anti-dumping and countervailing duties. The contracting parties made a somewhat ambiguous pronouncement in February 1955 about the Swedish anti-dumping duty on Italian nylon stockings. They urged Sweden to apply the system as flexibly as possible. A few months later, however, the duty was abolished.

There is not even agreement as to the definitions of subsidy and dumping. A classic definition of the latter term is given in the Agreement, but it is not generally accepted. An entrepreneur who obtains the equivalent of his fixed costs on his domestic market may be satisfied with having his variable costs covered on the export market. He must, indeed, pay due heed to changing conditions on world markets. Provided it is done consistently, permanent dumping of this kind is accepted by many economists; in such cases, other countries can acclimatize themselves to the situation and derive benefit from the lower prices.

To determine whether or not dumping is of an acceptable permanent or temporary character is not easy. It presupposes knowledge of the exporter's method of costing and his aims. Again, there is still no agreement concerning the determination of "injury". While other factors may be responsible for the difficulties of a particular industry, such difficulties are often attributed to subsidized imports.

In 1956 Czechoslovakia drew attention to the fact that the GATT definition cannot be used for countries with a collectivist system, where products are often sold on the domestic market at a much higher price than their cost. Hence, sale abroad at a price lower than the domestic one is to a certain extent understandable. Consequently, it was agreed that dumping in Article 6 relates to private commercial enterprises.

The term "social dumping" is frequently employed in the case of low-priced imports from low-wage countries. Actually, this is in most cases not dumping at all. At the GATT conference in 1959 the expression "market disruption" was introduced. This situation is generally characterized by a combination of the following factors:

a) a sharp and substantial increase or potential increase in imports of particular products from particular sources;
b) these products are offered at prices which are considerably below those prevailing for similar goods of comparable quality on the market of the importing country;
c) domestic producers suffer from or are threatened with considerable harm;
d) the price differentials do not arise from government intervention in the fixing or shaping of prices or from dumping practices.

In some situations other factors too are at work, so this enumeration is not to be regarded as an exhaustive definition of market disruption.

In July 1968 an Agreement on Implementation of Article 6 (the Anti-Dumping Code) came into force. It was a compromise which resulted from the Kennedy negotiations among the United States, the United Kingdom, Canada and the EEC.

Under the GATT a government has the power to protect enterprises in its own country, but not in other markets. If an exporting country is supplanted on a foreign market owing to the fact that another supplying country subsidizes its exports, it has no means of defence available, unless it too has recourse to subsidies. In such a case, the importing country could be granted permission to levy a countervailing duty benefiting one of its supplier countries, although it is rather improbable that it will do so: if the importing country does not itself produce the article in question, it has no interest in practicing such a policy. The Anti-Dumping Code provides explicitly for such a procedure, but the decision whether or not to proceed with a case rests with the importing country (Article 12). Each party to the Anti-Dumping Code must align its laws, regulations and administrative procedures on the provisions of the Code.

A Committee on Anti-Dumping Practices was established in November 1968 for the purpose of reviewing annually the application of the Code.

Provisions with respect to international trusts and cartels are not found in GATT. In November 1960 the member countries undertook to negotiate in connection with complaints relating to restrictive action by such trusts and cartels. So far, no such consultations have taken place.

In the Tokyo Round a Code on Subsidies and Countervailing Duties was set up. The Code requires a finding of material injury from subsidization before countervailing duties may be imposed. The required injury is determined in the same manner as when anti-dumping duties are considered. In contradiction to the Anti-Dumping Code, the authorities of the exporting country must be given an opportunity for consultations. An annex to the Code gives examples of export subsidies which should not be granted. The

Anti-Dumping Code was amended in order to bring it into line with the Code on Subsidies and Countervailing Duties.

The determination of injury must be based on positive evidence involving an examination of the volume of the dumped imports (and their effect on domestic prices of like products) and of the impact on domestic producers (Article 3,*1*).

Whereas in the 1968 Code the dumped imports should be 'demonstrably the principal cause' of the injury to the domestic industry, according to the revised Code the injury caused by the dumping must be segregated from the injuries caused by other factors. The assessment has to be made on the injury caused by the dumping alone (Art. 3,*4*).

The new Code provides for the possibility of retroactive application of anti-dumping duties.

Among the 24 signatories ofo the Anti-Dumping Code 354 anti-dumping cases have been initiated (89 of which by the United States) and 172 provisional actions have been imposed (97 by the United States, 79 by Australia, 78 by Canada, 76 by the EC) from 1 July 1986 to 30 June 1989.

In the field of countervailing actions the non-adoption of some panel reports has to be deplored.

e. *Other forms*

According to the Agreement on Trade in Civil Aircraft, technical barriers, subsidies and countervailing duties have to be eliminated.

Under the Agreement on Technical Barriers to Trade, or the Standards Code, in force since January 1980 technical regulations or standards relating to both agricultural and industrial products must not form unnecessary obstacles to trade. It has been signed by 36 member states.

The Agreement on Government Procurement reached in the Tokyo Round entered into force on 1 January 1981. It aims at bringing about more international competition in the government procurement market. For that purpose it contains rules on the way in which tenders for government purchasing contracts (of more than 150 000 SDR) are to be invited and such contracts awarded. There were 12 signatories only at the end of 1989.

Another Tokyo agreement relates to import licensing procedures, which are able to be simplified and administered equitably.

The Arrangement regarding Bovine Meat (26 signatories) is administered by an International Meat Council which proposes solutions to the governments concerned if a serious market imbalance develops. When the arrangement entered into force in February 1980 the International Meat Consultative Group was abolished.

The International Dairy Arrangement has similar objects. An International Dairy Product Council has been set up. The new Arrangement also replaces previous GATT arrangements to counteract subsidized competition (the

Arrangement concerning certain dairy products, the Protocol relating to milk fat).

E. *Consultations*

1. *Provisions*

Article 22 provides for consultation between the contracting parties with respect to any matter affecting the operation of the Agreement. There must likewise be consultation if one of the contracting parties considers that its interests are being damaged or threatened as a result of failure to observe the Agreement on the part of another GATT country (Article 23). If the discussions yield no result, the contracting parties may have recourse to arbitration. If need be, the adversely affected country may be authorized to withdraw concessions or suspend obligations to an equitable extent *vis-à-vis* the party which has not fulfilled its obligations (Article 23,2).

2. *Operation*

When bilateral discussion fails to produce a settlement, a panel of independent experts examines the disputes.

An understanding regarding notification, consultation, dispute settlement and surveillance adopted on 28 November 1979 strengthened the procedures concerned. It includes, for example, detailed provisions on establishment and composition of panels to examine complaints and on rules covering the handling of panels' findings.

Many complaints have been treated this way. They did not necessarily give way to results. A few examples are given below. In March 1982 the United States lodged a complaint against the European Community concerning the granting of production subsidies on canned peaches, canned pears and raisins. The Council discussed the report of a panel in March 1985. The report suggested that for the canned fruits the EEC should restore the previous competitive conditions. New discussions in November 1985 did not give way to an agreement. Finally, the United States and the EEC informed GATT in February 1986 that a settlement of the dispute had been reached (outside the GATT). In June 1982 a similar complaint relates to the tariff preferences granted by the EC on certain citrus products from Mediterranean countries. Here again the EC was asked in March 1985 to go back to its decision but the EC considered that this was "not politically viable". Finally, at the end of October 1985 the two parties made effective the announced retaliation measures.

F. *Escape clauses*

1. *Provisions*

Apart from the safeguard clauses already referred to (e.g., Article 12 see above), mention should be made of Articles 18 to 21 and Article 25.

a. *Article 19*

Deviations from the provisions concerning customs duties and any other trade restrictions may be made in order to check greatly increased imports which cause serious injury to domestic producers of similar or directly competitive products under Article 19. Article 19 is aimed mainly at facilitating the withdrawal of tariff concessions, but it does not rule out the suspension of other obligations.

This is, in fact, a general safeguard clause which was inserted at the request of the United States. Since 1947 a clause of this type has had to be included in all trade agreement to which the United States is a party. It has the effect of jeopardizing the stability of GATT agreements. In order to counteract this objection to the greatest possible extent, an intended withdrawal has to be notified to member states beforehand, and at the earliest possible moment. A government wishing to withdraw a concession discusses with the countries concerned measures to limit the adverse effects (Article 19,2). If no agreement is reached, the concessions may nevertheless be suspended, but the contracting parties affected may suspend a similar concession within ninety days, subject to written notice being given to the other contracting parties thirty days prior to the entry into force of the retaliatory measure (Article 19,3a). In this way, immoderate recourse to Article 19 is obviated.

b. *Article 18*

The escape clauses in favour of the less-developed countries are numerous. The desire for industrialization was so great in the case of many backward territories that they would not have acceded to the Agreement without the possibility of infant-industry protection. The entitlement of these countries to additional facilities is therefore expressly recognized (Article 18,2). In this connection, a rather vague distinction is made, depending upon the stage of economic development, between countries in the early stages, the economies of which can only support low standards of living, and those in a more advanced process of development.

The former may:

1. withdraw or modify concessions on customs duties, if this is required for

the establishment of a new industry which is likely to increase production and raise the standard of living (Article 18, *7a*);

2. restrict imports in order to keep its balance of payments in equilibrium and to obtain the necessary exchange for the purchase of goods for the implementation of development plans (Article 18, *9*; whereas Article 12 relates to a temporary shortage, this provision is more concerned with a structural deficit);

3. grant governmental assistance if this appears necessary to promote the establishment of enterprises which also help to improve the standard of living of the population (Article 18, *13*).

Here too, GATT has to be notified beforehand, and consultations have to be entered into with the countries affected in order to examine possible compensatory measures (Article 18, *7a* and *b* and *18*).

Once every two years an inquiry is made to ascertain whether the quantitative restrictions applied by a country under Article 18, *B* are still warranted in the light of the balance-of-payments trend and the execution of the development plan. If GATT considers that this is no longer the case, the country concerned is informed accordingly. If the latter refuses to suspend the restriction, GATT may grant permission to the countries which are adversely affected to take retaliatory measures (Article 19, *12*).

In the case of less-developed countries in the second category, exemptions are granted only with respect to governmental assistance. The procedure is somewhat different from that for the countries in the first category (Article 18, *22*).

c. *Articles 20, 21 and 25, 5*

Articles 21 and 25,5 aim at safeguarding certain national interests. Article 20, on the other hand, contains a number of exceptions, relating to such matters as the protection of public morals (*a*), the protection of human, animal or plant life or health (*b*), trade in gold and silver (*c*), and national art treasures (*f*). Furthermore, it is permissible to undertake certain obligations under intergovernmental commodity agreements (*h*), provided that they are not disapproved beforehand by GATT. Member states may also introduce quota arrangements for home-processed primary products in order to stabilize the domestic prices of such commodities (*i*). In this way, the commodity-exporting countries are afforded the possibility of cushioning the repercussions of a marked rise in world prices on the domestic market.

In exceptional circumstances not provided for in the other Articles, the contracting parties may, by a two-thirds majority of the votes cast comprising more than half of the contracting parties, exempt a member country from specific GATT obligations (Article 25, *5*). In such cases, serious damage to the other contracting parties has to be avoided. A precise definition of special circumstances, however, is not given.

2. *Operation*

a. *Article 19*

In the case of complaints, while the member states have in fact recognized the unilateral character of Article 19, they have not expressed disapproval of the countermeasures (e.g., by the EEC countries in 1962 after the increase in import duties on carpets and window glass). In 1978 Norway has invoked Article 19 to introduce temporary quota restrictions (on imports of textiles from Hong Kong); its invocation of the Article in this way was subsequently found by a panel to be unjustified.

When the Tokyo Round Agreement was initialled, one problem remained unsolved: the use of Article 19. The contracting parties could not find a solution before the summer of 1980, as agreed. While according to existing rules measures must be applied to all countries, the European Community favours a selective measure which would only concern major suppliers or suppliers concerned. The *erga-omnes* rule is responsible for the success of voluntary restraint agreements. The United States and many less-developed countries fear discrimination.

b. *Article 18*

The possibilities of derogation offered by Article 18 have been extended. Whereas previously trade measures could only be taken in the internal market of a particular industry, the "framework" agreement entitles the less-developed countries to do so for broader development objectives and without going through the prescribed processes of consultation or negotiation (decision of 28 November 1979 relating to "safeguard action for development purposes"). Developed countries complain about the arbitrary manner the Article is applied.

c. *Articles 21 and 25, 5*

The complaint by Czechoslovakia against the United States' disregard of Article 1 was rejected by the latter on the basis of Article 21. The contracting parties agreed to this in 1949, without accepting the United States arguments as such. In April 1982, during the conflict about the Falkland Islands between Argentina and the United Kingdom, the European Community, Australia and Canada suspended imports from Argentina. While Canada and Australia based their decision on a United Nations resolution, the Community referred to "inherent rights, of which Article 21 . . . was a reflection". In the GATT Council there were "widely differing views" on the question.

Article 25,5 has been applied for several purposes, notably:

1. For some preferences not provided for in Article 1 (ECSC: see above). Preferential arrangement between certain countries and their present or former overseas territories have been approved on several occasions by the other member states. On 25 June 1971 a ten-year exemption from the provisions of Article 1 was introduced to make it possible to apply the Generalized System of Preferences (see Chapter 4). During the Tokyo Round this exemption has been replaced by the enabling cause (see above) in order to continue the System.
2. For the raising of bound customs duties, for example, in connection with the introduction of a new customs tariff. The countries concerned include Brazil, Greece, Indonesia, Turkey, Nicaragua and Ceylon.
3. For the application of residual restrictions (see above).
4. For the raising of customs duties (see above).

G. *Action in favour of the less-developed countries*

1. *Provisions*

Although Article 18 contains scope for exceptional treatment of the less-developed countries, it was decided in 1965, upon the insistence of those countries, to impose greater obligations on the developed countries to contribute to the economic development of the new states. Part 4, which was added to the Agreement for this purpose, consists of three articles, the first of which (Article 36) summarizes the general principles (see above).

By the terms of Article 37, the developed countries undertake (without expecting reciprocity: Article 36,*8*):

a) to the fullest possible extent (i.e., except when this is ruled out by compelling reasons);

    1. to reduce and eliminate barriers to the export of products of the less-developed countries; to refrain from introducing such measures or increasing the incidence of those already in operation (1a and b);
    2. to reduce and eliminate fiscal measures which hamper the growth of consumption of goods originating in the less-developed countries, and to refrain from imposing new fiscal measures (1c);

b) to establish equitable trade margins if the resale price of the products in question is determined directly or indirectly by the governments (3a).

The less-developed countries agree to take appropriate action in the interest of trade with the other less-developed territories, provided that it is consistent with their individual present and future development, financial and trade needs, having regard to past commercial trends and the trade interests of these countries as a whole (Article 37,*4*).

The contracting parties undertake to further by joint action the implementation of the objectives set out in Part 4 (Article 38).

2. *Operation*

In November 1961 GATT approved a set of principles which were subsequently discussed in detail by the United Nations Conference on Trade and Development (UNCTAD) (see Chapter 4).

In May 1963 a programme of action which had been submitted by twenty-one countries was approved by a majority of the contracting parties. The developed countries would have to refrain from introducting any new trade barriers. Restrictions contrary to the General Agreement would have to be suspended within one year. The other barriers would be gradually reduced and eliminated, on the understanding that within three years customs duties would be lowered by at least 50 per cent. Revenue duties would cease to operate by 31 December 1965 at the latest.

The EEC countries were unable to agree to these proposals. They considered them to be focused too much on customs duties and quotas, and they thought that more general and positive measures aimed at increasing the export earnings of the less-developed countries would be more suitable. Other countries too formulated certain reserves (the United Kingdom pointed to its obligations towards the Commonwealth).

After further discussions, an agreement was nevertheless arrived at (UNCTAD had been held in the meantime) whereby less precise commitments were undertaken. Finally, these commitments were included in Part 4 of the GATT.

On 26 November 1964 a Committee on Trade and Development was created in order to follow up the application of Part 4. To help the less-developed countries participating in multilateral trade negotiations, a Technical Cooperation Division has been created.

In the context of trade expansion among less-developed countries, a Protocol Relating to Trade Negotiations Among Developing Countries came into force on 11 February 1973. Fifteen countries have ratified this Agreement, under which the countries concerned grant concessions in the form of a preferential duty rate or the binding of a margin of preference.

Textiles

Among the other measures in favour of the less-developed countries, mention should be made of the Arrangement of International Trade in Cotton Textiles and the Generalized System of Preferences (see Chapter 4).

After an initial Arrangement on International Trade in Cotton Textiles had been in force from 1 October 1961 to 30 September 1962, another came into effect for a period of five years. Although formally it is not a

GATT agreement, GATT was instrumental in its establishment, with the United States taking the initiative. It expired on 31 December 1973.

On 1 January 1974 the Arrangement Regarding International Trade in Textiles (referred to as the Multifibre Arrangement) entered into force. It was renewed subsequently till 31 December 1992.

The agreement provides that no new unilateral or bilateral restraints on trade in textiles may be introduced, while existing restrictions should be notified immediately and are to be phased out, justified or modified to conform with the Arrangement. Quotas, which must not be lower than actual trade during the preceding twelve-month period, may be introduced in case of market disruption; however, they are subject to a number of strict conditions (e.g., regular enlargement by a minimum of 6 per cent a year) and multilateral surveillance. Unlike those provided for in Article 19 of the GATT, the safeguard measures can be applied only "to the precise products and to countries whose exports of such products are causing market disruption".

The implementation of the Arrangement is supervised by a Textile Surveillance Body, which provides a forum for the settlement of disputes. It reports to the Textiles Committee (comprising all participating countries), which reviews the operation of the Arrangement at least once a year.

The Arrangement has been accepted by 40 countries. In world exports of textiles they account for about 75 per cent (89 billion dollars in 1987).

While a principal aim of the Arrangement is "to further the economic and social development of developing countries and secure a substantial increase in their export earnings from textile products", less-developed countries' exports of handloom fabrics or hand-made products of such fabrics are excluded from the agreement.

APPRAISAL

The General Agreement is a complicated text which contains so many vague obligations and escape clauses that it is an easy matter to circumvent commitments. It is therefore not surprising that, in addition to its advantages, there are a good many shortcomings to be pointed out.

Advantages

GATT is an initial code of "good behaviour" for international trade. In this way, member states have been induced to exchange ideas with their partners about national decisions with international repercussions. Regular consultation among the contracting parties has several times helped to avoid measures prejudicial to international trade. When the EEC and EFTA were set up, for example, account was taken of the comments of GATT countries.

Progress has been made in the elimination of discrimination and more in particular in the reduction and stabilization of customs duties. The main industrialized countries have bound well over 90 per cent of all their duties on industrial products.

Drawbacks

Little progress has been made in the elimination of non-tariff distortions (e.g., technical and ecological provisions, health and security measures, retaliatory duties and government procurement). Hence special attention was given in the Tokyo and Uruguay Rounds to the abolition of non-tariff barriers.

Moreover, the agricultural sector almost entirely escapes the GATT rules. The problem of subsidized exports is now central.

While customs unions and free-trade areas referred to in Article 24 constitute a breach of the most-favoured-nation clause, they lead to complete abolition of customs duties between the member countries, a result which would not normally be reached through GATT action. Nevertheless, the discrimination against non-members is a drawback. For example, the Lomé Convention provides for duty-free imports from all African, Caribbean and Pacific (ACP) countries (see Chapter 8), while the less favourable System of Generalized Preferences (see Chapter 4) applies to imports from other less-developed countries.

At all events, the importance of international trade between members of various customs unions cannot be denied. Trade on which most-favoured-nation duties are applied is estimated to account for 50 to 75 per cent of the GATT members' total trade, the rest being subject to reduced rates. Preferential treatment has to a large extent replaced the principle of non-discrimination.

GATT has been unable to prevent the rise of protectionism during recent years: besides protection of agriculture trade (accounting for about 10 per cent of world trade), trade in textiles (5 per cent) has been more and more restricted since the beginning of the sixties. Since 1974, this has also been the case with steel products, shipbuilding, ball-bearings and consumer electronics (again 5 per cent). In addition, more and more "voluntary" export restraints or "orderly marketing agreements" are being applied, Japan, South Korea, Hong Kong, Brazil, Taiwan and Singapore being among the main "volunteers".

As an agency which has no supranational authority and which has to operate mainly by consultation and persuasion (there are no sanctions, and retaliatory measures are not always possible), GATT has been unable to prevent repeated and frequently unjustified recourse to the escape clauses. These safeguard clauses were indeed inevitable in order to ensure large-scale accession to the General Agreement.

Less-developed countries

Through the application of the most-favoured-nation clause, the developed countries have in fact, without any compensation, granted the less-developed countries the benefits of the GATT tariff reductions. Some of these less-developed countries have now become serious competitors but are themselves protected by high tariffs (for example: tariff on shoes in the United Kingdom: 15 per cent and in Brazil: 175 per cent). The GATT rules have ceased to apply to the trade with less-developed countries although many of them, like the new industrialized countries (for example, South Korea) are successful exporters. Instead of having recourse to escape clauses, western countries would do better to raise barriers to imports from these less-developed competing countries, in order to strengthen their negotiating position for more favourable reciprocal arrangements in trade relations.

The diversity of the membership means that it is almost impossible to establish general rules. GATT started with 23 members, now there are 100. As in other international organizations, GATT discussions are characterized by the antithesis between the developed and the less-developed countries; the latter are clamouring for greater help. As a consequence, however, economic motives have become entangled with political motives, giving rise to new forms of discrimination. Large-scale deviation from the most-favoured-nation principle leads to arbitrary action and confusion in international trade relations, without much benefit for the less-developed countries. Part 4 is inconsistent "with the freer trade goal of the GATT. At best it can be viewed as an exception necessary to enable less-developed countries to deal with their balance-of-payments or development problems, but for that purpose a special procedure focusing on the balance-of-payments or development needs of the applicant contracting party would be preferable" (K. W. Dam).

Matters are not made easier by the fact that the less-developed countries do not form a homogeneous group. Moreover, it has to be borne in mind that countries such as Australia, New Zealand and South Africa occupy a special position. Even the interests of the United States sometimes run parallel to those of certain less-developed countries.

Hence the proposal to divide the world into traders and (semi-planned and basically anti-trade) non-traders and the suggestion of "a free trade area, using the GATT's flexibility to create a perfectly legal way of separating the traders from the non-traders". It would "ensure that only market-oriented countries would be included, which immediately contains the problem of non-commercial subsidization, state trading and having to compete with foreign treasuries. The tighter rules would ensure better surveillance of non-tariff measures, fewer departures from the general rules and more rigorous procedures for dispute settlement" (G. and V. Curzon). The United States have already declared that they could promote trade liberalization with "like-minded" countries.

Conditions for further progress

In addition further progress calls for:

1. Improvement of exchange-rate stability. Continuing exchange-rate fluctuations may have a considerable influence on both a country's competitive position and its export prospects. The effects of tariff cuts on prices over a period of ten years for most goods will be less than the changes that the foreign-exchange markets can cause in two or three weeks. Hence GATT and IMF ought to cooperate more closely. At present, GATT only consults the IMF if a contracting party asks to introduce or to maintain quantitative restrictions for balance-of-payments reasons.

   During the Uruguay Round discussions the Community proposed to its partners 'that a joint Gatt/IMF/World Bank declaration be adopted concerning the need for compatibility in policy-making and a network of inter-institutional links to enable the three bodies to cooperate to some extent'.

2. More importance to be accorded to the non-tariff barriers to trade. As tariffs are reduced, quotas and other barriers to trade become more significant. The GATT codes governing non-tariff distortions of trade "should be improved and vigorously applied to make trade more open and fair". Agriculture does not require "special treatment for particular countries or commodities. Efficient agricultural producers should be given the maximum opportunity to compete" (*Trade policies for a better future*, GATT 1985).

3. A curbing of the escape clauses: stability of international trade can only be achieved by a limited and clearcut application of the safeguard facilities. Trade policy measures for balance-of-payments purposes, for example, should no longer be so readily authorized. In this respect an acceleration of the consultation procedure is required: the protracted nature of inquiries and discussions means in most cases that the contracting parties publish their findings very belatedly, by which time the circumstances that gave rise to the dispute have completely changed.

   Since panels' reports must be adopted by consensus parties to a dispute tend to block recommendations which are detrimental to them. Moreover there are no rules about what happens when a panel's recommendations are not implemented.

4. The weighting of partner countries' votes in accordance with their economic importance (in the political world organizations as well, the principle of "one country, one vote" is unrealistic). The votes of the EEC and the associated nations, for example, exceed the two-thirds required for a waiver. This explains the American distrust of the GATT voting process. Nevertheless, in practice GATT never votes unless consensus has already been reached.

Bibliography

A. *GATT publications*

1. *Basic documents*

The present text of the General Agreement on Tariffs and Trade is reproduced in Volume 4 of *Basic instruments and selected documents* (Geneva, March 1969). Earlier versions of the Agreement are given in Volume 1, the revised Volume 1 and Volume 3. Volume 2 contains the resolutions, statements and reports relating to conferences and committee meetings from 1948 to early 1952. *Basic instruments and selected documents. Supplements* contain similar documents subsequent to 1952. Beginning with the fourteenth supplement (July 1966), an index to the contents of Volumes 1 to 4 and the supplements is provided.

An *Analytical index* (3rd ed., April 1970) contains notes on the drafting, interpretation and application of the General Agreement. In October 1971 the *Status of legal instruments* was published in loose-leaf form; this describes the legal instruments drawn up by the contracting parties or under their auspices.

2. *Operation*

Successive reports on activities from January 1948 to December 1951 appeared under the following titles: *The attack on trade barriers; A progress report on the operation of the General Agreement from January 1948 to August 1949* (September 1949); *Liberating world trade. Second report on the operation of the General Agreement* (June 1950); *GATT in action. Third report on the operation of the General Agreement* (February 1952).

From 1952 to 1958 annual reports, issued under the title *International trade 195—*, consisted of three parts, devoted respectively to a survey of world trade, trade policy and the activity of the contracting parties. In 1957, however, the first part was not dealt with and the title was accordingly changed to *Commercial policy 1957*, including a report on recent activities of the contracting parties. The subject matter of this first part was discussed in the subsequent annual report, *International trade 1957—1958*. From 1959 onwards, the annual reports relate solely to the subject matter of the former Part 1 (changes in the structure of World trade). Since the 1973 report, the title has been *International trade 19—/19—*.

Publications on the operation of GATT include *The activities of GATT for* 1959/60, 1960/61, 1961/62, 1964/65, 1967/68. In June 1970 the title was changed to *GATT activities 197—*. This publication reports the most important events (detailed data being given in the supplements referred to above). The principal aspects of the member countries' commercial policy (formerly contained in Part 2 of *International trade*) were at first published in the half-yearly *Developments in commercial policy* (1960—62) and subsequently in *Certification of changes to schedules to the GATT*, the latest edition of which was published in October 1974; *Basic documentation for tariff study* (July 1970) contains detailed information on the level of post-Kennedy-Round duties.

Since December 1964, the International Trade Centre has issued a quarterly review, *Forum*, and a large number of other publications on marketing and export promotion.

On the Kennedy Round, see *Legal instruments embodying the results of the 1964—67 tariff conference* (Geneva, June 1967), five volumes; and on the Tokyo Round, *Geneva (1979) Protocol to the General Agreement on Tariffs and Trade* (Geneva, 1979), four volumes.

The results of some of the studies undertaken by the Secretariat of the GATT on current issues in the field of international trade are published in *GATT studies in international trade*, for example, *Network of world trade by areas and commodity classes 1955—76* (1978); *Trade relations under flexible exchange rates* (1980).

B. *Other publications*

On the ITO and the origins of GATT: W. A. Brown, *The United States and the restoration of world trade. An analysis and appraisal of the ITO Charter and the GATT* (Washington, The Brookings Institution, 1950).

General surveys: T. Flory, *Le GATT. Droit international et commerce mondial* (Paris, Librairie Générale de Droit et de Jurisprudence, 1968); K. Kock, *International trade policy and the GATT 1947–67* (Stockholm, Almqvist & Wicksell, 1969); K. W. Dam, *The GATT law and international economic organization* (Chicago, University of Chicago Press, 1970); R. Senti, *GATT: Allgemeines Zoll- und Handelsabkommen als System der Welthandelsordnung* (Zürich, Schulthess, 1986); A. Comba, *Il neo liberalismo internazionale. Strutture giuridiche a dimensione mondiale* (Giuffré, Milano, 1987); O. Long (a former director-general), *Law and its limitations in the GATT multilateral trade system* (London, Dordrecht, Boston, Graham & Trotman / Martinus Nijhoff, 1987); A. Oxley, *The challenge of free trade* (New York, London, Toronto, Harvester Wheatsheaf, 1990).

See also H. G. Johnson, *The world economy at the crossroads. A survey of current problems of money, trade and economic development* (Oxford, Clarendon, 1965); G. Patterson, *Discrimination in international trade. The policy issues 1945–1965* (Princeton University Press, Princeton, 1966); G. and V. Curzon, Defusing conflict between traders and non-traders, *The World Economy*, 1969, No. 1; G. and E. Patterson, Importance of a GATT review in the new negotiations, *The World Economy*, 1986, No. 2; M. Wijkman, Informal systematic change in the GATT, *The World Economy*, 1986, No. 1; P. Moser, *The political economy of the GATT* (Gruesch, Rueegger, 1990).

On the Kennedy Round: H. G. Johnson, The Kennedy Round, *The World today*, August 1967.

On the Tokyo Round: H. G. Johnson, *Trade negotiations and the new international monetary system* (Geneva, Graduate Institute of International Studies, 1976); A. V. Deardorff and R. M. Stern, *The effects of the Tokyo Round on the structure of protection* (Chicago, University of Chicago Press, London, 1984).

C. *The Customs Cooperation Council*

While GATT is concerned with problems of economic policy, the Customs Cooperation Council (CCC) is a technical body for the study of customs problems. The convention establishing the CCC was signed in Brussels on 15 December 1950 and came into force on 4 November 1952. Its main purpose is to assemble the executive machinery for the interpretation and application of two other conventions signed also on 15 December 1950 — the Convention on Nomenclature for the Classification of Goods in Customs Tariffs and the Convention on the Valuation of Goods for Customs Purposes.

The first convention, which entered into force on 11 September 1959, set up the Brussels Tariff Nomenclature (BTN). The tariffs of many countries and regional organizations (including the EEC and EFTA) are based on the BTN. The aim of the second convention, which came into force on 28 July 1953, is to achieve maximum uniformity in the valuation of goods for customs purposes.

The International Convention on the harmonized commodity description and coding system was signed by the EEC states and 18 other countries on 10 June 1985. The Convention was developed over 10 years by experts from 60 countries. The harmonized system brings together in a single, integrated instrument the descriptions needed for customs tariffs, statistical nomenclatures and transport classifications. It will replace the Customs Cooperation Council Nomenclature.

See *In brief . . . The Customs Cooperation Council* (Brussels, November 1969), published by the CCC and an article by a former secretary-general, G. Annez de Taboada, "CCC: oiling the wheels of trade", *Forum*, supplement (UNCTAD-GATT), April 1969.

The extracts quoted are from: K. W. Dam, *op. cit.*; G. and V. Curzon, *art. cit.*

4. The Commodity Agreements. The United Nations Conference on Trade and Development (UNCTAD)

The possibilities of commodity agreements are rather limited, since the technical and economic characteristics of many commodities and the nature of the trade in them preclude the useful application of international commodity agreements.
HARRY G. JOHNSON

The following section deals with the commodity agreements. The one after that concerns UNCTAD, not only because this organization seeks to coordinate negotiations regarding these agreements, but also because it has attracted attention by its tendency to broach numerous subjects of a general nature.

THE COMMODITY AGREEMENTS

Experience has shown that a disequilibrium between supply and demand on the commodity markets may give rise to considerable price fluctuations. This holds true particularly for the agricultural commodities, production of which is influenced by changing weather conditions and cannot be adapted to changes in demand immediately. Efforts have been made to achieve greater stability on the commodity markets.

In the 1920s international cartels were created for rubber, sugar, tin and tea (e.g., the Rubber Growers' Association in 1920, the Bandoeng Pool in 1921 and the Tin Producers' Association in 1929), but they yielded no lasting results. Nor did cooperation between the governments of exporting and importing countries (e.g., in the International Wheat Agreement 1933 and the International Sugar Agreement 1937) serve to attain the desired goals during the subsequent depression years.

After World War II the Interim Coordinating Committee for International Commodity Arrangement (ICCICA) came into being as a result of a resolution adopted by ECOSOC in March 1947. This was followed in May 1954

147

by the setting-up of the Commission on International Commodity Trade. While the Committee dealt mainly with problems concerning individual commodities, the Commission's tasks consisted rather in examining general questions in this field. Since 30 December 1964 the Committee on Commodities of the Trade and Development Board (UNCTAD) has carried out the functions which were previously performed by the Commission on International Commodity Trade and by the ICCICA.

In order to preclude neglect of consumer interests in the drafting of agreements, ECOSOC, in March 1947, formulated a few general principles and requested the United Nations to pay due heed to them. Subsequently, these principles were included in the Charter of the International Trade Organization. They are:

1. any government may call for and participate in discussions on matters in which it claims to have a major stake;
2. adequate representation of importing (consumer) countries has to be guaranteed;
3. full publicity must be given to the terms of agreements proposed or concluded;
4. "control agreements" (regulation of production or foreign trade) may only be introduced in the event of considerable surpluses, general unemployment or inadequate employment opportunities;
5. in the case of a control agreement there has always to be a sufficient supply available and, as a general rule, increasing use must be made of the most efficient production sources; no serious disturbance must be caused to the economic and social organization of any country.

When account is taken of the interests of both producers and consumers, the term "commodity agreement" is employed, although it is also used less restrictively (in the sense of an international cartel).

Up to the present, endeavours to achieve stabilization of commodity prices have mainly assumed three forms — the multilateral contract agreement, the quota agreement and the buffer-stock agreement. Transactions are effected at world market prices. When a minimum or maximum price is reached (or approached), efforts are made to ensure that prices remain within the two limits. Each of the three methods (which are not mutually exclusive) has its own way of doing this.

1. In the multilateral contract system, consumers and producers mutually undertake to buy or sell certain quantities at the minimum and at the maximum price respectively (the Wheat Agreements of 1949, 1953 and 1956), or at a price within the price range (but not at the maximum) and at the maximum price respectively (the 1959 and subsequent agreements).
2. In the quota method, the quantity negotiated is determined by a previously fixed quota when a minimum or maximum price is exceeded. When

there is a surplus, the producers restrict their exports or production, while in the case of shortage quotas are allotted to the consuming countries.
3. With the third method, stability is ensured by a buffer-stock arrangement. It may be supplemented in certain circumstances by a limitation of export. The buffer stock buys when the market price is in the lower sector or at the floor price set in the Agreement; the buffer stock sells when the market price is in the upper sector or at the ceiling price.

The following passage deals with the main commodity agreements.

1. THE WHEAT TRADE CONVENTION

In 1933 a quota-type International Wheat Agreement was concluded among nine exporting and twelve importing countries. The Agreement came to a formal end in 1935, largely because it proved impossible to obtain the full cooperation of all major exporters in adhering to the agreed export quotas (Argentina, for instance, was not satisfied with its quota and exported more). Only the Wheat Advisory Committee (set up at the 1933 Conference to watch over the application of the Agreement) continued to perform its task up to 1939.

After the end of the hostilities, as and when production was stepped up in Europe and the United States, the danger of overproduction became acute. The exporting countries were therefore prepared to negotiate a new agreement. The idea of a multilateral type of agreement, raised for the first time, was favourably received at an international conference in 1947. This contained what were to be the basic principles of the 1949 Wheat Agreement. It met with opposition — especially on the part of Britain — because the minimum and maximum prices were considered to be too high. A revised version led to another agreement of the multilateral type in 1948, but it did not come into effect because the United States failed to ratify. A conference held in January 1949 finally drew up a text (a lower maximum price was provided for) which was signed on 1 March 1949 and came into effect on 1 August of that year for a period of four years. Revisions and three-year extensions were enacted in 1953, 1956, 1959 and 1962.

The 1962 Agreement, which was originally due to expire in the summer of 1965, was subsequently extended by protocol (without amendment) for two years. Meanwhile, the cereals discussions which had been proceeding since 1963 in GATT within the context of the Kennedy Round came to a conclusion in May 1967 with the adoption of a Memorandum of Agreement on basic elements for the renegotiation of a world grains arrangement. An International Wheat Conference was called which led to the negotiations of the 1967 International Grains Arrangement, consisting of two legal instruments, the Wheat Trade Convention (limit prices were provided for) and the Food Aid Convention. Pending the entry into force of the Arrangement on 1

July 1968, the 1962 Agreement was further extended for one year by protocol in respect of its administrative provisions only: i.e. the "commercial" obligations of the Agreement relating to prices and rights and obligations were suspended between 1 August 1967 and 30 June 1968. The two conventions arising out of the 1967 Arrangement expired on 30 June 1971.

From 18 January to 20 February 1971 a United Nations Wheat Conference established a new International Wheat Agreement, again consisting of a Wheat Trade Convention and a Food Aid Convention. It came into force on 1 July 1971 for a three-year period and was renewed ever since (the last time till 30 June 1991).

The Wheat Trade Convention, however, contains no price provisions or related rights and obligations but it maintains the International Wheat Council in being. The Convention also requires the Council to examine "at an appropriate time, the questions of prices and related rights and obligations; and, when it judges that these matters are capable of successful negotiation with the objective of bringing them into effect within the life of the Convention, to request the Secretary-General of UNCTAD to convene a negotiating conference".

Under the Food Aid Convention, Argentina, Australia, Canada, the European Economic Community, Finland, Japan, Sweden, Switzerland, and the United States have undertaken to contribute annually wheat, coarse grains or derived products totalling almost 7 600 000 metric tons. The progress of the programme is kept under review by a Food Aid Committee established under the Convention.

2. THE INTERNATIONAL SUGAR AGREEMENT

As far back as 1902 an agreement was concluded in Brussels by the terms of which the leading beet sugar producers undertook, for a period of ten years (starting from 1 September 1903), not to grant any further production and export subsidies and to prevent or prohibit the import of sugar subsidized by non-member countries (the production costs of cane sugar being lower than those of beet sugar).

After 1918 the Agreement was allowed to lapse under the influence of growing protectionism.

On 9 May 1931 the Chadbourne Plan was signed by Belgium, Cuba, Czechoslovakia, Germany, Hungary, Java and Poland (subsequently also by Peru and Yugoslavia). It aimed at the elimination of surpluses by the regulation of exports and production. Although some results were achieved in this respect, a fall in prices could not be avoided on account of the fact that the production of non-member states followed an upward trend. In 1935 the convention in question was not extended. A new International Sugar Agreement of a restrictive nature came into being in 1937, with a few large importing countries (e.g., Britain, the United States) among the participants.

Owing to the outbreak of World War II, the significance of this agreement is difficult to assess.

After a brief period of shortage, the prewar production level was topped as early as 1948/49. During the Korea boom prices achieved a record figure, but they subsequently fell back. Purchases were restricted in the dollar area (owing to the dollar shortage) which provided 80 per cent of world supplies (Cuba alone accounting for 50 per cent). For this reason, too, Britain concluded the Commonwealth Sugar Agreement in January 1952 (with retroactive effect from 1 January 1950) for a period of ten years; it was extended yearly from 1962 to 1966. Owing to the discussions with the EEC this was not done in 1967, but a new agreement was finally concluded in December 1968 for an "indefinite" duration, subject to review every three years. The signatory Commonwealth exporting countries undertake to limit their exports of sugar to preferential and negotiated price markets to a total of 2 767 000 (long) tons. Of this total, Britain has undertaken to purchase 1 742 000 tons at a price negotiated every three years. The Commonwealth Sugar Agreement expired at the end of 1974 and was replaced by the Sugar Agreement attached to the Lomé Convention (see Chapter 8).

As the United States, by the terms of the Sugar Act, had since 1948 been withdrawing an annual quantity of nine million tons from the free market — quotas were allotted to producers in Cuba (four million short tons), the continental United States (two million tons) and Hawaii, Puerto Rico and the Philippines (one million tons each) — this market accounted for only 20 per cent of the international sugar trade. Cuba restricted its production and exports, but this did not cause the world supply surplus to disappear; competition became even more acute. (As it happened, pressure of high prices caused the Sugar Act to be repealed in 1974).

In these circumstances it proved easier to arrive at a new agreement in 1953. The International Sugar Agreement came into effect on 1 January 1954 for a term of five years. A few amendments were made in 1956. On 1 January 1959 a new five-year Agreement came into force. However, the Cuban affair in 1960 led to the suspension of the economic articles of the Agreement with effect from 1 January 1962. Only the International Sugar Council and some of the non-operational Articles remained applicable. Under reservation the second International Sugar Agreement was extended on 1 August 1963 until 31 December 1965, and afterwards until 31 December 1968, in the expectation that a new agreement would be drawn up. A new agreement was in fact concluded in Geneva on 24 October 1968 and entered into force on 17 June 1969, remaining operative until 31 December 1973. The new agreement was of a purely administrative character and designed to keep in being the body set up in the context of the International Sugar Agreement, i.e. the International Sugar Organization.

In October 1977 another agreement was approved (without the participation of the EEC). It became effective on 1 January 1978 (for a period of five years), but was extended till 31 December 1984. The International Sugar

Agreements 1984 and 1987 (extended till 31 December 1991), like the Agreement 1973, do not contain economic provisions in relation to trade in sugar. It provides "an appropriate framework for the renegotiation of a new agreement with economic provisions".

3. THE INTERNATIONAL COFFEE AGREEMENT

The conferences convened by the South American coffee producers before the Second World War yielded no tangible results. After 1945 prices rose continuously — record levels were reached in 1954 — and plantings were extended. When a degree of equilibrium was attained on the market (1955—57) and there was even a surplus — by 1958 Brazil's stock accounted for almost 40 per cent of world exports, compared with 10 per cent in 1954 — the producers again sought ways and means of counteracting the price decline.

After a series of short-term agreements between producing countries, a Coffee Study Group was formed in order to prepare the negotiation of an agreement including exporting and importing countries. This led to the first International Coffee Agreement (1963—1968), which operated through export quotas (later adjusted in the light of changes in indicator floor and ceiling prices). In the second Agreement (1968—1973), the price-regulating mechanism was refined but it collapsed under pressure of a heavy decrease in the supply by Brazil and steeply rising prices. The third Agreement entered into force on 1 October 1976 for a period of six years. Because of the high price level the export quota provisions have been applied since October 1980 only. Since no restrictions are placed on exports to non-members (the USSR and Eastern Europe countries, most less-developed countries), prices to these markets are approximately one half the level obtained in quota markets. A fourth Agreement (1983), for a further six years, is similar to the third one. The persistence of high coffee prices in 1986 triggered a suspension of the quotas on 19 February 1986. The coffee market thus returned to a free market. But in 1987 quotas were reintroduced. Producers even sold coffee outside the agreement in discount of up to 50 per cent. The 1983 Agreement was extended till 30 September 1992 (but without economic clauses and excluding the introduction of quotas).

4. THE INTERNATIONAL COCOA AGREEMENT

The main objective of the first two International Cocoa Agreements (1973 and 1976) was to keep prices within a pre-established zone through export quotas and a buffer stock. The third Agreement, which entered into force in August 1981 relies only on a buffer stock system. A levy on the cocoa trade is the primary source of financing the buffer stock. The major exporting and many importing countries (except the United States, which accounts for 20 per cent of world imports) are members of the agreement. The buffer stock manager has been purchasing cocoa since August 1981 but has not succeeded in raising prices. The 1986 new agreement entered into force in January 1987 but buffer stock operations were suspended in June 1987. On 15 April 1990 the economic provisions of the Agreement were suspended. The Treaty — without economic provisions — was extended till 30 September 1992.

5. THE INTERNATIONAL TIN AGREEMENT

Immediately after World War I, the Bandoeng Pool was established, grouping producers of the Malayan peninsula and the Netherlands East Indies. The depression of the 1930s led to a restrictive agreement (export quotas) among producers, which came into force for two years on 1 March 1931. A new agreement came into force in 1934 and was extended in 1937. After an initial increase the quotas were reduced in 1938 and then raised again in 1939. In 1938 a buffer stock was set up.

When the United States' strategic purchasing policy came to an end in 1953—54, prices suffered a considerable drop. Discussions about the establishment of an International Tin Agreement were then resumed. On 9 December 1953 the first International Tin Agreement was finally concluded at a UN conference; it did not become effective until 1 July 1956. The Agreement was renewed periodically but the essential provisions relating to a buffer stock and export controls have remained unchanged. The sixth Agreement entered into force on 1 July 1982. The United States, Bolivia and the USSR are no longer members to the sixth Agreement. The application of this agreement could not prevent violent price fluctuations which necessitated several price adaptations. In October 1985 the Council ran out of money and sales of tin were suspended on the London Metal Exchange. After an arrangement between the member countries, banks and brokers in respect of a debt of more than 500 million pound sterling, the Tin Council was dissolved on 31 July 1990. An agreement has been reached on 7 April 1989 to set up an International Tin Study Group to assemble and publish statistics about tin production, consumption and trade.

6. THE INTERNATIONAL NATURAL RUBBER AGREEMENT

The International Natural Rubber Agreement was the first agreement negotiated under the UNCTAD Integrated Programme for Commodities (see below). It entered into force on 15 April 1982 (provisionally on 23 October 1980). The instrument to avoid excessive price fluctuations is a buffer stock of 550 000 tons.

Prices declined sharply in 1981 and the lower prices prevailed in 1982 despite purchases in November 1981 and in 1982 for the buffer stock. The price range established in the Agreement was revised downward in May 1982. Subsequently the market remained weak. Oversupply persisted. The agreement was extended to October 1987. A new agreement was concluded on 20 March 1987 for a five-year period and entered into force on 3 April 1989 (provisionally on 29 December 1988). Its provisions are similar to those of the previous agreement (but loans in connection with buffer stock operations are not allowed). Due to the aids epidemy demand increased and the buffer stock was sold in 1988—89.

THE UNITED NATIONS CONFERENCE ON TRADE AND DEVELOPMENT

1. ORIGINS

At the perennial insistence of the new states, the United Nations General Assembly proclaimed the sixties as the first development decade and in 1962 it decided to convene a United Nations Conference on Trade and Development.

While the discussions could have taken place within the framework of ECOSOC or GATT, the less-developed countries urged the creation of a new institution. They argued that the problems discussed by these two bodies mainly concerned the economic interests of the developed countries and considered GATT as a "rich men's club". At that time (before Part 4 came into being) the GATT rules were based on the non-discrimination principle. However, even after the principle of a differential treatment had gradually come to be accepted, the less-developed countries' criticisms did not cease. Although in 1963 there were 43 international organizations dealing with commodity and other trade problems, the less-developed countries wanted a more satisfactory forum for an examination of their difficulties. Finally, the United Nations Conference on Trade and Development was held in Geneva from 23 March to 16 June 1964.

2. OBJECTIVES

Although no specific objectives were laid down at the first conference, the general function of UNCTAD is to formulate, negotiate and implement measures to improve the development process.

The specific standpoints and aims of the less-developed countries or the majority of the participating countries may be summarized as follows.

1. The share of the less-developed countries in world trade is decreasing. Their terms of trade with the developed countries are constantly deteriorating. More commodity agreements therefore need to be concluded, but in a new spirit, with the primary intention of helping the new countries. In the absence of effective agreements, compulsory and automatic compensatory measures should be introduced as soon as there is a decline in export earnings; the resources for this purpose should be provided by the developed countries. In GATT, only the less-developed countries should be allowed to invoke escape clauses.

2. In order to facilitate the industrialization of the less-developed countries, the western nations must open up their markets to the manufactured products of the new states, even to the extent of giving them preference over the products of the industrial countries. The provisions of GATT need be adjusted in order to make this possible.

3. Although the aid given by the developed countries to the less-developed countries has increased, the latter consider it to be inadequate. They need to be provided with 6 billion dollars more each year. The western nations would, indeed, also have an economic interest in bringing greater prosperity to the low-income countries, since their exports to these territories thus be stepped up. Moreover, support along these lines might be some kind of compensation for the "exploitation" of the former colonies.

The new international economic order

In fact, the target at which the less-developed countries are aiming is what they describe as "a new international economic order". As early as 1974, the UN General Assembly had drafted an action programme for the establishment of such a "new order" (which would give more consideration to the interests of the less-developed countries). It would appear that international civil servants and their national counterparts who conduct international negotiations are not exactly pressed for time, when one considers not only that this "new order" question has been examined by every possible international organization (e.g., GATT, the World Bank Group, IMF, FAO, UNIDO), but also that in December 1975 a North-South conference (officially known as "Conference for International Economic Co-operation") was convened. In the same way as many other organizations, the Conference studied the same problems and to this end set up four committees (Energy, Commodities, Development, Financial Assistance) whose activity — which yielded no result — was not discontinued until May 1977.

The new international economic order consists mainly in a demand for more cash and trade concessions from the developed countries. The international monetary system would have to be adapted in such a way that the less-developed countries would have more Special Drawing Rights at their disposal. Aid to less-developed countries, however, has nothing to do with the international monetary system. Furthermore, the less-developed countries have insisted on a maximum of assistance with the industrialization process, e.g., by applying capital, transmitting technology and granting preferential customs tariffs.

3. ORGANIZATION

The Conference was established as a permanent organ of the General Assembly; its second session was held in New Delhi in February—March 1968; the third in Santiago in April—May 1972, the fourth in Nairobi in May 1976; the fifth in Manila in May—June 1979, the sixth in Belgrade in June—July 1983, the seventh in Geneva in July—August 1987 and the eight will be held in 1992 in Cartagena (Colombia).

All member states of the United Nations and of its specialized agencies are members of the Conference.

Members are divided into the following groups:

Group A: The Asian countries (with the exception of Japan), Yugoslavia and the African countries.

Group B: The market-economy developed countries (the Western European countries and Australia, Canada, the United States, Japan and New Zealand).

Group C: The Latin American countries and the Antilles.

Group D: The USSR and the other communist countries of Eastern Europe. Since 1989 this is no longer a homogeneous group; Hungary even requested to become a member of Group B.

The less-developed countries of UNCTAD are known as the "Group of 77" which was created on 15 June 1964 and at present includes 128 members.

Conference decisions require a two-thirds majority but procedural matters a simple majority only. Board decisions are taken on a simple majority.

A Trade and Development Board is the permanent organ of the Conference (not to be confused with the GATT Committee of the same name). Its 126 members are elected at each conference on a geographical basis, but with representation of the principal trading countries ensured.

The Board's main committees examine commodities, manufactures, invisibles and financing related to trade, shipping, transfer of technology and economic cooperation among less-developed countries. There is also a special committee on preferences. An International Trade Centre has been operated, jointly with GATT (see Chapter 3).

A permanent Secretariat, headed successively by R. Prebisch (Argentina), M. Pérez-Guerrero (Venezuela), Gamani Corea (Sri Lanka) and K. Dadzié, operates in Geneva.

4. FUNCTIONS AND OPERATION

Nothing at all was achieved at UNCTAD I: not only were the meetings badly prepared, but there was also the fact that every conceivable subject was placed on the agenda and "discussed".

UNCTAD II was also a case of much ado about very little. On the basis of suggestions made during GATT session, agreement in principle was reached to grant "generalized preferences" to the less-developed countries. A formal agreement to that effect was concluded in 1970.

Following the second Conference, Secretary-General R. Prebisch criticized the long-winded and laborious discussions within the various 100 strong committees and working parties. It had, however, proved impossible to limit the number of participants and working parties. An attempt to curtail the number of items on the agenda also met with failure. Nor did there seem to be any way of eliminating time-consuming repetitions in working parties and during plenary sessions. Hence the viewpoint expressed by R. Prebisch that "a serious effort was required to improve the effectiveness of UNCTAD and thus achieve practical results".

This note of warning passed unheeded, for the third Conference too was attended by thousands of delegates and comprised innumerable subjects for discussion, each of which, taken separately, would have provided sufficient material for a realistically conceived conference. The resolutions are a typical example of *parler pour ne rien dire*. What obtained unanimous agreement, however, was a recommendation to enlarge the Trade and Development Board. In the same vein, it was decided at UNCTAD IV that the Rapporteur of the Conference should be assisted by a group of eleven "Friends of the Rapporteur" and that a "Contact Group of the President of the Conference" was required.

It was agreed to extend UNCTAD's jurisdiction to cover discussions and agreements relating to commodities. The dominant theme at UNCTAD IV was, in fact, the commodities problem, which did not prevent any number of other international topics from being brought up once again.

As with previous Conferences, the agenda for UNCTAD V was, in the words of the Secretary-General himself, "wide-ranging": every imaginable topical question was discussed, but, in contrast with UNCTAD IV, which concentrated on commodities, no priority was given to one particular item. Consequently, results have suffered as before.

The actual negotiations were delayed by a week owing to considerable differences among the less-developed countries. Some attached special importance to commodity agreements; others preferred direct aid; others again stressed the need for liberalization of trade. A great deal of time was lost in discussing subjects which had nothing to do with UNCTAD, such as Israel and South Africa. For the first time, the less-developed countries pointed an accusing finger at the communist countries and the negligible amount of aid supplied by them.

Understandably, a great many "problems" remained unsolved, such as the debt position, the extension of preferences and the improvement of the international monetary system.

The developed countries are being encouraged to increase their aid to the less-developed countries and to refrain from protectionism. They ought to double their assistance to the least-developed nations; no agreement, however, has been reached on a timetable for achieving this. Notwithstanding a 'substantial new programme of action' for the 1980s, adopted in 1981, the growth rate in these countries was lower than in the 1970s.

UNCTAD VI and VII did not adopt any major initiative but reiterated support for several programs approved at previous conferences. Even when decisions are in dependence of the less-developed countries, no progress is made, a good example being the economic cooperation and integration among these countries. Only in 1988 62 less-developed countries adopted the Global System of Trade Preferences, a trading system under which members of the Group of 77 will exchange trade concessions among each other on a wide range of products. It entered into force in April 1989.

A. *Transfer of technology*

Since 1970 UNCTAD has been working on an international code of conduct on the transfer of technology to less-developed countries "on fair and reasonable terms and conditions". The new states believe that the fees charged for the use of patents and licences are too high. So far no agreement has been reached.

However, the willingness to transfer technology will decrease if the fees are subject to control. Accordingly, the developed countries are opposed to a legally binding code.

B. *Trade in manufactures*

In order to stimulate exports of manufactured goods from the less-developed countries to the industrial states, the Trade and Development Board adopted on 13 October 1970 the conclusions of the Special Committee on Preferences. The Generalized System of Preferences (GSP) is a system under which the developed countries (either separately or in association, such as in the EEC) grant unilateral preferences for imports of industrial goods; these preferences remove customs duties either wholly or in part. Many developed countries have established preferential systems since 1971. These show marked differences, both as regards the preference concerned and in respect of the favoured products and countries. For the import of the favoured goods it is also possible to invoke escape clauses.

Some countries, whose competitive position was deemed to be solid enough, were excluded (Hong Kong, Taiwan, Korea but not by the United

States); in addition, preferences were granted to countries who did not belong to the Group of 77 (e.g. Israel, Portugal, Spain, Albania, North Korea).

It is not easy to define what constitutes a "product from less-developed countries". Hence, industrial nations require a minimum of processing of the goods concerned.

Imports into developed countries under GSP arrangements have risen substantially; they represent approximately fifty per cent of these countries' dutiable imports. The less-developed countries want an extension of the product coverage and less use of the limitations and safeguards.

In fact, the GSP amounts to a subsidy on the products involved; it also serves to undermine the Lomé Convention, which, in itself, is not a bad thing.

Most of the GSP schemes were established for a ten-year period, although a few had no time limit. In 1981 the schemes approaching expiration were renewed for another ten-year period. The less-developed countries would like to see the temporary GSP become "a permanent feature of trade policies of developed countries".

C. *Shipping*

A Committee on Shipping was set up in 1965. Its programme aims at establishing and strengthening the merchant marines of less-developed countries. A convention on a Code of Conduct for Liner Conferences (shipowners' conferences) adopted in 1974 attempts "to regulate the operations of a particular set of international cartels". Among its objectives is: "a balance of interests between suppliers and users of shipping services". The convention entered into force on 6 October 1983.

The effectiveness of shippers' councils in less-developed countries has been limited "by lack of adequate knowledge" about the feasibility and cost of alternative methods of shipment.

At UNCTAD V it proved impossible to agree on ways of enabling less-developed countries to obtain a larger share of the world's shipping. The developed countries voted against a resolution adopted by the Conference on "a set of principles for 'equitable participation' in bulk shipping" because "the text was in direct opposition to the fully competitive environment which was an essential feature of the bulk market". A resolution on ship financing and technical assistance was also unsupported by the developed nations because of its provisions on cargo sharing in bulk trade.

D. *Commodities*

At its Nairobi session UNCTAD adopted an Integrated Programme for Commodities in order to establish and maintain "prices at levels which, in real terms, are equitable to consumers and remunerative to producers" and to reduce "excessive fluctuations in ... prices and in the volume of trade". The programme refers to seventeen commodities, ten of which (coffee, cocoa, tea, rubber, sugar, cotton, jute, sisal, copper, tin) are storable; the stocks would be financed by a Common Fund of 6 billion dollars.

An agreement *in principle* on the establishment for such a fund was not reached until March 1979, but the budget for the fund was set at 750 million dollars. The fund consists of two windows, the first (400 million dollars) being aimed at buffer stock operations and the second (350 million dollars) at helping poorer countries with other measures, such as marketing. The agreement entered into force on 19 June 1989. Amsterdam is the seat of the Fund.

At UNCTAD V the industrial states considered, however, that the determining factor in the price of commodities should be market forces rather than artificial measures. One of these artificial measures is the "indexation" of commodity prices on prices of industrial goods.

More particularly, the less-developed countries claim that the general trend in terms of trade between less-developed countries and developed countries is to their disadvantage. This is by no means a foregone conclusion, especially when one considers exactly how the relevant statistics are compiled. As a result of a drop in transport costs, which sometimes assumes considerable proportions, many commodity prices have been reduced, without leading to a decrease in the revenue derived from the commodities in question. Over the past few decades, the improvement in the quality of industrial products has been more marked than in that of commodities, as a comparison between a Boeing 747 and a DC3 will bear out. Moreover, a widening of the gap in the terms of trade between commodities and its manufactures is not in itself a "favourable factor", and may be a consequence of shortages or of an increase in commodity prices through inflation, which both lead to the use of substitution goods.

As regards "index-linking", this involves the danger of prices becoming divorced from the cost of production, which will lead to overproduction at a time when consumers seek to a acquire substitutional goods.

The fact that UNCTAD seems to be oblivious of the unsatisfactory outcome of such commodity agreements as have been concluded to date gives cause for much disappointment.

An International Agreement on Jute was adopted in 1982 and another on Tropical Timber in 1985 within the framework of the Integrated Programme, but they contain no measures concerning price stabilization, buffer stock or export controls.

APPRAISAL

The commodity agreements

The commodity agreements have not succeeded in obstructing the functioning of the market mechanism. Market conditions, moreover, differ from product to product. In the case of sugar and wheat, demand is fairly stable, but supply is not; as regards tin (and, indeed, the majority of metals), the converse is true (in the case of industrial commodities, such as cotton, there are fluctuations in both supply and demand). Political factors sometimes have an important bearing (as in the Sugar Agreement). Numerous national regulations have made the international sugar market, in the final analysis, a residual market that is hypersensitive to comparatively minor changes in supply and demand. In the case of tin the United States strategic stockpile exerted an influence. The existence of important outsiders may cause difficulties.

Prices

The most intractable of the difficulties lies in the fixing of the price range. In view of the fact that future market conditions are not easily foreseeable, the possibility of errors cannot be ruled out and regular adjustment of the price ranges proves necessary.

In the Tin Agreement ceiling prices have generally not been respected; they have in fact been adapted to (high) market prices. Later it proved impossible to halt a sharp price decrease.

When it comes to determining the price range, the importing and exporting countries do not systematically advocate low and high prices respectively. Certain importing countries are not opposed to a relatively high price because the difference between the international price and their own protected price is thereby reduced (wheat in the United States); exporting countries, which are in a more favourable competitive position, are sometimes in favour of lower prices so as to enable them to increase their share of the market at the expense of less competitive countries.

A low market price is generally required to induce producer countries to conclude an agreement. Even then negotiating positions may be different. The position of a country that sells most of its sugar under one of the regional arrangements is, for example, stronger than that of a country which depends heavily on the "free" market.

In concluding an agreement, the fact has to borne in mind that complete price stabilization is impossible. Indeed, it would be undesirable; in the long run, supply and demand need to remain in equilibrium; the necessary adjustments in the economies concerned must not be precluded. Price fluctuations do not necessarily imply failure.

The method of stabilization

The multilateral-purchase-contract and buffer-stock systems offer the advantage of not requiring any restrictions on production; new producers with improved technical equipment may participate. The consumer still has a free choice. With export quotas, on the contrary, the existing production conditions are crystallized and the most efficient producers are handicapped. Price stability is obtained at the expense of production stability.

A buffer stock needs to be sufficiently large if it is to achieve its purpose. In the case of tin it was not. Owing to the perishable nature of certain commodities and the high storage costs, a buffer stock is not always advisable. In fact, the Tin Agreement provides also for export control; there has been no long-term buffer-stock activity not associated at one stage or another with export control. The supervision of the implementation of an agreement is particularly difficult where agricultural commodities are concerned.

Beneficiaries

As many commodities are exported by developed countries (about 58 per cent of commodity trade except fuels), the establishment of a commodity agreement does not *ipso facto* benefit the less-developed countries. In the case of wheat, for example, few of the latter stand to benefit, except indirectly through the export of American production surpluses under favourable conditions.

So far as the producing countries, and more particularly the less-developed territories, are concerned, stabilization of incomes, rather than of prices, is the main factor. Although the commodity agreements may contribute to this, their relatively limited success has caused other proposals to be advanced. For instance, the establishment of an international insurance fund has been recommended; should export earnings decline, it would pay out a certain portion of the "loss". But fluctuations in exports are often accounted for by domestic factors (e.g., bad economic policy).

As regards a multi-commodity agreement, its administration would be highly complex.

A. I. MacBean has pointed out that the significance of export instability has been exaggerated and that most of the economies concerned have suffered no serious damage from it. Consequently, the resources devoted to countering price fluctuations and compensatory financing would be better employed in, say, investment or technical assistance.

Not all less-developed countries have the same opportunities as the Oil Producing and Exporting Countries (OPEC). Circumstances vary from commodity to commodity. In the case of commodities such as coffee, tea, cocoa and bananas, which are only produced in the less-developed countries and for which practically no substitute exists, action to increase prices can easily be taken if demand is inelastic (which is to a large extent the case) by levying an export duty, for example. But all producers need to apply similar measures in this respect: otherwise, changes occur in the pattern of trade.

There are industrial substitutes (e.g., synthetic rubber) for a few goods, though none of them can be said to be a perfect replacement. Nevertheless, the opportunities of increasing prices here are more limited than in the first case. In fact, the majority of commodities, which account for approximately 50 per cent of the value of the producer countries' exports, meet with competition from the developed countries — either the same commodities (e.g., sugar, cotton) or goods which are in varying degrees substitutable (e.g., butter and groundnut oil).

UNCTAD

Most less-developed countries' ideal is planning on a worldwide scale which would result in a new international division of labour and income.

Hence their rejection of the market mechanism and their failure to understand the industrialized nations when they claim that transfer of technology is the preserve of the private sector. This also explains the proposals for commodity funds, which have understandably met with little enthusiasm from the developed countries.

Moreover, UNCTAD never fails to take the opportunity to put the market mechanism in an unfavourable light. The same goes for most UN publications. However, a review of the publications concerned and of the policies pursued by various states over a period of 20 years have prompted D. T. Healey to conclude that "the result is sadly disillusioning for those who believed that planning was the only way".

The discriminatory measures to which the less-developed countries claim entitlement (e.g., through the GSP) disturb the market conditions. Since the less-developed countries do not need the GSP, it has had only very limited results.

The desire to see a "new international economic order" is to a certain extent symptomatic of international bureaucratic imperialism, especially in the case of UNCTAD. A number of authoritative economists, such as H. G. Johnson, have remarked on this subject that "the demand for a New International Order is to an important extent a demand for greater power for international bureaucrats, disguised as a demand for more justice for the ordinary people of the developing countries".

H. Grubel has interpreted the avalanche of reports published by UNCTAD as an attempt by the civil servants concerned — who in most cases are nationals of less-developed countries — to justify their activity and high salaries. For UNCTAD is "achieving little. Even the agency itself is wondering what it ought to be doing" (*The Economist*).

The necessity for more mutual cooperation only evokes a few vague statements. Time and again, UNCTAD publications maintain that "closer economic cooperation on a third-world basis is the essence of the idea of a new international economic order"; nor can one lose sight of "the need for much wider economic cooperation amongst the developing countries (Secretary-General Corea, in 1978 and 1979 respectively). Since their ever-growing surplus of products intended for export cannot be absorbed by the industrialized nations, the less-developed countries must "increasingly … look to one another for markets and for sources of supply, of raw materials and manufactured goods" (G. Corea).

Plans, agreements and conferences on regional integration have certainly not been found to be wanting either in Africa or in Latin America; to date, however, concrete results have been very few. The "colonial" frontiers have hardly been altered, which accounts for the existence in Africa of a large number of economically unviable miniature states. All are agreed that a new political division is necessary; not one head of state, however, will even consider giving up his office.

The authors of UNCTAD documents have lost sight of the fact that foreign aid is not a necessary element in economic growth (cf. Japan and, earlier still, the United Kingdom and the USSR), and can even have an adverse effect. Experience to date in the field of aid to less-developed countries has borne out the view that a political and economic effort on the part of the less-developed countries concerned is of greater importance than foreign aid (which is conducive mainly to projects commanding prestige and lines the pockets of politicians and civil servants). There are, moreover, nations for whom "economic growth" cannot be superseded by religious or other convictions (sacred cows, high birth-rate). This and other factors explain the lack of animation displayed by Western nations in relation to foreign aid. Moreover, several economists, such as Harry G. Johnson, doubt very much whether a reduction in official aid will be harmful of the less-developed countries.

The less-developed countries are beginning to forfeit a great deal of sympathy by their excessive, aggressively-worded and ceaseless demands. Some have gone so far as to describe UNCTAD as a class organization with member states who are engaged in a class struggle and a political circus.

At a time when there is a tendency for labour-intensive companies to be established in the less-developed countries, the latter have adopted a hostile attitude towards foreign capital; the Group of 77, for instance, have threatened to carry out nationalizations and take action against multinational companies. Furthermore, there is little sense in expecting results from leviathan conferences with approximately 2 000 participants and a disposition to discuss any subject under the sun. The cost of these conferences could have been used to serve more useful causes.

BIBLIOGRAPHY

A. *Commodity agreements*

Most of the relevant data (but naturally no criticism on the operation of the agreements) are to be found in the publications of the various commodity councils.

See also C. P. Brown, *Primary commodity control* (London, Oxford University, 1975); J. D. A. Cuddy, *International price indexation* (Westmead, D. C. Heath, 1976) and E. Brook *et al.*, Commodity price stabilization and the developing countries, *Banca Nazionale del Lavoro*, March 1978; A. Maizels, Selected issues in the negotiation of international commodity agreements. An economic analysis (*United Nations Conference on Trade and Development* 1982); W. Schug, Die Bedeutung von internationalen Rohstoffabkommen für die Verbraucherländer von agrarischen und mineralischen Grundstoffen, *Ordo Jahrbuch 1983*. F. Gordon-Ashworth, *International commodity control. A contemporary history and appraisal*, London, Croom Helm, 1984: A. I. MacBean and D. T. Nguyen, *Commodity policies. Problems and prospects*, London, Croom Helm, 1987. For wheat see N. Butler, *The international grain trade. Problems and prospects*, London Croom Helm, 1986; for tin: W. Fox, *Tin, The working of a commodity agreement* (London, Mining Journal Books, 1974).

B. *UNCTAD*

The most noteworthy of UNCTAD's publications are the *UNCTAD Commodity Survey*, 19—, and *Handbook of international trade and development statistics* (New York, UN, 19—); see also *Proceedings of the United Nations Conference on Trade and Development* (New York 1973 and 1978); Trade and Development Report (annually since 1981); *The history of UNCTAD 1964—1984* (United Nations, New York, 1985).

See also: B. Gosovic, *UNCTAD. Conflict and Compromise. The Third World's quest for an equitable world economic order through the United Nations* (Leyden, A. W. Sijthoff, 1972); *UNCTAD and the south-north dialogue. The first twenty years* (ed. M. Zammit Cutajar, Oxford, New York, Toronto, Pergamon, 1985).

The extracts quoted are from D. T. Healy, Development policy. New thinking about an interpretation, *Journal of Economic Literature*, Sept. 1972; H. G. Grubel, The case against the New International Economic Order, *Weltwirtschaftliches Archiv*, 1977, Heft. 2; Unloved, unuseful UNCTAD, *The Economist*, 13 April 1985.

5. The Organization for Economic Cooperation and Development

> *Without doubt the trade liberalization programme of the Organization for European Economic Cooperation . . . still stands out as one of the more solid achievements in the efforts towards Western European integration.*
>
> GUNNAR MYRDAL

As the Organization for Economic Cooperation and Development (OECD) is the successor to the Organization for European Economic Cooperation (OEEC), we should study the latter as a preliminary to any discussion of the former.

THE ORGANIZATION FOR EUROPEAN ECONOMIC COOPERATION

1. ORIGINS

The second World War had left Europe in critical economic situation. Agricultural and industrial production had fallen to a low level, open or repressed inflation was the general rule, and the necessary imports — especially those from the United States — could not be paid for. The hard winter of 1946—47 and the following dry summer did nothing to alleviate matters. The tough economic conditions furthered the growth of communism, which extended its influence more particularly in France, Italy and Greece.

After the unsuccessful attempt in Moscow in March 1947 (the conference between the United States, the USSR, Britain and France) to reach agreement on cooperation for the reconstruction of Europe, the American Secretary of State, G. C. Marshall, conceived the idea of a European recovery programme. On 5 June 1947 he enlarged on this idea in a speech at Harvard University, suggesting that the United States should be prepared to aid the European countries within the framework of a coordinated programme that the Europeans would draw up themselves. The proposal was favourably received in Europe but met with opposition from the Soviet Union. On 3 July 1947 the Foreign Ministers of France and the United Kingdom invited all European states except Spain to a conference in Paris in order to formulate a recovery programme (The Soviet Union and its Eastern European satellites declined the invitation).

The conference opened on 12 July, attended by sixteen countries, and led to the establishment of the Committee of European Economic Cooperation (CEEC) and of committees for food and agriculture, energy, iron and steel, transport, timber, manpower, balance-of-payments problems and finance. The CEEC was set up to work out the principles of the recovery programme, ways and means of implementing it, and how much foreign aid was required; on 22 September 1947, it adopted a report for submission to the American government.

In the United States the aid programme was examined by committees presided over by A. Harriman, J. Krug, E. Nourse and C. A. Herter. In the meantime the Interim Aid Programme supplied the most urgent of European needs. On 3 April 1948 the Economic Cooperation Act was signed by President Truman; for the first year (1948/49) 5 055 million dollars were allocated to the European Recovery Programme. During its entire period (1948—1952), Marshall aid amounted to 12 817 million dollars; 677.7 million went to Austria; 559.2 million to Belgium and Luxemburg; 273.1 million to Denmark, 2 713.8 million to France; 706.7 million to Greece; 29.3 million to Iceland; 147.4 million to Ireland; 1 508.6 million to Italy; 982.1 million to the Netherlands; 255.2 million to Norway; 51.3 million to Portugal; 107.2 million to Sweden; 225.1 million to Turkey; 3 819.9 million to the United Kingdom and 1 390.5 million to West Germany.

An Economic Cooperation Administration, with headquarters in Washington, and an Office of the Special Representative, in Europe, were set up to implement the Act. On 15 March 1948 the CEEC met to facilitate contacts between the Special Representative and the European countries and to ensure adequate coordination. After a working party composed of representatives of the sixteen countries and the Western Zones of occupied Germany had been formed to study the structure and functions of a possibly permanent organization, the Convention for European Economic Cooperation, which established the OEEC, was finally signed on 16 April 1948.

2. OJECTIVES

The aim of the OEEC was to build up a sound European economy through economic cooperation between its member states. For this purpose, it needed to ensure the success of the European Recovery Programme (Article 11), whose object was to enable OEEC countries to achieve, without any extraordinary outside aid, a satisfactory degree of economic activity and to increase their exports to non-member states as far as possible (Article 1).

3. ORGANIZATION

A. *Members*

The convention was successively ratified by the United Kingdom, the British and American Zones of Germany, Ireland, France, Austria, Iceland, Sweden, the French Zone of Germany, Denmark, Italy (initially, the Anglo-American Zone of Trieste was also an OEEC member; but on 26 October 1954 it was reunited with Italy) Norway, the Netherlands, Belgium, Turkey, Switzerland, Portugal, Luxemburg and Greece. On 31 October 1949 Western Germany was admitted as a member country in place of the three zones of occupation. After having participated in the activities of the Ministerial Committee for Agriculture and Food since 28 January 1955, Spain became a full OEEC member on 20 July 1959.

At the invitation of the OEEC Council, the United States and Canada accepted associated membership on 3 June 1950.

By a Council decision of 25 February 1955 Yugoslavia was asked to send observers to attend the meetings of the Council and its technical committees and subcommittees. From July 1959 onwards Yugoslavia took part in activities connected with agriculture and food; it had been a member of the European Productivity Agency (EPA) since 9 October 1957. Finland was represented on the Maritime Transport Committee from 1959.

B. *Administration*

The Council, the highest of the OEEC's organs, was composed of representatives from all member states (Article 15,*a*). Its decisions were normally reached by unanimous vote, though the Council was empowered to make an exception for special cases. Abstention by any country was no obstacle to the adoption of decisions, which then held good for the other member states (Article 14).

The Council was competent to conclude agreements with the OEEC countries, with non-member countries, with the United States and with international organizations (Article 13,*b*). It was assisted by an Executive Committee and a Secretariat and by such technical committees or other bodies as were required for its activities. All these bodies were responsible to the Council (Article 15,*c*).

The Executive Committee was composed of seven members appointed annually by the Council. If a country was not represented on the Executive Committee, it was allowed to participate in discussions and decisions where its interests were concerned. OEEC members were kept informed of the proceedings of the Executive Committee through the distribution of agenda and summary records (Article 16). Except with the consent of the Council, the Executive Committee was not authorized to take decisions. From 14 November 1956 onwards the Committee was charged with the coordination of the activities of the technical committees. There were technical committees for electricity, oil, coal, gas, iron and steel, non-ferrous metals, capital goods, chemicals, textiles, paper and paper pulp, timber, cement, leather, hides and skins, internal transport, maritime transport, manpower, tourism, overseas territories, and fiscal questions.

The Secretariat, headed by a secretary-general (R. Marjolin from 1948 until 1955, and then R. Sergent — both of France) assisted by two deputies (Article 17,*a*) and a staff of about 1 000, was located in Paris.

4. FUNCTIONS AND OPERATIONS

A. *General economic cooperation*

1. *Provisions*

In order to promote the coordinated recovery of the economies of the member countries, the signatories assumed the following general commitments:

a) to further, both individually and collectively, the expansion of production (Article 2);
b) to establish, as necessary, general production and trade programmes (Article 3);
c) to take the necessary steps to achieve or maintain currency stability, sound exchange rates and, in general, confidence in the monetary system (Article 7);
d) to provide all information requested by the Organization in order to simplify its task (Article 9).

If any country failed to meet its commitments, the others could continue to cooperate without that country (Article 26).

2. *Operation*

Initially, the OEEC's programmes were drawn up with a view to directing efforts towards and establishing criteria for the distribution of American aid. A comparison of national plans revealed discrepancies and shortcomings (e.g., in connection with the expansion of exports to one and the same region).

As a result of the Korean war, the focus of interest changed. In order to limit the detrimental effects of the speculative shortage of raw materials, the United States, Britain and France called an international conference at which the other OEEC countries were represented. One of the results was that, from February 1951 to mid-1953, the distribution of coal was controlled.

The numerous technical committees carried out a great many surveys, most of which were published. Real achievements were something of a rarity. This was also true of the activities of the Ministerial Committee for Agriculture and Food and the European Productivity Agency (set up on 22 May 1953). Special mention should be made of the Steering Committee for Nuclear Energy, which was responsible for the preparatory work in connection with the European Nuclear Energy Agency (ENEA), set up on 17 December 1957. It has the task of securing the harmonization of national legislation and programmes and the pooling of research and development projects for nuclear energy, in cooperation with the European Atomic Energy Community (EAEC or Euratom). Three major projects have been sponsored by ENEA: at Mol, Belgium (Eurochemic: European Company for the Chemical Processing of Irradiated Fuels; 1957, but the plant did not begin operating until 1966), at Halden, Norway (1958), and at Winfrith, Britain (1959).

The European Conference of Ministers of Transport, which created Eurofina (the European Company for the Financing of Railway Rolling Stock), did not come under OEEC jurisdiction, though its establishment was originally recommended by the OEEC Council.

In 1951 the Council estimated that a 25 per cent increase in the OEEC countries' overall production in the course of the next five years was desirable. With a view to securing better coordination of the economic policies of the member states, it was decided in March 1952 to examine collectively the policy of each individual country. The exchanges of ideas on this subject very often resulted in recommendations by the Council. In this way, the various countries were prompted to take more account of their partners' interests.

As the OEEC was unable to lay down rules and regulations concerning currency stability, it confined itself to stressing the necessity for bringing this about. Sharp price movements and fluctuations in demand, it pointed out, create balance-of-payments difficulties and entail recourse to escape clauses (see below). In specific cases, however, recommendations were made to the debtor countries (France, Britain) and creditor countries (Western Germany).

In June 1959 a group of experts was commissioned to study the question of constantly increasingly prices. Their report, *The problem of rising prices*, published in June 1961, was only intended as an explanatory statement.

B. *Liberalization of goods, invisible transactions and capital*

1. *Provisions*

The member countries agreed to pursue the study of customs unions and free-trade areas (Article 5) and, more specifically in connection with the movement of persons, goods and capital:

a) gradually to facilitate free movement of persons (Article 8);
b) as far as possible by common agreement, to expand trade between

themselves and to that end to intensify efforts to bring into operation a multilateral system of payments and to reduce restrictions on trade and payments (Article 4);

c)   to cooperate in lowering tariffs and other barriers to trade (Article 6).

2. *Operation*

As nothing was actually done to liberalize the movement of persons, this section will be devoted to examining what measures were adopted as regards trade in goods (for example, prevention of artificial boosting of exports), invisible transactions and capital. It will be followed by a discussion of the establishment of a system which went a long way towards making multilateral payments possible.

a. *Goods*

Whereas GATT's activities were concentrated mainly on the lowering and stabilization of customs duties, the OEEC was primarily concerned with quantitative restrictions.

In July 1949 the Council recommended that the member states should gradually abolish import restrictions. On 2 November 1949 they agreed to liberalize 50 per cent of the value of private imports in 1948 before 15 December 1949. The percentage accounted for by each product in the total value of the 1948 imports being determined beforehand, trade in such a manner of products had to be liberalized as would ensure that the sum of the corresponding percentages calculated on this basis equalled 50 per cent. (In other words, the fact that the relative proportions of the total value of imports had changed in the meantime was of no importance as regards determination of the liberalization percentages.) For Western Germany the base year was 1949, for Austria 1952. As the Belgium-Luxemburg Economic Union was already pursuing a flexible import policy in 1948, it was at a disadvantage compared with other countries. Another year (1955) was therefore subsequently taken as a basis, and this also applied to the Benelux countries when acting jointly.

State-controlled trading was not taken into account for the determination of the import values. In addition, each country was allowed to draw up different lists of products applicable to every other OEEC state. Such discrimination was inevitable owing to the lack of a multilateral payments system.

This state of affairs was changed by the adoption of the Code of Liberalization of Trade on 18 August 1950 and the establishment of the European Payments Union on 19 September 1950. On 4 October 1950 the degree of liberalization was increased to 60 per cent. In order to secure harmonious liberalization, the percentage was extended, from that date, to each of the main categories of goods — foodstuffs and products of animal origin, raw materials and manufactured articles.

Discrimination was forbidden (Article 7 of the Code of Liberalization), though exceptions were allowed in the case of special customs or monetary systems, obstacles to exports and dumping (Articles, 8, 9 and 10). In the event of balance-of-payments difficulties (Article 3) or for reasons of national interest or equity (Article 5), member states could be released from the obligations. To this end, a justification procedure was instituted (Part 3 of the Code of Liberalization). In no case whatsoever could the interests of other countries be unnecessarily harmed.

From 1 February 1951 total imports had to be liberalized as to 75 per cent. Member countries were authorized to maintain the figure of 60 per cent in respect of each of the three main categories of goods (Article 2). At the request of a member country, the Organization may decide that, for the purpose of calculating the percentage, another member country must take account of imports liable to high rates of duty which frustrate measures of liberalization (Article 32). The lists of liberalized goods were consolidated as from 30 April 1951; in other words, the point of no return had been reached, except in cases where the escape clauses could be invoked (as did Greece and Austria because of balance-of-payments difficulties). The member countries were required to apply common liberalization regulations for textiles and certain raw materials before 15 August 1951.

On 14 January 1955 further important decisions were taken. At least 10 per cent of the restrictions still applying to private imports as at 30 June 1954 were to be abolished. From 1 April 1955 the overall liberalization was to be provisionally raised to 90 per cent and that for the three main categories of goods to 75 per cent. As a result of repeated extensions, these percentages remained in operation until 30 June 1960. It was also decided that an increase in the disparity of customs tariffs could be considered a reason for countries placed at a disadvantage to obtain exemption from the liberalization regulations. Finally, state-controlled trade could be regarded as a quantitative restriction. In July 1956 the Council arrived at the conclusion (see the *Report on the possibility of creating a free-trade area in Europe*, published in 1957) that a further reduction of quantitative restrictions would be difficult to achieve in view of the divergent levels of customs duties.

The desired aims were for the most part attained. By 1960 approximately 95 per cent of intra-European trade and 90 per cent of trade with the dollar area had been liberalized. No liberalization percentages had been stipulated in connection with the liberalization of trade with the dollar area (although they had been calculated — see Table 15). On 22 December 1954 the Council issued instructions for restrictions to be decreased, and laid down a procedure for following up their implementation.

Although most countries fulfilled their obligations (Table 16), considerable exceptions had to be granted in respect of intra-European trade, owing to internal difficulties.

"Structural" debtors were temporarily freed from their obligations. This was the case with Austria in 1951 and 1952, and with Greece from 1950 onwards. (The latter, however, reintroduced its liberalization measures in

April 1953 on its own initiative.) An adverse balance of payments caused Turkey to suspend the previously agreed liberalization regulations in April 1953. These were replaced by a system of aggregate quotas, the amounts of which were, in general, equivalent to imports for the preceding period. With the advent of the Korean crisis, various countries were compelled to invoke the safeguard clauses. On 21 February 1951 Western Germany contracted out of its commitments (until 21 April 1952). On 8 November 1951 Britain decreased its liberalization percentage from 90 to 61 per cent and to 46 per cent on 11 March 1952 (but raised it to 75 per cent on 29 October 1953). On 1 March 1952 France reverted to freedom of action as regards quantitative restrictions and maintained it until the second half of 1953. It did so again from 18 June 1957 to 1 January 1959.

As quantitative trade restrictions were abolished, the importance of eliminating practices tending to distort competition increased. The only practice condemned in the Code of Liberalization was dumping (Article 10).

Table 15. Liberalization percentages for the OEEC countries' trade with the United States and Canada (1953 = 100; 1953—59).

Country	1 January 1953[a]	30 September 1954	1 January 1956	1 May 1957	1 January 1958	1 January 1959[a]
Denmark	—	—	55	55	55	66
Germany (Western)	—	54	68	90	94	78
France	—	—	11	11	—	(50)
Greece	—	99	99	99	99	99
Ireland	—	—	15	15	15	15
Iceland	—	33	33	33[b]	33	33
Italy	—	24	24	39	68	68
Netherlands BLEU	57	86	86	86	86	86
Norway	—	—	—	84	87	91
Austria	—	—	8	40	40	45
Portugal	—	—	53	53	53	53
Turkey	—	—	—	—	—	—
United Kingdom	(7)	49	56	59	62	73
Sweden	—	—	64	68	68	68
Switzerland	(98)	98	98	99	99	99
Total for member countries	(11)	44	54	61	64	(73)

[a] The figures appearing between parentheses relate to autonomous liberalization measures not notified to the OEEC.
[b] This percentage does not take into account the February 1957 liberalization.
Source: *A decade of cooperation. Achievements and perspectives. 9th Annual economic review* (Paris, 1958); *Policies for sound economic growth. 10th Annual economic review* (Paris, 1959).

It was on this basis that action was taken in respect of the double prices of Swedish and Norwegian paper pulp.

On 14 January 1955 it was decided that the member countries (with the exception of Greece and Turkey) would abolish their main artificial export promotion regulations by 31 December 1955 and enact no fresh provisions in the intervening period. This decision (which was not complied with by Denmark or France) was subsequently extended. A further decision taken on 17 February 1959 laid down a general code of procedure in which the following practices in particular were prohibited: allocation to the exporter of part of the proceeds of an export, direct subsidizing of exports, reimbursement of direct taxes and social security charges, refunding of an amount higher than the indirect taxes on a product, subsidized supplies of raw materials, interest subsidies in connection with or contributions towards the cost of export credits and, in general, all regulations that tended to distort normal conditions of competition. Exceptions were allowed within the framework of agricultural policy. In actual fact, these recommendations were not followed to any great extent.

Table 16. Liberalization percentages for intra-OEEC trade (1948 = 100; 1950—58).

Country	1950	1951	1952	1953	1954	1955	1956	1957	1958
Denmark	50	65	75	76	76	78	86	86	86
Germany (Western)[a]	63	0	81	90	90	91	92	93	91
France	66	76	0	18	65	78	82	0	90
Greece[b]	—	—	—	90	97	95	95	95	96
Ireland	67	75	73	77	77	90	90	90	90
Iceland	15	41	0	29	29	29	29[c]	29[d]	29[c]
Italy	76	77	100	100	100	99	99	99	98
Netherlands	66	71	75	93	93	96[d]	96[d]	96[d]	96[d]
BLEU	64	75	75	87	88				
Norway	45	51	75	76	75	75	78	81	81
Austria[e]	66	0	0	51	82	89	90	90	90
Portugal	61	84	85	93	93	94	94	94	94
Turkey	60	63	63	0	0	0	0	0	0
United Kingdom	86	61	44	75	83	85	94	94	95
Sweden	69	75	85	91	91	93	93	93	93
Switzerland	85	85	91	92	92	93	91	91	91
Total to member countries[f]	67	61	65	77	83	86	89	83	89

[a] 1949 = 100.
[b] Autonomous, unilateral liberalization not notified to the OEEC.
[c] This percentage does not take into account the December 1956 liberalization.
[d] 1955 = 100.
[e] 1952 = 100.
[f] Excluding Greece, Benelux imports are based on the 1948 figure.
Source: *A decade of cooperation. Achievements and perspectives. 9th Annual economic review* (Paris, 1958); *Policies for sound economic growth. 10th Annual economic review* (Paris, 1959).

b. *Invisible transactions*

The obstacles to invisible transactions in connection with liberalized goods were abolished in August 1951. They related mainly to the transfer of profits resulting from commercial transactions, dividends from securities and interest on mortgages, the contractual amortization of long-term loans, the participation of subsidiaries and branches in the overhead expenses of parent companies, freight and emigrants' funds. As it was not possible to compute liberalization percentages for them, invisible transactions were subdivided into thirty-two headings. As far as the remaining invisible operations (fourteen headings) were concerned, member states were recommended to adopt a flexible attitude. Departures from these regulations could be permitted when necessitated by serious economic disorders and balance-of-payments difficulties. Discrimination had to be avoided (except in the case of customs and monetary unions).

In June 1955 the fourteen remaining headings were liberalized. The possibilities afforded by the escape clause in the event of balance-of-payments difficulties were limited in time (Article 20,*d* of the Code of Liberalization): the rule which had been suspended had to be partially reinstated within twelve months and wholly restored within eighteen months (except when an extension was granted by the Council). The minimum amount of currency allowed for certain transactions (e.g., in respect of tourism) was increased. The restrictions imposed by a number of countries were regularly examined. Despite considerable progress, there remained restrictions on insurance, films and transport. Greece, Iceland, Spain and Turkey were unable to implement their commitments in full.

In 1960 the Committee for Invisible Transactions was requested to draw up a new Code of Liberalization of Current Invisible Operations to be applied by the OECD.

c. *Capital*

In order to promote investment in Europe, proposals were put forward in 1950 for a relaxation of the regulations and controls on the payment of dividends and interest and on the repatriation of capital. The same ideas were advanced in 1954.

On 25 March 1955 the Council issued a recommendation to the member countries concerning the liberalization of specific capital movements. It urged, in particular, that the repatriation of capital, capital gains and income relating to all new direct investments made by the OEEC countries should be facilitated. From 1955 to 1956 a great many restrictions on capital movements were abolished or eased. Regulations governing investment in securities by residents of the dollar area were relaxed in several countries. Growing interest in these measures was shown by American and Canadian firms.

In December 1957 it was decided that the member states should permit any import or export of capital in connection with direct investments made by the partner countries. Exceptions to this rule could only be made when detriment was caused to a member country's economic and financial interests.

In every case, however, permission to transfer the proceeds of the liquidation of and capital gains on investments made after 6 December 1957 had to be granted unconditionally. Blocked credits could be used by foreign creditors for direct investments and investments in domestic securities (except when re-expressed in foreign currency), for the purchase of property, for assistance to needy persons and for personal expenses (up to a specific amount); transfers in connection with these operations were also permissible. Some countries made reservations in respect of certain clauses.

The Code of Liberalization of Capital Movements was adopted in December 1959. It was taken over by the OECD in slightly amended form (see below).

d. *Multilateral settlements*

In the immediate postwar period, trade restrictions were inevitable in order to alleviate balance-of-payments difficulties. In each bilateral trade and payments agreement the provisions were aimed at minimizing, on the one hand, exports of the most necessary goods or of goods in short supply and, on the other hand, imports of less essential products. Within certain limits, the net balances were not the subject of a settlement but of the granting of credit. Subsequently, payments had to be made in gold or in dollars.

This system was threatened with extinction by the fact that certain countries had accumulated surpluses with some partners and deficits with others. After the ill-starred effort in July 1947 to restore sterling convertibility, intra-European trade was financed with American credits.

With the coming into operation of the European Payments Union (EPU) on 1 July 1950, a system of multilateral payments between the member states was set up. (Its effect was retroactive, since the agreement was signed on 19 September 1950). Under this scheme, each country's debts and claims towards each of the other countries were recorded by the central bank concerned. At the end of each month, the balances were notified to the Bank for International Settlements in Basel, which acted on behalf of the EPU. All net claims or debts were compensated so as to leave only a credit balance or a debit balance for each country with the EPU (Articles 5—6 of the Agreement establishing the EPU). In order to determine the cumulative position, this balance was added to the preceding balance (Article 7). This system made it possible, for example, to use credit balances to reduce previous deficits.

Initial credit balances were assigned to the "structural" debtors, viz. Greece (115 million dollars), Austria (80), Norway (60), the Netherlands (30), Turkey (25) and Iceland (4). A number of countries — the United Kingdom (150), the BLEU (29.4) and Sweden (21.2) — began with an initial debit balance in exchange for conditional aid under the Marshall Plan. In other words, they received dollars on condition that they made an agreed amount in their national currency available to the debtor countries.

These initial amounts were taken into consideration when the cumulative positions referred to above were evaluated. This did not, however, apply to balances existing on 30 June 1950, the use of which was determined by bilateral negotiations.

In addition, each country was allocated a quota equivalent to approximately 15 per cent of its payments in respect of visible and invisible intra-European trading operations in 1949 (e.g., United Kingdom; 1 060 million dollars, France: 520 million dollars, Western Germany: 500 million dollars) and divided into five equal parts. If the cumulative deficit was still equivalent to the first part, the debtor country received 100 per cent credit. In each of the following portions this credit was reduced by 20 per cent, and the remainder had to be paid in gold (Article 13). The Union could discharge this obligation to make a payment of gold (payments being allowed in dollars, the currency of the country concerned or another currency — Article 14). An aggregate of 60 per cent was thus obtainable. The creditor countries gained 100 per cent credit in respect of the first part and only 50 per cent in respect of the following portions (Table 17). All entries were expressed in units of account having the same value in gold as the dollar.

Table 17. Credits granted and payments made in gold in the European Payments Union, in per cent of quotas, 1950—51.

Portions of quotas	Creditors		Debtors	
	Gold received from the Union	Credits granted to the Union	Gold paid to the Union	Credits received from the Union
Between 0 and 20		20		20
Between 20 and 40	10	10	4	16
Between 40 and 60	10	10	8	12
Between 60 and 80	10	10	12	8
Between 80 and 100	10	10	16	4
Total quotas	40	60	40	60

Source: EPU, *First Annual Report of the Board of Management* (Paris, OEEC 1951).

The Union was administered by a Managing Board of seven members appointed for a year by the Council (Article 20,*a*). Its capital (350 million dollars) was supplied by the United States: it was thus possible, if so required, to pay out more to the creditor countries than was received by the EPU from the debtor countries.

The life of the EPU, which was initially established for a period of two years, was repeatedly extended. These extensions were usually accompanied by adjustments to the Agreement. In 1952 the system of settlements was modified. The credit ceiling remained at 60 per cent but payments in gold had to be made more promptly. All member states could be called upon to make a (temporary) payment of gold to the EPU if this proved necessary in order to maintain its reserves at the required level.

In June 1954 further important decisions were taken. In order to reduce the amount of outstanding loans the debtor countries were authorized to conclude agreements directly with the creditor countries. Generally speaking, 25 per cent of the debt was repaid immediately and redemption of the remainder spread over a period of several years; each payment reduced *ipso facto* the debtor's debt to the EPU and the EPU's debt to the creditor. Ceilings for credits granted by the creditor countries were raised. In addition credit facilities were broadened for the debtor countries which had concluded bilateral payments agreements. From 1 July 1954 onwards half of the balances were settled in gold and half covered by loans; quotas were increased by 20 per cent.

Quotas were again expanded on 29 July 1955, when payments in gold were increased to 75 per cent. Abolition of EPU and its replacement by the European Monetary Agreement (EMA) was envisaged at this time, but the EPU was given further leases of life with hardly any modification in 1956, 1957 and 1958.

During the EPU's existence, the cumulative total of the debts and claims notified to the Bank for International Settlements was 46 400 million dollars (Table 18). Of this sum, 43 per cent was covered by reciprocal compensation, 27 per cent by compensation in time, 1 per cent by the allocation of other funds, 23 per cent by payments in gold or dollars and 6 per cent by credits.

During the Korean war the amount of credits granted rose considerably (Table 19). During most of the following years, on the other hand, repayments of previous debts were higher than new credits. The part paid in gold followed a steady upward trend, from 46 per cent on 30 June 1952 to 70 per cent on 27 December 1958 in the case of the creditor countries, and from 47 to 80 per cent in that of the debtor countries.

The European Monetary Agreement had already been signed on 5 August 1955 but only came into operation on 27 December 1958. This development was actuated by thirteen European countries, introducing external convertibility (see Chapter 1).

The new Agreement retained the EPU'S multilateral payments system and provided for the formation of a European Fund. It was modified several times and was finally adopted by the OECD (see below).

Table 18. Bilateral balances within the EPU, in billion units of account (1950—58).

Description	1950/ 51	1951/ 52	1952/ 53	1953/ 54	1954/ 55	1955/ 56	1956/ 57	1957/ 58	July—Dec. 1958	Totals[c]
1. Total bilateral balances (sum of claims and debts)	6.3	8.7	5.3	3.9	3.5	3.9	5.7	6.5	2.6	46.4
2. Multilateral compensation	3.0	3.5	2.9	1.9	1.7	1.4	2.0	2.6	1.0	20.0
3. Compensation in time	1.0	3.0	2.0	0.9	1.4	1.1	0.9	2.1	0.3	12.6
4. Special assimilation[a]	0.7	—[b]	—[b]	—[b]	—[b]	—[b]	—[b]	—[b]	—[b]	0.5
5. Balance (1—2—3—4)	1.6	2.2	0.4	1.2	0.5	1.4	2.8	1.9	1.3	13.4
6. Settlements in gold or dollars	0.4	1.3	0.3	1.3	0.6	1.5	2.3	1.8	1.0	10.7
7. Credits granted	1.2	0.9	0.1	−0.1	−0.1	−0.1	0.4	0.1	0.3	2.7

[a] This represents the settlements by the initial balances, the existing balances at the inauguration of the EPU, interest and the special loans in gold.
[b] Nil, or negligible amounts. (This accounts for the difference between 0.7 and 0.5 in item 4.)
[c] July 1950 to December 1958.
Source: *Final report of the Managing Board of the European Payments Union* (Paris, OEEC, 1959).

Table 19. EPU credits, in million units of account (1950—58).

Period (end)	Granted to the EPU	Granted by the EPU
1950/51	73	700
1951/52	1058	1081
1 July 1952	—	2
1952/53	360	174
1953/54	417	259
1 July 1954	—	—
1954/55	312	242
1955/56	263	184
1956/57	412	436
1957/58	372	297
July—Dec. 1958	175	197

Source: *Final report of the Managing Board of the European Payments Union* (Paris, OEEC, 1959).

THE ORGANIZATION FOR ECONOMIC COOPERATION AND DEVELOPMENT

1. ORIGINS

The establishment of the EEC resulted in a split among the OEEC countries. It confronted the non-EEC states with the threat of a drop in their exports to the EEC countries.

With the progress in external convertibility, moreover, the role of the OEEC in the field of international payments had greatly diminished. At world level, new problems had arisen, more especially that of aid to the less-developed countries — a matter in which the United States wanted the other developed countries to take a greater interest.

In order to thrash out these problems, the President of the United States, the President of the French Republic, the Prime Minister of the United Kingdom and the Chancellor of Western Germany held a meeting in December 1959. With a view to studying future cooperation, a Special Economic Committee, consisting of representatives of thirteen countries and of the EEC Commission, met on 12 and 13 January 1960. It instructed a working group to inquire into the most appropriate methods for attaining the new aims, to draft an agreement and to specify those functions of the OEEC which ought to be maintained. The group's report, *A remodelled economic organization*, was published on 7 April 1960.

The conference on the adaptation of the OEEC took place on 24 and 25 May 1960. A working group was again formed to draw up a project which was examined by a meeting of ministers on 22 and 23 July 1960. It was also resolved to provide for the creation of a new Trade Committee. The Development Assistance Group, which had been set up in January 1960 on the advice of the Special Economic Committee, was converted into a Development Assistance Committee (DAC). It was also agreed that the ENEA and the EMA should be continued under the new organization, whereas the EPU was wound up.

In order to determine the procedure for replacing the OEEC by the OECD a preparatory committee was formed, headed by T. Kristensen of Denmark. Its activities were completed on 23 November 1960; the committee's report was approved by a meeting of ministers in Paris on 13 December, and the OECD Convention was finally signed on 14 December 1960. By 30 September 1961 there were sufficient ratifications for the Convention to come into force.

2. OBJECTIVES

The aims of the OECD are very general: achievement of the highest and soundest possible growth in the economies of the member countries and also of non-member states in the process of development, expansion of employment, raising of living standards, maintenance of financial stability, growth of the world economy, extension of world trade on a multilateral and non-discriminatory basis in accordance with international obligations (Article 1).

3. ORGANIZATION

A. *Members*

Initially, the member countries were the same as those of the OEEC, except that Canada and the United States were full rather than associate members. Yugoslavia and Finland maintained their special position, and Finland became a full member on 28 January 1969. Japan joined on 28 April 1964, Australia on 7 June 1971 and New Zealand on 29 May 1973.

B. *Administration*

1. *The Council*

As in the OEEC, the Council is the highest authority; it represents all OECD countries and meets from time to time at ministerial level and regularly at permanent representative level (Article 7). The Council appoints a chairman and two vice-chairman each year (Article 8).

As a general rule decisions and recommendations are made by all the member countries. Exceptions to this rule may be granted in special cases by unanimous vote. Where a member does not vote, the decision or recommendation is binding only on the other members (this provision encourages non-European members to abstain in purely European matters). No decision needs to be implemented by a member until its required constitutional procedures have been complied with (Article 6).

2. The Executive Committee

The Executive Committee (Article 9) is composed of fourteen members, with permanent membership of seven countries (Canada, France, Germany, Italy, Japan, United States, United Kingdom) and a rotating membership of seven others.

The Committee makes a preliminary study of matters submitted to the Council. It receives directives from and is responsible to the Council. The Committee can take no decisions without the Council's authorization.

In 1972, the Executive Committee in Special Session consisting of senior officials in charge of international economic relations was created in order to bridge the work of the more specialized committees.

3. The Secretariat

The Secretariat (located in Paris) is responsible for the proper functioning of the Organization. The secretary-general is appointed by the Council for a period of five years; the first incumbent was T. Kristensen (see Sec. 1 above)., and he was succeeded on 1 October 1969 by E. van Lennep, of the Netherlands. Since 30 September 1984 J. C. Paye, of France, is the third secretary-general. The secretary-general is assisted by one or more deputy or assistant secretaries-general who, on his recommendation, are also appointed by the Council (Article 10,1). The secretary-general takes the chair at meetings of the permanent representatives (Article 10,2) and attends, or is represented at, meetings of the Executive Committee or other OECD bodies. He prepares the ground for decisions by the Council and the Executive Committee and is responsible for ensuring that they are implemented. The secretary-general's task also embraces the Organization's relations with the outside world. The Secretariat has a staff of over 1 800.

There are in addition numerous committees, which may also meet at ministerial level. This is being done more and more. The committee's work relates to economic policy, economic and development review, energy policy, industry, steel, agriculture, fisheries, maritime transport, tourism, scientific and technological policy, manpower and social affairs, education, environment, trade, competition law and policy, capital movements and invisible transactions, fiscal affairs, international investment and multinational enterprises, insurance, consumer policy, financial markets, development assistance, information, computer and communications policy. In addition there are autonomous and semi-autonomous bodies and programmes: the International Energy Agency, the Nuclear Energy Agency, the Centre for Educational Research and Innovation, the Development Centre.

Furthermore, each committee has set up working parties or expert groups.

A Business and Industry Advisory Committee and a Trade Unions Advisory Committee make their views known on the positions adopted by member countries.

The Commission of the EEC takes part in the work of the Organization.

4. FUNCTIONS AND OPERATION

A. *General economic cooperation*

1. *Provisions*

To attain the objectives of the OECD, the member states must, both individually and jointly, make proper use of available resources, promote scientific research and vocational training, endeavour to achieve economic growth and both internal and external financial stability (thereby obviating situations which could endanger their own economies or those of other countries), and make further efforts to lower barriers to the exchange of goods and services and current payments, and to capital movements. Finally, help must be furnished to less-developed countries, more particularly by the provision of capital, but also by technical assistance and the widening of markets (Article 2).

Member states pool their information and provide the OECD with all the data needed for the accomplishment of its task. They are in constant contact with each other and work in close collaboration on joint projects (Article 3).

2. *Operation*

a. *General economic policy*

The Economic Policy Committee consists of the leading officials responsible for economic policy decisions in each OECD country, meeting at regular intervals, and has in practice become the forum where problems of coordination of economic policies of member countries are the most thoroughly discussed. The Committee has several working groups: Working Party No. 3 on Policies for the Promotion of Better International Payments Equilibrium for example, has particular responsibility for overseeing balance-of-payments and exchange-rate adjustment.

Of course, opinions are influenced by the general political climate. This is reflected in OECD advice: Keynesian points of view are succeeded by 'classical' statements.

In 1975 an "expert group of economists to examine the policy issues involved in the pursuit of non-inflationary economic growth" was set up. Its report *Towards full employment and price stability* (8 April 1977) concludes that the recession was the result of an "unusual bunching of unfortunate disturbances" and advises an active, but cautious demand management policy, accompanied by the establishment and publication of budgetary and monetary targets. Although rejecting detailed intervention in price and incomes determination, it is in favour of an incomes policy, including measures to reward or penalize those who conform to the policy guidelines or fail to do so.

Three years later the Council meeting at ministerial level made vague statements in the same vein: "Belgium, Canada, France, Germany, Italy, Japan, Switzerland and the United Kingdom should ensure, by appropriate measures . . . , that the expansion of their domestic demand is significantly greater than in 1977 or, where capacity is already fully utilized, should ensure that the total demand increases in line with productive capacity".

In 1979 the Council was less one-sided: "Cautious demand management policies should . . . be combined with action — or the unwinding of previous actions — to improve the supply side by benefiting from lower cost imports, encouraging investment, and facilitating necessary structural adjustment". The following year it stressed that "the basic aim is to restore price stability and to promote in both the short and the medium term the conditions for investment-led supply-oriented growth in output and employment". And to quote a report on activities of OECD in 1980: "The best 'social' policy is probably an economic policy that provides more jobs. But this means that we have to accept constraints on total welfare spending in order to provide increased investment, and concentrate on making the best use of the welfare we can afford".

Each year an important number of publications come out. They include projections and country studies.

The economic projections of the OECD emphasise international consistency. An inbuilt assumption in the forecasting is that neither oil prices nor economic policy will vary over the forecast horizon (18 months). The results are published in the bi-annual OECD *Economic Outlook*. The *Employment Outlook*, published yearly, complements the *Economic Outlook* by spelling out their labour-market implications.

According to the Economic Outlook of June 1989 ". . . projections embody the view that monetary tightening has been broadly sufficient to cause output growth . . . to moderate and inflation to stabilise. Specifically, growth is projected to slow to a little over 3 per cent this year and a little under that in 1990."

The economic policy of each member country is discussed once a year by the Economic and Development Review Committee. It makes recommendations to the country being examined, in the light of the broader policy framework agreed among OECD countries. The related documents are published as the OECD's *Economic Surveys*.

b. *Energy*

The importance attached to energy problems has increased since the energy crisis in 1973.

On 18 November 1974 an agreement on an international energy programme was signed. The main aims are security of oil supply, the setting up of an information system on the oil market, long-term cooperation and a dialogue between oil-producing and oil-consuming countries. To carry out the programme an International Energy Agency (IEA) was established.

The IEA is an autonomous body within the OECD. The IEA Agreement is open for accession by any member of the OECD (Article 71,*1* of the Agreement). Finland, France and Iceland have not acceded; Norway participates under the terms of a special agreement.

The administrative structure of the IEA consists of a Governing Board, a Management Committee, four Standing Groups and a Secretariat (Article 49,*1* and *3*). The Governing Board, composed of one or more ministers or their delegates from each of the member countries, is the principal vehicle for decision-making (Articles 50—52). It is assisted by the Management Committee, composed of one or more senior representatives of each participating country (Article 53), and by four standing groups, which are responsible for emergency questions, the oil market, long-term cooperation and relations with producer and other consumer countries (Article 49,*1*).

The Secretariat assists the Governing Board and standing groups; it is also responsible for arriving at the findings required to activate emergency measures and for coordinating the on-going work of the Programme (Articles 59—60).

There are three types of weighted votes in the Governing Board:

a) voting weights which are the same for each country (general voting weights);
b) weights based on each country's consumption of oil; and
c) combined voting weights; i.e. the sum of (*a*) and (*b*) (Article 62,*2*).

Where the Agreement calls for binding decisions by a "majority" (mostly operational decisions), it requires votes of countries with sixty per cent of the total combined voting weights and fifty per cent of the general voting weights cast (Article 62,*3*). Fresh commitments of a substantial nature require unanimous decision (Article 61).

To meet oil supply emergencies each participant must maintain stand-by demand restraint measures (Article 5,*1*) and oil reserves which would be sufficient to sustain consumption for 60 days (Article 2,*1*). Pursuant to Article 2,*2*, the emergency reserve commitment was raised as from 1 January 1976 to 70 days and from 1 January 1980 to 90 days.

Emergency allocations are possible when the participants as a whole (or one or several countries) sustain (or expect to sustain) a seven per cent reduction in oil supplies (even though oil supplies to the group as a whole have not declined) (Article 13 and 17,*1*). According to the case, each country (or the country concerned) would be required to reduce oil consumption by seven per cent or by ten per cent if the aggregate shortfall were twelve per cent or more (Article 13 and 17,*1*). So far the emergency system has not been put in operation.

The IEA has to proceed with plans for the development of an extensive oil market data-gathering system (Article 25). A standing group on the oil market reports on oil prices and oil company finances and organizes consultations with these companies.

In order to reduce their dependence on imported oil, the members have undertaken cooperative programmes in four main areas:

a) conservation of energy;
b) development of alternative resources;
c) energy research and development, and
d) uranium enrichment (Articles 41 and 42).

The projects are financed by the participants and not by a central IEA fund. In order "to assure that only activities of high mutual interest and value will be undertaken", projects are either task-sharing (each participant bears their own costs) or jointly-funded (all project members contribute to a common fund). The exchange of technical information may be either of the task-sharing or of the jointly-funded type.

By the end of 1975, IEA members had committed themselves to reducing imports of oil by 8 per cent in 1976 and 6 percent in 1977 below the level of 1973. As it happened, oil imports into the IEA region were 1.8 per cent below the 1973 level in 1976 and 1.8 per cent above the level in 1977. Subsequent projects overestimated oil import requirement.

On 30 January 1976 the Ministers adopted a long-term cooperation programme. It provided *inter alia* protection for investment in energy production in IEA countries through a "minimum safeguard price". The measure aimed at reducing the investment risk in more expensive conventional energy sources which would have resulted from a sudden fall in the price of lower-cost oil produced outside the IEA area. Imported crude oil could not be sold in the IEA markets below a safeguard price. As one might expect, there was no further mention of this measure in later reports.

The Steering Committee for Nuclear Energy and the ENEA continued to operate within the framework of the OECD. As a result of the admission of Japan in 1972, the Agency's name was changed to Nuclear Energy Agency (NEA). At present, the NEA groups all OECD countries except New Zealand.

The Eurochemic plant at Mol ceased reprocessing operations in 1974 and is now carrying out a research programme. On 30 October 1978 a convention between Belgium and Eurochemic came into force in order to transfer progressively to that country the industrial site owned by Eurochemic. The Dragon project at Winfrith came to an end on 31 March 1975. Continued support was given to the Halden project.

Since 1973 greater attention has been given to such problems as safety of nuclear installations and radioactive waste management. The NEA Incident Reporting System contained approximately 1250 event descriptions. On 22 July 1977 a multilateral consultation and surveillance mechanism for sea dumping of radioactive waste was set up. NEA sponsors an experiment in Sweden, designed to examine how deep geological formation can be used to dispose of radioactive waste. On 1 January 1978 a NEA Data Bank was created at Saclay (France).

NEA joint projects include the Halden project (see above), the Loft project (United States), the examination of the damaged core of the TMI reactor (Three Mile Island — United States), the TMI vessel investigation project, the programme on inspection of steel components and the decommissioning of nuclear facilities.

c. *Environment*

The Environment Committee set up in 1970 reviews and confronts projects undertaken or proposed in member countries in the field of environment and proposes solutions for the problems concerned.

In May 1971 an "early warning" system came into force under which any member country has to notify member countries of any measures which might affect the trade or economic interest of those countries to a substantial extent. The formal procedures of this system have largely been replaced by the more informal procedures of an information exchange provided for in a 1977 chemicals programme.

In May 1972, the Council meeting at ministerial level adopted a set of "guiding principles concerning international economic aspects of environmental policies". National measures to combat pollution have to aim at better management of scarce environmental resources and should not create distortions in international trade. In addition, the "Polluter pays principle" must be adhered to. (Exceptions and special arrangements, particularly for transitional periods, are possible.) Where there are no reasons for differences, governments should harmonize their environmental policies. Environmental measures should avoid the creation of non-tariff barriers to trade. If products liable to cause pollution enter into international trade, governments must determine common product standards.

According to the Notification Procedure of Financial Systems for Pollution Prevention and Control the OECD has to gather the most recent information on the amount and the nature of various aid given for pollution control. Member countries regularly reply to an appropriate questionnaire.

A recommendation of 1974 contains a set of principles relating to transfrontier pollution. Those responsible for transfrontier pollution should be treated in the same way as polluters in their own country. There should be prior consultation between the countries concerned before any new activity is undertaken which could be harmful to the environment in another country.

The Council has approved a system for testing chemicals before they come onto the market. It has created standards so that tests made in one member country are accepted by the others. In addition, it has made numerous recommendations or decisions on noise abatement, water management, transfrontier pollution and control of international shipment of hazardous wastes. OECD publications in this field include *The macro-economic impact of environmental expenditure* (1985). In 1985, 1987 and 1989 the OECD published an *Environmental Data Compendium*. There is little or no progress with respect to water pollution by nitrates, air pollution from transport activities, exposure to noise and the hazards related to toxic chemicals.

d. *Central and Eastern Europe*

The Organization has set up a Centre for Cooperation with European Economies in Transition (to a market economy and a pluralistic democracy) on 4 June 1991 agreements for technical assistance were signed with Poland, Hungary and the Czech and Slovak Federal Republic.

B. *Liberalization of goods, invisible transactions and capital*

1. *Provisions*

Apart from the above-mentioned provisions relating to general economic cooperation, there are no specific provisions on liberalization of goods, invisible transactions and capital. In fact, the codes established by the OEEC in respect of invisible transactions, capital movements and multilateral settlements were duly adopted by the OECD, on the understanding that the United States and Canada had decided to allow European cooperation to continue as before without their participation.

2. *Operation*

a. *Goods*

The member countries agreed to consult each other about any difficulties that may arise as a result of any of the member states repealing certain liberalization measures.

The Trade Committee examines, in the light of the OECD's aims (the expansion of world trade on a multilateral and non-discriminatory basis), trade policy questions which are of practical and topical interest (e.g., the relation between the EEC and the EFTA countries). When a country ascertains that it is suffering prejudice through the regulations obtaining in another member country, the former may request the Committee to carry out an immediate investigation with a view to eliminating the regulations concerned and limiting the prejudice.

At the Council meeting at ministerial level in May 1974, the so-called "trade pledge" was adopted, by virtue of which the Member Governments committed themselves to take no unilateral protectionist measures for a period of one year. The pledge also applied to the restriction or stimulation of exports. The commitment has been extended, successively for one-year periods. In June 1980 the Council (at ministerial level) adopted a Trade Declaration to supersede the Trade Pledge. The Declaration is wider-than the Pledge, unlimited in time and contains provisions for follow-up procedures.

Studies of problems associated with credit and export insurance, government purchasing and export controls have been instituted.

In June 1972 the Council established an exchange-of-information system relating to export credits of terms of more than five years. Each country can grant the most advantageous terms envisaged by its partners for a given transaction but may not exceed these terms without notifying the other participants. The Council also instituted a prior notification procedure applying to credits between industrialized countries and supported by the European countries (except for Austria, Finland, Greece, Iceland and Portugal) in the OECD, as well as Canada and Australia. Each participant must notify every other participant of the terms envisaged for credits of more than five years' duration; before it can take its decision it has to hear of the views of its partners, which must be formulated within a prescribed time-limit.

An "Arrangement on guidelines for officially supported export credits" came into effect on 1 April 1978 (an amended text on 15 July 1988); it is implemented by all OECD countries (except for Iceland and Turkey). It is still called the "Consensus" like a similar agreement of July 1976. It tries to prevent an export credit race by providing the framework for an orderly export credit market. The most important conditions are: (a) at least 15 per cent of the contract is to be covered by cash payments; (b) the maximum repayment terms are five years for relatively rich countries, eight-and-a-half year for 'intermediate' countries and ten years for relatively poorer countries; (c) minimum rates for interest are set for up to five and eight-and-a-half years and are subject to changes in January and July (Table 20; for relatively rich countries the commercial interest rate, determined each month according to the currencies being used is the only minimum). Several sectors (e.g., agriculture) remain outside the scope of the Arrangement. Others, including power and aircraft, are covered by separate agreements.

The Trade Committee encourages member states to open up their markets for products from the less-developed countries. Studies on this subject, especially in connection with the GSP, are made in cooperation with UNCTAD.

Table 20. OECD guidelines for officially supported export credits (since 15 January 1991).

Classification of country	Number of years in maximum repayment terms	
	Over 2—5	Over 5
Intermediate	10.05	10.55
Relatively poor	9.20	9.20

Sourc : OECD.

A *Guide to legislation on restrictive business practices* is kept up to date by the Committee of Experts on Restrictive Business Practices.

In 1967 the Council recommended a notification and exchange-of-information procedure and in 1973 a consultation and conciliation procedure in the field of restrictive business practices affecting international trade.

b. *Invisible transactions*

The Council approved the Code of Liberalization of Current Invisible Transactions on 12 December 1961.

By accepting the Code the member states agree to approve all payments made in connection with the transactions listed in an appendix to the Code (Article 2,*a*). This list concerns such items as costs incurred in repairs and processing, technical assistance, patents and copyrights, wages and salaries, the participation of subsidiaries in the parent companies' overheads, social security contributions, investment income, private travel, immigrants' remittances. All liberalization measures and amendments thereto are notified to the Organization (Article 11,*a*).

Each member has the right to stipulate reservations in respect of these obligations (Article 2,*b* and Appendix). Such reservations are subjected to regular scrutiny (Article 12,*b*). In cases in which the Code is not applicable, the member states are urged to take as liberal a view as possible (Article 1,*b*). Discrimination is prohibited (Article 9). Countries which are members of a special monetary system or customs union, however, are allowed to take additional reciprocal liberalization measures without including other members states in their scope (Article 10).

Efforts must be made to extend the liberalization measures to overseas territories and to all members of the IMF (Article 1,*c* and *d*).

The provisions of the Code do not represent an obstacle to the maintenance of public order, the protection of public health, morals and safety, or the fulfilment of obligations relating to international security or peace (Article 3). Nor do they conflict with obligations resulting from international multilateral agreements such as the IMF (Article 4).

Escape clauses are allowed if justified by an unfavourable economic and financial position or an adverse balance of payments. In the latter case, a time limit of twelve months is fixed for the resumption of partial liberalization and eighteen months for the resumption of full liberalization. No detriment may be unnecessarily caused to the interests of other member countries, and discrimination is to be avoided (Article 7); the procedure for notification and examination is governed by Articles 13, 14 and 15. To the extent that all these factors are taken into account, the liberalization measures remain applicable to the countries concerned (Article 8).

When a country has reason to believe that a partner state is using internal measures to evade regulations, that state may bring the matter before the OECD, which makes any proposals that may be required (Article 16). An appeal to the OECD is also permissible when a country fails to fulfill its obligations (Article 17,*a*).

Withdrawal of a member state's adherence to the Code must be notified twelve months in advance (Article 23). The Committee for Invisible Transactions (subsequently changed to Committee on Capital Movements and Invisible Transactions) supervises the implementation of the Code (Articles 19 and 20); its reports are examined by the Payments Committee (Article 21).

In September 1972, the Council extended the provisions of the Code to printed films and similar material. The decision was extended to video-cassettes in 1973.

The Committee on Capital Movements and Invisible transactions examines the reasons why some governments maintain obstacles to trade and investment.

In the insurance sector the impediments concern restrictions on establishment; others relate to specific insurance transactions between residents and non-residents. The Council approved a number of revisions and amendments to the insurance section of the Code in 1985. It also extended the tourism section of the Code in the same year (e.g., the unlimited use of credit cards abroad for tourism purposes). In 1989 the coverage of the banking and financial provisions was completed (they include short-term capital movements and cross-border services).

c. *Capital*

By the terms of the Code of Liberalization of Capital Movements, adopted on 12 December 1961, member states must gradually remove obstacles impeding capital movements to the extent necessary to ensure efficient economic cooperation (Article 1,*a*). More specifically, they will sanction transactions and transfers of the type referred to in List 1 of Annex A (Article 12,*a*). Among these are direct investments, the use and transfer of non-resident owned funds, and the transfer of securities, the issuing of credits and the granting of loans. Here again, any member state may stipulate reservations (Article 2,*b*); a list of those permissible is given in Annex B. All reservations lodged are regularly reexamined (Article 12,*b*).

In so far as their balances of payments and monetary reserves allow, member states must approve transactions and transfers as specified in List 2 of Annex A (Article 2,*a*); these relate to the liquidation of direct investments, including capital gains, and certain credits and loans (Article 2,*c*).

When, in accordance with a regulation or an international agreement, loans are authorized between the residents of various member countries (other than by the issue of national negotiable securities or by the use in the borrower's country of currency subject to transfer restriction), repayment may be effected in the currency of either of the two member countries concerned (Article 2,*d*).

Member states follow the same policy in respect of the assets of non-residents, regardless of the date on which acquired, as they do in respect of their own nationals, especially as regards the liquidation of such assets and the transfer of assets or their liquidation proceeds (Article 1,*b*).

All other provisions conform to the stipulations of the Code of Liberalization of Current Invisible Transactions.

The Committee on Capital Movements and Invisible Transactions is also responsible for supervising the fulfilment of the provisions concerning the liberalization of capital movements (cf. Articles 18 and 19).

The Code concerning capital movements was amplified in 1964 (new categories were incorporated and others were liberalized to a greater extent), in 1973 to include collective investment securities and the admission of securities on all recognized markets, and in 1989 when nearly all capital movements were liberalized, the only exceptions being mortgage and consumer credits and operations by governments on their own account.

On 12 October 1967, a Model Convention on the protection of foreign property was adopted. The Council put into effect recommendations on international security issues (14 March 1972), on standard rules for the operations of institutions for collective investment in securities (11 April 1972) and on the minimum disclosure and procedure rules to be complied with before securities may be offered to the public (22 February 1976).

In 1977, a revised version of a 1963 Draft Convention, the "Model convention for the avoidance of double taxation with respect to taxes on incomes and on capital", was approved. In 1982 a similar convention with respect to taxes on estates and inheritances and on gifts was published.

On 21 January 1975, a Committee on International Investment and Multinational Enterprises was set up. On 21 June 1976, the Council recommended to multinational enterprises the observance of the Guidelines established by the Committee, i.e., rules of conduct as to the disclosure of information, competition, finance, taxation, employment and industrial relations, science and technology. The Guidelines also prohibit bribing holders of public office.

In addition, the governments concerned agreed that foreign enterprises operating in their territories should receive treatment no less favourable than that accorded in similar situations to domestic enterprises.

The Committee on International Investment and Multinational Enterprises is in charge of the consultations on matters relating to the Guidelines. A member country may ask the Committee to give individual enterprises the opportunity to comment on the application of the Guidelines. An individual enterprise, however, is not obliged to accept such an invitation and the aim of the consultations is not "to lead the Committee to reach conclusions on the conduct of individual enterprises":

Since it is "rather difficult to discern any substantial systematic differences in the behaviour of national and international firms" (A. Lindbeck) one wonders why the Code is confined to the latter. Moreover, no nationalized multinational enterprises have subscribed to the Code. So far, the Committee meetings have taken the form of Court sessions (the trade unions acting as prosecutors), which is not the function for which it was set up, creating at the same time hostility towards the procedure among the multinational enterprises.

d. *Multilateral settlements*

Any member state could be authorized by the OECD to adhere to the EMA (Article 28,*a* and *b*, of the Agreement); Australia, Canada, Finland, Japan and the United States did not accede.

The European Fund provided the member countries with the credits necessary to withstand temporary balance-of-payments difficulties and to maintain liberalization. The Fund was also intended to facilitate the operation of the multilateral settlements system (Article 2).

The capital of the Fund was formed by the transfer of capital from the EPU (271 575 000 dollars) and by contributions from the member countries (335 925 000 dollars). The initial amount of 600 million units of account, was brought up to 607.5 million units when Spain joined in July 1959. The largest contributions were those of Britain (60 575 000), Western Germany (50 million) and France (50 million). Payment deferments up to 56.85 million units of account were granted to certain countries (Denmark, Greece, Norway, Turkey and Iceland) until such time as the other member states had paid their contributions in full.

The maximum credit term was originally two years; from 1 January 1962 this was extended to three years (Article 7).

The Agreement comprised three obligations for the member states:

1. To fix buying and selling rates in their own currency for gold, the dollar or another currency in order to avoid variations in exchange rates. These rates are taken as a basis for the monthly settlements (Article 9,*a*). Should there be a variation in the exchange rate, the unexpended balances

in the currency concerned are settled at once at the earlier rate (special settlement; Article 13).

2. To make available to the other member states, when requested and during the periods between settlements dates, a specific amount in their own currency (interim finance) without demanding payment in gold or foreign currency (Article 10,*a*); an equivalent amount may be borrowed from member countries (Article 10,*b*). Outstanding sums bear interest (Article 10,*c*).

In principle, a bilateral settlement is incompatible with the multilateral settlements system. It is, however, permissible between member states whose currencies are non-convertible or between one such state and a convertible-currency country.

3. To notify each month advances made in connection with the intersettlement credits, holdings of the currencies of the other member states and balances resulting from bilateral payments agreements, in so far as the credit margins are exceeded (Article 11,*a*). In contrast with the system employed in the EPU, transactions are regularly settled on the exchange market at the rate of the day (except in the case of the bilateral balance referred to above, which are adjusted at the agreed exchange rate). The new agreement does not entail the automatic granting of credits (Article 11,*b*).

The balances were calculated at the end of each month by the Bank for International Settlements, which acted on behalf of the EMA, on the basis of the above-mentioned information. Bilateral claims and debts were compensated reciprocally; the balance was a debt due to or owed by the European Fund. Payments were made in dollars (Article 12).

Where a debtor failed to pay, the Fund became substitute for that country to the extent of 50 million dollars. Above this amount, the creditor countries paid the Fund and had bilateral claims as regards the defaulting member. As soon as the debtor country had extinguished its debt, the creditors were reimbursed (Article 12,*c*).

The EMA was operated by a Board of Management under the authority of the Council (Article 17). The Board was composed of a maximum of eight members appointed by the Council. Representatives of the United States, the IMF and the Bank for International Settlements, as well as the chairman of the Payments Committee, attended meetings but had no vote (Article 19).

At first the Agreement was extended every year. On 1 January 1966, it was renewed and revised for three years. The changes introduced were as follows: credits up to the equivalent of 50 million dollars to member countries for up to one year, which had previously needed a unanimous vote in the OECD, were to be granted by the Board of Management of the EMA; and small credits made available by individual member countries to other member states, hitherto repayable at the end of the month in which borrowed, could be extended for two months. At the end of 1968 the EMA was renewed until 31 December 1971, with its provisions broadly unchanged. The EMA was renewed for the last time at the end of 1971, until 31 December 1972.

Up to the time of liquidation, only 38 million units of account in member states' contributions had been called up; together with the unexpended EPU balance of 148 037 000 units of account, therefore, the available capital amounted to 186 037 000 units of account.

Most of the credits granted were for Turkey; this country received sixteen credits (498.9 million units of account or 75 per cent of the total credits granted). In 1962 a consortium was formed to implement the aid to Turkey; this consortium was composed of representatives from fifteen member countries and from the IBRD. Representatives of the IMF and the European Investment Bank (EIB) attended as observers. A consortium was also set up for aid to Greece in 1962 (eleven members countries, the IMF and EIB sending observers and the IBRD associating itself with the consortium's activities). This country received two credits (totalling 45 million units of account). Three credits have been granted to Iceland (22 million) and one to Spain (100 million).

The most recourse to the interim finance scheme was had by Greece (99 per cent), but as repayment was made before the end of the month, no notification (for the purposes of the multilateral settlements system) needed to be given. The largest suppliers were Western Germany (37 per cent) and Italy (19 per cent). Interest was raised from 2 to 2.5 per cent on 1 July 1959 and to 3 per cent on 1 February 1960. Since 31 March 1963 there have been no further calls on the scheme.

All the central banks established the exchange rates for their currencies and the permitted margins (approximately 0.75 per cent).

The faculty of declaring foreign currency balances (in connection with the exchange guarantees attaching to them) was used only in case of exchange-rate changes. When there is no danger of a change in the exchange rate, it is more advantageous to carry out transactions in the more favourable exchange market.

Up to February 1963 there were no limits on the amounts of the balances which could benefit from the exchange guarantee. Britain requested the abolition of this guarantee, mainly on the grounds that convertibility had been restored (and also that the guarantee does not apply to sterling balances of non-EMA countries). Other states felt that this guarantee made for currency stability. Finally, the guarantee was maintained but only up to a certain limit (in respect of the sterling balances and of equivalent amounts in EMA countries' currencies with the Bank of England).

From 1959 balances under bilateral settlement agreement with credit margins, which also have to be declared within the framework of the multi-lateral settlements system, decreased from year to year. The number of these agreements declined too. The last of them (between Greece and Turkey) terminated on 31 October 1964.

All this explains why the multilateral settlements system's role has been only a minor one. The cumulative total of settlements amounted to 94.5 million units of account (see Table 21).

In view of the IMF facilities for balance-of-payments assistance, it was decided on 13 December 1972 that the European Fund was no longer needed and could be liquidated.

The Fund's capital has been distributed to members; the "residual capital", which originated in a contribution by the United States to the founding of the EPU, has been returned to that country. The outstanding assets represented by claims on Turkey (114 million dollars) have been consolidated into a 30-year credit. In April 1979 OECD countries pledged special aid for Turkey and agreed on a new rescheduling of Turkish debts.

An agreement between the central banks of the European OECD countries and Australia provided an exchange guarantee of the amounts held by a central bank on account with another central bank, in the latter's national currency, which were used as working balances. This agreement was concluded on 13 December 1972 for an initial period of three years; it was extended for a further period of three years on 7 November 1975, but only the claims and liabilities outstanding on 1 January 1976 remained in effect. (No new claims or liabilities could arise.) The agreement expired at the end of 1978.

In 1975 an agreement was signed on the creation of a Financial Support Fund (the so-called "safety net"), which had to be used only as a last resort (after members had made use of other facilities, such as are available in the IMF). The quotas totalled 20 billion SDR. The maturity of the loans was not to exceed more than seven years. As the United States postponed ratification however, the Agreement did not come into force.

C. *Relations with less-developed countries*

The DAC does not give financial assistance but endeavours to stimulate and coordinate financial aid to the less-developed countries. Most OECD member countries and the Commission of the EEC are members of the DAC. (Greece, Iceland, Luxemburg, Portugal, Spain and Turkey are not.)

Since 1962 the Committee has also carried out a comparative survey of the various member states' programmes.

Research on development issues is the main function of the OECD Development Centre, created in 1962.

The programme of technical assistance to four member countries (Greece, Portugal, Spain and Turkey) and one associated country (Yugoslavia) covers policy formulation, planning and innovation of suitable methods and techniques.

The Club des Amis du Sahel was set up in December 1975, with the assistance of the OECD, "to provide an informal framework for bringing

Table 21. Payments by (+) or to (−) the European Fund, within the EMA multilateral settlement, in thousand units of account, 1959—72.

Country	1959	1960	1961	1962	1963	1964	1967	1968	1969	1972	Total 1959—71	Net payments
Austria	+10527	+8676	+5880	—	—	—	+823	—	+30	—	+25936	+25936
	—	—	—	—	—	—	—	—	—	—	—	
Belgium	—	—	—	—	—	—	+633	—	+129	+124	+886	—
	—	—	—	—	—	—	—	—	—	—	—	+886
Denmark	+10	+207	+23	—	—	—	+1830	+9	+171	1783	+4033	—
	−67	−83	—	—	—	—	−2434	—	—	—	−2584	+1449
France	—	—	—	—	—	—	+1383	—	—	+2471	+3854	—
	—	—	—	—	—	—	—	—	−24995	—	−24995	−21141
Germany (Western)	—	—	—	—	—	—	+3444	—	+285	+4470	+8199	—
	—	—	—	—	—	—	—	—	—	—	—	+8199
Greece	−10707	−9283	+262	—	+286	+141	+1210	—	+116	+1121	+3315	—
	—	—	−4924	−2314	−736	−799	—	—	—	—	−28762	−25627
Ireland	—	−1	—	—	—	—	+306	—	+5	—	+312	—
	—	—	−23	—	—	—	−9	−9	—	—	−42	+270
Italy	+243	—	—	—	—	—	+1047	—	+514	+1936	+3739	—
	—	—	—	—	—	—	—	—	—	—	—	+3739
Netherlands	+1400	—	—	—	—	—	+1604	—	+21	—	+3025	—
	−1378	—	—	—	—	—	—	—	—	—	−1378	+1647
Norway	+44	+343	+274	+97	+130	—	+12	—	+4	—	+906	—
	−876	−1045	−251	−323	−10	—	—	—	—	—	−2505	−1600
Portugal	—	—	—	—	—	—	+1926	—	+20813	—	+22739	—

Table 21. (Continued)

Country	1959	1960	1961	1962	1963	1964	1967	1968	1969	1972	Total 1959—71	Net payments
Spain	—	—	—	—	—	—	+53	—	+1 237	+13	+1 303	—
	—	—	—	—	—	—	—	—	—	—	—	+1 303
Sweden	−243	—	—	—	—	—	+2 447	—	+28	—	+2 475	—
	—	—	—	—	—	—	—	—	—	—	−243	+2 232
Switzerland	—	—	—	—	—	—	+2 338	—	+212	—	+2 550	—
	—	—	—	—	—	—	—	—	—	—	—	+2 550
Turkey	+2 350	+2 202	+654	+2 539	+667	+799	+132	—	+734	—	+10 078	—
	−1 304	−1 016	−1 895	—	−337	−141	—	—	—	—	−4 694	+5 384
United Kingdom	—	—	—	—	—	—	+624	—	+696	—	+1 320	—
	—	—	—	—	—	—	−17 368	—	—	−11 918	−29 286	−27 966
Totals	14 574	11 428	7 093	2 636	1 083	940	19 812	9	24 995	11 918	94 489	—

Source: *European Monetary Agreement. Annual Report of the Board of Management, 1959—72.*

together actual and potential aid donors, African regional organizations and the Sahelian countries" in order to discuss the long-term development of the Sahel.

Most OECD members adopted the UN target of 0.7 per cent for concessionary aid. Following the untying of contributions to multilateral institutions agreed upon in October 1973, a majority of DAC members joined on 4 June 1974 a Memorandum of understanding on untying of bilateral development loans. In fact, in 1982—83 56.9 per cent of the official development assistance was untied.

In 1987 the total resource flows to less-developed countries totalled 89 billion dollar of which 59 billion official development finance and 30 billion private flows. The DAC countries provide approximately 80 per cent of official development finance, the OPEC and the CMEA contribute each about 10 per cent.

In a review of 25 years development cooperation (1985) the OECD states that "one of the compelling lessons of experience is that aid can only be as effective as the policy, economic and administrative environment in which it operates . . . Self-reliance in the sense of independence from major reliance on external subsidies remains the ultimate objective of aid . . . Particular care must . . . be taken with forms of aid which tend to prolong aid dependence. Forms of aid which carry that risk include in particular food aid, open-ended budget support, other prolonged recurrent-cost financing, and major reliance on expatriate experts for regular operational tasks".

APPRAISAL

For the purposes of appraisal, OEEC and OECD must again be treated separately.

The Organization for European Economic Cooperation

It cannot be denied that the OEEC achieved something as regards the recovery of the European economy (during the few years covered by the European Recovery Programme approximately 13 billion dollars were allocated) and the liberalization of trade and payments. Although exceptions had to be granted in the case of certain states because of internal economic difficulties, the majority of the member countries met their commitments. As the liberalization percentages were stepped up, additional obligations became increasingly difficult to meet. *Ipso facto*, tariffs often became more important than quantitative restrictions as barriers to trade. Little account was taken of the ban on artificial means of promoting exports.

The EPU's function was an important one. The reciprocal credit system did much to stimulate the recovery of the European economy. Progress was made in the liberalization of invisible transactions and capital movements.

In addition, the OEEC (it will be the sole task of its successor, the OECD) acted as a kind of permanent economic conference, providing an opportunity for discussion of such matters as the repercussions of each member state's measures on its partners. On the occasion of each yearly justification of their economic policies, the member states were prevailed upon to view them in an international context. The harmonization of national recovery programmes, e.g., in respect of investments, was attained to only a very limited extent: it was not possible to persuade the member states to alter their plans materially.

The Organization for Economic Cooperation and Development

Owing to the establishment of EEC and EFTA the OECD no longer had an important role to play in matters relating to European economic integration. Indeed, liberalization of goods was almost completed and invisible transactions largely liberalized. Further liberalization of capital movements, on the other hand, proved impossible at that time, many countries fearing the huge pool of free funds in the Eurodollar market.

The main requirement for progress in economic integration is coordination of economic policies of the members concerned. But such coordination is also desirable with the non-member countries. Coordination of the economic policies of all developed countries has, in fact, become the principal aim of the OECD. But it is also the aim of the Groups of Five, Seven and Ten. So far such coordination has not being achieved (small wonder, if one considers that this was not even possible in the EEC). Since the OECD does not allocate money, it has little influence on its members' policies. Some countries such as Germany and Japan give priority to fighting inflation; other countries prefer job-creating policies, even if these involve "easier" monetary and fiscal policies, not realizing that in the longer run these policies will endanger employment.

The regular exchange of useful information (the OECD pioneered comparable economic statistics) and discussion of the problems concerned has, however, in many cases contributed to the adoption of national decisions which have avoided harmful consequences for other economies. But the Organization has often given wrong advice to its members. For example, the OECD predicted zero growth for the Swiss economy in 1977 and the recommended policy was based on that assumption: in fact, a growth rate of 4.3 per cent was achieved. No wonder the Swiss did not follow the OECD's advice. A similar observation can be made about the biannual forecasts of the OECD.

Until 1978 the OECD's views on economic policy has been invariably

Keynesian. The advantages of monetary policy are ignored. Since 1978 they have been less unilateral and the Organization is less suspicious concerning the efficiency of the market.

One of the major drawbacks of the OECD (as well as of many other international organizations) is that it concerns itself with all conceivable problems. In 1969 the Council even called on the Organization to pursue its efforts to solve "the problems of modern society" and in 1980 a high-level conference discussed "The role of women in society"! Notwithstanding the existence of UNESCO, Ministers of Education of OECD countries met in 1978 to discuss "Future education policies in changing social and economic context". The activities of the FAO, the EEC and the ILO do not prevent the OECD from discussing agricultural and social problems.

The OECD has, in fact, become a huge publishing house. When its own publications — mostly of high quality — are judged to be insufficient in number, 'publications' are ordered from outsiders. And these publications are open to many criticisms even if "the opinions expressed and arguments employed ... are the responsibility of the authors and do not represent necessarily those of the OECD". Why, for example, is a poor person "one whose income is below two-thirds of the average per capita disposable income of the country"? (cf. "Public expenditures on income maintenance programs", OECD, 1976).

The OECD demonstrates remarkable activity but one searches in vain for concrete decisions.

The declarations and recommendations of the OECD are full of generalities and one wonders why expensive meetings are needed for that purpose. An example is a declaration made after a meeting of the ministers of national education in 1978. They agreed that "the following aims deserve priority consideration ... to promote the continuous development of educational standards as conceived within each country, and to ensure that all young people are helped to acquire the basic competences needed to embark successfully upon adult life". Another example: "Governments of OECD countries agree that trade policy has a major role to play in the framework of an overall strategy for sustained and non-inflationary growth in the world economy" (1980), "The situation and performance of developing countries vary widely. However, central to the prospects of all is a global economic environment conducive to strong and sustainable growth" (1988).

Also the numerous centres set up by the OECD, such as the IEA, yield very few results. "Some of the more significant 'IEA' projects have essentially been limited United States-German projects, that could have been developed by those two governments apart from the IEA framework" (R. O. Keohane). In 1979 and despite IEA regulations, member states competed with each other for the reduced supplies of oil after Iran's shut-down of production.

Whether the above-mentioned exchange of information and discussion of the problems concerned requires the creation of a special international organization is doubtful. Non-institutional groupings such as the Groups of

Ten, Seven or Five have been set up for this purpose. The OECD owes its origin more to the desire to preserve the administrative machinery of the OEEC than to the necessity of resolving urgent problems. Its "infinitesimal productivity, given the efforts made" (F. Couigneau) has been regretted.

BIBLIOGRAPHY

A. *The OEEC*

1. *OEEC and OECD publications*

The *Annual reports* of OEEC, especially the 9th report: *A decade of cooperation. Achievements and perspectives* (Paris, 1958); the *Annual reports of the EPU*. See also *The OEEC. History and structure* (8th edn, Paris, 1960). The numerous publications issued by the Organization are listed in the 1958 catalogue. *From Marshall Plan to global interdependence. New challenges for the industrialized nations* (Paris, OECD, 1978) is more forward-looking than historical.

2. *Other publications*

There are comparatively few recent studies on the OEEC: most of the articles were published during the years 1950—55. Reference may be made to the relevant chapters in J. L'Huillier, *Théorie et pratique de la coopération économique internationale* (Paris, Editions Génin, 1957) and in M. Palmer *et al.*, *European unity. A survey of European organizations* (London, George Allen & Unwin, 1968).

On the origins of the OEEC and the policy of the United States: M. Beloff, *The United States and the unity of Europe* (London, Faber & Faber, 1963) and E. van der Beugel, *From Marshall aid to Atlantic partnership. European integration as a concern of American policy* (London, Elsevier, 1966), Chapters 2 and 3. On the application of the OEEC Code of Liberalization see I. B. Kravis, *Domestic interests and international obligations. Safeguards in international trade organizations* (Philadelphia, University of Pennsylvania, 1963), Chapter 3, and G. Patterson, *Discrimination in international trade. The policy issues 1945—1965* (Princeton University Press, Princeton, 1966), pp. 75—119.

About EPU: W. Diebold, Jr, *Trade and payments in Western Europe* (New York, Praeger, 1952); R. Triffin, *Europe and the money muddle* (Yale University Press, New Haven, 1957).

B. *The OECD*

1. *OECD publications*

The *Annual reports of EMA, Activities of OECD in 19.. Report by the Secretary General, The OECD Observer* (bimonthly), *OECD. History, aims, structure* and *OECD. Organization for Economic Cooperation and Development. Economic Outlook* (twice a year since 1967 with one-year forecasts, since 1980 with 18-month forecasts). *International Energy Agency*. For a detailed review of DAC-activities see the yearly published *Development Cooperation. Efforts and policies of the members of the Development Assistance Committee*. For the numerous publications issued by the OECD, see the 1986 catalogue and the Supplements to the Catalogue.

2. *Other publications*

H. J. Hahn and A. Weber, *Die OECD. Organisation für wirtschaftliche Zusammenarbeit und Entwicklung* (Baden-Baden, Nomos-Verlag, 1976).

On the IEA: R. O. Keohane, The International Energy Agency. State influence and transgovernmental politics, *International Organization*, Autumn 1978, The extracts quoted are from: R. O. Keohane, *art. cit.*; A. Lindbeck, "Possible future conflicts in a growing world economy" in *Economic science and problems of economic growth* (North-Holland, Amsterdam, 1974), F. Couigneau, La nécessité de l'impertinence, *Le Monde*, 21 October 1986.

PART 2

European Organizations

6. Benelux

. . . sie erlaubt den drei Ländern . . . auf solchen
Gebieten tätig zu werden, die nicht oder noch
nicht von der EWG erfasst werden.

HANS MÖLLER

The experience acquired in Benelux has proved very useful in the formulation of subsequent integration plans. The present chapter gives an outline of the most important stages in this, the first experiment in Western European integration, followed by an appraisal.

1. ORIGINS

A. *Preparatory phase*

As early as 18 July 1932 the Netherlands, Belgium and Luxemburg signed the Ouchy Convention, by which customs tariffs were to be stabilized and therefore gradually reduced. The infringement of the most-favoured-nation principle drew protests from the United States and the United Kingdom, as a result of which the Convention became a dead letter.

In 1943—44 the foundations of postwar cooperation were laid. On 21 October 1943 the governments in exile signed a monetary agreement, which laid down a fixed exchange rate for the two currencies concerned (BF 16.52 to the Dutch guilder) and the terms of a bilateral agreement. On 5 September 1944 a customs convention was signed. This aimed solely at forming a tariff union, since excise duties were not unified. Although on the economic level there were only two contracting parties the Netherlands and the Belgium-Luxemburg Economic Union, Luxemburg was always treated as an equal in all discussions and institutions.

The Convention of 5 September 1944 provides for the setting-up of three councils, namely the Administrative Council on Customs Duties, the Administrative Council for the Control of Foreign Trade (renamed in April 1946 the Council for the Economic Union) and the Commercial Agreements Council.

Upon the final liberation of the Netherlands in May 1945 the monetary agreement came into operation, but, owing to the unpropitious economic conditions, the customs convention did not. During ministerial discussions at The Hague in April 1946, however, it was decided that its introduction should be speeded up, as any delay would mean further divergence of the economic and social structures of the countries concerned. In addition, a secretariat for the three councils was set up. At a later date a Board of Presidents (of these councils) was also established.

The 1944 common tariff was first of all adjusted to the new situation (protocol of 14 March 1947). Parliamentary ratification also took some time, and the customs convention only came into force on 1 January 1948.

On 9 May 1947, in anticipation of a common agricultural policy, the ministers concerned signed a protocol introducing greater freedom of trade in agricultural commodities between the Benelux countries, subject to the observance of certain minimum prices. This amounted to protection of Belgian and Luxemberg agriculture against the more competitive Dutch agriculture.

The attempts at unification of excise duties came to naught, the Belgian government not relishing the idea of a shrinkage of its revenue. A protocol of 16 December 1948 for partial unification (not affecting alcohol, sugar, petrol, matches or lighters) was not ratified by the Belgian Parliament on account of opposition to the raising of the excise duties on beer.

The abolition of internal customs tariffs had, however, little effect on the expansion of intra-Benelux trade; owing to financial difficulties and despite credits from Belgium, the Netherlands was obliged to cut down its imports appreciably. Belgium, for its part, kept an eye on exports of goods obtained from the dollar area, as the Netherlands was unable to apply a similar import policy in trade with the United States.

Accordingly, efforts from 1948 onwards were directed to eliminating quantitative restrictions. It was also announced that an economic union was envisaged. This intention found its main expression in June 1948 during the Château d'Ardenne Conference, where the problems were given a thorough airing. Agreement was reached on the need for:

1. the abolition of rationing;
2. a reduction of subsidies on production and consumption;
3. reciprocal notification and coordination of investment plans. This point had already been agreed upon in January 1948, but nothing had actually been accomplished, mainly because the Belgian Government did not possess the necessary powers to make notification of investment projects compulsory;

4. further studies on the necessary harmonization of taxation and social policies;
5. the maintenance of monetary equilibrium.

B. *Pre-Union*

In 1949 the inception of the economic union, which had originally been scheduled for 1 January 1950, was fixed for 1 July 1950. A "pre-union", with gradual liberalization of intra-Benelux trade, was to be set up on 1 July 1949. Since an expansion of trade hinged on the granting of further credits to the Netherlands, in particular under the Marshall Plan (see Chapter 6), and the latter had been delayed, the introduction of the Pre-Union was postponed to 1 October 1949 (Luxemburg Agreement of 15 October 1949).

In point of fact, the Pre-Union was only a sort of permanent trade agreement. The chief object was to show world opinion that Benelux was moving ahead, despite the deferment of the economic union. There were a number of exceptions to the principle of unhampered trade between the partner countries, notably in connection with:

1. goods originating from outside countries (there was as yet no joint trade policy);
2. a wide range of agricultural products (under the protocol of 9 May 1947);
3. imports of coal and coke into Belgium.

By such means as the European Payments Union, liberalization was also to be extended, so that only one year after the establishment of the Pre-Union about 90 per cent of intra-Benelux trade had been freed. BLEU exports to the Netherlands followed a marked upward trend: in 1950 they accounted for 22.4 per cent of the total exports in value, as compared with 14.6 per cent in 1949, despite the fact that in September 1949 the exchange rate had been adjusted to BF 13.16 to the Dutch guilder.

Little progress was made along the road to economic union in 1950. The protocol of 18 February 1950 concerning excise duties provided for complete unification of duties but gave no indication as to the timing to be followed (nor was this to be carried out simultaneously by the partner countries). An adjustment was made on 27 May 1952 (see also below).

At the end of July 1950 a decision was taken at Ostend to enter into joint commercial agreements, thus opening up the way for the liberalization of foreign goods in intra-Benelux trade. It was not until September 1956, however, that the first joint commercial treaty (with Denmark) was concluded.

Agricultural problems were discussed at a conference of ministers of agriculture in October 1950. No departure was made from the basis principles agreed upon in 1947, though there were important modifications to the actual provision which had been drawn up in that year. In the case of several products (List A), imports from partner countries could be limited for the purpose of maintaining prefixed minimum prices. The latter were thenceforward to be determined jointly, and provision was also made for arbitration. The difference between the price in Belgium and the lower price in the Netherlands, from which the latter derived the entire benefit, was now to be split on a fifty-fifty basis.

The arbitration arrangements elicited protests in Belgium; it was accordingly decided in December 1950 that the governments themselves should be permitted to take the necessary measures as soon as the national price dropped below the minimum. A waiver was included for Luxemburg, making the protocol non-operative in the Grand Duchy. The adjusted agricultural protocol became effective on 1 January 1951.

After having had to contend with serious balance-of-payments difficulties in 1951, the Netherlands experienced a more favourable economic trend in 1952 and its sales on the Belgian market increased steadily, a major factor being its lower wages. In Belgium, many industries encountered keen Dutch competition (the Netherlands' share in BLEU's total exports fell to 15.3 per cent in 1952, while that of BLEU in Dutch exports rose from 13.5 per cent in 1950 to 15.6 per cent in 1952); unemployment swelled and the Benelux idea itself came under fire.

In October 1952 the Benelux ministers admitted that an economic union could not be brought about until the wide disparities in the economies of the Benelux countries, especially as regards wages and prices, had been ironed out. Subsequently, a raising of Dutch wages was recommended. To remove the difficulties suffered by many sectors of Belgian industry, no action was taken to restrict imports from the Netherlands but contacts between Dutch and Belgian industrialists were encouraged.

The necessity of a coordinated commercial policy was re-emphasized in July 1953. At the same time the cases in which special arrangements could be made to help certain hard-hit sectors were duly specified. In December 1953 a common commercial policy was once again recommended in order to ensure free intra-Benelux trade in goods imported into the Union; this did not, however, apply to agricultural products, which were subject to control at internal Benelux frontiers. From 1 June a joint policy was adopted towards the dollar area, and from 24 June 1955 concerted action was taken by the Benelux partners within the Organization for European Economic Cooperation (common liberalization list).

In July 1954 a protocol on the liberalization of capital movements provided for greater transferability of capital within the Union. This really added up to increased freedom for Dutch capital, since a fairly flexible system already existed in Belgium. Henceforward it was possible to repatriate invested capital, make new investments and transfer securities without restriction.

On 3 May 1955 agricultural policy came up for discussion once again. It was decided that harmonization should be carried out, and that after seven years unrestricted exchange of agricultural products should be introduced, for which purposes agricultural funds were to be created in Belgium and Luxemburg. An escape clause was maintained.

A few months afterwards on 5 November 1955, a protocol was signed which provided for the setting-up of a Consultative Interparliamentary Council of forty-nine members designated by the three Parliaments (twenty-one from Belgium, twenty-one from the Netherlands and seven from Luxemburg).

In 1956 two important decisions were taken. On 7 June 1956 approval was given to a Labour Convention, which was to become effective at the same time as the Treaty of Economic Union and ensured the free movement of wage-earners within the Union. In anticipation of this development, an interim agreement was signed on 30 March 1957. A protocol concerning the attitude of the public authorities to tenders invited and goods purchased by them came into force on 6 July 1956. Henceforth, contractors tendering in any partner country must be treated in the same way as nationals of that country.

C. *Economic union*

Nothing further had been said about the Treaty of Economic Union since 1950. In the meantime, integration had forged ahead in a broader Western European context. When it was clear that spectacular progress in the solution of outstanding problems — especially in agriculture — could not be expected in the immediate future, the Benelux countries decided that all commitments into which they had thus far entered should be incorporated in a single document and to assume that the Economic Union was already a going concern.

On 17 September 1957 the draft text was approved, and on 3 February 1958 the Treaty was signed at The Hague. Because of the protracted business of ratification by the three Parliaments, it was not until 1 November 1960 that the Treaty actually became effective. Economic union in its present form may be said to have come into force some four years earlier. An Implementing Protocol relates the existing Protocols to the Treaty. In order to allow for temporary derogations from the Treaty, a Transitional Convention (TC) was also concluded.

The provisions of the EEC Treaty constitute no obstacle (according to Article 233) to the completion of the Benelux Union in so far as the objectives of this union are not achieved by application of the EEC Treaty.

A governmental conference held on 28—29 April 1969 advised more active cooperation in order to complete the economic union before 1 November 1970. It was intended to hold a meeting every year but only four government conferences have taken place (in 1969, 1970, 1975 and 1982).

2. OBJECTIVES

By establishing the Economic Union, the three countries concerned hope to attain "the most satisfactory level of employment and the highest standard of living . . . compatible with the maintenance of monetary stability" and secure "the favourable expansion possible in the exchange of goods and services" with other countries (Preamble to the Treaty).

On the occasion of the governmental conference of 1975, the governments stated that a new direction and stimulus should be given to Benelux cooperation. The key issues in this context were the coordination of the economic, financial and social policies and the removal of the remaining custom formalities.

3. ADMINISTRATION

Unlike the European Communities, Benelux has no common or supranational institutions other than the Secretariat. Decisions are taken as a result of direct negotiation between the three governments.

A. *Executive institutions*

The Committee of Ministers is responsible for attainment of the Treaty's objectives (Article 16; see also Article 19). It includes at least three members from each government (Article 17,*1*). Decisions are taken by unanimous vote only. They are not invalidated by the abstention of any one country (Article 18), though their terms do not then apply to that country.

Preparations for the Committee's meetings are made and its decisions implemented by the Council of the Economic Union. This executive organ also coordinates the activities of the committees and special committees. There are committees for foreign economic relations; monetary and financial questions; industry and trade; agriculture, food and fisheries; customs tariffs and taxes; transport; and social questions (Article 28). The special committees cover coordination of statistics; comparison of public-sector budgets; tenders; public health; and small business (Article 29). A number of other committees have also been established: the free movement and establishment of persons, tourism, town and country planning, environment and energy (see below). The Secretariat, with its headquarters in Brussels, is directed by a secretary-general (E. D. J. Kruytbosch; since 3 September 1990 B. M. J. Hennekam) and acts for all the executive institutions (Articles 33, 34 and 36). Joint services may be set up (Article 40). It employs 90 people.

On 29 April 1969 an Action Group (*Collège d'impulsion*) was set up to advise the Committee of Ministers on the possibilities of completing the realization of the Union. It includes two members from each country. Its term of office was extended until 1 January 1977. Then the Group's duties were taken over by the Secretary-General and the Assistant Secretary-General, who were accorded the right to take the same initiatives since the third governmental conference.

B. *Consultative and arbitration bodies*

In addition to the Consultative Interparliamentary Council (see above, Convention of 5 November 1955), there is an Economic and Social Advisory Council (Article 54), the twenty-seven members and twenty-seven alternate members (nine for each country) of which are appointed by the three governments in consultation with the bodies representing their countries' economic and social organizations. The Council gives advisory opinions at the request of the Committee of Ministers or on its own initiative.

The Arbitration Tribunal settles disputes between the contracting parties in connection with the application of the Treaty and the agreements relating to it (Article 41). It is made up of different sections, dealing with different types of dispute. Each section consists of the national arbitrator of each party to the dispute and one person appointed in rotation from a list drawn up by the Committee of Ministers (Article 42).

Should one of the parties fail to implement a decision of the Tribunal, the other party may appeal to the International Court of Justice (Article 50). The Committee of Ministers may also request the Tribunal to give opinions on matters of law arising out of the Treaty or other Benelux agreements (Article 52,*1*).

In addition, a treaty signed on 31 March 1965 provided for the establishment of a Benelux Court of Justice. The Treaty came into operation on 1 January 1974 and on 11 May 1974 the Court of Justice was set up. This Court has the task of ensuring equity in the interpretation of common rules of law to be further determined either by treaty or by a decision of the Committee of Ministers. Some of them have already been specified in a protocol of 29 April 1969 (jurisdictional authority). The ministers may also ask the Court for opinions on the interpretation of these common rules (advisory authority). It has done so in 24 cases.

4. FUNCTIONS AND OPERATION

A. *Liberalization of goods, services and capital*

The Treaty provides for free movement of persons, goods, services and capital (Article 1). Freedom of movement must not be hampered by laws or regulations, including public health regulations (Article 6); nor may conditions of competition be distorted by legal provisions or measures (e.g., subsidies) (Article 7). Within five years, the necessary coordination must be brought about (Article 9 of the TC).

1. *Goods*

a. *Provisions*

Intra-Benelux goods traffic, irrespective of the origin, the last country of exportation or the destination of the goods, is exempt from all import, excise or other duties of any kind, and also of all taxes, charges or dues (Article 3,*1*), as well as being free from all prohibitions or restrictions of an economic or financial nature (Article 3,*2*). Goods from the partner countries are treated in the same way as home-produced goods (Article 3,*3*).

Restrictions in force at the time of establishing the Economic Union may be maintained but must be abolished within five years (Article 10 of the TC).

Many agricultural products come within the scope of the former agricultural protocols. The provisions of the latter are incorporated in the Transitional Convention. Imports from other Benelux countries may be restricted or prohibited (Article 11 of the TC). Duties or licences can be applied to imports and exports provided they are also applied in respect of non-Benelux countries (Article 12 of the TC). Minimum import prices (Schedule A: e.g., cattle, meat, dairy produce, potatoes, some classes of vegetables and fruit) are fixed by the Committee for Agriculture, Food and Fisheries on the basis of costs (Articles 13 and 14 of the TC). If prices fall below the fixed minimum level, imports may be suspended (Article 15 of the TC). The partner countries accord each other preferences as regards imports of agricultural products for which minimum prices are in operation (Article 17 of the TC). There are also special arrangements for Schedule B goods (mainly cereals and sugar products). In the case of Schedule C goods (which include cattle, dairy produce and potatoes), Luxembourg is permitted to maintain an autonomous import system provided the other Benelux states are always granted most-favoured-nation treatment (Article 20 of the TC).

The special arrangements for agricultural produce were to last for only five years (Article 23 of the TC), provided that agricultural policies had been coordinated in the meantime.

As regards public tenders, there is to be no discrimination (Article 62). This represents a step forward in comparison with the agreement of 6 July 1956: non-discrimination now applies to local authorities also (Article 63), though exceptions to this provision were permissible for three years (Article 4 of the TC).

b. *Operation*

Since the date of introduction of the Economic Union is in a sense fictitious and somewhat arbitrary, no outline of the operation of Benelux since 1

January 1948 is called for. As a start with this had already been made (see 1, B above), what follows below is by way of continuation.

As required by the Treaty of Union, the transitional provisions contained in Article 3,6 and 7 (of the TC) were abolished on 1 November 1965, though the transitional period for Articles 9 and 10 had to be extended to 1 November 1967.

Up to the end of 1970, industrial products were still subject to autonomous restrictions, such as quantitative restrictions on imports of lignite and coal from non-ECSC countries, light and medium-heavy oils, gas oil and fuel oil from Eastern Europe.

The divergences between national rules governing the composition, packaging, conservation, transport and denomination of certain products remain obstacles to the free movement of goods. The approximation of certain provisions in this field (e.g., as regards sanitary, phytosanitary, quality and packaging requirements) have already yielded beneficial results. A further approximation of laws constitutes the last stage in the process of total liberalization of trade between the Benelux countries.

Since the establishment of the EEC (see Chapter 8), a solution to the problems posed by agriculture (Article 11 to 23 of the TC) has been found within the framework of this organization's activities. The EEC is, after all, based on the Benelux system in this respect. As far as possible, the three countries grant each other preferential treatment and as a general rule there is prior consultation. The actual impediments in Benelux agriculture are mainly in the veterinary and plant health sectors, though some provisions have been harmonized (e.g., for imports of fresh meat from 1 July 1969).

As agricultural policies had not yet been coordinated (see below), the Committee of Ministers extended the transitional period for two years on 18 April 1966 but agreed that from 1 November 1967 national provisions should not hamper intra-Benelux trade. Although by 1 November 1968 agricultural policies were far from being coordinated, the transitional period was not extended any longer.

In 1950 a special committee was set up to supervise observance of the protocol on public tenders. This committee examines complaints but has, of course, no authority to make the ministers concerned reverse decisions which they have already taken. Since 1 July 1964 the protocol has also applied to local authorities (see above).

The volume of contracts placed with foreign enterprises has in recent years been insignificant. This is not necessarily due to discrimination by the authorities but is traceable mainly to the scant interest shown by such enterprises in undertaking work abroad.

On 19 March 1962 a Benelux convention on trademarks and brands was signed and on 25 October 1966 the Committee of Ministers further approved a Benelux treaty and a Benelux standard law on designs and models (amended on 31 May 1989), and in 1967 a Benelux standard law on agency contract was published. On 1 July 1969 the convention on trademarks and brands, and on 1 January 1970 a uniform Benelux law on trademarks and brands came into force. One of the provisions of this law is for a single register for the whole Benelux territory, thereby guaranteeing the exclusive use of certain trademarks and brands to their owners throughout Benelux. A joint Benelux Trademark Bureau was set up in The Hague on 1 January 1971 and marked the entry into force of the Benelux standard Law on Designs and Models, as well as the establishment of the Joint Benelux Designs and Models Bureau. On 11 May 1974 a protocol on the legal protection of persons in service of the two Bureaus was signed. It came into operation on 1 November 1978.

A start was made with the standardization of customs documents by the introduction on 1 September 1965 of a transit document for the whole of Benelux territory. Finally, in April 1969 the Committee of Ministers decided to abolish all customs formalities at intra-Benelux frontiers before 1 November 1970; in July 1970 this time limit was extended to 1 February 1971. It went into force on 29 January 1971. Benelux became a single customs territory.

Since 1 July 1984 intra-Benelux trade requires a single document only. It implies further simplification of formalities at the frontier.

Partly as a result of the abolition of customs duties, intra-Benelux trade recorded a marked expansion, but it fell off again as progress was made within the EEC. Before the war the Netherlands was the BLEU's third largest customer and fourth largest supplier; in 1966 it was the BLEU's major trade partner. In 1990 it occupied third place as regards exports and second place as regards imports: 13.7 per cent of the BLEU's exports went to the Netherlands, as compared with 11.7 per cent in 1936—38 (and 22.2 per cent in 1966), while 17.6 per cent of its total imports came from the Netherlands, against 8.6 per cent in 1936—38 (and 14.6 in 1966). The BLEU's share in Dutch imports increased from 11.6 to 17.7 per cent between 1936—38 and 1969 but in 1990 dropped back to 13.9 per cent; the corresponding share in Dutch exports rose from 10.9 per cent in 1936—38 to 13.9 per cent in 1969 and stayed at that level (14.7 per cent in 1990).

2. *Services*

a. *Provisions*

Services, too, are free of taxes and all other charges, nor may they be hampered by restrictions of an economic or financial nature (Article 5).

The Committee of Ministers determines the conditions governing participation in road and inland-water way transport (Article 85). Within three years, quantitative restrictions on road haulage and unscheduled passenger services by road must be abolished (Article 34 of the TC).

For a period of five years, the existing situation may be maintained as regards transport by water of river sand and gravel from the Netherlands to Belgium (Article 35 of the TC).

Efforts will be made to secure coordination of official provisions concerning transport (Article 9,*1* of the Implementing Protocol). All support or protective measures benefiting one or more enterprises must be eliminated (Article 9,*2* of the Implementing Protocol). This, however, is without prejudice to arrangements for the reorganization of national railway finances or the modernization of a transport sector (Article 9,*5* of the Implementing Protocol).

b. *Operation*

On 21 May 1962 the Committee of Ministers took three decisions, which came into force on 1 October 1962, facilitating road transport considerably.

Under this "liberalization decision", road haulage between the Benelux countries is subject to no restrictions in the case of carriers who are authorized to operate in their own country. An additional permit in the partner country is not required.

By the terms of the provision on rates, a common tariff has to be observed in this field. This is based on the average between the Belgo-Luxemburg and the Dutch costs. The Committee may fix special rates for the transport of certain goods or for haulage in special circumstances. The 1962 Benelux tariff for road haulage was replaced by a new tariff on 10 March 1971, which was amended in 1976 (coming into force on 1 March 1976). To ensure application of this decision, a standard document has been introduced.

The third decision (amended in 1967 and 1974) lays down the dimensions and weights with which commercial vehicles must comply.

The decisions taken on 21 May 1962 are designed not only to eliminate unfair competition but also to restrict competition with the railways. Negotiations for a settlement on inland waterways charges have so far proved abortive. In 1965, all negotiations were discontinued when it was decided to establish a reference tariff for inland navigation.

As from 1 February 1979, a common railway tariff per truck load was established for Belgium and the Netherlands. Since 1 February 1982 it is also applicable in Luxemburg.

On 18 October 1972, a Joint Service for the Registration of Pharmaceutical Products for Human Consumption was established by the Committee of Ministers. It became operational as from 1 January 1973. In order to remain in line with the directives issued by the European Communities, as well as for practical purposes, the rules of governing this service were amended on 30 November 1977, with effect from 1 January 1978. It was discontinued as from 1 January 1983.

Insurance companies operating in one of the Benelux states may not pursue their activity in the partner countries without fulfilling the latter's requirements concerning the setting-up of such enterprises. This will cease to be necessary as soon as coordination of supervision over insurance has been effected. Efforts to achieve this, however, have been taken over by the EEC. Because of the divergent and complex nature of the regulations on the subject, the aim is to secure not identity but equivalence of systems of supervision.

No spectacular results are to be expected in the future as steps to liberalize services — and particularly transport — are taken over by the EEC.

3. *Capital*

a. *Provisions*

Freedom of capital movements (Article 4) has already been guaranteed by the protocol of 8 July 1954. Complete liberalization is not yet to be introduced; however, the member countries undertake to remove conflicting provisions "as soon as and in such measure as the international payments situation permits" (Article 30,*1* of the TC).

b. *Operation*

The protocol of 8 July 1954 is still in force. While in the field of current payments a large measure of concordance exists between the Dutch and BLEU regulations, this is not the case with capital transfers, supervision of which is stricter in the Netherlands.

As the EEC's directives are more far-reaching than the provisions of the Benelux Treaty, liberalization of capital is no longer a Benelux issue.

B. *Free movement of persons*

a. *Provisions*

The nationals of each of the partner countries are able to enter and leave the territory of other member countries without restriction (Article 2,*1*). They are accorded the same treatment as nationals of the other Benelux states as regards:

a) freedom of movement and settlement;
b) carrying on a trade or occupation, including the supply of services;
c) capital transactions;
d) labour conditions;
e) social security benefits;
f) taxes and charges of any kind;

g) exercise of civil rights, and legal and judicial protection of their person, rights and interests (Article 2,*2*).

This list is restrictive. Thus Dutch nationals in Belgium are not entitled to reduced railway fares, even if they belong to the privileged categories.

Equal treatment also applies as regards legislation on rents (Article 57) and the taxation of companies (Article 59; see also Article 58). However, this does not apply to insurance companies, savings banks or building societies.

b. *Operation*

On 11 April 1960 an agreement was reached on confining frontier checks at the external frontiers of the Benelux area. This agreement entered into force on 1 July 1960, as from which date identity checks at internal frontiers were abolished. A common visa policy was introduced. The agreement will apply as long as the Treaty of Union remains valid. It further provides for a special Committee, which was established on 3 November 1960 (see 3A).

It defined in greater detail the rights of nationals of a Benelux country in the territory of other partner states (cf. Articles 55 and 56). They may freely enter these countries (cf. Article 2) but have to be in possession of identity papers (Article 1, as amended on 1 October 1963). Since this requirement is mandatory only in Belgium and Luxemburg, Dutch nationals in these countries must also be able to offer evidence of their identity. Agreements have been drawn up with most industrial countries and with many less-developed countries on the abolition of visas (e.g., Israel, Yugoslavia) and visa charges (e.g., Iraq) for foreign tourists.

Permanent settlement in another state is permissible provided the persons concerned have adequate means of support and are of good character (Article 2). Extradition is only possible on grounds of public policy or national security (Article 4); an appeal may be lodged with the Minister of Justice; furthermore, the competent authorities of the country of which the person concerned is a national must be duly notified (Article 7).

Adaptation of laws on the establishment of commercial enterprises will probably not be feasible in the shorter term. Whereas provisions on the subject were issued in the Netherlands as far back as 1937 (a new law was brought out in 1954), Belgian legislation is of more recent date (1958). Only a quarter of the relevant sectors in Belgium are subject to regulation.

With a view to easing the right of nationals of each Benelux country to set up in business in another Benelux country, the recognition of specified degrees and diplomas (as proof of the general and professional knowledge and commercial experience required in that country) may be useful. Since 18 January 1967 the Committee of Ministers has been making recommendations on these lines to the Benelux governments.

On 12 December 1968 the Committee of Ministers proposed an agreement that would give lawyers of each member country the right to plead before the courts in the other two countries, provided they were assisted by a lawyer of the country where the case was being heard. It came into force on 1 September 1971.

The transitional provision (which come within Articles 2 and 8) were abolished on 1 November 1965.

Although population pressure is greater and wages have been lower until 1965 in the Netherlands than in BLEU, there has been virtually no migration of Dutch labour to Belgium and Luxemburg.

C. *Coordination of economic policy*

The Benelux countries conduct a coordinated economic, financial and social policy in close consultation (Article 8,*1*). The statistics which are essential for appraisal of the economic, financial and social situation are duly collected and pooled (Article 90). The substance of economic policy is not dealt with systematically in the Treaty. Certain aspects are, however, touched upon; they are specified below. The government conference of 1975 aimed at filling that gap by formulating the lines of the coordination in the field of economic, financial and social policy as well as in those of road infrastructure, environment and country and road planning. Since 1982 priority is given to border-crossing cooperation (e.g., in the fields of Employment Exchange, nature reserves). On 12 September 1986 a convention was signed organizing cooperation between municipalities and provinces in frontier areas.

1. *Abuse of economic power*

a. *Provisions*

As regards private business agreements, and also the disadvantages arising out of market dominance, a coordinated policy is followed and measures are taken to counteract abuse of economic power (Article 8,*2*). There must be prior consultation if a member state is requested by one of its partners to take measures in this connection. This is also the case if any one of the partner countries contemplates action which is of major concern to one of the others (Article 11,*1* and *2* of the Implementing Protocol). The member countries assist each other in the detection of abuse (Article 11,*3* of the Implementing Protocol).

b. *Operation*

The three countries have different legislations, but the problems concerned are dealt with in an EEC setting.

2. *Agriculture*

a. *Provisions*

In the field of agricultural policy, efforts are directed to obtaining harmonization of production and marketing, job security for farmers and farm workers in well-run and economically and socially viable enterprises, promotion of technical progress and productivity and the lowest possible level of costs. This policy is aimed at the satisfaction of internal requirements and the acquisition of a strong position on external markets (Article 65).

Although the Treaty contains a general escape clause (see below), it was considered necessary to insert a special safeguard provision for agriculture. If a critical situation threatens, the Committee of Ministers may take the necessary preventive or remedial measures (Article 66,1). If possible, the Committee first of all obtains an opinion from the Consultative Interparliamentary Council and the Economic and Social Advisory Council (Article 66,1 and 2).

Harmonization was to be completed within a period of not more than five years (Article 22,1 of the TC).

On account of the less favourable production conditions in Luxemburg agriculture, the latter is given protection against competition from the other Benelux countries (Articles 67 and 20 of the TC — see above).

b. *Operation*

While agriculture in Belgium has traditionally been geared to supplying the home market, the main outlets for Dutch farming are on export markets. The Netherlands consequently sets considerably greater store by the maintenance of low costs and the stepping-up of productivity. This has resulted in a rather complicated policy, with some types of produce dutiable and others subsidized. In Belgium, the authorities have been content to make imports of certain agricultural commodities subject to quantitative restrictions in order to protect the domestic price level.

After the introduction of the agreement of 3 May 1955 (see above), Belgium and Luxemburg increasingly followed the example of the Netherlands, notably by setting up agricultural funds (in the case of Belgium, under the law of 25 July 1955). The segregation of the home market had generated ever-growing production surpluses, for which — sometimes by subsidization — outlets had had to be found abroad.

Although the levels of some cost factors became more closely aligned, little was achieved as regards coordination of agricultural policy and, as has already been mentioned, the transition period had to be extended. Activity has been confined to the compilation of numerous studies and repeated affirmations that coordination is being sought in certain sectors. Benelux attempts to harmonize agricultural policy have in fact been overtaken by the corresponding efforts in the EEC.

As from 1 January 1977, customs formalities and checks at internal frontiers were reduced, except for imports of tomatoes, grapes and potatoes in the BLEU-countries, by abolishing the internal import and export licences imposed by the three countries.

The EEC Commission has empowered the BLEU to exclude from Community treatment imports of such quantities of grapes, tomatoes and potatoes as move freely within the Community. The current system of potato export licences remains applicable as long as this matter is not dealt with at EEC level.

The monetary compensatory amount which had to be introduced in 1982 after the revaluation of the Dutch guilder, the devaluation of the Belgian and the Luxemburg francs, could be suppressed in 1983.

3. *Investment*

a. *Provisions*

The Committee of Ministers is required to decide as to the desirability of adopting investment aims, whether for the entire economy or for one or more sectors. Ways and means of implementing such aims (e.g., standardization of investment legislation) are to be determined (Article 64).

b. *Operation*

The provisions on this subject have not been applied. The only agreements which have been concluded in the field of public investment are those on the waterway links between Ghent and Terneuzen (20 June 1960), Liège and Maastricht (24 February 1961) and the Scheldt and the Rhine (13 May 1963). The canal linking Ghent with the sea at Terneuzen was opened to traffic in 1969, the Scheldt-Rhine project in 1975.

Informal arrangements have been made, notably concerning road construction (e.g., the building of the E3 motorway in Belgium, which started in 1969 and was completed in 1973).

In April 1969 harmonization of policies on investment (especially foreign industrial settlement, town and country planning, seaports and the road system) and energy, was again recommended.

4. *Transport*

a. *Provisions*

Coordination of policy is designed to bring about harmonization of conditions of competition (as regards both charges and advantages) and to ensure the profitable operation of public and private transport undertakings (Article 68). More particularly, it is directed to promotion of the harmonious development of and active cooperation between seaports (Article 69).

Joint implementation and control measures, especially in connection with prices, for road haulage and passenger transport will be taken by the Committee of Ministers (Article 86,*1*).

b. *Operation*

The principal developments in this field have been the decisions of 21 May 1962 and 1 February 1969 (see 4A2b).

5. *Monetary policy*

a. *Provisions*

The Benelux countries only alter their exchange rates by mutual agreement (Article 12). Monetary stability must not be jeopardized, nor must any of the countries be forced to suffer a shrinkage of its foreign exchange reserves in a way which is incompatible with its responsibility for its own currency, or to acquire non-convertible currencies or grant credits (Article 12).

The central banks take a hand in the shaping of policy (Article 71). If joint commercial and financial relations with certain non-Benelux countries involve the granting of credit or the acceptance of non-convertible currencies, the resultant charges must be shared by the contracting parties in a manner to be determined (Article 77).

b. *Operation*

Since it was no longer compatible with the prevailing conditions, the Monetary Agreement of 21 October 1943 was terminated on 5 June 1967.

Divergences as regards discrimination against the dollar area (see Chapter 5) led to quantitative restrictions on intra-Benelux trade for balance-of-payments reasons. Although a common dollar import programme was worked out later on, some exceptions had to be maintained. This, of course, prevented complete liberalization of intra-Benelux trade.

In 1971 the Benelux monetary policy was directed especially at cushioning the difficulties raised by the dollar crisis.

From 21 August 1971 to 10 March 1976, the margins of fluctuation between the Member States' currencies were reduced to 1.5 per cent. In the other EEC countries this margin was 2.25 per cent as from 24 April 1972 (see Chapter 1).

6. *Tax policy*

a. *Provisions*

Turnover and purchase tax arrangements are to ensure freedom of movement (Article 79), but there is no reference to a common policy, each
country retaining its autonomy in this field (Article 32 of the TC).

Excise and hallmark duties are also fixed by each country individually.

b. *Operation*

The Committee of Ministers reached agreement on 25 May 1964 that from 1
January 1968 turnover or purchase tax should no longer be charged at the
frontier but within the country. In 1967, however, general principles for a
system of taxation on value added were laid down in the EEC to supersede
the multistage turnover tax systems.

The Netherlands switched to this system on 1 January 1969, Luxemburg
on 1 January 1970 and Belgium on 1 January 1971.

The Benelux Agreement on the Harmonization of Excise Duties was
signed in Luxemburg on 29 May 1972. Subsequently, it was amended on
three occasions, i.e., by the Protocols of 6 March 1973, 19 July 1976 and 22
September 1978, but it was not applied.

At the third Government Conference it was stipulated that the so-called
"authentic document" only would be used for the purposes of supplying data
regarding trade within Benelux, and provided the system contained adequate
safeguards as regards tax inspection. From 1 January 1984 information
relating to statistics, VAT and *l'Institut Belgo-Luxembourgeois du Change*
could be given on one document.

High officials hold regular consultations on the progress made in implementing the action programme for the removal of internal customs formalities.

7. *Social security*

a. *Provisions*

Policy in this field must be directed to the furthering of social progress and to
providing the peoples of Benelux with the greatest possible degree of
protection and social security (Article 70). This will be done in consultation
with both sides of industry.

b. *Operation*

A large-scale comparison of the various social insurance systems and their
financial consequences has been carried out. Under Dutch law, a greater

proportion of the burden of social charges is borne by the employee than under Belgian law.

On 10 April 1965 an agreement was signed concerning sickness, disability and unemployment benefits for merchant seamen.

Although such a measure is not envisaged by the Treaty, the Government Conference of 1975 put in a strong plea for more harmonious development of the national provisions governing social security.

8. *External relations*

a. *Provisions*

To the extent necessary for achieving the aims of the Union, the three countries consult together on attitudes and commitments towards non-Benelux countries and international organizations (Article 9). They undertake a common policy in the field of external trade (including customs tariffs) and payments (Article 10). Policy is determined by the Committee of Ministers, which lays down in particular joint import and export quotas (Article 72). Before taking measures to encourage exports, the three countries consult each other (Article 75).

The partner countries render each other assistance in the application of statutory provisions governing imports, exports, goods in transit and the relevant payments, and in preventing and combating offences against such provisions (Article 76,*1*).

In respect of goods imported from or exported to non-member countries, the same import, excise and other duties are levied (Article 11,*1*). Provisions relating to import, excise, and other duties, taxes or dues charged on imports, exports or goods in transit must therefore be jointly determined (Article 78,*1*). If a devaluation or a revaluation by a partner country distorts the equivalence of the duties, this country must immediately adjust them (Article 81,*1*).

Licences and quota systems for imports, exports and goods in transit are identical (Article 11,*2*).

b. *Operation*

As was said above, joint commercial agreements have been concluded since 1956. The date upon which the common trade policy was to be effectively introduced, i.e., 1 January 1959 (Article 26 of the TC) was later postponed to 1 January 1961. There has also been prior consultation within the framework of the EEC and GATT negotiations. In 1956 a joint liberalization list was submitted to the OEEC (see Chapter 5). The Benelux governments have also endeavoured to work together in the promotion of exports (economic information, trade mission, trade fairs, exhibitions, chambers of commerce in other countries). The private sector, however, has not proved willing to lend its cooperation in this field.

Finally an agreement between the Benelux-states, France and Germany signed at Schengen (Luxemburg) and in force since 15 June 1985 organizes the gradual abolishment of controls at the common frontiers (cf. Chapter 8).

The transition period had to be extended for two years (until 1 November 1967), but even then the liberalization of trade in goods was not put into effect. Since 1 January 1971, however, nearly all import licences have been abolished (except for grapes, tomatoes and potatoes — see above)

D. *Escape clauses*

a. *Provisions*

If the "vital interests" of one of the Benelux countries are in danger, the Committee of Ministers, after obtaining the opinion of the Consultative Interparliamentary Council and the Economic and Social Advisory Council, may take measures which for a certain time deviate from the provisions of the Treaty (Article 14,*1*). In cases of urgency, such opinions are not requested, but the Committee reports without delay to the two Councils on the measures taken and the circumstances which have prompted them (Article 14,*2*).

In the case of agriculture, there are safeguard provisions, which apply even if the vital interests of one of the partner countries are not at stake (see above).

Each year, the Committee of Ministers reviews the escape clauses with a view to abolishing them (Articles 36 of the TC). All transition periods referred to in the Transitional Convention may be extended for two years by the Committee (until 1 January 1963) (Article 37 of the TC).

b. *Operation*

The Committee of Ministers was obliged to make use of its power to extend the transition period. In April 1969 a new target date (1 November 1970) was fixed for the full completion of the Treaty. Subsequently it was postponed till 1 February 1971 (even then exceptions relating to the value added tax were provided for).

APPRAISAL

In view of the difficulty of distinguishing between effects due to economic integration and those resulting from favourable general developments in the economies concerned, it is scarcely possible to draw up a really accurate balance sheet of the Benelux experiment.

Advantages

One might, for instance, be inclined to attribute the substantial increase in intra-Benelux trade (in industrial goods, at all events) to economic integration. It may also, however, derive from the overall expansion of the member countries' economies, which would have occurred even without customs union.

Compared with the other EEC internal frontiers, customs formalities for goods and persons have been reduced to a minimum.

Investment projects, such as those relating to automobile assembly and oil refining, would appear to have taken more account of the larger market. There has been greater specialization in both durable consumer goods (textiles) and the metal manufacturing industries.

On the international scene, the Benelux countries have something upheld their interests more successfully than they would have been able to do acting individually. They have taken the initiative in important measures to stimulate the liberalization of European trade. The Benelux Union has, in fact, served as a model for the EEC. In some fields it is still ahead of the Communities (transport, free movement of persons, trade marks and brands, procurement).

Drawbacks

Insufficient coordination of economic policy

Although prescribed by the Treaty of Economic Union, a coordinated economic policy has not yet been worked out. Despite regular Benelux conferences, the governments usually lose sight of the firm resolutions taken at the Benelux meetings. Important decisions (such as the revaluation of the Dutch guilder in 1961) are often taken without first contacting partner countries.

In other words, the frontier remains a frontier, even for industrial products. The consequence is that in most cases marketing subsidiaries need to be maintained in the partner countries and prices of the same goods frequently show disparities.

The inadequate coordination of economic policy has also been a barrier to closer liaison in international economic relations.

More interest in the EEC

Little progress has been achieved since 1958; advances have for the most part been of a preponderantly technical character and in limited fields. This must be ascribed mainly to the greater interest that is being shown for the EEC, the establishment of which has certainly diminished the significance of

Benelux. An instance of this is the solution of the Benelux countries' problems of agricultural policy within the EEC framework.

This does not mean, however that the Benelux countries no longer have a role to play. If two areas with roughly the same economic structure are unable to achieve a minimum of coordination, there can surely be little hope of this being done in a wider context. The Benelux countries must, of course, having regard to the requirements of EEC integration, continue to gain "integration experience", and this may prove beneficial to the Community.

BIBLIOGRAPHY

All the Treaty texts, together with comments, subsequent conventions, ministerial decisions, etc., are incorporated in the loose-leaf work *Union économique Benelux. Textes de base*, published by the Benelux Secretariat, supplements to which are issued at regular intervals.

Periodicals published by the Secretariat include *Bulletin Benelux* (since June 1957) — published up to March 1960 under the title of *Bulletin Trimestriel* (six issues per year) — and *Bulletin Trimestriel de Statistique Benelux* (since January 1954). There are also separate publications dealing in particular with wage policy and comparative budgets. See aiso *Rapport Commun des Gouvernements belge, néerlandais et luxembourgeois au Conseil interparlementaire consultatif de Benelux sur la réalisation et le fonctionnement d'une Union économique entre les trois états* (yearly). In English: *the Benelux economic union. A pioneer in European integration* (1987).

A good historical survey up to 1956 is found in J. E. Meade, *Negotiations for Benelux: an annotated chronicle 1943–1956* (Princeton, Princeton University, 1957). A more systematic exposition is provided by J. E. Meade and S. J. Wells, "The building of Benelux 1943–1960", in J. E. Meade, H. H. Liesner and S. J. Wells, *Case studies in European economic union. The mechanism of integration* (ed. J. E. Meade) (Oxford, Oxford University Press, 1962).

Note: the Belgium-Luxemburg Economic Union. The convention establishing an 'economic union' between Belgium and Luxemburg was signed on 25 July 1921 and came into force on 6 March 1922. Since 1921 the Treaty has been amended several times. The most important of these amendments relate to the control of foreign trade (1935), a new institutional structure, stressing mutual agreement instead of consultation (1963) and — in the same spirit — monetary association instead of consultation in the monetary field (1981).

See: M. A. G. van Meerhaeghe, *The Belgium-Luxemburg Economic Union* (SUERF, Tilburg, 1987).

7. Central and Eastern European Cooperation

> ... *the need arises for coordination of the plans of economic development, for a division of labour, for coordinated investment policies, etc. Also, there are the political considerations ... of defence against imperialism...*
>
> OSCAR LANGE

This chapter deals with the Council for Mutual Economic Assistance, established as a parallel to the OEEC by the Eastern European countries. The commonest English abbreviation for this organization is Comecon, but we shall use the officially preferred CMEA. The CMEA was abolished in 1991 and was to be succeeded by the Organization for International Economic Cooperation (OIEC). But at the time of writing no decision was yet taken. This chapter examines first the CMEA, then, briefly the envisaged OIEC.

THE COUNCIL FOR MUTAL ECONOMIC ASSISTANCE

1. ORIGINS

After the USSR had refused to be included in the European Recovery Programme and to become a member of the OEEC (see Chapter 5,1) — and Czechoslovakia, which had already formally accepted membership, was even compelled to withdraw — it felt bound to establish a separate organization for the communist countries. The Cominform (1947) being a union of the communist parties, there was not at that moment any formal assembly of communist states. So the Council for Mutual Economic Assistance was founded in January 1949. While in Western Europe the necessity of handing over certain national powers to supranational bodies was emphasized (cf. the ECSC: Chapter 8), in the CMEA the principle of national sovereignty was stressed from the beginning. Later, some countries were to appeal to this principle in order to check proposals for supranational cooperation.

229

No charter was drawn up for the new body in January 1949, however; only a communiqué was issued, and for ten years this was to be the only document in which the aims of the CMEA were explicitly formulated. As a matter of fact, it was not until December 1959 that a CMEA charter was adopted, taking effect on 13 April 1960. Amendments to this Charter, relating on the one hand especially to the Executive Committee and the Secretariat and on the other hand mainly to the Council Committees (see below), were adopted in 1962 and in 1974 respectively, but are still awaiting ratification. Nevertheless, these amendments are in fact applied and will consequently be considered in this account.

The relatively short "founding" communiqué stated that the CMEA was created in order to establish "wider economic cooperation between the countries of people's democracy and the USSR".

Initially, however, the establishment of the CMEA had a political import only: the intention was to show the non-communist world that in Eastern Europe, too, economic cooperation was being aimed at. Until 1954, there was very little to show for this cooperation. The trade agreements that had been made by then would have been concluded even without Comecon. Because of the strong domination exerted by the USSR, coordination was automatically effected in favour of this nation. The end of the Korean War and Stalin's death brought about a gradual change in this situation. As the negotiations on the establishment of the EEC progressed, more importance was attached to economic cooperation within the CMEA.

2. OBJECTIVES

The main aim was to promote a constant improvement in the welfare of the peoples of the member countries and the gradual equalization of the levels of well-being; other aims were the acceleration of economic and technical progress, a steady increase in the productivity of labour, the promotion of industrialization in states with less-developed industries, more cooperation between the member countries and the development of socialist economic integration (Article 1,*1*), though these are rather means of achieving the first objective. In the preamble mention is also made of other merits of economic cooperation (strengthening the unity and solidarity of the countries concerned, building socialism and communism, ensuring lasting peace throughout the world).

3. ORGANIZATION

A. *Members*

The original member states (Article 2,*1*) were Bulgaria, Czechoslovakia, Hungary, Poland, Romania and the Soviet Union. Albania joined in February

1949 and Eastern Germany in September 1950. China (in 1956), North Korea (1957), North Vietnam (1958) and Mongolia (1958) were admitted as observers. As a result of its dispute with the USSR, China had not made use of its observer status since 1966. This example was followed by North Korea and North Vietnam until 1972. Membership was offered to the Asian observers in June 1962, but only Mongolia became a member country (after the Charter had been amended; previously, only European states could be member countries). Albania, which supported China, ceased to be invited to the CMEA meetings, but never expressed its intention of withdrawing from the CMEA. Yugoslavia, which had already attended some meetings as an observer from 1956 until 1958, refused full membership in 1961 but participated in several activities after an association agreement had been concluded (1964). Cuba became a member in 1972 and Vietnam in 1978.

Some countries had been granted observer status: Laos and Angola (1976), Ethiopia (1978), North Yemen (1979), Afghanistan (1980) and Mozambique (1981).

The explanation of the early accession of Eastern Germany (1950) was to be found in the fact that Western Germany was represented in the OEEC, and especially in the fact that the Anglo-American-French agreement to end the state of war with Western Germany had just been concluded.

Member countries agreed to ensure compliance with the recommendations of the CMEA organs, to inform them about progress in carrying out these recommendations and to submit the materials and information necessary for the tasks of the Council (Article 2,*4*).

There were no provisions for the suspension or expulsion of member countries. Members could withdraw, however, six months' notice being required (Article 2,*3*). Non-member countries could be invited to take part in the work of CMEA organs or enter into cooperation with them in other forms (Article 11). Multilateral cooperation agreements existed with several countries.

B. *Administration*

The organs of the CMEA were the Council Session, the Executive Committee, the Committees, the Standing Commissions and the Secretariat.

1. *The Council Session*

The Council Session discussed all matters within the jurisdiction of the CMEA. It consisted of delegations from all member countries. A regular session was held not less than once a year in the capital of each of the member countries in turn and was presided over by the head of the delegation of the host country.

Recommendations were made on matters of economic, scientific and technical cooperation and were implemented by decisions of the member governments or other competent authorities in accordance with their national legislation (Article 4,*1*). Decisions related to organizational and procedural matters (Article4,*2*).

There was no question of supranational powers or majority decisions. The Charter made it clear that the CMEA was established on the basis of the principle of sovereign equality of all member countries (Article 1,*2*). The effects of recommendations and decisions did not extend to countries which have declared their lack of interest in the question concerned. Each such country could, however, subsequently accept recommendations and decisions adopted by the other member countries (Article 4,*3*).

Although there was no mention of them in the Charter, the consultations of the leaders of the Communist and Workers' Parties were in many cases just as important as the Sessions of the Council and in many cases they determined their decisions.

2. *The Executive Committee*

The Executive Committee, created in 1962, consisted of one representative of each member country (Article 7,*1*) and held meetings, at least as a rule, once very quarter (Article 7,*2*).

The Executive Committee directed all work relating to the functions of the CMEA and supervised the implementation by member countries of the recommendations of the Council (Article 7,*4a*). More particularly, it directed the work of coordinating plans for national economic development and for specialization and cooperation in the field of production (Article 7,*4b*). The Committee also organized the formulation of basic guidelines for the division of labour in the key industries (Article 7,*4b*). It drew up ground rules for the expansion of trade in goods and services and for cooperation in the scientific and technical field (Article 7,*4d*), and considered proposals from member countries and from the organs of the Council concerning cooperation (Article 7,*4c*).

The Executive Committee directed the work of the Committees, the Standing Commissions and the Secretariat (Article 7,*4e*). It approved the budget of the Secretariat and established agencies for checking the Secretariat's financial activities. It also approved the regulations governing the Committees, the Standing Commissions, the Secretariat and the other organs of the Council (Article 7,*4f* and *g*).

The Executive Committee was empowered by its terms of reference, to adopt recommendations and decisions. It could submit proposals to the Council Session (Article 7,*3*).

3. *The Committees*

The Committees "ensure comprehensive consideration and solution . . . of the most important problems . . . in the sphere of the economy, science and technology" (Article 8,*1*). Four committees have been established in the field of planning (the former Bureau for Integrated Planning Problems), science and technology, material and technical supply and machine building. Their seat was in Moscow.

4. *The Standing Commissions*

Standing Commissions were established by the Council Session in order to promote further development of economic relations and cooperation in individual sectors of the economies of the member countries (Article 9,*1*).

The first Standing Commissions were set up in 1956. There were more than twenty of them. Nine were located in Moscow (statistics, foreign trade, currency and finance, telecommunications, electric power, peaceful use of atomic energy, iron and steel, health and civil aviation), three in Berlin (chemicals, construction, standardization), two each in Budapest (non-ferrous metals, radio engineering and electronics), Warsaw (coal and transport), Prague (engineering and light industry) and Sofia (agriculture and food industry) and one each in Ulan Bator (geology) and Bucharest (oil and gas).

There was also a CMEA Institute of Standardization (1962), an International Institute on Economic Problems of the World Socialist System (1971) and an International Research Institute for Management Problems (1975). In addition, several conferences regularly discussed questions relating to internal trade, water conservation, shipping and freight organizations (there was also a Bureau for the coordination of ship freighting; 1962), legal problems, prices, inventions and patents and labour agencies.

5. *The Secretariat*

The Secretariat consisted of the secretary of the Council, his deputies and a staff. The secretary was appointed by the Council Session and the deputies by the Executive Committee. The staff was recruited from citizens of the member countries. The secretary and his deputies could take part in all meetings of the organs of the Council (Article 10,*1*). Since 20 October 1983 the secretary was V. Sichev (USSR).

The Secretariat prepared and helped with the conduct of meetings held within the framework of the Council and by other organs of the Council. It also prepared economic surveys and studies based on material from the member countries and proposals on individual problems arising in the work of the Council for consideration in the appropriate organs of the Council. It organized or assisted in working out the drafting of multilateral agreements (Article 10,*2*). It has no executive power (such as that exercised by the EEC Commission).

The headquarters of the Secretariat was in Moscow (Article 10,*4*). The proportion of the cost to be borne by each member country was determined by the Council Session (Article 13,*1*).

4. FUNCTIONS AND OPERATION

The general function of the CMEA was the organization of economic cooperation and the development of integration (see A below). Special attention was given to specific aspects of cooperation (B and C below).

A. *General economic cooperation and integration*

1. *Provisions*

The overall task of the CMEA consisted in the organization of comprehensive economic, scientific and technical cooperation between the member countries and the development of "socialist economic integration" (Article 3,*1a*). The concept that the CMEA shall adopt measures in order to study the economic, scientific and technical problems of member countries (Article 3,*1c*) was implicit in Article 3,*1a*.

2. *Operation*

As was mentioned above, a gradual relaxation of the predominating pressure of the USSR on the economy of the other Eastern European states only came about after Stalin's death. The former enemy countries were required to furnish reparations. Eastern Germany in particular was confronted with heavy obligations, and nothing was changed in this respect by the creation of the CMEA. Before the war Germany was an important stockholder in many Eastern European firms. These shares were taken over by the countries themselves in Czechoslovakia, Yugoslavia and Poland, and by the USSR in Hungary, Romania and Bulgaria.

From 1954 onwards, the network of Soviet-owned and mixed companies was dismantled (with few exceptions). More importance was attached to the division of labour among communist countries. Before, the USSR had imposed its economic viewpoint on the other CMEA countries; heavy industry had complete priority (even Albania was obliged to provide for a steel smelter but abandoned this plan after Stalin's death) and autarky remained the ideal. After the USSR had returned to the old view for about a year, from February 1955 onwards, it aimed at applying the autarky principle no longer within its own territory but within the communist world as a whole.

The relaxation of the USSR's grip in the economic field was offset by closer military cooperation: in May 1955 the Warsaw Pact was established. During the same month the *rapprochement* with the Western World was promoted by the Austrian State Treaty, and a Soviet state visit to Yugoslavia took place.

Only from May 1956 onwards was there evidence of cooperation in the proper sense within the CMEA context.

The "integration" phase was announced by the "comprehensive programme of further extension and improvement of cooperation and the development of socialist economic integration" of 1971 (approved by the CMEA Session of June 1971). The "comprehensive programme" of 1971 was the outcome of the desire of the USSR, after the invasion of Czechoslovakia, to tighten the bonds with the smaller central and East-European countries and even to set up supranational organs. In the latter aim it has failed, as the comprehensive programme stresses that "socialist economic integration takes place on the basis of complete free will and does not lead to the creation of supranational organs".

Since the 1970s the growth of the Soviet economy is declining. The poor performance of agriculture contributes to it. But industry's productivity is also very low. For a turn in this evolution the Soviet leaders rely on western technology.

The Cold War initiated a substantial military effort of the United States. It gave way to major technological progress in many sectors. The USSR tries to acquire the military innovations. Knowledge of the West is easily obtainable through literature and conferences. Buying hardware is no problem. At this moment the Soviet Union is familiar with the most important new military and civil innovations. Generally the United States have a qualitative lead. In the field of military technology the Soviet Union has a leeway of at least two to three years (although the military sector gets top priority).

The delays in the implementation are inherent to the Soviet economic system. Research is in high esteem but the economic system does not favour initiative and innovation. Motivation is limited, planning not flexible enough and managers avoid risk. Why introduce robots when the hidden unemployment amounts to 25 per cent? A purchase proposal or the choice between western goods has to go through a whole bureaucracy.

The new leaders try to promote innovations. But initiatives in that field — e.g. a bonus for inventors — meet opposition. In December 1985 the CMEA Council approved a Complex Programme of Scientific and Technical Progress.

B.   *Coordination of economic plans*

1.   *Provisions*

Article 3,*1b* prescribed coordination of national economic plans, specialization and cooperation in production as means of improving the internal socialist division of labour.

2.   *Operation*

Although coordination of the plans of the various communist countries was already contemplated in 1954, it was not until 1956, as mentioned above, that a start was made. In all member states, consumer goods were in short supply, while capital goods often remained unsold. The revolt in Hungary (quelled with the help of Soviet troops) and the analogous difficulties in Poland in October 1956 meant that these countries could not put their plans into effect and that the other partner countries were therefore sometimes obliged to modify their own foreign trade to a large extent.

Little attention had been paid to the fundamentals of specialization among the communist countries. In 1950 it was agreed that Hungary and the Balkan countries were to specialize in fruit, vegetables and early potatoes and the USSR in wheat and meat. However, it soon became evident that each country wanted to supply its own needs. In 1957, and especially in 1958, it was again emphasized that the plans should be made to cover the same period and that advance coordination was essential. It was not until December 1961 that a document was approved concerning the division of labour among the communist countries; this was published in June 1962. To judge by these *Basis principles*, division of labour appears to have been attained through the coordination of economic plans. No concrete rules were laid down. With the following rule, for instance, little can be done in practice: "Estimates of the relative economic effectiveness of capital investments and production ... and of the economic effect of foreign trade are used in coordinating national plans as an important, though not the only, criterion in substantiating rational ways of developing the international socialist division of labour". One of the reasons why this is impractical is that cost comparison between the various countries is very difficult. The drafters of these *Basic principles* seemed to be aware of this: "The system of price formation on the world socialist market must be continuously improved ... simultaneously creating the conditions for transition to a price basis of its own".

Where somewhat precise rules were found, they were not necessarily accepted. When the document declares that "it is expedient to develop complete-cycle metallurgy above all in countries which are fully or largely provided with ores and technological fuel or with at least one of these basic types of raw materials", it is clearly Poland that the authors had in mind. But countries like Romania certainly did not wish to give up their industrialization plans. Hence the fact that this country had little sympathy with the Khrushchev proposals of 1962, in which mention was made of joint planning and shared factories. In April 1964 Romania in fact pronounced itself once more in favour of economic independence, relying upon the sovereign equality of member countries stressed in the CMEA Charter.

There was a limited degree of coordination (on a bilateral basis) for the period 1966—70 and 1971—75. It applied mainly to trade arrangements. Since 1975 the CMEA endorsed "Agreed plans for multilateral integration measures" and since 1976 "Long-term special purpose programmes for cooperation".

The Agreed Plans grouped a number of major economic integration projects in several fields (see C2). Moreover, they stimulated multilateral (and bilateral) specialization and cooperation agreements. Over 150 multi-lateral and more than 700 bilateral agreements were in force, especially in the engineering, the chemical and the electronics and computing equipment industries.

Long-term target programmes of cooperation focused on selected activities with a time horizon of about ten years or even more. Such a programme has been adopted for five areas, of special significance for long-term growth: engineering; energy and raw materials; agriculture and food industry; industrial consumer goods and transport. The implementation of these long-term programmes which were to be worked out by Agreed Plans, needed more than 300 bilateral and multilateral projects. "These schemes are in fact means of including each country into Soviet planning, through structural adaptation required by the long-term special purpose programmes for cooperation" (M. Lavigne).

C. *Joint undertakings*

1. *Provisions*

The CMEA assisted member countries in mapping out, coordinating and implementing joint action in respect of:

a) the development of industry, agriculture and transport;
b) the most effective utilization of investment allocated by the member countries for the "development of extractive and processing branches of industry" and for the construction of major projects of common interest;
c) the exchange of scientific and technical knowledge and advanced production experience;
d) the expansion of trade in goods and services (Article 3,*1d*).

2. *Operation*

a. *Development of industry, agriculture and transport*

The joint enterprises in this field may be seen as part of the coordination of economic plans. Apart from non-CMEA economic agencies, including the Conference of Directors of Danube Shipping Lines (1955), the Joint Institute for Nuclear Research (1956), the Organization for Railway Cooperation (1956) and the Organization for the Cooperation in Telecommunications and Posts (1957), a distinction should be made between intergovernmental economic organizations and international economic associations. The latter were based on agreements not between member states but between enterprises or economic organizations and could have financial autonomy. (Where the joint enterprise is concerned, they are also referred to as international economic organizations *sensu stricto*.)

The most important intergovernmental economic organizations were the Common Waggon Pool (1964), Agromash (agricultural, especially horticultural, machinery; 1964), Intransmash (transportation equipment; 1964), Intermetall (iron and steel industry; 1964), the Organisation for Cooperation in the Ballbearing Industries (1965), Medunion (medical equipment; 1967), Interkhim (parachemical industry; 1969), Interport (port activities; 1973), Interelektro (electrotechnical equipment; 1973), Petrobaltik (oil and gas exploration venture; 1975) and Interlichter (ocean and river shipment; 1978). Initially Romania and Mongolia declared their lack of interest in these organizations (Romania was only a member of the Common Waggon Pool), but later Romania became a member of the Organization for Cooperation in the Ball-bearing Industries and Interkhim and an associated member of Intermetall. Mongolia is not a member of the Common Waggon Pool, its tracks being broadgauged. This is also true of the USSR, but it constructs standard-gauge waggons for the Pool.

The intergovernmental economic organizations had limited activity. (Intermetall and Interkhim, for example, played a coordinating role only in the case of specific products). They were not even qualified to deal with industrial and/or commercial exploitation. The international economic associations too performed limited functions. Between 1972 and 1974, eight international economic associations were created for the coordination of research, production and sales of nuclear machine construction (Interatominstrument), textile machinery (Intertextilmash), atomic power station (Interatomenergo), photography (Assofoto), measurement equipment (Interetalonpribor), electrical installations (Interenergorement), artificial fibers (Interchimvolokno) and household chemicals (Domochim). No data on the results of their operation were available. Interatominstrument and Interatomenergo were dominated by the Soviet Union and Interatomenergo "has obviously been established . . . to control primarily the research activities of the other Comecon member countries" (H. Machowski).

Joint enterprises, as in the Hungarian-Polish Haldex Corporation (set up in Katowice in 1959) for the processing of coal slack, were rather an exception. On the other hand, multilateral investment in which there is joint technical control but financing by each country in its own territory was more common. Cooperation was most advanced in the energy sector. The establishment of a CMEA electricity grid was approved in 1959, and in 1962 the governments of Bulgaria, Czechoslovakia, Eastern Germany, Hungary, Poland and the USSR signed an agreement establishing a United Power Systems Distribution Centre for the parallel operation of the power systems. The Centre, with headquarters in Prague, started operations in January 1963.

In 1958, agreement was reached for the construction of the *Druzhba* (Friendship) crude oil pipeline from the Urals to Poland and Eastern Germany. The pipeline was finished in 1964 and the branch line to Hungary and Czechoslovakia in 1963. On the pattern described above, each country financed the section of the pipeline on its own territory. The capital invested was recouped as early as 1966 (transport costs being 80 per cent less than by rail and 50 per cent less than by inland waterway). Pipelines have also been built for transporting natural gas from the USSR to the other European CMEA member countries. The large-scale "Soyuz" gas pipeline delivers annually since 1980 15.5 billion cubic metres of gas from the Soviet Union (Orenburg) to Bulgaria, Czechoslovakia, the German Democratic Republic, Hungary and Poland (each 2.8 billion cubic metres) and Romania (1.5 billion cubic metres). Other large projects were completed at the end of the eighties, e.g., a 5 600 km gas pipeline from the Yamburg peninsula in northern Siberia to eastern Europe with a capacity of 22 billion cubic metres.

The most important joint projects in other sectors include the Ust'-Illinisk cellulose complex in the Irkutsk region (all European member states, except Czechoslovakia), the Kiyembaev asbestos mining and processing complex in the Orenburg region and the nickel and cobalt production in Cuba. A Soviet-Hungarian 750-kV line from the Ukraine to Hungary was the initial phase of a joint Comecon high-voltage grid.

While the *Druzhba* installations as well as the oil fields remain Soviet property, in the Orenburg project (Soyuz) this is only the case with the gas field (not the installations). Most joint enterprises, however, were constructed on a compensatory basis: the credits are paid for by part of the production (in proportion to these credits).

b. *Financing of projects of common interest*

Capital movements between the member countries have been of little significance. Where they have occurred it has been mostly in the interests of the countries providing the capital. This has been the case in several joint investment projects. Under an agreement between Eastern Germany and Poland, Eastern Germany has supplied capital for the building of new mines in Poland and the latter repays the loan and the interest from whatever is produced. Romania has received capital from Eastern Germany and Hungary for chemical projects and from Eastern Germany. Czechoslovakia and Poland for the construction of a paper mill. The USSR has given technical assistance and Czechoslovakia has furnished credits to Bulgaria for the building of copper mines and a smelter. Since 1965 the credits have been repaid by deliveries of copper and copperware to Czechoslovakia. Czechoslovakia has also supplied Poland with a loan for building copper and sulphur mines and processing facilities. The loan is being repaid in the form of copper and sulphur.

Proposals to establish investment banks — emanating from Romania, for instance — met with no success for a long time, but agreement was finally reached in May 1969. Romania refused, however, to join the International Investment Bank (which was set up in July 1970 and began operations on 1

January 1971) since decisions — contrary to the practice in other CMEA organs — are taken by majority vote (each member state having one vote). However, it became a member in 1971 (Cuba in 1974, Vietnam in 1977).

The International Investment Bank (IIB) grants medium- and long-term credits to the member countries, preferably for projects beneficial to them all. The capital of the Bank is 1 071.3 million transferable roubles (TR). The contributions of the member states have been determined on the basis of the ratio of their exports to members' total mutual exports.

The lack of interest in the IIB is to be explained by the fact that the richer countries, given their own capital needs, did not wish to contribute in large measure to the development of the poorer member countries. In point of fact, the activity of the IIB could have been performed by the International Bank for Economic Cooperation (see below).

c. *Exchange of scientific knowledge*

Although agreement on closer scientific cooperation was reached in 1949, it was the end of 1956 before any worthwhile advance was made. More progress has been made since 1973. New capital goods from member countries are tested jointly at regular intervals, and only those that give most satisfaction are recommended to be produced.

Until 1956 licences had to be paid for in the form of deliveries of goods and services. Since then, the exchange of technological information has developed considerably; industrial blueprints and technological processes were at one time provided free to other CMEA members. In 1967 the principle of free transfer was challenged and in 1971 it was abandoned.

d. *Trade in goods and services*

The CMEA has not brought about a relative expansion of trade between the member countries: approximately half of CMEA exports and imports (excluding Mongolia, Cuba and Vietnam) in the late eighties did go to partner countries, a share lower than thirty years before.

Notwithstanding the specialization agreements and the establishment of the International Bank for Economic Cooperation (see below), intra-CMEA trade remained largely bilateral in nature. Each member country's share in total intra-CMEA trade (excluding Mongolia, Cuba and Vietnam) has remained fairly stable. The share of the OECD countries in the European CMEA countries' foreign trade increased continuously.

Trade within the smaller CMEA countries was rather limited. More than half Bulgaria's trade was with the USSR. Hungary's and Poland's exports to and imports from the developed market economies were more important than similar operations with the USSR (Table 22).

At the end of 1947 the United States, and later also the Western European countries, placed an embargo on exports of strategic goods to

Table 22. CMEA trade flows (1988) in per cent of total exports and imports.

Country	Exports			Imports		
	Six[a]	USSR	Developed market economies	Six	USSR	Developed market economies
Bulgaria	18.1	62.8	6.4	20.1	53.7	15.5
Czechoslovakia	29.9	43.1	16.3	32.3	40.3	18.6
German Dem. Rep.	26.1	34.8	29.9	25.3	36.8	31.8
Hungary	17.0	27.6	39.5	18.7	25.0	43.3
Poland	16.2	24.5	43.3	17.2	23.4	45.7
Romania	16.8	24.0	33.7	24.6	24.0	13.5
USSR	48.9	—	21.9	54.1	—	25.1

Source: official statistical yearbooks of the countries concerned and UN estimates.
[a] Six: Bulgaria, Czechoslovakia, German Democratic Republic, Hungary, Poland and Romania.

Eastern European countries. In 1951 this embargo was reinforced in the United States through the Battle Act. Coordination between the Western countries is effected by the Coordinating Committee of the Consultative Group (COCOM) which holds its meetings in Paris. It is *not* an emanation of NATO, the North Atlantic Treaty Organization (the original EC countries, the United Kingdom and Denmark, Greece, the Iberic countries, Iceland, Norway and three non-European countries: Canada, Turkey and the United States): Ireland is not a member of COCOM, whereas Japan and Australia are. In 1954 the embargo was reduced to approximately 10 per cent of tradable goods.

The Western European countries gradually reduced the embargo list as from 1954 but the United States did not follow until more than ten years later. It brought its embargo list more into line with that of Western Europe in the period 1972—74. Even so, its attitude was more stringent.

After the Eastern bloc reform control on many goods had been dropped, but the war with Iraq gave rise to control on exports of strategic products to less-developed countries.

In 1987 a group was formed to prevent missile proliferation in less-developed countries (Missile Technology Control Regime). Members are the United States, Japan, Germany, the United Kingdom, France and Italy, Canada, the Benelux countries and Spain.

After ignoring the EEC for a long time and even rejecting it as a discussion partner, the CMEA countries reconsidered their attitude (without recognizing the EEC *de jure*). On 27 August 1973 the Secretary of the CMEA urged the President of the EC Council to start talks. The subsequent talks with the Commission have been concluded on 25 June 1988 (see Chapter 8).

Economic relations between the Eastern European countries and the less-developed countries cover at present practically all major sectors, from geological prospection and exploration through implementation of infrastructure projects to the establishment of large-scale multibranch industrial complexes.

The East-West economic relations included not only specialization in production, sub-contracting, joint ventures but also cooperation in third countries. The tripartite cooperation, involving partners from socialist countries, developed market-economy countries and less-developed countries, was a relatively new form of multilateral cooperation. At present the three groups of countries are participating in over 200 projects of tripartite industrial cooperation. Examples include: Romania built jointly with firms from the Federal Republic of Germany a mineral fertilizer plant in the Syrian Arab Republic; Poland and Switzerland participated in the development of coal mining in Peru; Hungarian and Swedish companies constructed a bus assembly plant in Iraq; the USSR and the United Kingdom participated in the construction of an oil pipeline in Nigeria.

e. *The International Bank for Economic Cooperation (IBEC)*

In order to overcome the disadvantages of the bilateral system of intra-CMEA trade, some member countries in 1949 made a number of trilateral clearing arrangements, but their operation did not prove satisfactory. Schemes for multilateral clearing were drawn up in Warsaw in June 1957 and in Moscow in October 1963. The operations of the clearing house set up by the Gosbank (the USSR's central bank) in 1957 were never significant. More progress was made when the International Bank for Economic Cooperation (IBEC) was created in October 1963. It started operations on 1 January 1964.

The IBEC's authorized capital is 304.4 million TR — which is a unit of account (distinct from the internal rouble in circulation but corresponding to the same gold definition = 0.987412 g) and is not convertible into gold, for instance.

Though trade negotiations between CMEA countries are conducted in such a way that the value of each country's prospective exports to the other CMEA countries equals the value of the corresponding imports of those countries (except, for instance, for transactions covered by IBEC credits), a deficit may arise. Temporary assistance from the IBEC is then possible. The IBEC grants settlement credits (comparable to the swing limits of bilateral agreements and normally repaid within a month; the limit is 2 per cent of the volume of settlements on trade turnover with all other authorized banks for previous years) and term credits (up to three years). In 1984, 75 per cent of credits were settlement credits.

Since 1970 the IBEC charges an interest rate of 2 till 5 per cent on credits according to time (0.5 to 2 per cent for Mongolia, Cuba and Vietnam). The rates for creditors vary from 1.5 to 4 per cent.

In each country one authorized bank notifies the IBEC at the end of each day of total export transactions with the member countries. The IBEC credits the account of that bank and debits the accounts of the authorized banks of the importing countries. In this way each authorized bank has one net accounting surplus or deficit with the IBEC.

As has been said above, trade between CMEA countries did not rise faster after the establishment of the IBEC. Nor did the multilateral arrangements in the framework of the Council and the IBEC give rise to a substantial change in the fundamentally bilateral character of the intra-Eastern trade.

APPRAISAL

There seems to be no question of integration in the CMEA. Indeed, it was — *when* a definition is given — a nebulous concept. Hence the CMEA cannot be compared to the EEC, but rather to the OECD.

Although the CMEA was one of the oldest of the European economic organizations, there are relatively few achievements — apart from standardization in some fields and the exchange of technical information — of which it can boast. This was partly due to the following factors.

a) Notwithstanding recent reforms, prices in the member countries have little relation to costs. And exchange rates do not bear much relation to purchasing-power-parities. It is therefore difficult to determine the cost advantage of imports and exports. Consequently, intra-CMEA trade has as a rule been based on free-market prices (which differ from domestic prices). In order to obviate too frequent fluctuations (which hinder planning), these were adjusted only periodically, but one of the results is that substantial differences between these prices and world market prices may occur. The possibility of gradually switching to a price system based on the cost structure of the CMEA countries has been under examination for a long time. Nonetheless, "the need to establish a system of foreign trade prices that best promotes cooperation based on planning and mutual advantage" is as yet an ". . . unsolved problem" (B. Csikos- Nagy).

b) This would appear to imply that political considerations would be ignored in price determination, which has not been the case so far. Between 1946 and 1953, for instance, Polish coal was delivered to the USSR at a price which only covered the cost of transport. Different prices are often charged for one and the same product. A significant factor here is the CMEA countries' economic dependence on the USSR. O. von Gajzágó, for example, has shown that in 1955—63 some countries (including Eastern Germany, Poland, Bulgaria, Yugoslavia) were systematically favoured while others (Hungary, Romania, China, Czechoslovakia, and in particular Finland) were discriminated against. Since the rise in prices of some raw materials, and more specifically of petroleum, in the early 1970s, the Eastern European countries have had the advantage of being supplied with these raw materials by the Soviet Union, though this country has gradually raised the prices. In return, therefore, the USSR has, among other things, to accept industrial products which are usually of defective quality.

c) There is no automatic clearing of imbalance (unanimity being required). So far, the IBEC has been a mere bookkeeping organization. Surpluses cannot be converted into Western currencies, so there is little incentive to build up such surpluses. (This is why the member countries, even the USSR, prefer to try to develop their trade with the West.) Multilateralism is therefore impossible.

There are major differences between the IBEC and the EPU arrangements, which were associated with trade liberalization and required part settlement in gold or convertible currencies. Though no data are available, it is accepted that about 5 per cent of intra-CMEA trade was settled in convertible currencies. Even if convertibility did exist, it is questionable whether multilateral relations would be promoted, since planning is thereby hampered. As to the IIB its principal function "is the management of the inflow of Western capital to assist, and in many respects to make possible, the realisation of joint investment and specialisation projects" (V. Sobell).

d) Many difficulties arose from the heterogeneity and the extreme diversity in the economic importance of the CMEA countries. There are the "richer" ones (Eastern Germany, Czechoslovakia, the USSR), and there are the "poorer" ones (the non-European CMEA states), who primarily expect aid from the CMEA.

There was no integration with CMEA at the industrial sector level. "The Soviet Union's position as raw material supplier and its vast market determine the structure of integration. In addition, political relations and bilateral economic relations with this country have a decisive impact on integration" (K. Pécsi).

The population of the USSR (286 million) accounts for 60 per cent of the total population of the CMEA. Much the same kind of disparity holds goods in the case of production figures, though it is difficult to be accurate on this score, partly because of unrealistic exchange rates. It is not surprising that there has been opposition to economic supranationality from countries which were already militarily integrated and had to face up to the possibility of intervention along the lines of what happened in Hungary in 1956 and Czechoslovakia in 1968. This explains why some authors believe that integration without the USSR could be more successful.

In any case, such cooperation as there is should be accompanied by a greater measure of *effective* competition, the absence of which means that the goods produced are not as good as they might be or do not match requirements and are therefore not competitive on Western markets, for instance.

Organization for International Economic Cooperation

The Executive Committee of the CMEA met from 2 to 5 January 1991 in order to prepare a meeting of the Council during which the CMEA would be abolished and the treaty in respect of the succeeding organization would be signed. After several postponement, the CMEA was finally abolished on 28 June 1991, but an agreement on the articles of the successor organization has not been reached.

With the exception of the former German Democratic Republic, the former CMEA members would become members of the new organization. However, membership of this organization would not be an obstacle to membership of western European organizations, such as the OECD.

The International Investment Bank and the International Bank for Economic Cooperation would be privatized.

Hungary, Poland and the Czech and Slovak Federal Republic would prefer the new organization to be strictly European. Moreover, they do not see the new organization as a legal successor to the CMEA and prefer its competence to be purely consultative.

BIBLIOGRAPHY

A. *CMEA publications*

The following documents have been published in English by the CMEA Secretariat: *Charter of the Council for Mutual Economic Assistance* (Moscow, 1968); *Basic principles of international socialist division of labour* (Moscow, 1962); *Comprehensive programme for the further extension and improvement of cooperation and the development of socialist economic integration by the CMEA member countries* (Moscow, 1971); *The Council for Mutual Economic Assistance 25 years* (Moscow, 1974); *Survey of CMEA activities* (Moscow, annually from 1967, mimeogr.); *IBEC 19- [Annual Report]* (Moscow, annually from 1968); *International Investment Bank 19- [Annual Report]* (Moscow, annually from 1973).

B. *Other publications*

G. Schiavone, *The institutions of Comecon* (London, MacMillan, 1981); L. Csaba, Integration into the world economy and the cooperation of the CMEA countries in planning, *Osteuropa*

Wirtschaft, 1983, No. 2; A. Köves, *The CMEA countries in the world economy: Turning inwards or turning outwards* (Akadémiai Kiado, Budapest 1985); V. Sobell, *The red market. Industrial co-operation and specialisation in Comecon* (Gower, Aldershot 1984); H. Wienert and J. Slater, *East-West technology transfer. The trade and economic aspects* (OECD, Paris 1986); J. M. van Brabant, *Economic integration in Eastern Europe. A handbook* (New York, London, Toronto, Harvester Wheatsheaf, 1989).

On foreign trade: O. von Gajzágó, *Preisentwicklung und Preispolitik im sowjetischen Aussenhandel* (1955—1963) (Cologne, Wissenschaft und Politik, 1966); J. M. P. van Brabant, *Bilateralism and structural bilateralism in intra-CMEA trade* (Rotterdam, Rotterdam University Press, 1973); E. Hewett, *Foreign trade prices in the Council for Mutual Economic Assistance* (London, Cambridge University Press, 1974) is a chronicle of an unsuccessful attempt to replace the working of the market with command and social goodwill; W. N. Turpin, *Soviet foreign trade. Purpose and performance* (Lexington, Mass., Lexington, 1977).

M. Lavigne (ed.), *Stratégies des pays socialistes dans l'échange international* (Paris, Economica, 1980); O. Bogomolov, The international market of CMEA countries, *Problems of Economics*, 1980; M. Lavigne, The Soviet Union inside Comecon, *Soviet Studies*, 1983, No. 2; A. Tiraspolsky, L'énigme des prix des échanges à l'intérieur du CMEA, *Courrier des pays de l'Est*, 1983, No. 271; *Financial reforms in socialist economies* (ed. C. Kessides et al., IBRD Washington DC, 1990).

On East-West trade J. Wilczynski, *The multinationals and East-West relations. Towards transideological collaboration* (London, Macmillan, 1976); M. Lavigne, *Les relations économiques Est-Ouest* (Paris, Presses Universitaires de France, 1979); B. Csikos-Nagy, East-West trade from the aspect of prices, *Economies et Sociétés*, 1979, Nos. 7/8/9/10; *East-West trade: the prospects to 1985* (Washington, U.S. Government Printing Office, 1982); *East-West Trade, Recent developments in countertrade* (Paris, OECD, Oct. 1981); H. Wienert and J. Slater, *East-West technology transfer. The trade and economic aspects, op. cit.*

The extracts quoted are from J. M. van Brabant, *East-European cooperation. The role of money and finance* (New York, Praeger, 1977); M. Lavigne, The Soviet Union inside Comecon, *art. cit.*; K. Pécsi, *The future of socialist economic integration* (edited with a foreword by Paul Marer, Armonk New York 1971, translated for the Hungarian edition of 1977), W. Sobell, *op. cit.*

8. The European Communities

*L'Europe ne sera jamais faite par les fonctionnaires;
elle ne sera fait que par des hommes politiques qui
prendront des décisions politiques.*

JEAN REY

On 8 April 1965 the member states of the three European Communities signed the "Merger Treaty" for the amalgamation of the three European "Executives" — the High Authority of the European Coal and Steel Community (ECSC), the Commission of the European Economic Community (EEC) and the Commission of the European Atomic Energy Community (EAEC or Euratom) into a single Commission of the European Communities. At the same time the three Councils of the three Communities were merged into one. Hence, since 1 July 1976 when the Merger Treaty came into force, the unified Commission of the European Commission has taken the only executive authority. Western European economic integration, however, started much earlier in the fifties, on a sectoral level.

1. ORIGINS

A. *The European Coal and Steel Community*

In the immediate postwar period it was thought that the aim of preventing any renewal of German aggression could best be pursued by exercising control over the Ruhr. To this end, an International Ruhr Authority was set up with responsibility for the distribution of coal, coke and steel production. However, this organization, which was highly unpopular with both France and Germany, never played a very significant part. For the rest, Germany in course of time progressively regained more and more independence; when, eventually, a body of opinion came to urge her rearmament, it was thought desirable to reduce the risks by amalgamating French and German economic interests (Schuman declaration of 9 May 1950 to pool coal and steel of France and Germany).

247

Negotiations opened on 20 June 1950, on the draft of a treaty (based on the so-called "Schuman Plan") to run for fifty years (Article 97), which was laid before the respective governments early in December. The discussions were markedly influenced by the Korean hostilities begun in June 1950: in view of the boom conditions prevailing, there was less apprehension of the stiffer competition which would normally result from the abolition of impediments to trade, and also greater importance was attached to the economic and military recovery in Western Germany.

After the Foreign Ministers had settled a number of organizational points, including the number of members of the High Authority, the method of voting in the Council of Ministers and the allocation of seats in the Common Assembly, they signed the Treaty in Paris on 18 April 1951 (Treaty of Paris). On 23 June 1952 the ECSC became operational.

Over a transition period scheduled to expire on 9 February 1958 all practices incompatible with the common market which had not been abolished forthwith (import and export duties, quantitative restrictions, certain subsidies and discriminations) were eliminated; during this time, under the Convention containing the Transitional Provisions (annexed to the Treaty), marginal enterprises — the Belgian collieries in particular — received assistance. The Transitional Provisions concerning "readaptation" (tiding over the retraining redundant workers) remained in force until 9 February 1960.

B. *The European Economic Community and the European Atomic Energy Community*

When France proceeded unwilling to subject other sectors of the economy to supranational control and the efforts towards political unification in the form of the European Defence Community failed in August 1954, the ECSC looked for less radical means of furthering economic integration. This is how the European Economic Community came into being.

The various possible ways of proceeding further with European cooperation were set out in a Benelux memorandum and debated in Messina on 1 and 2 June 1955; it was there decided to give priority to economic rather than political integration. The economies of the member states were to be brought closer together by establishing common institutions and by creating a single market. Recommendations were also made for the study of partial integration in sectors such as transport and energy.

The report that was eventually drawn up, including provisions concerning a common agricultural policy, common rules of competition, free movement of capital and labour, and atomic energy — *Rapport des chefs de délégation aux ministres des Affaires Etrangères* (Spaak Report) — was submitted to the Foreign Ministers at the Conference of Venice (29–30 May 1956). It was accepted as the basis for further negotiations.

Because of French demands in respect of social policy (equal pay for men and women, for instance) and especially in respect of the treatment of overseas territories, little progress was made at the outset, and negotiations nearly broke down at the last moment over the second of these two points. However, the Treaty was finally signed in Rome on 25 March 1957 (Treaty of Rome). It was concluded for an unlimited period (Article 240).

The Treaty setting up the European Atomic Energy Community (EAEC or Euratom) was concluded at the same time as the EEC Treaty. Initially, the structure of the Euratom Treaty seemed very supranational, giving extensive powers to the organs of the Community. Little has remained of this in the definitive text. Each country works out its own programme; the Community plays more of a supplementary role, because its research programme has to be approved unanimously.

The EEC Treaty was ratified by the member states — Belgium, the Federal Republic of Germany, France, Italy, Luxemburg and the Netherlands — in the course of 1957 and came into force on 1 January 1958. It does not detract from the ECSC, Euratom or Benelux Treaties (Articles 232 and 233).

Before the internal customs tariff of all goods (not only coal and steel products as in the ECSC) was abolished there was a transition period of twelve years, which could be extended to fifteen years. Provision was made for three stages, each lasting four years. Transition from the first to the second stage was conditional on the objectives of the first having been attained. Failing this, the first stage could be extended by two successive periods of one year (Articles 8,*1—3*). This turned out to be superfluous, since the Council decided on 14 January 1962 — when the basic decisions as to an agricultural policy were taken — that the second stage should begin with effect from 1 January 1962. The second and third stages could not be extended or curtailed except by unanimous decision by the Council, acting on a proposal from the Commission (Article 8,*5*). As no such decision was issued, the transition period came to an end on 31 December 1969.

Brussels was provisionally chosen as the headquarters of the Commission and of the Council; the Court of Justice was established in Luxemburg, and the Parliament continued to meet in Strasbourg and Luxemburg, some of the Parliament committees also meeting elsewhere (Brussels). When the ECSC, EEC and Euratom Executives were merged, it was agreed, as compensation for the transfer of some ECSC departments to Brussels, that Luxemburg should keep certain ECSC and be given certain EEC and Euratom departments and the European Investment Bank, and that the Council should meet there every April, June and October.

2. OBJECTIVES

As the Merger Treaty only provided for unification of the various Community institutions, the specific objectives of each Community were not altered.

Article 32 of the Merger Treaty shows that the merging of the three Communities into a single European Community once was envisaged. But it did not occur.

A. *The ECSC*

The purpose of the ECSC is to contribute to the expansion of the economy, the development of employment and the improvement of the standard of living in the participating countries. The Community must progressively establish conditions which will in themselves assure the most rational distribution of production while avoiding the creation of fundamental and persistent disturbances in the economies of the member states (Article 2).

   This statement of general principle is particularized in Article 3 as follows. The Community is required:

a) to ensure that the common market is kept regularly supplied, due account being taken of the needs of third countries (3,*a*);
b) to afford to all consumers in comparable positions within the common market equal access to the sources of production (3,*b*);
c) to ensure that prices are as low as is possible without sending up either the same enterprises' prices for other transactions or the price level as a whole at another period, while at the same time permitting the necessary amortization and normal returns on invested capital (3,*c*);
d) to ensure the maintenance of conditions which will encourage enterprises to expand and improve their production potential and to promote a policy of rational development of natural resources (3,*d*) without protection against competing industries except in response to unfair competition on their part (3,*g*);
e) to promote the levelling-up of the "living and working conditions" (i.e. general conditions, working conditions proper and terms of employment) of the labour force (3,*e*);
f) to foster the expansion of international trade and ensure that prices charged in foreign markets are kept within equitable limits (3,*f*).

Article 4 specifies the arrangements and practices, such as discrimination, deemed incompatible with the common market. Article 5 stipulates that the Community's activities must be carried out "with a minimum of administrative machinery and in close cooperation with the parties concerned".

B. *The EEC*

The Treaty was concluded to promote the harmonious development of economic activity within the Community, continuous and balanced expansion, greater stability, a steady improvement in living standards and closer relations between the member states. The means of achieving these aims are the creation of a common market, the gradual alignment of economic policies (Article 2) and, more specifically (Article 3):

a) the elimination between member states of customs duties, of quantitative restrictions on imports and exports of goods and other measures equivalent in effect, and of obstacles to the free movement of persons, services and capital;
b) the establishment of a common customs tariff towards third countries;
c) the approximation of member states' legislation to the extent required for the common market to function;
d) the coordination of economic policy, including policy to remedy balance-of-payments disequilibria, and the prohibition of practices that distort competition; the adoption of common policies for agriculture, transport and commerce towards third countries;
e) the creation of a European Social Fund to improve employment opportunities and to raise living standards;
f) the establishment of a European Investment Bank to promote economic growth;
g) the association of overseas countries and territories with a view to expanding trade and contributing to social and economic development.

However, no definition is given of 'common market' (it is not an instrument, but the result of economic integration).

The Single Act signed at Luxemburg on 17 February 1986 and The Hague on 28 February 1986 specifies some of these objectives (see infra), gives a legal basis on policies already applied (environment policy, regional policy, monetary policy), imposes majority voting and consultation of the European Parliament in a limited number of fields.

Any discrimination on the grounds of nationality is prohibited (Article 7). This general rule of non-discrimination is reflected in several other articles of the Treaty (as in the required approximation of member states' legislation, mentioned above).

The member countries aim not only at the establishment of a customs union, but also — though this is not explicitly stated — at the establishment of an economic union. There is no agreement concerning a notion introduced in 1974: European union. Even in EEC reports on European union no precise definition is given. The Ministers of Foreign Affairs have to communicate, in annual reports to the Commission and the European Council, the progress made towards the attainment of European union.

They also consider the "common market" to be a means, just as the gradual alignment of economic policies, to attain the Community's aims. In fact, the common market is *not* a form of economic integration, it is rather the ultimate result of such a process. It is the result of an economic union in which movements of persons, goods and capital are unrestricted and where the necessary coordination is achieved in the determination and implementation of economic, financial and social policy. In the Single Act too, the common or internal market and the coordination of economic policies are considered separately, whereas the first cannot be realized without the achievement of the latter.

According to the Single Act, the Community adopts measures with the aim of progressively establishing an internal market over a period expiring on 31 December 1992. The internal market comprises "an area without internal frontiers in which the free movement of goods, persons, services and capital is ensured" (Article 8A).

The Commission reports to the Council before 31 December 1988 and again before 31 December 1990 on the progress made towards achieving the internal market. The Council, acting by a qualified majority on a proposal from the Commission, determines the guidelines and conditions necessary to ensure balanced progress in all the sectors concerned (Article 8B).

When drawing up its proposals, the Commission takes into account the extent of the effort that certain economies showing differences in development will have to sustain during the period of establishment of the internal market and it may propose appropriate provisions. If these provisions take the form of derogations, they must be of a temporary nature and must cause the least possible disturbance to the functioning of the common market (Article 8C).

C. *Euratom*

The specific task of Euratom is to create the conditions necessary for the speedy establishment and growth of nuclear industries (Article 1). The Community must accordingly promote research, set up uniform safety regulations, facilitate investment, ensure regular and equitable supplies of ore and fissionable material (Article 2), and institute a common market, with a common external tariff established on 1 January 1959 (Article 94).

D. *The subsidiarity principle*

Although not mentioned in the Treaty, nor in the Single Act, 'subsidiarity' is used more and more in respect of the Community to denote that decisions should not be taken at a higher level, if they can be taken at a lower level. In other words, the Commission should not do things that member states can do better. The level (town, province, state) at which a function can be efficiently performed, is the right level of government. In fact, the subsidiarity principle is implied in the anti-interventionist philosophy of the Treaty of Rome.

The Report on economic and monetary union in the European Community (Delors Committee) refers to the principle of subsidiarity as follows: An essential element in defining the appropriate balance of power within the Community would be adherence to the "principle of subsidiarity", according to which the functions of higher levels of government should be as limited as possible and should be subsidiary to those of lower levels. Thus, the attribution of competences to the Community would have to be confined specifically to those areas in which collective decision-making was necessary. All policy functions which could be carried out at national (and regional and local) levels without adverse repercussions on the cohesion and functioning of the economic and monetary union would remain within the competence of the member countries.

3. ORGANIZATION

A. *Members*

The provisions of the EEC Treaty extend to those European countries — Monaco and Andorra — for whose external relations individual member states are responsible (Article 227). Any European state may apply for membership of the Community. Applications must be addressed to the Council, which has to decide on such matters by unanimous vote after consulting the Commission and after receiving the assent of the Parliament which act by an absolute majority of its component members (see 3.B3). A treaty is then worked out concerning conditions of admission and any amendments that need to be made to the Treaty (Article 237).

In May 1967 the United Kingdom, Denmark, Ireland and Norway for the second time applied for membership of the European Communities. (Their first application in 1961—1962 was rejected). On 22 January 1972 the Council agreed to the accession of the four countries as from 1 January 1973. Since the Treaty was not ratified by Norway, some changes had to be made (especially on institutional matters) at the last moment. Membership having been called into question in the United Kingdom, a referendum was held in that country on 5 June 1975 and 67.5 per cent voted to stay in the Community. Following a referendum held in Greenland in February 1982 the Danish Government asked the Council in May 1982 to take out Greenland of the geographical scope of the Treaties and to apply the association provisions to the island. The treaty concerned went into effect on 29 November 1985 (Greenland left the Community on 1 February 1985).

At the request of Greece, Portugal and Spain (in June 1975, March 1977 and July 1977 respectively) negotiations were opened on the conditions of their possible accession to the Community.

The association treaty with Greece was signed on 28 May 1979 and Greece became the tenth member state on 1 January 1981. A five-year transitional period was agreed for the progressive elimination of customs duties and the alignment of the Greek tariff on the Common Customs Tariff. Quantitative restrictions on fourteen products may be maintained during the transitional period but the relevant quotas must be progressively increased. A special transitional period of seven years has been laid down for fresh and processed tomatoes and fresh and preserved peaches.

The accession treaties with Spain and Portugal were signed on 12 June 1985 only and these countries became members on 1 January 1986. In customs matters a seven-year transitional period is introduced. Spain has three or four years to abolish import quotas on a dozen sensitive products, including tractors, colour televisions, sewing machines and guns. Portugal has similar facilities to phase out its quotas on car imports. Two sectors are sensitive for the other EC-countries: steel and textiles: Spain and Portugal exports of steel and some textile products will be limited for three years (meanwhile subsidies in the steel sector are allowed in the new member states).

In order to avoid disruption or disturbance of agricultural markets, traditional transitional measures were not considered sufficient. Some special measures extend over ten years. Thus it will be 1996 before Iberian farmers are integrated in the Community agricultural market. The measures relate to wine, olive oil and other fats, fruits and vegetables. Moreover the Community is to finance a development programme to help Portuguese agriculture (700 million ECU in ten years).

Given the size of the Spanish and Portuguese fleets a strict control on fishing effort is considered necessary. The size of the Spanish Atlantic fleet will be gradually adapted to fishing opportunities.

Some countries want to join the Community — Austria (application submitted on 17 July 1989) and Turkey — and some are considering it — Norway, Cyprus and Malta.

B. *Administration*

Where originally each Community had its own Council and Executive Authority, a single Council and Commission of the European Communities came into being on 1 July 1967 (see Merger Treaty). Accordingly, some articles of the basic treaties, the Protocols on the Statute of the Court of Justice and the Convention on certain institutions common to the European Communities (the Parliament and the Economic and Social Committee) were amended or repealed. Further amendments were necessitated by the enlargements of the Communities.

1. *The Council*

The Council is composed of representatives of the member states; as a rule each government delegates one of its members to attend Council meetings, depending on what is on the agenda. Sometimes two or even more ministers per country take part. In the autumn of 1974 the last summit took place. It decided to meet from then as "European Council" (see below). Meetings of, for example, the Ministers of Finance not held at Community headquarters (Brussels or Luxemburg) are not Council meetings. The office of president is exercised for a term of six months by each member in rotation (Article 2 of the "Merger Treaty" — MT). The president convenes the Council on his own initiative or at the request of one of the members or of the Commission (Article 3 of the MT).

The Council is entrusted with the coordination of the general economic policies of the member states; it also has the power to take other decisions (Article 145). It can request the Commission to carry out inquiries and put forward proposals for the attainment of the Community's objectives (Article 152); it also draws up the terms of reference of the committees provided for in the Treaty (Article 153) and fixes the salaries, allowances and pensions of the members of the Commission and of the Court of Justice (Article 6 of the MT).

Depending on the Articles concerned, Council decisions have to be reached by simple or qualified majority or by unanimous vote. Where a qualified majority is needed, especially in respect of common policies, the votes are weighted as follows (based partly on population and partly on economic strength): Germany, France, Italy and the United Kingdom ten each; Spain eight; Belgium, the Netherlands, Greece and Portugal five each; Denmark and Ireland three each and Luxemburg two. Decisions taken on a proposal from the Commission must obtain at least fifty-four votes. If the Council takes a decision for which no proposal from the Commission is required, again fifty-four votes are required but they must come from at least six members.

In order to strengthen the decision-making process the Single Act provides for majority voting to be extended to certain decisions, particularly in relation with the completion of the internal market, research and technology, regional policy and improvement of the working environment.

Where the Council acts on a proposal of the Commission, unanimity is required to amend this proposal. Where the Council acts in cooperation with the European Parliament, it adopts a common position by a qualified majority, on a proposal from the Commission and after obtaining the opinion of the Parliament. This common position is communicated to the Parliament. Within three months of such communication the Parliament may propose amendments or reject the common position by an absolute majority of its component members. In case of a rejection unanimity is required for the Council to act on a second reading.

Within a period of one month the Commission reexamines the Council's position by taking into account the Parliament's amendments. The Council adopts by a qualified majority the proposal reexamined by the Commission; unanimity is required to amend this proposal (Article 149).

The Council (just like the Commission) can make regulations, issue directives, take decisions and make recommendations or deliver opinions (Article 189).

A regulation has general application; it is "binding in its entirety and directly applicable in all Member States". A directive is only binding "as to the results to be achieved" but leaves to the national authorities the choice of form and methods. A decision is "binding in its entirety upon those to whom it is addressed". Recommendations and opinions have no binding force. While Article 189 of the EEC-Treaty and Article 161 of the Euratom Treaty have an equal wording, the terminology is different in Article 14 of the ECSC Treaty. An ECSC (general) decision corresponds to a regulation, an ECSC recommendation to a directive (but it can also be addressed to individuals).

Council meetings are prepared by the Permanent Representatives Committee (Article 4 of the MT). The Council has its own Secretariat (2 076 people on 31 December 1989) and is assisted by a number of working parties and committees. In practice, the Permanent Representatives Committee plays an important role in policy-making since the Ministers rely more and more on its advice.

2. *The European Council*

At the Paris Summit (9—10 December 1974), the Heads of State or Government agreed to meet regularly three times a year (the European Council) in the capitals of the member states. It was also decided to apply the unanimity rule less strictly (the "Luxemburg compromise" of 30 January 1966 provided that if a country considers a matter of very great importance, a decision in the Council can only be taken by unanimous vote).

The European Council is an institution which is neither mentioned nor even envisaged in any way in the Treaty of Rome. The Single Act, however, stipulates that the European Council brings together 'the Heads of State or of Government of the Member States and the President of the Commission of the European Communities'. They are assisted by the Ministers of Foreign Affairs and by a Member of the Commission. The European Council meets at least twice a year (Article 2).

3. *The Commission*

The Commission consists of seventeen members (France, Germany, the United Kingdom, Italy and Spain, two each, the other member states one each) selected for their general competence and indisputable independence. The Council can change the number of members by unanimous vote, but there may not be more than two members per country (Article 10 of the MT). They are appointed — not by the Council but by the national governments — for four years by common accord of the governments of the member states; their terms of office may be renewed (Article 11 of the MT).

By the same procedure, a president and five vice-presidents are appointed from among the members for two-year periods (Article 14 of the MT).

The Commission is responsible for implementing the provisions of the Treaty and the enactments of the institutions, and it exercises the powers conferred on it by the Council. It makes proposals and recommendations or issues formal opinions whenever it thinks fit or where required by the Treaty. Under the conditions laid down in the Treaty it has its own power of decision (Article 155), exercised *inter alia* in respect of competition and some aspects of trade. The decisions of the Commission are reached by majority vote (Article 17 of the MT). The powers of the Commission are more circumscribed than those of the ECSC High Authority (partly because the EEC Treaty, unlike the ECSC Treaty, is more of an "outline agreement" — see 4). Though it has a practically unlimited right of initiative, its proposals need the agreement of the Council. Such approval is only required in some cases under the Treaty of Paris.

Each year, at least one month before the opening of the Parliament session, the Commission publishes a report on the activities of the Community (Article 18 of the MT). As the Parliament annual session opens in March (Article 138), that means February.

Since 6 January 1989, J. Delors (France) is president of the Commission, the vice-presidents are F. Andriessen (Netherlands), H. Christophersen (Denmark), M. Marin (Spain), F. Pandolfi (Italy), M. Bangemann (Germany) and L. Brittan (United Kingdom); the other members are C. Ripa de Meana (Italy), A. Cardoso e Cunha (Portugal), A. Matutes (Spain), P. Schmidhuber (Germany), C. Scrivener (France), B. Millan (United Kingdom), J. Dondelinger (Luxemburg), R. Mac Sharry (Ireland), K. Van Miert (Belgium) and V. Papandreou (Greece).

The Commission is assisted by a number of advisory committees; some of them are mentioned in the Treaty — e.g., the Monetary Committee (Article 105,2) which also assists the Council, the Transport Committee for negotiations with non-member countries (Article 113,3). Its staff consists of 17 257 people (31 December 1989).

In 1974 the Economic Policy Committee took over the activities of the Short-term Economic Policy Committee (1960), the Medium-term Economic Policy Committee (1964) and the Budget Policy Committee (1964). Also worth mentioning are the Committee of Governors of the Central Banks (1964) and the various management committees (one for each product group) which assist the Commission in administering the common agricultural policy.

4. *The European Parliament*

Provision had already been made in the ECSC Treaty for an Assembly consisting of "representatives of the peoples of the member states" (Article 20). It consisted of 78 members, appointed and delegated by the six national parliaments.

When the EEC and Euratom came into being, a single Assembly with jurisdiction over the three Communities was established. The number of seats was increased subsequently to 518 members.

The concept "European Parliament" cannot be found in the EEC and EAEC Treaties; however, on 20 March 1962 the Assembly decided to rename itself the "European Parliament".

The Parliament supervises the operation of the Community (Article 137), debating the Commission's annual report in open session. It has power to compel the Commission to resign in a body on a vote of censure. Should a motion of censure be tabled, voting cannot take place until three days later, and in order to be carried the motion requires a two-thirds majority out of an attendance representing a majority of the total membership (Article 44). There have been four proposals of motions of censure; two were withdrawn and two were not successful.

Another means of control is the right of the Parliament or its members to put questions to the Commission (now about 5000 a year), which may be answered either in writing or orally. Members of the Commission must be heard at their request (Article 140). The Treaties do not provide for control over the Council, although it takes the most important decisions.

The Parliament advises on most proposals made by the Commission to the Council. Such advice is compulsory in many cases, e.g. measures to be taken in the common agricultural policy (Article 43), common transport policy (Article 75), conclusion of an association agreement (Article 228), any amendment of the Treaty (Article 236), but the Council decides freely whether the opinion of the Parliament is to be taken into account.

On budgetary matters, the power of the Parliament has been extended. The procedure for the preparation and approval of the European budget is laid down in Article 203 (in effect from 1977) as altered by the Treaty amending certain budgetary provisions (1970) and the Treaty amending certain financial provisions (1975).

The draft budget is forwarded to the Parliament not later than 5 October of the year preceding that in which the budget is to be implemented. Amendments by the Parliament (to be made within 45 days) on compulsory items of expenditure (those which necessarily arise from the Treaty or from acts adopted in accordance therewith) are discussed by the Commission and the Council (within 15 days), the latter deciding by a qualified majority on any proposed change. The Council has the last word in determining the amount of expenditure of this category.

In the case of non-compulsory expenditure (about 15 per cent of the total) the Commission fixes a maximum rate of increase each year (taking into account the movement of the gross national product, the member states' budgets and the trend of the cost of living). The amount of these items of expenditure is fixed by the Parliament, on condition that the maximum rate of increase is complied with.

The Treaty of 22 July 1975 extended the authority of the Parliament in this field. The Parliament is entitled to reject the entire draft budget "for important reasons" and to require the presentation of a new draft (Article 203,*8*). It did so once, in 1979. Only the Parliament can discharge the Commission in respect of the implementation of the budget, since the Commission implements the budget (Article 205).

After numerous proposals and endless debates concerning the number and the distribution of the seats and procedural matters, the Council decided on 20 September 1976, in accordance with Article 138, that the Parliament must be elected by direct universal suffrage. The number of seats (518) is broken down as follows: Germany, France, Italy and the United Kingdom each 81; Spain 60; the Netherlands 25; Belgium, Greece and Portugal each 24; Denmark 16; Ireland 15 and Luxemburg 6. The first elections were held on 7 and 10 June 1979, the second on 14 and 17 June 1984, and the third from 15 to 18 June 1989.

The seats are distributed as follows: Socialists 180, European People's Party 121, Liberal, Democratic and Reformist Group 49, European Democratic Group 34, Greens 29, European Unitarian Left 28, European Democratic Alliance 22, European Right 17, Left Unity Group 14, Rainbow Group 14, Non-affiliated 10.

The Parliament meets in plenary in Strasbourg, in committees in Brussels, its Secretariat being located in Luxemburg (about 3 300 people on 31 December 1989). Various committees have their meetings in Brussels.

The Parliament has been criticized for the slowness of its procedures.

5. *The Court of Justice*

As was the case with the Parliament, a single Court of Justice for the three Communities was established on 1 January 1958, with jurisdiction over the three Communities (Article 3 of the Convention on certain Institutions common to the European Communities). The function of the Court is to ensure that in the interpretation and application of the Treaty the law is observed (Article 164). Judges must perform their duties "impartially and conscientiously".

The Court consists of thirteen judges, appointed by the governments for a term of six years. Every three years a partial renewal of the bench takes place but the outgoing judges may be reappointed (Article 167). The Court is assisted by six independent advocates-general, who make reasoned submissions on cases brought before the Court (Article 166).

Subject to limitations set forth in the Treaties, the Court may hear disputes between member states, between the Commission or the Council and member states, or between private persons and the Commission or the Council. The Commission (Article 169) or a member state (Article 170) may bring a matter before the Court if it considers that a member state has failed to fulfil an obligation under the Treaty. This right cannot be exercised by private persons, the Parliament or the Council. Hitherto there have been no direct confrontations between member states before the Court; on the other hand, the Commission has often invoked Article 169 and 170.

If the Court finds that there has been an infringement, the obligation to remedy the situation flows from Article 171; however, no other sanctions than the cost of judgment are laid down for a country failing to take such action.

The Court has unlimited jurisdiction in regard to the penalties provided for in the Council regulations (Article 172).

Article 173 assigns to the Court the task of reviewing the legality of acts of the Council or the Commission other than recommendations and opinions. It has jurisdiction in actions brought by a member state, the Council or the Commission on grounds of lack of competence, infringement of an essential procedural requirement, infringement of the Treaty or of any rule of law to its application, or misuse of power. Any natural or legal person (provided the decision is addressed to that person or, although in the form of a regulation or a decision addressed to another person, is of direct and individual concern to the former), the Commission, the Council or a member state can bring cases before the Court. Any act which is found to be illegal will be declared void by the Court.

Failure to act on the part of the Commission or the Council, in contravention of the Treaty, may give rise to a complaint by the member states, the institutions of the Community or any natural or legal person to the Court of Justice (Article 175). On 22 January 1983 the Parliament brought an action before the Court for failure to act by the Council in the field of transport policy. In its judgment of 22 May 1985 the Court declared these proceedings admissible and to a certain extent well-founded.

Moreover, the Court may rule on questions of Community law submitted to it by national courts. The Court gives preliminary rulings (not to be confused with decisions in appeal) concerning the interpretation of the Treaty, the validity and interpretation of acts of the Community institutions, and the interpretation of the statutes of the bodies established by the Council (Article 177). Furthermore, in matters of non-contractual liability, the Court has jurisdiction in disputes relating to compensation for damage caused by the Community institutions or by its servants in the performance of their duties (Article 178), in disputes between the Community and its servants (Article 179) and in disputes relating to the activities of the European Investment Bank (Article 180). The seat of the Court of Justice is in Luxemburg.

At the request of the Court and after consulting the Commission and the

Parliament, the Council may, acting unanimously, attach to the Court of Justice a court with jurisdiction to hear and determine at first instance, subject to a right of appeal to the Court of Justice on points of law only, certain classes of action or proceeding brought by natural or legal persons (Article 168A of the Single Act).

6. *The Economic and Social Committee*

The Economic and Social Committee is made up of representatives of the various economic and social groups (Article 193). The members are appointed by the Council for a term of four years (twenty-four members each from Western Germany, France, Italy and the United Kingdom; twenty-one from Spain; twelve each from Belgium, the Netherlands, Greece, and Portugal; nine each from Denmark and Ireland; six from Luxemburg) and may be reappointed (Article 194). From 1973 to 1975 the British trade unions (8 seats) refused to attend the Committee's meetings.

The Committee appoints from among its members a chairman for a period of two years. The chairman convenes the Committee at the request of the Council or of the Commission (Article 196). Provision is made for specialized sections, including an agricultural and a transport section (Article 197).

The Committee must be consulted by the Council or the Commission in certain cases, and it may be consulted in others (Article 198). Since 1972, the Committee has been able to advise on its own initiative on all questions affecting the Community.

7. *The Consultative Committee (ECSC)*

The Consultative Committee consists of not less than seventy-two and not more than ninety-six members, who are appointed for two years by the Council. It comprises three numerically equal groups, representing producers, workers, and consumers and dealers (Article 18 of ECSC Treaty).

The Commission consults the Committee whenever it thinks fit; in cases specified by the Treaty it is obliged to do so. It submits to the Committee the general objectives and regular programmes drawn up under Article 46, and keeps it abreast of the broad outlines of its work in connection with industrial investment and with restrictive agreements and mergers (Article 19 of the ECSC Treaty).

4. FUNCTIONS AND OPERATION

The EEC Treaty is more of an "outline agreement" than the ECSC Treaty: only general directives are laid down, and only for a limited number of items

— such as the establishment of a customs union — does the Treaty go into detail. Consequently, the EEC Treaty is a more flexible instrument on the whole.

A. *The creation of a customs union*

As the provisions concerning the liberalization of trade in manufactures differ substantially from those relating to agriculture and ECSC products, the three categories are treated separately.

The creation of a tariff union involves the elimination of customs duties and charges with equivalent effect, and of quantitative restrictions and measures with equivalent effect in trade between EEC countries. In addition, a common customs tariff and a common commercial policy are to be adopted. Finally some contend that a common policy on indirect taxation is required.

1. *ECSC products*

a. *Provisions*

Liberalization of trade in iron and steel products was one of the objectives of the ECSC. Import and export duties, charges with equivalent effect and quantitative restrictions are prohibited (Article 4,*a*).

As regards commercial policy towards non-member states, the powers of the High Authority (the former executive body) are rather limited. In principle the Treaty does not encroach upon the member states' sovereignty in matters of commercial policy (Article 71,*1*).

Governments are required to notify the High Authority in advance of proposed trade agreements concerning coal or steel or the importation of raw materials or specialized equipment for their production. If the effect of such agreements would be to interfere with the implementation of the Treaty, the High Authority has to issue the necessary recommendations within ten days of receiving the advance particulars; otherwise, it may issue opinions without binding force (Article 75).

The member countries are further required to assist one another with measures which the High Authority deems to be in accordance with the Treaty and existing international agreements (Article 71, third paragraph). This is part of the general undertaking to coordinate the member states' economic policies through the Council (Article 26).

The Treaty makes no provision for a common external tariff: the most that it does in this direction is to allow that, on the proposal of the High Authority or of a member state, the Council may, by unanimous vote, fix maximum and minimum duties, the governments then charging their own rates within the range. The High Authority can, on its own initiative or at the request of a member state, issue opinions suggesting tariff modifications (Article 72), since disparities in the rates of duty charged on imports from non-ECSC countries could interfere with trade.

In any measures to safeguard the common market against imports from abroad, GATT rules must be observed. The High Authority is empowered to take any steps consonant with the Treaty, and to issue appropriate recommendations to the governments, in the event of:

1. dumping or other practices prohibited by the GATT;
2. undercutting from outside made possible by competitive conditions not allowed in the Community by the Treaty;
3. a rise in imports causing or liable to cause serious injury to production in the common market (Article 74).

Action with regard to exports to non-ECSC countries is also permitted in some circumstances. Should a serious shortage develop, the High Authority may, on the advice of the Consultative Committee and with the agreement of the Council, require the member countries to impose export controls (Article 59,5) or, subject to certain conditions, maximum or minimum export prices (Article 61,*c*).

b. *Operation*

On 10 February 1953 the frontiers between member countries were opened for coal, iron ore and scrap: quantitative restrictions on the import and export of these products were abolished. The common market for steel was introduced on 1 May 1953, and for special steels on 1 August 1954.

Importers and exporters were still required, as before, to comply with the regulations regarding customs clearance and statistical checking of the merchandise.

In April 1959 the Assembly pressed the High Authority, in cooperation with the governments, to frame a common commercial policy in respect of coal imports from non-ECSC countries. However, the governments declined, as they had already done in October 1958, to accept the High Authority's suggested importation programme, and made their own individual arrangements. The High Authority has since been endeavouring at any rate to ensure as far as possible that these arrangements do not conflict.

Following consultations between the Council and the High Authority, the governments decided on 6 June and 15 July 1963 respectively to impose quotas on imports of steel and pig iron from countries with Soviet-type economies, up to the end of 1964; the timelimit was subsequently extended each year. Community producers are forbidden to align prices on the lower quotations from these countries.

This step, rendered necessary by deterioration in the state of the market, could not be taken *vis-à-vis* GATT countries. Accordingly, from 15 February 1964 the rate of duty on iron and steel imports was raised to an average level of 9 per cent (corresponding to the Italian minimum rate), and in addition a specific duty of at least 7 dollars per ton was imposed on imports of foundry pig iron, GATT procedure of course remaining valid. Exemptions, permitting importation at the former rate of duty and without payment of the specific duty, were granted subsequently. On 1 January 1967 the specific duty was lowered from 7 dollars to 5 dollars. After the Kennedy Round (see Chapter 3) it was decided to reduce the rate of duty from 9 per cent to 5.7 per cent (the US rate from 7.5 per cent to 5.9 per cent, the UK rate from 10 per cent to 8 per cent; in the UK, the £4.50 specific duty was cut by 20 per cent).

Without being obliged to do so, the member states harmonized their customs duties on products covered by the ECSC Treaty (from 1 January 1972 on). The unified tariff on ECSC products had to be applied by the new members.

2. *Manufactures other than ECSC products*

a. *Elimination of customs duties*

1. *Provisions*
The member states are required to refrain from introducing new import duties or charges with equivalent effect and from increasing those already in force (Article 12), while existing import duties (and similar charges) are to be gradually abolished in the course of the transition period (Article 13). A detailed time-table for reducing import duties is laid down in the Treaty (Article 14).

Not later than the end of the first stage, customs duties on exports and charges with equivalent effect had to be abolished between the member states (Article 16). Duties designed essentially to produce revenue are also cut by at least 10 per cent every time the basic duty is reduced (Article 17,*1*); they can be replaced by internal charges as long as this involves no discrimination or indirect protection (Articles 17,*3* and 95).

These provisions could not be implemented immediately by the countries joining the European Community subsequently. Accordingly, transitional measures had to be decided upon.

2. *Operation*
Customs duties were reduced in accordance with the pre-established table. In pursuance of two speed-up decisions taken on 13 May 1960 and 15 May 1962, additional cuts were made on 1 January 1961 and 1 July 1962. Although the Treaty provides for a minimum cut of only 5 per cent on each duty, the reduction generally amounted to 10 per cent on each occasion.

On the whole, the member states have met their obligations. There have only been a few failures to do so. In some countries internal charges were introduced or raised as tariffs on certain products were dismantled. Where the governments concerned refused to terminate such measures, the Commission brought the matter before the Court of Justice.

On 1 July 1968 (eighteen months ahead of schedule) all common duties on industrial products traded within member countries were abolished. Notwithstanding the difficulties inherent in the general economic situation, duty-free trade within the nine member countries was achieved on 1 July 1977.

The Commission has done its utmost to secure the removal of charges equivalent in effect to customs duties. Hundreds of such charges have been listed (e.g. licensing charges, statistical dues, stamp duties, duties on the loading and unloading of goods, charges and dues the revenue from which is intended to finance the activities of organizations which are partly government-controlled).

As the requirement to abolish these charges before the end of the transition period was not met completely, the Commission continued to enact directives for the elimination of such charges. At the final date for the elimination of the like charges imposed by the new member states (e.g., 1 July 1977) similar difficulties arose.

By the end of the first stage of the transition period, all export duties have been abolished. The elimination of export charges with equivalent effect caused more problems. The Court of Justice has been asked to rule on Article 16 on several occasions.

b. *Elimination of non-tariff barriers*

1. *Provisions*
Quantitative restrictions on imports and all measures equivalent in effect are prohibited between member states (Article 30). New restrictions are also prohibited. This applies only to the degree of liberalization attained in pursuance of the decisions reached by the OEEC Council on 14 January 1955 (Article 31). Exceptions to this rule may be made on grounds of public morality, the preservation of public order and public security, and on certain other grounds such as the protection of national treasures or of patents and trademarks (Article 36). New restrictions are permitted only under the safeguard clauses written into the Treaty (e.g., Articles 108, 109 and — during the transition period — 226).

Existing quotas are gradually to be abolished during the transition period (Article 32). Measures equivalent in effect to quantitative restrictions are set aside as directed by the Commission (Article 33,7). Export restrictions are prohibited after the first stage (Article 34).

Quantitative restrictions on trade between the original and new member countries, and between the new members themselves, are to be abolished from the date of accession. Measures with equivalent effect must also be eliminated.

Government monopolies may also restrict international trade in the same degree as quantitative restrictions. Such monopolies of a commercial character are therefore gradually to be adjusted so that by the end of the transition period there is no discrimination between the nationals of member countries as regards the purchase or sale of goods (Article 37,1); the time-table for adjustment is harmonized with that for the removal of quantitative restrictions. If there is a monopoly in only one or some EEC countries, protective measures can be authorized in the other states of the Community (Article 37,3). Similar measures have been introduced at the accession of the new member states.

2. *Operation*

There have been many infringements on Articles 30 to 34 but the countries involved have complied with the Treaty after intervention by the Commission and/or a ruling by the Court of Justice.

Quantitative restrictions on exports were removed shortly after the end of the first stage. After the removal of quantitative restrictions, the Commission's chief purpose has been to abolish measures equivalent in effect. These include practices whereby imports are linked to the export or purchase of home-produced goods and those involving discrimination in respect of public tenders.

In 1974 the Court of Justice stated that "all trading rules enacted by member states which are capable of hindering, directly or indirectly, actually or potentially, intra-Community trade are to be considered as measures having an effect equivalent to quantitative restrictions". This view has been specified in 1979 (*Cassis de Dijon* case) and in 1981: "the authorities of the importing State are ... not entitled unnecessarily to require technical or chemical analyses or laboratory tests when the same analyses or tests have already been carried out in another Member State and their results are available to those authorities or may at their request be placed at their disposal".

Although progress had been made in the field of removal of technical barriers to trade, the Council adopted a new approach to technical harmonization and standards on 7 May 1985. This approach is based on the following principles:

a) harmonization of legislation is confined to the adoption of the essential safety requirements (or other requirements in the general interest) to which products must conform in order to enjoy freedom of movement throughout the Community;

b) the task of drawing up the technical specifications needed to ensure the manufacture and marketing of products that conform to the essential requirements is entrusted to industrial standardization organizations;

c) these technical specifications are not mandatory;
d) this means that a manufacturer may choose not to manufacture products conforming to the standards, but in that case he must show that they do conform to the essential requirements of the relevant directive.

Decisions under the new approach have been taken in the case of pressure vessels, toys and construction products and machinery. However, as things stand there is little hope of getting hundreds of standards ready for 1993.

Article 34, on export restrictions, which was long considered of minor significance, acquired increased importance in 1974 when several member states introduced a system of administrative authorization for the export of petroleum products. Hence the Dutch government had to abolish the reservation of gas for Dutch users.

With regard to the implementation of Article 37 difficulties have arisen as a result of national monopolies in France, Italy and Western Germany. The Commission has repeatedly urged the governments concerned gradually to liberalize imports and to eliminate discrimination in marketing conditions.

Certain state monopolies have been eliminated: e.g. in Italy on sulphur, bananas, quinine, lighters, flints, cigarettes, paper, salt and matches; discriminatory measures on matches have been eliminated in France. Negotiations with France (on tobacco, alcoholic beverages and petroleum products) and with Italy (on tobacco) to prevail upon the governments in question to adapt their legislation on Article 37 took much time. At the end of 1981 only the Commission decided not to proceed with its action before the Court concerning the French and Italian monopoly in manufactured tobacco and the Italian match monopoly, after the governments concerned agreed to take measures by the end of 1983. So far the Greek government has not taken steps to adjust its monopoly in petroleum products, notwithstanding a condemnation by the Court in 1990.

The Commission has tried to open up public procurement markets (except those relating to offensive weapons, munitions and war-related materials), representing 500 billion ECU, or 15 per cent of Community GDP. The rules adopted in the 1970s (relating mainly to publicity) were largely flouted.

Directives on public supplies and on public works came into force respectively in 1989 and 1990 (1991 for Greece, Spain and Portugal), others relating to compliance measures will come into force in 1992 (1996 for Spain and 1998 for Greece and Portugal). As from 1993 public procurement markets for water, energy, transport and telecommunications (previously excluded from Community legislation) must be opened up.

The inefficiency of the relevant industries is demonstrated by their low rates of capacity utilization. Hence large price differences. The price per installed telephone ranges between 225 and 500 dollars in the EC, against 100 dollars in the US. In the power and railway equipment sectors restructuring is particularly necessary.

c. *Establishment of a common customs tariff*

1. *Provisions*

The member states are ready to reduce the common duties "on a basis of reciprocity and mutual advantage" in order to "contribute to the development of international trade and the lowering of barriers to trade" (Article 18). As a general rule, the duties in the common customs tariff are calculated on the arithmetic mean of the duties applied in Benelux, Western Germany, France and Italy on 1 January 1957 (Article 19,*1—2*).

Several exceptions to this rule are mentioned in Article 19. For six lists of products (Lists A—F) the common external tariff will be calculated in a different way. For List G goods the common tariff will be determined at a later date (Article 20).

The timetable for the gradual alignment of national tariffs to the common tariff is laid down in Article 23,*1*. The common tariff is to be implemented not later than the end of the transition period (Article 23,*3*). The member states are free to align these duties at a faster pace (Article 24).

To obviate harmful economic consequences, two safeguards are provided for — the opening of tariff quotas, i.e. quotas at a reduced rate of duty or duty free (Article 25), and the authorized postponement of the introduction of the common tariff (Article 26).

The Council decides by qualified majority vote on any *autonomous* alteration or suspension of duties in the common tariff of the Commission (Article 28). The member states are prepared to reduce the external tariff in order to contribute to the development of world trade and the removal of obstacles to trade (Article 18).

Before the end of the first stage, EEC countries are required to approximate their provisions imposed by law, regulation of administrative action in respect of customs matters (Article 27).

The new member countries had to apply the common customs tariff according to the accession provisions.

2. *Operation*

On 13 February 1960 the Council approved a draft common tariff. On 2 March 1960 an agreement was signed concerning List G duties (including vegetable oils, oil products, synthetic rubber, wood and motor-vehicle parts). At the beginning of 1962 the only outstanding points were duties on manufactured tobacco and oil products.

The average of duties in the external tariff was about 12.5 per cent on the basis of EEC imports in 1958. For the countries with low tariffs — the Benelux countries and Western Germany — this meant an increase in customs protection, while for the others — France and Italy — the result was less protection.

The speed-up decisions mentioned above (see 4A,*2a*) also applied to the external tariff. Consequently, national tariffs were brought more in line with the common tariff on 1 January 1961 (one year ahead of schedule) and on 1 July 1963 (thirty months ahead of schedule). On each occasion the difference between the external tariff and the national tariffs was reduced by 30 per cent.

From 1960 on changes were made in the external tariff as a result of tariff conferences in GATT (see Chapter 3). The EEC states were prepared to make concessions during the Dillon Round amounting to a 20 per cent cut in the external tariff, to show that they had no protectionist aims. In fact, the tariff negotiations brought about a reduction of some 8 per cent. As a result, the average of duties in the external tariff was 11.7 per cent in 1963 (17.8 and 18.4 per cent for the United States and the United Kingdom, respectively).

The Council finally approved a common customs duty for manufactured tobacco on 6 February 1962 and for oil products on 8 May 1964. This decision made the common customs tariff complete.

As elimination of internal customs duties was reached on 1 July 1968, member states were bound to apply the common external tariff from that date (eighteen months before the end of the transition period).

After the conclusion of the Kennedy Round — in which the EEC took part as a single entity — the common external tariff was cut by 32 per cent (as was the United States tariff, against 35 per cent for the United Kingdom tariff), so that on 1 January 1972 the common external tariff averaged 8.1 per cent compared with about 12 per cent for the US tariff and 11.5 per cent for the UK tariff.

The various trade and association agreements concluded between the EEC and non-member countries, the GSP and the Lomé Convention in most cases provide for a reduction of or exemption from the common customs tariff on specific EEC imports (see 4.D).

Applications for tariff quotas, mainly emanating from Western Germany, related only to industrial products at first, but also to farm products since 1962. The number of quotas applied for (278 at the end of March 1962, 16 at the end of 1970) and granted (104 and 9) declined after 1962. Since 1972 no national tariff quotas have been granted. Community quotas have been substituted for these national quotas in due course because tariff quotas disrupt tariff unity and obstruct the establishment of a customs union. Since July 1971 Community tariff quotas have been applied in the GSP on so-called sensitive and semi-sensitive products imported from the less-developed countries (e.g., textile products).

The Commission prefers as a rule to grant suspension of customs duties, particularly if this benefits manufacturing industries in the EEC. During last years the common customs tariffs on about a thousand products or groups of products (particularly chemicals, plastics, medical supplies and products of the aircraft and electronics industries) were suspended.

On 27 June 1968 the Council adopted regulations with a view to reducing as much as possible the differences in the methods by which the value and origin of goods are assessed. Since 1981 the Customs Valuation Code has been adopted (see Chapter 3).

Though the common customs tariff has been applied since 1 July 1968, the sets of customs legislation are still not harmonized (notwithstanding Article 27). A proposal has been made in 1990 for this purpose.

Since 1 January 1970 a regulation on Community transit has been in force, reducing considerably controls and formalities. Since 1 October 1969 the storage of goods from non-member countries without payment of custom duties must be governed by the same conditions throughout the Community. The Council adopted on 25 July 1988 two regulations, one on customs warehouses and the other on free zones and free warehouses.

Processing arrangements allow industrialists to import goods temporarily from non-member countries without payment of customs duties, to process the goods, and to re-export the products to markets abroad. In the member countries that purchase these processed products, the conditions of competition are distorted because these member states levy customs duties on goods from non-member countries consumed or utilized on the home market. As a consequence, countervailing charges were instituted on 1 January 1969.

The Council decision of 21 April 1970 provided that from 1975 onwards all customs receipts, with the exception of a ten per cent fee for costs of collection, would go to the Community. Hence the Community had a strong fiscal interest in seeing that customs duties were collected both fully and fairly.

Not only harmonization but also simplification is needed. In 1987, the Commission approved a new tariff nomenclature.

On 18 February 1985 the Council adopted a single administrative document. From 1 January 1988 the amount of documents and required data is standardized.

d. *Establishment of a common commercial policy*

1. *Provisions*
In the preamble to the Treaty the member states underline their desire 'to contribute, by means of a common commercial policy, to the progressive abolition of restrictions on international trade' (see also Article 18 above). In the setting up of the common customs tariff they will be guided by 'the need to promote trade between member states and third countries' (Article 29 (a)).

Since the common market applies to goods imported from outside the Community (Article 9,2), a common commercial policy towards non-EEC countries is essential.

The content of the common policy could hardly be foreseen and was therefore not laid down in the Treaty (Article 113,*1* states that it should be based on uniform principles). Only one general directive is given: account is to be taken of the likelihood that the abolition of customs duties between member states will make firms in the EEC more competitive (Article 110); the removal of obstacles to the growth of world trade should therefore not be feared (cf. also Article 29,*a*). Article 110 repeats an objective of the customs union: "to contribute, in the common interest, to the harmonious development of world trade, the progressive abolition of restrictions on international trade and the lowering of customs barriers".

During the transition period trade relations with non-member countries must be coordinated so that a common commercial policy can be implemented by the end of the period. The Commission submits the appropriate proposals to the Council (Article 111,*1*; see also Articles 113,*2* and 114).

Although many powers have been transferred to the Community (tariff rules, conclusion of tariff and trade agreements, achievement of uniformity in measures of liberalization, export policy, anti-dumping and countervailing duties), the remaining member states' powers may give rise to differing degrees of liberalization. Nevertheless, the member states are to aim at securing as high a level of uniformity as possible in liberalizing trade with non-EEC states (Article 111,*5*). Protective measures may be authorized in cases of difficulty (Article 115).

Export subsidies are to be harmonized to the extent necessary to ensure that competition is not distorted (Article 112,*1*). This does not apply to the normal drawback of customs duties or indirect charges on goods exported (Article 112,*2*). The Protocol on German internal trade and connected problems (Annex to the EEC Treaty) established, in fact, free trade between the then two German states (unified on 3 October 1990).

2. *Operation*

Several Council decisions aiming at harmonization of the member countries' commercial policies have already been dealt with in the previous section. Accordingly, only the measures concerning the conclusion of trade agreements with non-member countries and the establishment of common liberalization lists are set out below.

It was not until 1960 that the first decision was taken on the principles of the common commercial policy. The member states were asked to include an "EEC clause" in bilateral agreements with non-member countries whereby any amendment to these agreements necessary under the common commercial policy may be negotiated without delay.

A procedure was instituted in 1961 whereby joint consultation is obligatory before a member country concludes trade agreements with, or amends liberalization arrangements in respect of, non-member states. Further efforts were made in subsequent years to institute systematic coordination of the commercial policy of the member states, but there was not much progress. The Community's first trade agreement was signed on 14 October 1963 with Iran (not reconducted in 1972).

On 5 April 1968 the Council adopted a regulation on defence against dumping practices, bonuses or subsidies on the part of non-member countries. It follows closely GATT rules (see Chapter 3).

The latest legislation dates from 11 July 1988. It relates to protection against dumped or subsidized imports from countries not members of the Community, but it does not apply to services, such as banking and insurance. An additional duty may be imposed if it can be shown that the foreign exporter chooses to bear the cost of the anti-dumping duty himself, rather than pass it on in the form of a higher price for his product on the Community market.

Anti-dumping duties could also be extended on products assembled in the Community. The objective was to prevent non-EC exporters from avoiding anti-dumping duties by importing components for the assembly of products identical to the imported products (which are subject to the duties) in Community 'screwdriver' plants. A GATT panel ruled in March 1990 that such EC action is inconsistent with GATT, because the duties are not levied at the borders, but are internal charges.

Where, during the course of an investigation, acceptable undertakings are offered, the investigation may be terminated without imposition of duties. (In undertakings foreign exporters promise, for example, to respect minimum export prices and agreed-on conditions of sale.)

Recent investigations involved mainly Japan, Yugoslavia and Korea. Anti-dumping duties relate, for example, to video-recorders (Korea and Japan), circumvention duties to electronic scales and typewriters (Japan). The few cases of anti-subsidy proceedings have been essentially directed against Spain and Brazil (steel products).

According to a Council regulation of 22 December 1986 on unfair pricing practices in maritime transport, a regressive duty may be imposed when an unfair price practice causes a major injury. On 4 January 1989 the Commission imposed a regressive duty of 450 ECU pro container on the South Korean Hyundai Merchant Marine for undercutting freight rates to Australia of Community shippers.

Harmonization of the member countries' export arrangements has been attained almost completely. Only for a few common customs tariff headings are there export restrictions (e.g., products in short supply in the Community, certain oil products, chemical products that may be used for the production of chemical weapons).

On 16 December 1969, the Council confirmed, on the basis of Article 113, that the conduct of trade negotiations should be the responsibility of the Commission. Trade agreements have been gradually aligned (see also External relations). In addition, the Community participates in a variety of multilateral agreements (e.g., on textiles).

As a result of the delay in the realization of a common commercial policy, intra-Community controls on imports of the products from non-member countries and even from member countries were needed after the transition period to establish the origin of the products.

Article 115 has been used mostly in respect to textiles and other products from Japan (for example, video-recorders) and the state-trading countries. In 1989 authorizations were given to France (73), Italy (sixteen), Spain (twelve), the United Kingdom (three), Greece (two) and Portugal (one). In 1990 the Commission authorized France to stop imports (via other member countries) on TV receivers from Japan and South Korea. Italy obtained a similar authorization in respect of industrial sewing machines from Japan.

A typical example of a market influenced by different national import regimes is the car market. Italy, France, Spain, Portugal and the United Kingdom limit their imports of Japanese cars (for example, France three per cent of the market, Italy 3.000 cars a year plus 14.000 units from other member countries).

The realization of the internal market does not imply the elimination of Article 115, but the progressive abandonment of its use. However, if the economic difficulties in the country or countries concerned are substantial, the Community may be obliged to communitarize the national contingents.

On 9 February 1982 new rules for imports from non-member countries other than state-trading countries, China, and Cuba, and on 5 July 1982 new rules for state-trading countries and China, entered into force. The new arrangements establish the principles of a formal investigation, at Community level, prior to the adoption of surveillance or protective measures. The new arrangements are uniform throughout the Community for all products. Protective measures may only be adopted by the Community authorities.

Under the Multifibre Agreement (see Chapter 3) the quotas of textiles and clothing are partitioned into intra-EEC quotas.

On 17 September 1984 the Council adopted a "new commercial policy instrument" enabling the Community to respond to any illicit commercial practice with a view to removing the injury resulting therefrom. It refers to any practice attributable to non-member countries which are incompatible with international law or commonly accepted rules of international commerce, such as restrictive administrative practices contrary to international rules, restrictions on imports of raw materials and certain other restrictions on imports.

A complaint under this regulation (16 March 1987) by the Association of European members of the International Federation of Phonogram and Videogram Producers related to the unauthorized reproduction of sound recordings in Indonesia. The Commission terminated (11 May 1988) the examination procedure after Indonesia's undertaking to give sound recordings by EC nationals the same protection as those by Indonesian nationals.

3. *Agricultural products*

a. *Provisions*

Agricultural products are taken to include the products of the soil, stock-farming and fisheries, together with products of first-stage processing directly related to them (Article 38,*1*); they are listed in Annex 2 to the Treaty. Within two years of the Treaty's coming into force this list may be extended (Article 38,*3*). It was agreed from the outset that the general rules for the establishment of a common market could not simply be taken over and applied to agricultural products since farming conditions and government intervention varied too much from country to country. This explains the special provisions set out below concerning general policy, prices and long-term agreements.

In the replacement of national market regulations by a common policy, the objectives are to increase productivity, and thus "a fair standard of living for the agricultural community", stabilize markets, guarantee supplies and ensure reasonable prices for consumers (Article 39,*1*).

The common policy to be put into effect during the transition period (Article 40,*1*) may take one of the following forms — common rules of competition, compulsory coordination of member states' market regulation arrangements, or a Community system of market regulation (Article 40,*2*). Measures that can be taken to achieve these objectives include price regulation, subsidies, arrangements for stockpiling and stabilization of imports and exports, guidance and guarantee funds (Article 40,*3—4*). Provisions may also be made for coordination in vocational training, research and dissemination of information and for promoting the consumption of certain products (Article 41).

The rules of competition (Articles 85—94) apply to agriculture only where the Council so stipulates. The Council can also authorize protection for undertakings handicapped by structural or natural conditions or assistance within the framework of development plans (Article 42).

The Council issues regulations, directives or decisions relating to the common agricultural policy on proposals by the Commission and after consulting the Parliament, the Economic and Social Committee and sometimes other committees (e.g., the Committee of Governors of the Central Banks). Account must be taken of the work of the agricultural conference to be convened within two years of the Treaty's coming into force (Article 43,*1—2*).

The enactments of the Council have to be adopted by unanimous vote during the first two stages and thereafter by qualified majority vote (Article 43,*2*). Community regulations can be substituted for the member states' regulatory arrangements if equivalent guarantees are offered regarding employment, living standards and trade (Article 43,*3*).

In addition to the common market regulations, two transitional measures have been instituted. The first relates to the possibility of applying *minimum prices* to particular products in a non-discriminatory manner and in substitution for quotas. A table of minimum prices still in force must be drawn up at the end of the transition period (Article 44). The second consists in the introduction of long-term agreements (Article 45,*1*).

All systems of common market regulation are to be adopted gradually by the new members.

b. *Operation*

1. *Abolition of internal trade restrictions*
The speed-up decisions (see 4A*2a*) also provide for a reduction of customs duties on agricultural products traded between member states.

On 4 April 1962 the Commission determined criteria for the establishment of minimum prices. In 1969 minimum prices for some products were changed into countervailing duties to be determined by the Commission.

On 1 July 1968 customs duties on farm products covered by common market regulations were replaced by levies. As some regulatory arrangements had still to be introduced, however, customs duties (not exceeding 25 per cent of the basic duty) on the forty or so agricultural products concerned were still applied within the Common Market. On 1 January 1970 these duties were abolished (with the exception of compensatory levies for certain fishery products).

In the case of some products (e.g., grain, butter, condensed milk, certain cheeses, rice, sugar) quantitative restrictions were replaced by a system of levies at the national frontier which were to be gradually reduced (except for the levies on imports from outside the Community) as national prices were aligned. The levy was equal to the difference between the price in the exporting country (the price at the frontier of the importing country) and what is known as the threshold price. Since 1 January 1970 the only remaining import restrictions have been on goods from non-member countries.

Long-term arrangements between member states have been abolished since the various common market regulations came into being.

2. *Common market regulations*
Annex 2 was extended to sugar, alcohol and vinegar, according to Article 38,*3*. The agricultural conference referred to in the Treaty was held in Stresa from 3 to 11 July 1958. It was not until 1959 that the Commission put proposals on the common agricultural policy to the Council. These were recast a number of times to take account of the views of the Economic and Social Committee and of the Parliament.

Difficulties arose chiefly because France (with the lowest prices) wanted the common market to be introduced as quickly as possible, while Western Germany (with the highest prices) tried to hold matters back. On 14 January 1962, after long negotiations, the Council reached agreement on the first set of regulations concerning a number of products. Common market regulations came into effect on 30 July 1962 for grain, pigmeat, poultrymeat, eggs, fruit and vegetables, and wine. Agreement was reached on 5 February 1964 for rice (with effect from 1 September) and for dairy produce and beef and veal (with effect from 1 November).

It was a long time before the prices of regulated products — particularly the price of grain, which more or less determines all the others — were aligned, meaning free movement of these products within the Community. Agreement was finally achieved on 15 December 1964: common (target) prices for grain, pigmeat, poultrymeat and eggs would take effect on 1 July 1967 (on 1 September for rice; in the case of pigmeat, intra-Community levies were not completely abolished until 1 October 1967).

Owing to political difficulties (see 4E2b), no further decisions were taken before 11 May 1966. Common market regulations came into effect on the following dates: olive oil, 10 November 1966; fruit and vegetables (additional arrangements), 1 July 1967; sugar, 1 July 1967 (new rules on 1 July 1981); oilseeds, 1 July 1967 (except sunflower seeds 1 October 1967); fruit and vegetables (not already regulated), 1 July 1968; live trees and other plants, bulbs, cut flowers, etc., 1 July 1968; wine (final arrangements), 1 June 1970; tobacco, 1 June 1970; fishery products, 30 October 1970; sheepmeat (mutton), 20 October 1980. Common prices for beef and veal, milk and milk products were established on 20 July 1968.

At the moment a few agricultural products are still subject to national market regulations such as potatoes and alcohol (with a view of the single market some form of harmonization is envisaged). On 8 June 1983 the Parliament approved an amended proposal (the first proposal dated already from 1972) from the Commission for the regulation of the market in ethyl alcohol of agricultural origin.

Three basic principles govern the operation of the common market regulations:

1. *common prices* expressed in a common denominator so as to guarantee free movement of agricultural products between the member countries;
2. *Community preference* (achieved through variable customs duties and/or levies) in order to protect farmers in the Community against lower and sometimes heavily fluctuating prices on the world market;
3. *financial solidarity* by means of the creation of the European Agricultural Guidance and Guarantee Fund, which finances the common agricultural policy.

These principles resulted in the establishment of a complex system of price concepts (see Figure 2). *Target prices (prix indicatifs)*, regarded as normal (politically "wanted") prices, are fixed by the Community (during the transition period this was done by the member governments). For cereals, this is the wholesale price (including profit margin and any taxes) obtained in the

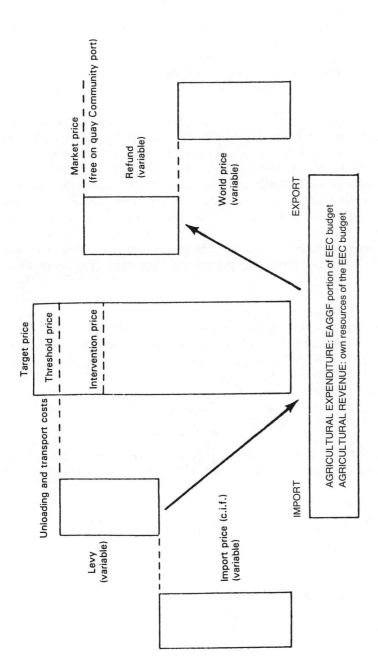

Figure 2. Levy and refund system for wheat (EEC).
Source: *The agricultural policy of the European Community*, European Documentation, third edition, 1983, p. 17.

Community on the market of the area with the greatest deficiency (Duisburg, in Germany). This is in fact a maximum price.

In order to protect the farmers against price decreases within the Community there is also a common *intervention price (prix d'intervention)*, which is guaranteed to producers by the appropriate national agencies. The latter must buy in the products concerned on the market at the intervention price at any time. The intervention price is approximately 9 per cent lower than the target price.

The target prices determine the level of the *threshold prices (prix de seuil)* below which imports from outside the Community are prohibited. The threshold price is equal to the target price less transport and distribution costs from the frontier (Rotterdam) to the market with the greatest deficiency. Variable levies are calculated on a daily basis to bring the prices of imported grain up to the threshold price. In the beef and veal and wine sectors the target price is called the *guide price (prix d'orientation)*, in the pigmeat sector the *basic price*, in the tobacco sector the *norm price*. It is a non-guaranteed price, but efforts must be made to attain it. If the market price falls below 93 per cent of the guide price, intervention purchases are to be made.

About 70 per cent of agricultural products enjoy guaranteed prices and sales. They include soft wheat, barley, rye, maize, rice, sugar, dairy products, beef, sheepmeat, pork, some fruits and vegetables and table wine.

Twenty-one per cent of produce is protected only by measures to prevent low-priced imports from outside the Community. It includes other cereals, other wines, fruit and vegetables, eggs and poultry.

A system of subsidies is used for products predominantely imported by the EEC. It keeps prices down for the consumer and guarantees a minimum income for the producer. It applies to only 2.5 per cent of production (hard wheat, olive oil, certain other oils and tobacco).

Flat rate aid by hectare or quantity produced covers only 0.5 per cent of production (cotton seed, flax, hemp, hops, silk worms, seeds and dehydrated fodder).

Price support for the main types of fish is provided by a "withdrawal price" set at 70—90 per cent of the guide price. Fish withdrawn from the market is used to manufacture fish flour for feed. The support arrangements are implemented by producers' organizations. Protection from non-member countries is ensured by reference prices below which imported products may not enter the Community.

For each of the products mentioned above, a Management Committee has been set up, composed of representatives of the member states and the Commission. If the Committee disagrees the Commission can nevertheless enact the envisaged measure. But it has to inform the Council and the Council can decide otherwise within one month.

Efforts are also being made to work out uniform rules for competition (government support for farms; cf. Article 42) and to harmonize legislation concerning agriculture, foodstuffs and forestry. The Council has issued directives on health requirements for intra-Community trade in beef, veal and pigmeat, on the use of certain preservatives for the surface treatment of citrus fruit, on specific purity standards for preservatives approved for use in foodstuffs for human consumption, on colouring matters for use in these preservatives.

Given the permanent surpluses the Community pursues a more prudent policy and no longer guarantees prices or subsidies for unlimited quantities (see also below). In order to restore market balance several decisions were taken: obligatory distillation in the wine sector, financial co-responsibility of producers, who pay part of cost of storage or disposal through a tax or levy in the milk sector; production quotas, again in the milk sector; guarantee thresholds, which bring a reduction in guaranteed prices when a certain volume of production is exceeded (for cereals, colza, sunflower seeds, processed fruit and raisins); similar mechanisms have been introduced for sugar and cotton.

3. *Monetary compensatory amounts*

As the common agricultural prices are expressed in ECU (since 1979) (see B2b2), they have to be converted into national currency. Originally this conversion was based on the gold parity declared to the IMF.

The French devaluation and the German revaluation in 1969 gave rise to a series of problems for the common agricultural policy. Normally, devaluation and revaluation should have caused, respectively, an automatic increase and a reduction in prices and incomes (in national currency). The countries concerned wanted to avoid a sharp increase (danger of wage rises) or decrease (with repercussions on the agricultural incomes) and preferred a gradual rapprochement of prices. Since common prices are set by the Council, authorization by the Council was needed to delay the changes in price. Thus, France was authorized not to increase its agricultural prices (except for certain products, such as milk and beef), to apply compensatory levies on exports and processed products and to grant subsidies on imports (provided France financed these operations). The introduction of levies and subsidies (called monetary compensatory amounts; MCA's) was necessary to avoid deflection of trade: French exports were artificially cheap, while exports to France were equally hampered. Alignment of the common agricultural prices was completed within two years (before 1 July 1971). The MCA's introduced by a council decision on 12 May 1971 that has been modified several times, level out the difference between the "green" rates and the market exchange rates.

Positive MCA's (e.g., subsidies on exports) are applied after a revaluation, negative MCA's (e.g., a levy on exports) after a devaluation. Since MCA's enable countries with a high price level to stimulate production they lead to an inefficient allocation.

The persistent instability of the international monetary situation has hampered the abolition of the MCA's, intended to be strictly temporary.

From 1 July 1972 they were financed by the Community (Guarantee Section of the Agriculture Fund: see below).

4. The Agriculture Fund

A European Agricultural Guidance and Guarantee Fund (EAGGF) came into operation at the beginning of 1964. The Guidance Section contributes to improvements in the structure of farming (see B2b6). The Guarantee Section makes refunds on exports to non-member countries and finances interventions on the internal market. The expenditures in 1985 amounted to 20 billion ECU, of which 6.5 billion for milk products, 4.5 billion for cereals and rice, 4 billion for meat and 3.2 billion for fruit and vegetables.

The EAGGF is in fact not a separate fund but part and parcel of the Community budget. In the 1989 budget it accounted for about 75 per cent of the total Community expenditure.

B.   The creation of an economic union

1.   Free movement of persons and services

a.   Provisions

The member states were already required by the ECSC Treaty to make provision for free movement within the Community of workers possessing the necessary skills for jobs in the coal and steel industries (Article 60,1). To this end, the member governments undertake to establish a common definition of skilled jobs and conditions of qualification, to settle among themselves any limitations necessary for purposes of public health and public policy, and to work out procedures for bringing the Community labour supply and demand into balance (Article 69,2).

Should shortage of labour interfere with the expansion of production, member states are to adjust their immigration regulations so as to facilitate re-employment of miners and steelworkers from other member states (Article 69,3). These provisions are not to encroach on the observance of the member states' international obligations generally (Article 69,6).

As well as in regard to the engagement of these men, the member states must prohibit all discrimination between them and their own nationals with regard to wages and terms of employment: in addition, special arrangements are to be observed for cross-frontier commuters (Article 69,4).

As regards the EEC Treaty, free migration of workers is to be secured within the Community by the end of the transition period (Article 48,1). Discrimination on grounds of nationality as regards employment, remuneration and other conditions of work and employment is prohibited (Article 48,2). Subject to limitations on grounds of maintaining public order, safety, security or health, workers have the right to accept offers of employment, to move freely within EEC territory and to reside in a member country for the purpose of employment. Provided they comply with conditions to be laid down by the Commission, workers may remain in a member state after having been employed there (Article 48,*3*). These provisions do not apply to employment in the public services (Article 48,*4*). Exchange of young workers is to be encouraged (Article 50).

On a proposal by the Commission, in cooperation with the Parliament and after consulting the Economic and Social Committee, the Council enacts the requisite measures by a qualified majority, including setting up clearing machinery and abolishing administrative obstacles, qualifying periods and other impediments (Article 49). The Council has to act unanimously, on a proposal from the Commission, to introduce a system of social security for migrant workers (Article 51).

Freedom of establishment covers the right to engage in activities as a self-employed person and to set up and manage undertakings (Article 52, second paragraph). New restrictions on these matters may not be introduced (Article 53).

Restrictions on freedom of establishment are gradually to be abolished during the transition period (Article 52, first paragraph) except on grounds of maintaining public order, safety, security or health (Article 56,*1*). This also applies to the establishment of agencies, branches or subsidiaries (Article 52, first paragraph).

On a proposal by the Commission, in cooperation with the Parliament and after consulting the Economic and Social Committee, the Council must issue directives as appropriate (by unanimous vote during the first stage and by qualified majority vote thereafter) (Article 54,*2*). The principles to be taken into account are laid down in the Treaty (Article 54,*3*). Directives are also to be issued for the mutual recognition of degrees and the like (Article 57,*1*) and the coordination of the provisions imposed by law, regulation or administrative action governing establishment (Article 57,*2*). Again, the exercise of public authority constitutes an exception (Article 55).

Companies or firms "formed in accordance with the law of a member state and having their registered office, central administration or principal place of business within the Community shall, for the purposes of this Chapter" (Right of establishment) "be treated in the same way as natural persons who are nationals of member states" (Article 58).

For services too, no new restrictions may be introduced once the Treaty comes into force (Article 62). Existing restrictions are gradually to be abolished during the transition period in accordance with the Council's programme (Article 59 and 63,*1*). As long as restrictions have not been abolished, they must be applied without distinction on ground of nationality or residence (Article 65). The member countries are prepared to speed up liberalization if their economic situation permits (Article 64).

A number of articles refer to transport (Articles 61,*1*, 74, 83). They will be dealt with below.

b. *Operation*

As regards the ECSC provisions, an agreement came into force on 1 September 1957 entitling various categories of skilled workers to take employment in the coal and steel sector of other member countries: the list of jobs concerned was subsequently extended.

On 16 August 1961 a regulation was issued containing the first measures to introduce freedom of movement for workers within the Community (EEC Treaty). A new regulation came into force on 1 May 1964. All priority for the home labour market is henceforth to be abandoned, and workers from other EEC countries are to be given the same treatment as regards access to employment. They will have priority over workers from non-member states.

On 29 July 1968 the Council decided to remove the last restrictions. In other words, employees need not be in possession of a labour permit; they need only apply for a residence permit (valid for five years). It also extended the free movement of workers to the French overseas departments (Guadeloupe, Martinique, Réunion and Guiana).

In 1974 the Council adopted two directives concerning the right of foreign workers to remain in the country of immigration after having been employed in that country. Problems arose in connection with the accession of the United Kingdom. Since British legislation was fairly liberal as regards the influx of persons from former British territories, the original members feared that persons from African or Asiatic countries might insist that the rules on free movement of workers should be applied to them. Accordingly, the term "nationals" was defined in an Annex to the Accession Treaty. Article 48 only applies to citizens of the United Kingdom and to Commonwealth citizens who are actually living in the United Kingdom and have a permanent right to reside. The Joint Declaration on the Free Movement of Workers (Annex to the Accession Treaty) provides that if the enlargement of the Community causes certain difficulties in the social situation in a member state, the matter can be brought before the institutions to find a solution. This escape clause has not yet been invoked.

In 1974 the Court of Justice ruled that Articles 59 and 60 may be directly invoked before national courts in certain cases; the law of a member state may not require a person established in another member state to have a permanent residence in its territory as a precondition for providing services there.

In order to facilitate the practice of economic activities and of professions which are governed by or subject to training conditions many directives have been adopted. The main items covered are: liberal professions; banking, finance, insurance; agriculture, forestry and horticulture; commercial activities; manufacturing industries.

In most cases it was sufficient to open access to the jobs concerned or to introduce transitional measures to facilitate such access, through the recognition in the host country of the experience acquired in the country of origin.

For some professions, however, measures involving the harmonization of the conditions for exercising the profession (especially at the training level) were necessary. This is the case in the health sector.

Freedom of establishment and freedom to provide services exists for doctors (1976), for nurses and for dentists (1979), for veterinarians (1980), for midwives (1983), pharmacists (1987) and for architects (1988). Since March 1979 lawyers may plead jointly with a lawyer from the host country and provide other legal services, but there is no free professional establishment in the countries for which they do not have a diploma (because in some member states the legal profession is considered to be, directly or indirectly part of official authority; Article 55).

After legal proceedings that started in 1977, the Court ruled in May 1982 that Article 48,4 refers to positions assuming a special solidarity relation between the official and the state and a reciprocity of rights and duties constituting the basis of the nationality relation. According to the Court this is not the case for workers with the railway company and with local authorities.

On 19 June 1990 five member states (France, Germany and the Benelux countries) signed the Schengen agreement (after a Luxemburg village). It removes all checks on people travelling across borders between the five countries and shifts these controls to their external borders. The five agreed on a common visa and asylum policy, to let their police hotly pursue criminals into each other's territory, to minimize the differences in their antinarcotics policies and to pool crime data in a huge computer database (the Schengen Information System). Italy joined the five on 27 November 1990, Spain and Portugal on 25 June 1991. The agreement could enter into effect at the end of 1991, after ratification by the parliaments of the countries concerned.

Several directives have been adopted under Article 58; they have been confined largely to limited companies. The First directive of 1968 provides a system of publicity for all companies, the Second directive of 1976 common standards and procedures for the raising, maintenance and alteration of the capital of public limited companies. The Third directive of 1978 introduces in the legal systems of the member countries the transaction of merger (it avoids cumbersome procedures by way of winding-up). The Sixth directive of 1982 provides for the process of scission whereby an existing company divides into entities. The Third and Sixth directives apply to transactions confined to a company or companies in the same member country.

The Fourth, Seventh and Eighth directives constitute a codex of European accounting law. The Fourth directive of 1978 covers the accounts of limited companies, the Seventh directive of 1983 deals with the consolidated accounts of groups of undertakings, the Eighth directive of 1984 defines the qualifications required of those who audit the accounts required by Community law.

In December 1989 the Council adopted the 11th and 12th Company law directives concerning disclosure requirements in respect of branches opened in a member state by companies governed by the law of another state, and single-member private companies.

So far no agreement has been reached on the proposed fifth directive relating to the European company, due to different views in respect of employee participation.

In the field of insurance, markets remain largely segmented. Hence, the appreciable differences in premiums. Although the right of establishment in member countries is assured, companies cannot directly contract across frontiers.

In 1986 the Court of Justice ruled that harmonization of essential regulations concerning prudential standards is necessary prior to the insurance market's liberalization. In the co-insurance sector, however, the Court judged that competition on the basis of 'home country control' was justified, the market parties needing no special protection.

The same principle explains why, as from July 1990, large commercial non-life risks are liberalized. According to another directive individuals are allowed to take life cover in other EC member states, but on their own initiative (and at their own risk). Finally in February 1991 the Commission adopted the third directive which will enable insurance groups to operate freely throughout the Community according to their own country rules. If approved by the member countries, it will come into effect in 1993.

The right of establishment for banks is also assured (second banking directive of 15 December 1989), as from 1 January 1993, but many restrictions on its exercise persist. At the same date directives on banks' own funds and solvency will enter into force.

The Commission philosophy relating to financial services (insurance, banking, securities) involves (a) harmonization of the essential requirements of prudential supervision and (b) freedom to provide services in the Community by any member-country company on the basis of mutual recognition of supervisory standards and 'home country control' (foreign financial products or institutions being monitored by the supervisory authorities of the parent company's country).

2. *Coordination of economic policies*

a. *General economic policy*

1. *Provisions*
Though this is not stated explicitly, the Treaty of Rome aims at the creation of an economic union, which requires coordination of the member states' economic policies. The provisions in this respect are very general, and the Treaty does not deal with all aspects of economic policy.

The economic policies of member states are to be directed towards ensuring balance-of-payments equilibrium, maintaining confidence in the currency and ensuring a high level of employment and stable prices (Article

104). In so doing, the member states take account of the experience acquired in cooperation within the framework of the European Monetary System and in developing the ECU (Article 102A).

The Council (which ensures coordination of the general economic policies of the member states — Article 145) acting unanimously on a proposal from the Commission issues directives for the approximation of provisions affecting the establishment or functioning of the Common Market (Article 100). In order to achieve the objectives set out in Article 8A (see above), the Council may issue directives by a qualified majority on a proposal from the Commission in cooperation with the Parliament and the Economic and Social Committee. This qualified-majority vote does not apply to fiscal provisions, to those relating to the free movement of persons nor to those relating to the rights and interests of employed persons.

If a member state wants to apply Article 36 it informs the Commission. The Commission confirms the provisions involved after verification that they are not a means of arbitrary discrimination or a disguised restriction on trade between member states (Article 100A).

During 1992, the Commission shall, together with each member state, draw up an inventory of provisions which have not been harmonized. It submits appropriate proposals in order to allow the Council to act before the end of 1992 (Article 100B).

The coordination of economic policies (Article 6) is achieved by cooperation between the appropriate government departments and the central banks (Article 105,*1*: cf. also the role of the Monetary Committee — Article 105,*2*).

Short-term economic policy is regarded as a matter of common concern (Article 103,*1*) on which the EEC countries consult each other and the Commission. The Council is authorized to take appropriate measures on a proposal by the Commission (Article 103,*2*).

Article 235 should also be mentioned in this context: where action by the Community is needed to achieve one of its objectives, and where the Treaty does not provide the necessary powers, the Council can adopt appropriate measures by unanimous vote (on a proposal by the Commission and after consulting the Parliament).

2. *Operation*

The Council established successively a Conjunctural Policy Committee (9 March 1960), a Medium-term Economic Policy Committee (15 April 1964) and a Budget Policy Committee (8 May 1964) but, owing to the overlapping of responsibilities and duplication of work, the three committees were merged on 18 February 1974 into an Economic Policy Committee; this analyses the development of the economies in order to discover the reasons for any divergence from the medium-term economic policy programme.

On 17 July 1969 prior consultation on important aspects of economic policy was made mandatory. On 22 March 1971 the Council decided to hold three sessions a year in order to coordinate more closely the short-term economic policies of the member states. It also agreed to the setting-up of a system of financial aid (cf. balance-of-payments policy). The Convergence Decision (18 February 1974) stressed once again the need of a high degree of economic-policy convergence.

Whereas the Paris Treaty provides that the Community must accomplish its mission with limited intervention and with as little administrative machinery as possible, the Rome Treaty prescribes the coordination of several aspects of economic policy. Some "policies" have merely given rise to mountains of reports (regional policy, social policy) and often the absence of "action" (transport policy) has been due to a battle between those in favour of "dirigisme" and those in favour of a free market.

The coordination of economic policy was supposed to be realized through Community programmes and through prior consultation. The medium-term programmes of the Communities — just like the national plans of some of the member countries — are at the moment no more than manifestations of wishful thinking. Like the High Authority in the ECSC, the new Commission felt obliged to make medium-term and long-term forecasts. Like corresponding ECSC exercises, they were often very misleading. In 1975 "Forward estimates of future demands for steel in the medium term indicate that present capacities are inadequate to cover maximum expected requirements in 1980; consequently, the present situation is of a distinctly cyclical nature" (Annual Report 1975). Later on, however, the crisis in the steel sector is considered to be "structural" (Annual Report 1977).

At the Hague summit meeting in December 1969 it was formally decided to establish an economic and monetary union. On 9 February 1971 the Council again expressed its political resolve to achieve such a union before 1980. It was even provided that by 1980 definite exchange rates would be established. During a first three-year phase, ending at 31 December 1973 (which could be extended by two years) a series of measures had to be taken: the gradual coordination of monetary and financial policy, especially an approximation of tax systems, closer cooperation between central banks, a reduction in exchange rate margins and a gradual liberalization of capital movements, medium-term economic assistance. It was agreed that even during the first phase the Parliament would be given limited control over Community decisions.

On 14 and 15 December 1973 the Summit failed to agree on the adoption of measures for the transition to the second stage of the monetary and economic union. As is usual in such a situation, a commission was set up under the chairmanship of Professor R. Marjolin, a former vice-president of the Commission. According to the commission report of March 1975 the failures since 1969 are caused mainly by a "lack of political will" and by "intellectual shortcomings, in that efforts had been started to move towards Economic and Monetary Union without any clear understanding of what was involved". Typical of the last-named phenomenon is the Tindemans report

(19 December 1975) on European Union, which does not even give a definition of this "union".

Notwithstanding numerous reports and resolutions pleading for more coordination of economic policies, this objective has still to be achieved (on 15 October 1985 the drachme was devalued without prior notification).

The Hanover Council of June 1988 appointed a Committee under president Delors to propose the stages needed to achieve an economic and monetary union. The Committee proposed to set up a European System of Central Banks as a way to create a monetary union and a common single currency. The Committee admits, however, that an economic and monetary union does not require a single currency (see below).

b. *Balance-of-payments policy and monetary policy*

1. *Provisions*
Payments connected with the movement of goods, services, capital or persons that has been liberalized are authorized by the member states in the currency of the country in which the creditor or the beneficiary resides. If the economic situation and the balance of payments permit, payments may be liberalized to a greater extent (Article 106,*1*). If the further liberalization of these operations is limited only by restrictions on payments, the restriction must be abolished in accordance with the provisions for the elimination of quantitative restrictions and the liberalization of services and capital movements (Article 106,*2*).

Where a member state is in difficulties (or in serious danger of difficulties) with its balance of payments, and this is liable to prejudice the operation of the common market or the gradual introduction of the common commercial policy, the Commission institutes an inquiry and recommends measures to the country concerned. If necessary, the Commission, after consulting the Monetary Committee, recommends to the Council that mutual assistance be provided (Article 108,*1*). The Council decides on this last point by qualified majority vote. Assistance may take the form of:

a) a concerted approach in other international organizations;
b) measures to avoid deflection of trade when quantitative restrictions in respect of non-member countries are maintained or imposed;
c) the granting of credits.

If the Council rejects the proposal for mutual assistance, or if the support and assistance provided are inadequate, the Commission authorizes the country concerned to take protective measures as determined by the Commission. The Council may revoke or amend this authorization by qualified majority vote (Article 108,*3*). Where there is a sudden balance-of-payments crisis, the state involved can take action on its own initiative (Article 109,*1*), provided the other EEC countries and the Commission are kept informed

(Article 109,*2*). The Council may also decide to amend, suspend or abolish these measures (Article 109,*3*).

Each member state must treat its policy with regard to exchange rates as a matter of common interest (Article 107,*1*). If a member state makes an alteration to its exchange rates that is incompatible with the objectives of economic policy outlined above and which seriously distorts conditions of competition, the Commission may, after consulting the Monetary Committee, authorize other member countries to take for a limited period the necessary measures to meet the consequences (Article 107,*2*).

2. *Operation*

As post-war history shows, coordination of member countries' economic policies leaves much to be desired (see Chapter 1). There was, for example, no prior consultation before the revaluation of the Dutch and the German currencies (6 and 7 March 1961). Since Article 107,*1* does not explicitly provide for prior consultation, in April 1964 the member countries agreed to joint consultation before modifying exchange rates, but again in 1969 the announcement of the French devaluation (8 August) came as a surprise. Yet, a few days before, on 17 July 1969, the Council had decided to strengthen the coordination of short-term economic policies (see above).

a. *Very-short-term and short-term financing.* Following an agreement reached by the Governors of the central banks, an arrangement for short-term monetary assistance came into effect on 9 February 1970. The scope for support measures was increased in 1974, 1977, 1979 and 1987.

In order to enable the member states' governments to intervene in their foreign exchange markets in the way required by the "snake" arrangement, the Governors agreed on 10 April 1972 on a scheme for financing and settling any balances arising out of such intervention in Community currencies; under this scheme the central banks granted each other lines of very-short-term credit. On 13 March 1979 this facility was modified in order to comply with the EMS. (For a description of the foreign exchange arrangements in the EEC, see Chapter 1, 4B2).

On 6 April 1973 a European Monetary Cooperation Fund (EMCF) came into effect in Luxemburg in order to promote the proper functioning of the progressive narrowing of the margin of fluctuation of members' currencies against each other, interventions in Community currencies on the exchange markets and settlements between the central banks leading to a concerted policy on reserves; in particular, the EMCF has responsibility for the administration of very short-term and short-term financing. Each central bank contributes to the EMCF 20 per cent of its gold holdings and 20 per cent of its gross dollar reserves.

The maximum amounts of short-term support available for drawings by each of the central banks (debtor quotas) and of the short-term support financed by each central bank (creditor quotas) were fixed initially on 18

February 1974 and were raised subsequently (see Table 23). Extension beyond the debtor and creditor quotas (rallonges) may obtain 8.8 billion ECU. They are financed outside the creditor quotas when member states are prepared to do so.

Table 23. Community short-term financing, quotas by member states, 1991.

Country	Debtor quotas million ECU	Creditor quotas million ECU
Belgium-Luxemburg	580	1 160
Denmark	260	520
Germany	1 740	3 480
France	1 740	3 480
Ireland	100	200
Italy	1 160	2 320
Netherlands	580	1 160
United Kingdom	1 740	3 480
Greece	150	300
Portugal	145	290
Spain	725	1 450
Total	8 920	17 840

Source: EEC.

In July 1973 Italy was granted short-term support that was rolled over twice and on 17 December 1974 was converted into financial assistance for three years (1 159.2 million EMUA) under the decision of 22 March 1971. The last tranche was repaid ahead of schedule at the end of September 1978. On 11 May 1976 Italy was granted a short-term credit line, amounting to 400 million EMUA, but relinquished it after being granted a 500-million dollar loan in June 1977 (which it did not use).

b. *Medium-term support.* In 1971 the Council set up a system of medium-term financial aid, the principle of which is based on Article 108 of the Rome Treaty (member states experiencing balance-of-payments difficulties). Moreover, the Community raised the Community's lending possibilities in 1978 (the so-called New Community Instrument — NCI). At the end of 1989 total NCI loans amounted to 6 243 million ECU (3, 092 of which went to Italy).

On 24 June 1988 the Council decided to group the medium-term aid and the Community lending resources into a single medium-term financial assistance mechanism. Loans to member countries are limited to 16 million ECU. If conditions of capital markets or financial institutions are unsatisfactory member countries ensure Community lending up to certain maxima (France, Germany and the United Kingdom each 2 715 million ECU, Italy 1 810 million ECU, Spain 1 132 million ECU, the Netherlands 905 million ECU, Belgium 875 million ECU, Denmark 407 million ECU, Greece 235 million ECU, Portugal 227 million ECU, Ireland 158 million ECU and Luxemburg 31 million ECU).

c. European units of account. Different types of units of account used to be employed by the European Communities. Until 9 April 1979 common agricultural policy was expressed in terms of units of account/gold parity (0.88867088 g of fine gold), which coincided with the dollar until 1971 and was subsequently equal to 1.2 dollars.

The transactions in the context of the European Monetary Cooperation Fund had to be expressed in a European monetary unit of account (EMUA) of a value of 0.88867088 g of fine gold. Apart from some cases in which its value could change automatically, any change was to be decided by the Council.

The extensive use of floating exchange rates resulted in the creation of a European unit of account (EUA), which is founded on a basket consisting of all the member states' currencies. The EUA was introduced in 1975. It is the summation of fixed amounts of members' currencies and was calculated from day-to-day proceedings in the market rates and, as from 9 April 1979 it was applicable to all Community activities.

The EMS is also based on this unit, with the denomination of ECU (European Currency Unit). It came into being on 13 March 1979. In contradistinction to the EUA, which was a numéraire, the ECU has been created in order to play the role of reserve currency. The Council adopted a Regulation providing for the general use of ECU for all Community activities as from 1 January 1981. The ECU is defined in terms of a basket of Community currencies (Table 24).

c. *Competition policy*

1. *Provisions*

a. *ECSC rules.* The provisions of the ECSC Treaty relating to competition go further than those of the EEC Treaty.

1. Enterprises. a. Pricing Practices.
All pricing practices contrary to Articles 2, 3 and 4 are prohibited: two categories are specially mentioned, one of which relates to purely local or purely temporary price reductions offered in order to acquire a monopoly position within the common market. The High Authority is empowered, after referring the matter to the Consultative Committee and the Council, to issue decisions defining in more detail the practices ranking as prohibited (Article 60,*1*).

Table 24. Calculation of equivalents of the ECU for 20 October 1990.

National currency amounts composing the ECU	Central rates against the dollar	Equivalent in dollars of national currency amount	Equivalent in national currency of total dollar amount	Weight of currencies in the ECU basket, in per cent
(a)	(b)	(c) (a):(b)	(d) dollar total × (b)	(e) (c): total dollar amount
B/LFR[b] 3.431	31.0675	0.1104369518	42.4015	8.09
DKR 0.1976	5.7575	0.03432045158	7.85794	2.51
DM 0.6242	1.5090	0.4136514248	2.05951	30.31
DRA 1.440	152.0600	0.009469946074	207.534	0.69
PTA 6.885	94.8000	0.07262658228	129.385	5.32
FF 1.332	5.0530	0.2636057787	6.89642	19.31
IRL[a] 0.008552	1.7767	0.0151943384	0.768176	1.11
LIT 151.8	1130.5000	0.1342768686	1542.93	9.84
HFL 0.2198	1.7009	0.129225704	2.32142	9.47
ESC 1.393	133.2000	0.01045795796	181.794	0.77
UKL[a] 0.08784	1.9530	0.17155152	0.698831	12.57
Total of dollars amounts:	1.364817524			

[a] The dollar exchange rate from London and Dublin is the number of dollars per currency unit rather then the number of currency units per dollar. Column (c) is therefore found for each of these two currencies by multiplying the value in column (a) by that in column (b); and column (d) by dividing the dollar equivalent of the ECU (c) by the rate in column (b).

[b] Belgium (3.301) and Luxemburg (0.130) francs are taken together.

Source: EC.

The Treaty's requirements for the purpose of excluding prohibited pricing practices include:

1. *Adequate publicity.* Prices and conditions of sale must be disclosed to the extent and in the form prescribed by the High Authority after discussion with the Consultative Committee (Article 60,*2a*).
2. *Non-discrimination.* Producers, buyers and consumers in comparable positions must be treated on an equal footing by any one person or firm. Whereas in the EEC Treaty it is only discrimination on the basis of nationality that is prohibited, the ECSC Treaty provides also for the prohibition of discrimination within one and the same country (Article 4,*b*).

Enterprises are ordinarily free to choose the locality to serve as the basing point for their price schedules. If the basing point appears arbitrarily selected and results, for instance, in discrimination, the High Authority is required to issue appropriate recommendations to the enterprise concerned (Article 60,*2a*). The mode of quotation used must not be such that the prices actually charged are higher than those published. Rebates allowed in order to meet competition from sellers with a different basing point more advantageous to the consumer are permitted: in practice this means that the seller may assume part of the cost of transport. Where appropriate, the High Authority may, after hearing the Consultative Committee, fix limits to rebates, taking into account the origin and destination of the products (Article 60,*2b*).

b. Prohibition of restrictive agreements or practices.
There would be little sense in abolishing duties and quotas if private agreements resulting in restriction of competition and division of markets were to be allowed (Article 4,*d*). The Treaty accordingly makes provision against this. It takes a stronger line on restrictive agreements than on mergers and other forms of concentration.

1. *Restrictive agreements.* All agreements between enterprises, decisions by associations of enterprises and concerted practices tending directly or indirectly to prevent, restrict or distort the normal operation of competition within the common market are forbidden: these include more particularly price fixing, restrictions on production, technical development or investment, and allocation of markets, products, customers or sources of supply (Article 65,*1*). Here again, the ECSC Treaty goes further than the EEC Treaty: in the latter, agreements are prohibited only if they adversely affect trade between member countries; the ECSC Treaty also forbids agreements which only have domestic repercussions.

These provisions apply not only to the actual producers but also to distributor firms operating on the producers' behalf, except as regards sales to private households or small industry (Article 80). The purpose here was to prevent evasion of Article 65 by the device of setting up selling agencies. The Treaty does, however, permit contracts of sale between any one producer and his customers, and also agreements operative only outside the Community.

The High Authority can grant exemptions in respect of specialization agreements or joint buying and selling agreements, both to producer and to distributor firms, provided:

1. they are indispensable to a substantial improvement of production or distribution;
2. they do not put the firms concerned in a position to determine prices or to control or restrict production or sales on a substantial share of the market in the products in question, or to evade effective competition within the common market.

2. *Combinations.* Prior endorsement by the High Authority is required for concentration between enterprises of which one or more are under ECSC jurisdiction, whether by merger, acquisition of shares or assets, loan, contract or any other means of control, and irrespective of whether one product is concerned or several of them (Article 66,*1*).

The High Authority is expected to give its consent if it finds that the persons or enterprises in question will not be enabled by the proposed concentration to determine prices, control or restrict production or distribution, interfere with competition in a substantial part of the market, or evade the Treaty's rules on competition. If it wishes, it may give a conditional authorization. In accordance with the non-discrimination principle (Article 4,*b*), the High Authority has to take into account the size and influence of other Community enterprises of the same kind.

Existing enterprises in a dominant position in a substantial part of the common market must not abuse that position: if they do so, the High Authority has first to endeavor to stop them by issuing recommendations, and if they do not comply within a reasonable time, will proceed to fix their prices and conditions of sale, or impose compulsory production or delivery schedules, after consulting with the government concerned (Article 66,*7*).

2. Governments. In the coal and steel sectors, the ECSC Treaty provides that, basically, the member states retain their sovereignty in matters of general economic policy (Article 26): that is to say, the governments pursue their own course on finance, social affairs and trade, and on prices, wages and investments. Nevertheless, practically every decision by the public authorities does affect competitive conditions, militating to the advantage or disadvantage of the country's industries. It can thus happen that general measures — i.e., those not specifically directed at ECSC enterprises or products — have appreciable repercussions on conditions of competition in

the Community coal and steel industries; the High Authority must be notified of such measures (Article 67,*1*).

Any action that would substantially increase disparities in production costs (other than through changes in productivity) and so provoke a serious disequilibrium would be harmful to enterprises in the ECSC industries, either in the country concerned or in another member country.

In the first case, the High Authority, after obtaining the views of the Consultative Committee and the Council, can empower the government of the country in question to afford assistance to the enterprises affected, for instance in the form of a subsidy, the practical details — amount, terms and duration — having to be settled with the High Authority. This aid is also permitted in the case of changes in wages and terms of employment, even if the changes are not the result of government action.

In the second case (as with the effects of a devaluation), the High Authority, again after the necessary consultations, will address a recommendation to the country concerned with a view to getting the matter remedied by whatever measures appear most compatible with the latter's economic equilibrium (Article 67,*2*).

There is a blanket prohibition on subsidies, state aids and special charges (Article 4,*c*). However, as was pointed out above, conditional exceptions are allowed for the benefit of enterprises suffering serious damage to their interests (Article 67,*2*).

For a period of five years after the accession, the Commission will examine the measures in force in the new member states which come within the scope of Article 67. The Commission may, after consulting the Council, propose to the governments concerned appropriate action to correct such measures or to offset their effects (Article 134,*1*, AT).

Should the High Authority find that a discriminatory purchasing policy is being pursued — more especially by public bodies — it must address the necessary recommendations to the governments concerned (Article 63,*1*). It can also intervene if consumers make a regular practice of buying from domestic instead of from cheaper foreign suppliers.

b. *EEC Rules.* The Treaty's articles on competition rules are sometimes deliberately vague in order to give the Commission and the Council adequate scope in implementing them.

1. Enterprises. a. Restrictive agreements or practices.
All agreements between enterprises, all decisions by associations of enterprises and all concerted practices which are liable to affect trade between member countries and which prevent, restrict or distort competition within the common market are prohibited. Examples given are: the fixing of purchase or selling prices or any other terms; the limitation or control of production, markets, technical development or investment; market sharing or the sharing of sources of supply; discrimination (Article 85,*1*). Any agree-

ment or decision prohibited pursuant to this article is automatically void (Article 8,*2*).

These provisions may be waived if the measures involved help to improve production or distribution of goods or to promote technical or economic progress while allowing consumers a fair share of the resulting benefits. The enterprises involved must not be subjected to any restrictions which are not indispensable to the achievement of these objectives, nor must they be given the opportunity of eliminating competition in respect of a substantial proportion of the goods concerned (Article 85,*3*).

b. Abuse of dominant positions.
Any abuse by one or more firms of a dominant position within the common market or within a substantial part of it is prohibited in so far as trade between member countries is liable to be affected. Examples of this are the imposition of unfair purchase or selling prices, the introduction of restriction on production, markets or technical developments to the prejudice of consumers, and discrimination (Article 86). The application of Articles 85 and 86 implies identifying the market where trade between member states is affected and/or competition is restricted (the relevant market).

Article 86 is less restrictive than Article 85: dominance itself is not prohibited. Both articles lay down the basic rules: implementing provisions are contained in the following articles (Articles 87—89) and in many regulations of the Council or of the Commission.

Public enterprises are subject to the competition rules so long as these rules do not "obstruct the . . . fulfilment of the specific tasks entrusted" to them (Article 90,*1* and *2*).

c. Concentration.

In 1973 the Commission made a proposal for subjecting mergers to prior notification and again in modified form in 1981, but only in 1989 has the Council taken a stand on this issue.

On 21 September 1989 the Council adopted a regulation on the control of concentrations between undertakings (often referred to as the Merger Regulation). Concentration arises upon the merger of two previously independent undertakings or the acquisition of control over the whole or parts of an undertaking (Article 3,*1*).

Only those joint-ventures which have as their object or effect the coordination of the competitive behaviour of undertakings which remain independent, do not constitute a concentration (Article 3,*2*).

A concentration is considered to have a Community dimension when worldwide turnover of the companies concerned is 5 billion ECU and when the Community-wide turnover of each of at least two of the companies concerned is 250 million ECU. However, the regulation does not apply when each of the companies concerned obtains more than two-thirds of its turnover in the Community within a single member state (Article 1,2). These thresholds will be reviewed before 21 December 1993 (Article 1,3).

Concentrations are compatible with the common market if they do not create a dominant position (Article 2). According to the Preamble compatibility may be presumed where the market share of the companies concerned does not exceed 25 per cent either in the common market or in a substantial part of it.

When evaluating the concentration the Commission must also take into account other factors such as the interest of the consumers, the development of technical and economic progress. The vagueness of these and other terms adds to the uncertainty of the law for the firms affected.

The Commission has the prior control of the concentration operations. Companies must give prior notification of concentrations no more than one week after the signature of an agreement, or the announcement of a public bid, or the acquisition of a controlling interest (Article 4,1). Then the Commission has one month to declare the planned concentration compatible with the common market. If the Commission decides that there are doubts about the concentration's compatibility with the common market, it must take a final decision no later than four months after commencing the examination proceedings (Article 10).

The regulation went into effect on 21 September 1990.

2. Dumping within the common market. If, during the transition period, the Commission, at the request of a member state or of any other interested party, finds that dumping is being practiced within the common market, it must send recommendations to the party or parties involved to end these practices. Should dumping continue, the Commission authorizes any country adversely affected to take protective measures and determines the relevant conditions and details (Article 91,1). However, the treaty does not define dumping.

Dumping between member states is made difficult because the reimportation of goods must not be hampered by import duties, quantitative restrictions or measures equivalent in effect (Article 91,2, the so-called "boomerang provision").

3. Governments. Aid granted by a member country (or through state resources in any form at all) which distorts or threatens to distort competition (by favouring certain firms or the production of certain goods) is incompatible with the common market in so far as it adversely affects trade between EEC countries (Article 92,1).

The following are permitted: social assistance to individual consumers (granted irrespective of the origin of the products concerned), aid to make good the damage caused by natural disasters or other extraordinary events, compensation for the disadvantages caused to regions affected by the division of Germany (Article 92,2).

Some measures may be approved by the Commission if their purpose is:

1. to promote the economic development of regions with an abnormally low standard of living or serious underemployment (cf. also Article 80 on transport policy);
2. to promote the execution of an important project of common European interest or to remedy a serious disturbance in the economy of a member country;
3. to facilitate the development of certain economic activities or regions, provided this is not contrary to the common interest.

The Commission can also propose such other measures as may be considered permissible. The Council takes the appropriate decision by a qualified majority vote (Article 92,*3*). Furthermore at the request of a member state the Council may unanimously decide to waive Article 92 where exceptional circumstances warrant such action (Article 93,*2*, third paragraph).

In conjunction with the member states, the Commission examines all systems of aid existing in these states (Article 93,*1*). The Commission can order them to be abolished or modified. If no action is taken before the prescribed deadline, the Commission or any other interested state may refer the matter to the Court of Justice (Article 93,*2*, first and second paragraphs); in fact, a way equal to Article 169.

Any plans to grant or modify grants of aid must be made known to the Commission in good time. No measures may be implemented until the Commission has given its ruling (Article 93,*2*).

2. *Operation*

a. *ECSC rules.*

1. Enterprises. a. Pricing Practices.
    1. *Adequate publicity.* ECSC enterprises are required, by the terms of a number of High Authority decisions, to publish their price schedules and conditions of sale, including particularly shipping costs, rebates and commissions, dues payable and quality premiums.

High Authority spot-checks have revealed that these rules are frequently disregarded and that, for example, certain categories of customers receive preferential treatment, the prices of some products are not published, and unpublished rebates are allowed. Infringements detected have resulted in the enterprises concerned being cautioned or fined.

2. *Non-discrimination.* When the Treaty came into force, the enterprises' varying pricing systems were superseded by pricing as from a given point, or ex-works.

However, in order not to unbalance the market, the High Authority permitted the charging, of zone-delivered prices for coal up to 1958 (e.g., Aachen, Lower Saxony, the Saar, Lorraine). Since that time producers have again been allowed to align their delivered prices with those of their competitors.

Some producers have succeeded in evading ECSC rules with the aid of dealers, to whom the publication rule did not apply. On 11 December 1963, therefore, the High Authority issued a decision requiring selling agencies also to adhere to the published prices and conditions of the producer enterprises.

Application of Article 60 has become difficult because of changes in conditions on the coal and steel market. This is partly caused by the provisions of this article, which define discrimination as the charging of prices differing from those on the price list.

b. Prohibition of restrictive agreements or practices.
The Commission is applying the competition provisions in the EEC and ECSC Treaties according to the same criteria.

1. *Restrictive Agreements.* The ECSC provisions concerning agreements on restraint of competition came into force on 31 August 1953.

Many problems have arisen in connection with the joint selling of Ruhr and Belgian coal. The Comptoir belge des charbons (Cobechar) was permitted, after amending its articles of association, to continue selling on behalf of a large majority of the Belgian pits from 3 October 1956. For the Ruhr, the establishment of three selling agencies was authorized on 15 February 1956 — reduced on 20 March 1963 to two, Präsident and Geitling — on condition that they operated in entire independence of one another. The Dutch government appealed against the latter decision, but the Court dismissed the case. The decisions in favour of Präsident and Geitling were rescinded with effect from 31 December 1969.

Again, the French Association technique de l'importation charbonnière (ATIC) was requested at the end of 1955 to make changes in its rules for the purchase of coal in other member countries. Only the 14 February 1961, however, were French consumers at last allowed to buy direct from Community sources outside France.

Many joint selling agreements have been approved — for example (in 1967) the agreement between Arbed(Luxemburg), Cockerill-Ougrée-Providence (Belgium), Aciéries Beautor (France) and Sidmar (Belgium); and the agreement between German steel producers for joint sales of rolled products through four agencies (West, Westfalen, Nord and Sud). The specialization agreements authorized included those between the following Belgian and French iron and steel companies — Société métallurgique Hainaut-Sambre; Société des aciéries et tréfileries de Neuves-Maisons; Châtillon; Société métallurgique Espérance-Longdoz; and Phénix-Works.

Most of the approved agreements were in the coal sector; those approved in the iron and steel industry were mainly specialization agreements between a few enterprises.

2. *Combinations.* It is not easy to establish precise criteria relating to firm

market dominance. On the other hand, combinations generally give better results in terms of rationalization than restrictive agreements. This explains why, on 14 July 1967, the Commission dropped a number of rules constituting barriers to exemption: it increased the quantitative limits, exempted from prior authorization most combinations between producing firms and firms whose consumption of coal or steel is below specified amounts and exempted all combinations between distributors and firms not covered by the definition in Article 80.

The majority of the approved combinations related to production of and trade in iron and steel. Only in one instance did the High Authority rule that a position of dominance existed, in the production of brown-coal briquettes.

2. Governments. As soon as the Treaty came into force, the High Authority engaged in a drive to get rid of all special aids (subsidies) and special charges in the ECSC industries.

All special charges were abolished from 1 April 1954. Subsidization was allowed to continue in Belgium and Italy in consideration of the transition problems there. The various French official aids were progressively eliminated: subsidization of Saar and Lorraine coal sold to southern Germany ended in 1955 and of coking coal imported from other Community countries on 31 March 1956.

In order to avoid granting a wage increase in the coal industry Western Germany introduced a system of shift bonuses on 14 February 1956. The High Authority thereupon issued a recommendation, designed to secure the offsetting of this arrangement by a corresponding charge, and the Netherlands appealed to the Court of Justice, which ruled that the German action was counter to the Treaty. It was not, however, until November 1963 that the system was discontinued. The attention of the Italian government had also to be drawn to the unlawfulness of an indirect subsidy on home iron and steel products for use in shipbuilding.

Since the governments are debarred from influencing the pricing of ECSC products, the High Authority has been obliged to intervene on a number of occasions — to put a stop, for instance, to a compensation scheme in the Netherlands whereby each grade of coal was priced uniformly irrespective of origin or destination, to a price ceiling in Italy, and to price pegging in France, notably following the devaluation of 29 December 1958.

At the High Authority's urging, the governments did eventually, on 21 April 1964, undertake to line up their separate energy policies to some extent. In 1967 the Council agreed *inter alia* that the collieries should be granted special assistance in order to reduce prices of coking coal and coke for the Community iron and steel industry and that multilateral financial compensation should be introduced for the purpose.

The major part of the aid given by the member countries to their coal industries is accounted for by the part financing of high social-security charges.

Since the events of May and June 1968 faced the French steel industry with great difficulties, the Commission authorized the French government to grant the iron and steel enterprises, temporarily and in respect of exports up to 31 January 1969, limited compensation to offset wage increase. Imports could also be temporarily restricted (see below: industrial policy).

b. *EEC Rules*. 1. Enterprises. a. Restrictive agreements and practices.
It was not until 6 February 1962 that the Council adopted a regulation implementating Articles 85 and 86, i.e., "Regulation 17". This basic measure gave the Commission broad powers to implement its competition policy. All existing restrictions on competition had to be notified by 1 November 1962 or 1 February 1963, depending on the category. (For some agreements the closing date was 31 December 1966).

On 4 April 1962 it was decided that Articles 85 and 86 also covered production of and trade in agricultural products, though Article 85,*1* does not apply to restrictive practices forming part of a national system of market regulation ("Regulation 26").

A regulation on the hearing of parties directly concerned and of third parties, which came into force on 9 September 1963, sets out uniform rules for the treatment of cases. The first hearing took place in March 1964. At the end of 1962 the Commission published a practical guide. The latest edition appeared in 1986 (*Competition law in the EEC and the ECSC*).

Having notified their agreement to the Commission, parties to that agreement may seek a declaration from the Commission that their activities do not come within the scope of the competition rules (the so-called negative clearance). There exist also 'block' negative clearances. This is the case for the *de minimis* agreements: agreements between firms whose joint market share is less than five per cent and whose joint annual sales do not exceed 200 million ECU.

Contracts with a commercial agent, agreements between parent companies and their subsidiaries (or between subsidiaries amongst themselves), certain cooperation agreements (e.g., joint business or tax consultant agencies) and subcontracting are not caught by Article 85,*1*.

Some horizontal agreements have benefited from a group exemption. They relate to specialization and research and development. Not allowed are, for example, price fixing, market sharing, agreements to discriminate, collective boycotts, tie-ins.

Among the vertical agreements there are exclusive distribution agreements, exclusive purchasing agreements and selective distribution agreements. An agreement between a manufacturer in a member country and an exclusive distributor in another member state is not necessarily prohibited, because it may benefit distribution and market unification. However, it must not involve, for example, any territorial protection (e.g., by barring parallel imports into the sales area).

Exclusive purchasing agreements by which a reseller is obliged to buy its supplies exclusively from a stated manufacturer or other supplier (without being allotted an exclusive territory), can obtain a group exemption provided that:

a) the maximum duration of the exclusive purchasing obligation is limited to five (renewable) years;
b) the range of products covered by the obligation is limited to products connected to each other.

The group exemptions for exclusive purchasing agreements related to beer (and other drinks) sold for consumption on the spot and to petrol sold in service stations provide for a maximum duration of an exclusive tie for beer alone or for petrol for ten years.

In the field of selective distribution (only qualified dealers are 'selected') a block exemption (1985) relates to the motor vehicle sector. The motor dealer may not, for example, actively seek customers outside his allotted territory and the manufacturer not appoint other dealers or supply end-users direct in the allotted territory.

A block exemption (1988) for franchising agreements exempts the territorial protection granted to the franchisee, the location clause imposed on him and his obligation not to deal in goods competing with those manufactured by the franchiser or bearing his trade mark.

In the field of industrial property and in recognition of their beneficial effects the Commission adopted group exemptions for patent licensing (1984) and know-how licensing (1988).

Regulation 17 authorizes the Commission to institute an enquiry if it has reason to believe that competition in a given industry is being restricted or distorted within the common market. On 23 June 1965 it decided to investigate the margarine industry. The reason for this was that trade between the member countries was lagging behind the general expansion of trade, despite differences in prices. The inquiry was terminated five years later; different sanitary provisions explain the reduced trade.

Since 1972, the Commission has devoted a separate annual report to its competition policy.

Hundreds of cases have been investigated, not only by the Commission, acting in conjunction with the Consultative Committee on Cartels and Monopolies (composed of civil servants from the member countries), but also ruled upon by the Court of Justice. The large volume of case law thus obtained has given rise to general principles for the interpretation of Article 85.

1. Even if one of the parties to an agreement has its place of business outside the EEC, Article 85 still applies where the agreement has repercussions within the common market; this is also the case with contracts between firms in the production and distribution sectors.

2. Agreements which have effect only outside the Community (e.g., export cartels) do not come within the purview of Article 85.
3. Even if an agreement does only refer to the territory of one member state it may reinforce the compartmentalization of market, thereby upholding economic integration. The Vereniging van Cementhandelaars (Netherlands) recommended the prices at which the members of that association of Dutch cement dealers should sell in the Netherlands. The Court (1972) stated that the common market should be considered as a unit. The effect on trade between members should be combined in the light of Articles 2 and 3,*f* of the EEC Treaty (see however, below).
4. If a product goes through various stages of distribution, competition is held to be restricted where such restriction occurs at any one of those stages.
5. Agreements may not have the effect or object of maintaining, or preventing the removal of, national frontiers between member countries.
6. Restriction of competition must be detectable; in other words, it must have some effect, however slight, on firms not party to the agreement or on consumers, in comparison with the situation that would have existed if there had been no agreement. Limitation of the freedom of the contracting parties is in itself no evidence of infringement of Article 85.
7. Whilst parallel behaviour cannot by itself be labelled 'concerted practices', it is nevertheless liable to constitute a presumption that such a situation exists, when it leads to conditions of competition which do not match normal conditions of the market, having regard to the nature of the product marketed, the size and numbers of the firms in the industry, and the size of the market.

However, a firm reducing its price will be followed up by its competitors (unless there is shortage of supply). A price increase will be impossible to maintain if the competing firm do not follow suit. Even without collusion, competing firms may behave as if there is (conscious) parallelism. Taking account of competitor's behaviour does not amount to a concerted practice (unless the partners have been in communication about their market conduct). Parallel behaviour in an oligopolistic market is often a necessity. This parallelism is not dangerous as long as there are no barriers to entry (e.g., government regulations).

On 16 July 1969 the Commission decided for the first time to impose a fine under the Community's competition law. The parties to the International Quinine Agreement (a Dutch company, two German and three French companies), which involved price fixing, control of production and markets, and market sharing, were fined a total of 500 000 u.a. Since then, the Commission has not shrunk from regularly applying this sanction. On 7 June 1983 the Court of Justice stated that the fines are to be determined by several factors: the turnover of the enterprises (not only the turnover relating to the case), the duration of the infringement and its gravity.

b. Abuse of dominant positions.
From the outset, the Commission was faced with difficult problems in establishing what constituted a dominant position: the optimum size of production units varies from industry to industry. Nor can competition from non-member countries be disregarded. Big concerns with a dominant position are often a necessity if outside competition is to be met.

The Commission took action for the first time under Article 86 in 1971. The Gesellschaft für musikalische Aufführungs- und mechanische Vervielfältigungsrechte *GEMA*, a German composers' copyright company which has a *de facto* monopoly on the German market, was forbidden to impose abusive restrictions on the economic freedom of composers, authors or publishers (1971). A similar decision was taken in 1974.

In another famous case, United Brands Co. had to terminate abusive practices in relation to sales of Chiquita-brand bananas in the common market: market fragmentation through the ban on sales of green bananas, refusal to supply an importer/ripener who had taken part in an advertising campaign for a rival branch of bananas, price differentiation between customers on the Irish, German, Danish, Dutch and Belgian markets (1976). However, the Court seemed to ignore that a high market share is not necessarily proof of dominance. Moreover, the competition of other fruit than bananas was not taken into account.

The Commission and the Court have established the following principles:

1. A dominant position in the market for an intermediate product is being abused if supplies to an undertaking operating in the market for an end product derived from that intermediate product had been cut off (1972).
2. Article 86 is applicable to enterprises which have been given exclusive rights by a member state (cf. Article 90).
3. The exercise by a patent-holder of a right, conferred by the laws of a member state, to prohibit the marketing in that state of the patented produce marketed by or with the consent of the holder in another member state is incompatible with the Community rules on free movement of goods (1974).
4. The dominant position referred to in Article 86 "relates to a position of economic strength enjoyed by an undertaking which enables it to prevent effective competition being maintained on the relevant market by giving it the power to behave to an appreciable extent independently of its competitors, customers and ultimately of its consumers".

c. Concentrations.
In 1990 the Commission examined already twelve notifications and decided not to oppose them.

2. Governments. Many state aids fall outside the scope of Article 92,*1*,

because they are for charitable, social or cultural purposes or are admissible under Article 92,*2* or *3*.

Since the Treaty came into force the Commission has often been notified by member countries (by virtue of Article 93,*3*) of measures they were intending to introduce. Most of these were to promote economic expansion and investment, to which the Commission agreed (in so far as they did not have an unfavourable influence on intra-Community trade). The way aid was given to the textile industry by the French government was objected to on 18 July 1969 since it implies discrimination against producers in other member countries.

An important stage in the evolution of the Commission's attitude under Article 93,*3* was reached on 11 September 1973, when it prohibited plans by the Belgian Government to grant certain aids for extending an existing, and setting up a new, oil refinery in Antwerp. According to the Commission, there was no regional or sectoral justification and the aid seemed liable to distort trading conditions.

The Commission admits grants to ailing industries provided that assistance does not unduly delay the necessary adjustments or does not distort competition to an extent contrary to common interest. Given the required competitiveness of the textile and clothing industries they cannot longer be considered as crisis industries. The aids code for the steel industry should have reached its final year of application in 1985 but the deadlines were extended (till June 1988).

The Commission takes a positive attitude towards subsidies favouring common objectives such as research and development, energy conservation, the development of small and medium-sized business. Aid aimed at maintaining jobs is permissible only when it is linked to plans re-establishing the viability of the firm concerned. Aid granted in order to stimulate exports to the common market is contrary to the principles of the Community and the Commission requested, for example, the Italian government to withdraw such aid.

Total aid to the coal sector by Germany, France, Belgium and the United Kingdom totalled 3 025 million ECU in 1986. The amount per tonne ranges from 55.23 ECU in Belgium to 4.4 ECU in the United Kingdom. However 'these differences are not a measure of any distortion of competition between coal producers, for in reality the common market for coal is a series of national markets' (Commission Memorandum, 22 January 1988).

According to the above-mentioned regulation of 11 July 1988 the Community may impose a countervailing duty in order to offset any subsidy bestowed, directly or indirectly, in the country of origin or export, upon the manufacture, production, export or transfer of any product whose release for free circulation in the Community causes injury.

The few cases of anti-subsidy proceedings have been essentially directed against Spain and Brazil and related mainly to export subsidies for steel products.

3. *Transport Policy*
a. *Provisions.* The ECSC Treaty provides that all aspects of transport policy (including coordination among the different modes of transport) were to remain the province of the member states. Discrimination however, is prohibited (Article 4,*b*): users in comparable circumstances must be charged uniform rates, and in particular no differentiation is allowed in consideration of the country of origin or destination of the products carried. All schedules, rates and conditions of carriage have to be published or notified to the High Authority.

Special tariffs for the benefit of one or more producers have to be submitted in advance to the High Authority for its ruling whether they are compatible with the Treaty; its approval may, where appropriate, be given for a specified period only, or subject to stated conditions (Article 70).

The EEC provisions cover only transport by road, rail and inland waterway. A common transport policy is to be worked out (Articles 3,*e* and 74). However, the Council can enact appropriate measures for transport by air and sea by a qualified majority (Article 84).

On a proposal from the Commission, and after consulting the Economic and Social Committee and the Parliament, the Council (acting by a qualified majority vote after the second stage) lays down common rules for international transport within the Community and the terms on which non-resident carriers may operate transport services within a member country (Article 75,*1*). A unanimous vote is in any case required in respect of principles whose application could seriously affect the standard of living and the level of employment in certain areas or the use of transport facilities (Article 75,*3*). This vague wording may easily give rise to disputes.

Until these provisions have been enacted, nothing can be done to the detriment of carriers in other member countries (Article 76).

All discrimination (a single firm imposing different rates and terms for transporting the same goods along the same routes, because of the country of origin of destination of the goods) must be done away with before the end of the second stage (Article 79,*1*). From the beginning of the second stage, rates and terms intended to support particular firms or industries are prohibited. The Commission may authorize exceptions (Article 80,*1*). Account has to be taken of the requirements of regional economic policy, the problems of areas seriously affected by political circumstances, and the effect on competition between the various forms of transport (Article 80,*2*). These provisions do not apply to tariffs established as a result of competition within transport itself (Article 80,*3*).

Aid required to coordinate transport or to discharge certain obligations inherent in the concept of a public service is deemed to be consistent with the Treaty (Article 77).

Charges involved in crossing frontiers must not exceed a reasonable level, after taking the costs actually incurred thereby into account. Member states are required to reduce these costs gradually (Article 81).

b. *Operation.* 1. General Policy.

It was a long time before the principles of a common policy were stated. The Commission handed to the Council on 21 May 1962 an action programme for road, rail and inland waterway transport, accompanied by a timetable. Like the subsequent communications of 10 February 1967 and 8 November 1971, it sets out the objectives of a common transport policy: the harmonization of conditions of competition and the organization of a common transport market based on free competition by freeing access to the market, tariff arrangements and rules on competition.

The Council did not reach agreement on the Commission's proposals, the main difficulty being the conflict between the advocates of free markets and the champions of "dirigisme" and protectionism.

In 1973 the Commission felt obliged to state "that the common transport policy had reached an *impasse*" and on 24 October 1973 it placed before the Council a new communication to reactivate common transport policy: again the free market should be the primary regulating force of the sector. In the Community there should be guaranteed free choice and there should be coordination of transport policy with regional policy as well as with other Community efforts. More emphasis should be given to the infrastructure as the basis for a good functioning of the market and to the air and sea sectors.

2. Road. To avoid overcapacity the Commission wanted the liberalization of access to market to be accompanied by a regulation on capacity and proposed replacing the existing system of bilateral quotas by a system of Community quotas. The regulation of 19 July 1968 established a Community quota for road haulage between member states. It entered into force on 1 January 1969. Originally planned to operate for three years, the Community quota system was made permanent and the number of licences increased several times. The Community quotas represent now 25 to 30 per cent of total transported goods.

In June 1988 the Council decided to establish on 1 January 1993 a new system under which the existing quotas would be abolished. Meanwhile the Community quotas will be substantially increased. The liberalization will also be extended to cabotage (carriage of goods within each member country). On 21 December 1989 the Council adopted measures for the gradual introduction of cabotage.

Directives of 1974 and 1977 (revised by a directive of 1989), regulate access to the profession and provide for freedom of establishment and mutual recognition of road transport operators' diplomas and certificates. The directive of 1989 aims at replacing quantitative rules by qualitative conditions for practicing the profession.

A regulation of 30 July 1968 introduced a system of compulsory bracket rates applicable to road haulage. These rates were only in force at the end of 1971 and extended until the end of 1977. On 12 December 1977 the

Council adopted a regulation establishing for an experimental period a system which gives the member states the choice between a reference and a compulstory tariff for road haulage. The compulsory tariff has not achieved the transparency of the market and since 1 January 1990 the rates can be set by free agreement between the parties to the haulage contract.

3. Rail. While the road accounts for half of the transport of goods over land within the Community, rail represents only a sixth of the transported goods.

After lengthy discussions with the governments concerned, the High Authority issued a recommendation on 1 March 1961 to the effect that all transport rates for coal and steel must also be published; the legality of this requirement was confirmed by the Court in a judgment of 12 July 1962. The countries chiefly opposed to the publication rule were the Netherlands and Italy, where ECSC products are for the most part carried under undisclosed contracts.

In the field of state intervention in the railway sector the Council decided, by a Regulation of 26 June 1969, that railways should receive compensation for obligations imposed on them by the state; this would contribute to the financial independence of railways. The Council also established common rules for the standardization of railway accounts.

On 20 May 1975 the Council adopted a Decision on the improvement of the financial situation of railway undertakings and the harmonization of rules governing the financial relations between such undertakings and the state; railways should have sufficient independence to reach financial equilibrium by stages and they should operate along economic lines. The Decision was intended to be a major instrument for the harmonization of conditions of competition between modes of transport.

4. Air. Prices of European air services are substantially higher than would obtain in a competitive market. A comparison between the densest routes in Europe and the United States shows higher prices in Europe of 40 to 75 per cent. Moreover 50 to 60 per cent of the European passengers pay the full price, whereas in the United States only 15 per cent do so.

In 1987 and 1990 the Council adopted a set of measures providing for greater flexibility in the sharing of capacity and access to routes, relaxation of pricing rules and application to air traffic of the EC's competition rules.

5. Sea. In 1986 the Council adopted four regulations providing for the gradual implementation before 1992 of the free movement of services in traffic between member countries and with third countries. Existing national restrictions and cargo-sharing agreements are to be phased out by 1 January 1993. Maritime transport is brought within the scope of the competition rules, but because liner conferences have a stabilizing effect on the market they have been granted a block exemption (subject to certain conditions).

Community shipowners may complain to the Commission that they are suffering injury as a result of third-country shippers quoting freight rates which are below the normal rate charged by established and representative companies. The Community can impose licensing obligations or quotas or taxes/duties on third country shipping companies where third countries restrict or threaten free access by Community shipping companies to cargoes in ocean trades.

d. *Environmental policy*

Although the Treaty does not specifically provide for an environmental policy, the Summit of October 1972 instructed the Community institutions to draw up an action programme. The Council approved successively several Action programmes.

The Community has adopted two policy principles. The stand-still principle (Council Resolution of 19 July 1973) implies that measures to improve the environmental quality in one region of the Community may not negatively affect the environmental quality in other areas.

According to the polluter-pays principle (Council recommendation of 3 March 1975) the polluter should be charged with the cost of whatever pollution prevention and related control measures that are determined by the public authorities. In this way allocative efficiency is improved in the economies of the member countries and distortion in intra-community trade is avoided. The principle implies the abolition of subsidies paid to the polluters after a transition period ending 1986.

An agreement relating to the notification to the Commission and the member states on measures concerning the protection of the environment was concluded on 5 March 1973.

The Single Act (signed 1987) specifies the objectives of environmental policy:

a) to preserve, protect and improve the quality of the environment;
b) to contribute towards protecting human health;
c) to ensure a prudent and rational utilization of natural resources (Article 130r,*1*).

The principles on which it will be based are 'that environmental damage should as a priority be rectified at source, and that the polluter should pay. Environmental protection shall be a component of the Community's other policies' (Article 130r, *2*).

The environmental impact assessment directive (which came into force on 3 July 1988) tries to integrate ecological awareness into the decision-making process in all economic sectors. Certain projects, such as crude oil refineries, terminal power stations, chemical installations and motorway constructions, must be subjected to an impact assessment. Other projects undergo such an assessment under certain conditions only at the discretion of the member countries.

In 1988 the Commission argued that the Danish system for requiring returnable containers for beer and soft drinks, and for licensing new types of container, represented a barrier to trade. In a ruling of 20 September 1988 the Court accepted that there was a constraint but it said that the Danish measure could be justified on grounds of environmental protection.

The Council has taken numerous decisions in many fields: water pollution and more in particular the quality of surface water intended for the abstraction of drinking water, the pollution of the North Sea, the discharge of mercury in industrial sectors, the limitation of noise emission, the control of transfrontier shipments of hazardous waste.

Agreement in the Council proves often very difficult and member states apply the directives with great delay.

Fisheries

The first decisions relating to the fisheries were taken in 1970 only. Agreement was reached on the principle of common access to fishing grounds in the Community, on a common market organization and on financial help from the Community in order to modernize the fishing fleets. The common organization was revised on 20 December 1981 (see above).

After the extension of the fishing zones to 200 miles (370 km) on the Atlantic and North Sea (not Mediterranean) in 1977, the common fisheries policy had to be adjusted to this measure. An agreement had to wait until January 1983, when Denmark accepted a compromise plan to catch quotas. Member states may retain limits of up to 12 miles where fishing is reserved for their own fleets and those of member states with traditional rights. In addition, in an area beyond 12 miles around the Orkney and Shetland Islands, fishing for potentially endangered species is controlled by Community licences, limiting activities by larger boats to a given number of British, German and Belgian vessels. These measures apply for 20 years, but can be reviewed after 10 years.

The Council determines annually the total allowable catches (TACs) of Atlantic and North Sea fish for all species threatened by overfishing. These catches are divided into national quotas according to a key agreed upon on 25 January 1983. A stricter control of these quotas seems necessary.

Conservation measures are based on scientific advice, consisting mainly of limits on the fishing effort in certain zones, minimum mesh-size nets and, in certain cases, minimum sizes for fish landed. National governments are not prevented from applying extra conservation measures of their own, but such measures must not discriminate against other member states.

e. Violation of the subsidiarity principle

1. Direct tax policy

a. *Provisions*. As regards direct taxation, the Treaty contains only one concrete provision: the abolition of double taxation within the Community (Article 220), and not by Community legislation proper, but by international agreements between the member states.

b. *Operation*. Nevertheless the Commission felt it necessary to aim at harmonization of direct taxes.

On 8 February 1967 the Commission submitted a programme for the harmonization of direct taxes.

It put forward a large number of proposals but none of them has been adopted. In 1979 a directive on mutual assistance between tax authorities was approved, but it has not been widely applied.

In 1975 the Commission proposed that corporate tax rates should range from 45 to 55 per cent. These proposals went out of date, as tax rates have since fallen (within a band of 35—45 per cent). The Commission withdrew its proposal in April 1990. Competition between states was more efficient than Commission proposals.

2. Indirect taxation policy

a. *Provisions*. The autonomy of the member states in tax matters is normally respected, provided no discrimination is practised. Provisions in conflict with this provision existing when the Treaty comes into force have to be eliminated by the beginning of the second stage (Article 95). Where products are exported to other member countries, drawback of internal charges may not exceed the internal charges imposed (directly or indirectly) (Article 96). In the case of charges other than indirect taxation, drawback on exports and compensatory charges on imports are permissible only with the approval of the Council — given by qualified majority vote on a proposal by the Commission (Article 98).

Although Article 95 and 96 prohibit discrimination, they do not abolish tax frontiers, since each country still fixes the level of its own taxation. Consequently, the harmonization of tax legislation is dealt with in Article 99.

The original Article 99 has been replaced in the Single Act by the following text: "The Council shall, acting unanimously on a proposal from the Commission and after consulting the European Parliament, adopt provisions for the harmonization of legislation concerning turnover taxes, excise duties and other forms of indirect taxation to the extent that such harmonization is necessary to ensure the establishment and the functioning of the internal market within the time limit laid down in Article 8A";

b. *Operation*. The Commission has kept a check on the prescribed removal of discrimination. But in some cases the Community has had to take action against Italy and Belgium under Article 169 (which allows the Commission to bring a complaint against a member state before the Court of Justice).

Discrimination is not always a consequence of differing rates; it may result from differences in how taxes are applied. To remedy this, uniform directives have been formulated for excise duties on beer.

After numerous preliminary studies and proposals, the two first directives concerning the harmonization of turnover taxes were approved on 9 February 1967. They set out the general principles for the value added tax system (VAT) and laid down that it should supersede the multi-stage turnover tax systems applied in five member countries (Belgium, Western Germany, Italy, Luxemburg and the Netherlands). VAT is levied at each stage of the production process but only on the value added at that stage. The seller pays VAT on the total value of his sales but gets a rebate for tax already paid on the total value of his purchases. In multi-stage taxes no deduction is made for previous tax. VAT has no such cumulative effect and does not favour integrated firms. Exporters receive a rebate and importers pay, in addition to customs or other duties or levies, the same amount of tax as on comparable home-produced goods. Since the tax on capital goods is deductible, investment is encouraged.

The VAT system was modified in France (which already operated such a system but did not apply the common rules) and introduced in Western Germany on 1 January 1968, in the Netherlands on 1 January 1969, and in Luxemburg on 1 January 1970. The deadline for the adoption of the new system was originally set for 1 January 1970 but Belgium and Italy asked for authorization to postpone the introduction of VAT until 1 January 1971 and 1 January 1972 respectively, and a two-year extension was finally agreed. The new member states already implemented the VAT system (Denmark since 1967, Ireland since 1 November 1972) or planned to do so (United Kingdom from 1 April 1973) at the time of entry. Spain and Portugal implemented the system at the time of entry, but Greece waited till 1987.

Harmonization of the various national systems was intended to coincide with the programme adopted by the Council on 22 March 1971 to achieve an economic and monetary union. In an initial phase, rates exemptions would be fixed by each member state. In a second phase the systems would have to be harmonized (two rates; identity of tax base; harmonized operating rules). In a third stage the rates themselves would have to be harmonized enough to allow the removal of tax frontiers (this being compatible with small differences in rates). Nevertheless each country will still have the right to disallow, wholly or partially, tax deductions on capital goods.

The aim of arriving at an identical tax base was of great importance, since the council decided on 21 April 1970 that from 1975, the member countries would have to pay a share not exceeding one per cent of their VAT revenue to the Community in order to supplement the latter's own resources (see below).

In order to fulfil this condition the Commission submitted a proposal (the sixth VAT directive) to the Council on 29 June 1973. After considerable delay and numerous amendments this directive was accepted by the Council on 17 May 1977, and applied as from 1979 in the member states, with the exception of Western Germany and Luxemburg, who continued to make contributions based on their GNP share till 1 January 1980. Greece had to introduce the VAT system as from 1 January 1984 (later extended for three years) and in the meantime paid a contribution.

In order to avoid border controls the White Paper (1985) proposes that sales and purchases across national borders should be treated the same way as sales and purchases within a national market: exporters would charge VAT on exports and importers would reclaim that tax as an input tax. Since revenue should accrue to the authorities of the consuming country, the Commission proposes the use of a clearing mechanism. The White Paper favours a negotiated approximation of VAT rates (Table 25) within bands (low rates 4—9 per cent, high rates 14—20 per cent). Zero rates should be exceptional and provisional.

Table 25. VAT rates in EC countries 1 April 1991.

Country	Low	Normal	High
Belgium[a]	1 & 6	17 & 19	25 & 33
Denmark[a]	—	22	—
France	2.1; 4; 5.5; 13	18.6	22
West Germany	7	14	—
Greece	4 & 8	18	36
Ireland[a]	2.2; 10; 12.5	21	—
Italy[a]	4 & 9	19	38
Luxemburg	3 & 6	12	—
Netherlands	6	18.5	—
Portugal[a]	8	17	30
Spain	6	12	33
United Kingdom[a]	—	17.5	

[a] Zero rates for some products.
Source: EC.

Amended Commission proposals (1989) provide for a minimum limit to the standard rate without any upper limit. Each member state would choose a rate, having regard to its budgetary consequences and competitive position. No rate for the minimum limit is mentioned but the Commissioner responsible for tax questions has suggested 15 per cent. Zero rating would be admitted but only for a limited number of products and provided the member countries reach agreement on VAT rates. The clearing mechanism is abandoned in favour of a macro-economic approach. Lastly, the new rates would be introduced gradually, not abruptly in January 1993.

In the last quarter of 1989 the Council decided to maintain (till 1996) taxation in the country of destination. This does not require a clearing system;

but in order to prevent fraud some controls in the exporting and importing countries would be necessary (frontier controls will be replaced by importers' and exporters' reporting and comparison of these reports by tax authorities).

On 25 October 1989 the Commission abandoned former proposals to impose uniform excise duties in the Community. Now it wants minimum tariffs for tobacco, alcohol and petrol to be applied as from January 1993, but member states could levy higher duties. For diesel and fuel oil, however, if favours duties between tariff bands in order to avoid distortions.

In 1969 it was decided to increase the tax exemptions allowed on imported goods carried in travellers' luggage. Each traveller was allowed to take goods up to the value of 100 u.a. tax-free from one member country to another. This amount was raised several times (now 390 ECU).

3. *Industrial policy*
Is there any reason why the Community (or member states) should pursue industrial policy? According to the Commission it should help restructuring 'problem sectors'. The Commission proposed conversion measures in declining industries (e.g., in the Colonna report 1970), but the member states did not respond to it. Later, in the textile and shipbuilding sectors the common restructuring efforts were not successful. In the textile sector it restricted imports (Multi-Fibre Arrangement).

In fact, there has been no systematic common industrial policy, except — to a certain extent — in the steel sector. It was based on the provisions of the ECSC Treaty. In this sector it restricted production at the detriment of the most efficient producers. The steel cartel it created was in contradiction to the objectives of EC competition policy.

The Commission can help industry by creating the common market and by combating subsidies, not by tolerating, even authorizing them. In its 1985 White Paper the Commission deplores that large amounts of public funds are spent 'on state aids to uncompetitive industries and enterprises' (p. 39), but the Commission also wants the 'available resources' to be directed 'away from non-viable activities towards competitive and job-creating industries of the future' (p. 40). However, member states and Community resources have *not* to be directed to whatever industries. This is a task for the private sector which will be guided by the market. Neither the states, nor the Commission know better than business which are 'the industries of the future'.

Industrial policy in a market economy removes needless restrictions and promotes competition (e.g., by combating restrictive practices and by pursuing a free-trade policy). Industrial assistance may be justified if an economically well-founded activity is impossible because foreign companies receive government assistance, for example, in research and development.

No more than the OECD, the EC managed to develop a common energy policy. Its resolutions and directives in this field had, in fact, no influence on the policies of the member states.

Research and development policy

Most cooperation on EC companies in respect of research and development is with third-country enterprises. As the member states, the Community has only a slight influence on research and development technology. Its assistance to the programmes concerned represents no more than 0.2 per cent of the EC gross domestic product (GDP).

Among the Community programmes:

ESPRIT (European Strategic Programme for Research and Development Information Technologies) started in 1984 and helps Europe to respond to the challenge of foreign competition in information technology.

RACE (Research and Development in Advanced Communications Technologies for Europe) has as principal objective the development of the technology needed for wide band or high performance fibre-optic networks capable of transmitting simultaneously sound, picture and computerized information (thereby allowing the multiplication of new, integrated telecommunications services). The programme started in 1985 and concerns 440 million ECU.

BRITE (Basic Research in Industrial Technologies for Europe) encourages the development of new technologies, new processes of manufacture and new products in the "traditional" sectors.

4. *Regional policy*

a. *Provisions.* The Preamble of the Rome Treaty states that the member countries will try to "... ensure their harmonious development by reducing the differences existing between the various regions and the backwardness of the less-favoured regions". However, the Treaty does not contain any provisions regarding the establishment of a common regional policy although various articles (e.g., Article 92,*3*) state that deviation from the general rules is allowed in order to reduce regional disparities. In establishing the common agricultural policy and the free movement of workers, regional differences have to be taken into account. The European Investment Bank (see section E3) also gives priority to projects in less-developed areas of the Community.

According to the Single Act a Regional Development Fund is intended to help redress the principal regional imbalances in the Community through participating in the development and structural adjustment of regions whose development is lagging behind and in the conversion of declining industrial regions (Article 130C).

Once the Single European Act enters into force the Commission submits a proposal amending the structure and operational rules of the existing funds (European Agricultural Guidance and Guarantee Fund, Guidance Section, European Social Fund, European Regional Development Fund) in order to contribute to the achievement of this objective. The Council acts unanimously on this proposal within a period of one year, after consulting the European Parliament and the Economic and Social Committee (Article 130D).

Article 56 of the ECSC Treaty allows the Commission to grant conversion loans to encourage the creation of new activities in areas where employment in the coal and steel industries is declining.

b. *Operation.* Since 1969 numerous proposals in relation to regional policy have been submitted. Since 1975 the Regional Development Fund paid about 25 billion ECU to member countries. Nevertheless, national nor Community efforts have led to a decrease of regional welfare differences. Already in May 1973 a Commission report (1973) showed that, despite the high rate of growth achieved in the Community during the sixties (5.4 per cent per year), the ratio between the per capita income of the richest regions and that of the poorest regions had remained the same: 5 to 1. Regional disparities even worsened during the seventies. The Common agricultural policy, for example, benefitted the more prosperous regions.

5. *Social policy*

a. *Provisions.* Article 56,1 (to counter unemployment as a consequence of technical progress and providing, for example, resettlement allowances and grants for occupational retraining) is the major article of the ECSC Treaty which refers to social policy.

As regards the EEC, improvements in the living standards and working conditions of workers are expected to result from the operation of the common market, the procedures laid down in the Treaty and the approximation of laws and administrative rules (Article 117).

The Commission is required to promote coordination between member states in social matters such as employment, labour legislation and working conditions, occupational training (cf. Article 128), social security, protection against industrial accidents and occupational diseases, and the right of association and collective bargaining (Article 118), the working environment and the harmonization of conditions in this area. The Council, acting by a qualified majority on a proposal from the Commission, in cooperation with the Parliament and the Economic and Social Committee, adopts in this respect minimum requirements for gradual implementation (Article 118A of the Single Act).

During the first stage the principle of equal pay for men and women doing the same work is to be applied (Article 119). Once established, the principle must be maintained, as must the existing equivalence of paid holiday schemes (Article 120).

A European Social Fund has to increase the availability of employment and the geographical and occupational mobility of workers (Article 123).

The Fund is administered by the Commission, with the assistance of the committee made up of representatives of governments and of both sides of industry (Article 124).

At the request of a member state, the Fund makes good 50 per cent of the expenditure incurred after the Treaty comes into force by that country or by an official body for the purpose of:

a) granting aid to workers whose employment is reduced or removed as a result of conversion to other production;
b) ensuring productive re-employment by means of occupational training and resettlement allowances (Article 125,*1*).

After the end of the transition period the Council, on the basis of an opinion issued by the Commission and after consulting the Economic and Social Committee and the Parliament, may rule by qualified majority vote that all or part of this assistance should no longer be granted, or it can determine by unanimous vote to give new functions to the Fund (Article 126).

b. *Operation.* As provided by Article 118 of the EEC Treaty, regulations on social security for migrant workers came into force as early as 1 January 1959. Implementing measures were introduced at a later stage, covering sickness benefits and family allowances. On 1 and 2 April 1963 the Council approved similar provisions for frontier workers. On 11 July 1963 the Council finally gave its agreement to a regulation on social security for seasonal workers (supplementary provisions being added on 18 December 1963).

On 10 October 1972 regulations came into force which guarantee the application of national social security schemes to employed persons and their families moving within the Community. They take the place of other bilateral and multilateral agreements concluded between member countries, provided the latter are not more favourable for the workers. In 1981 the scope of this regulation was extended to self-employed persons and their families.

Directives have established minimum requirements with respect to mass redundancies (in force since 1977), the guaranteeing of established rights in the event of transfer (since 1979) and ensuring payment of salary and other claims when an employer ceases to pay (since 1983).

On 30 October 1961 the Council laid down a timetable for the introduction of equal pay for men and women. Differences between men's and women's pay had to be cut to 15 per cent by 30 June 1962 and to 10 per cent by 30 June 1963, with the abolition of all discrimination by 31 December 1964. These requirements have not yet been complied with in all member countries. The Commission has reminded the governments of their obligations on a number of occasions.

The European Social Fund began operations in 1961, refunding expenditure on vocational retraining and resettlement schemes carried out between

1958 and 1960. Reimbursement by the Fund totalled 379.4 million u.a. Up to the end of 1974, some 1 837 300 workers benefitted from such aid, the bulk being received by Germany (42.3 per cent) and Italy (36 per cent).

As a result of the Council Decision of 26 November 1970 a reformed Social Fund came into operation on 1 April 1972. The reformed Fund has two separate functions: financing measures to prevent unemployment resulting from Community policies, and helping to solve current structural and regional disequilibria. The latter measures are financed up to a maximum of 50 per cent, while the former can be financed up to 100 per cent. The functions and responsibilities of the Fund have been regularly enlarged: aid to persons other than workers (1971), aid to migrant workers (1974), specific measures for persons occupied in the textile and clothing industry (1976), aid to women (1977), aid for young unemployed under 25 (1978).

Total aid from the reformed Fund between 1972 and the end of 1989 amounted to about 26 billion ECU. Great Britain and Italy got each a quarter of this amount.

Since 23 October 1983 most credits are given in order to improve employment of young people (less than 25 of age). In addition, aid is concentrated on employment programmes in Greece, 10 Spanish regions, French overseas departments, Ireland, the Mezzogiorno, Northern Ireland and Portugal.

Here again the subsidiarity principle is ignored. As the Padoa-Schioppa report puts it: 'there are other areas were the Community expected role at least for harmonizing legislation, could be lessened: for example social policy and labour market regulations'.

6. *Agricultural policy*

As a consequence of the common agricultural policy, agricultural output was growing faster than demand for foodstuff. Surpluses existed for many commodities. In 1968, Commissioner S. Mansholt set out his plan for the reform of agricultural structures. The main aims of the plan were to modernize the structure of agriculture; to create new jobs (and vocational training) for young people wishing to leave agriculture and provide compensation for loss of income to farmers aged fifty-five and over who gave up farming on condition that their land is made available for the purpose of the Plan; to promote the establishment of types of farm that would ensure profitable investment (output should be guided by demand and come from rationalized farms; and to prevent price increases in the case of products of which there are structural surpluses. After 1975 support to individual specialized farms would only be given if they were profitable. Some 5 000 000 hectares should be assigned to other uses over a ten-year period — 60 to 80 per cent of them for afforestation, the rest for (recreational) parks.

Most agricultural organizations and Ministries of Agriculture reacted unfavourably to the Plan, which was considered by some to discriminate against small farmers.

On 20 November 1973 a directive was adopted on hill farmers and those working in naturally less-favoured areas. The farming concerned covers 25 per cent of the cultivable area in the EEC, comprises 15 per cent of the farm units, but accounts for only 12 per cent of the production. The directive has been put into effect on 28 April 1975. The aim of the directive is to enable the farms to be maintained and, as far as possible modernized. In the same line of thought, the Council has adopted a Regulation on a programme for the acceleration and guidance of collective irrigation works in the Mezzogiorno and a Directive on a programme to accelerate the restructuring and conversion of vineyards in certain Mediterranean regions in France (19 June 1978). On 19 December 1978, it approved a Directive on a programme for the acceleration of collective irrigation works in Corsica.

In order to reduce the production potential for some fruits which are in surplus (apples, pears, peaches) grubbing measures have been introduced in 1969—1973 and 1976—1977. On 6 March 1976 the Council set up a programme aiming at the reduction of excess supply of wine.

In the Commission's first report on the application of the agricultural reform (1977) the results of the implementation of the Mansholt Plan are said to be "very incomplete, unsuitable"; in 1978 the Plan was revised.

On 23 October 1981, the Commission pointed out in a communication on "Orientations for European Agriculture" that efforts must be continued to reduce permanent surpluses. Farmers must take over the financial responsibility for disposing of surpluses beyond a certain production threshold (see above). The difficulties of problem regions cannot be solved through agricultural development alone. This is why the Community has launched development programmes for rural areas in the Mediterranean regions including projects involving infrastructure, fishing, energy, tourism, small and medium-sized enterprises.

A Green Paper of the Commission (23 July 1985) points once again to the continuing imbalance between supply and demand for agricultural products and to the limited resources which have to be shared by an increasing number of beneficiaries. The classical measures advocated in order to balance the agricultural market are reiterated (i.e. set-aside of farmland). The last years some progress has been made in the fields of price restraint, flexibility of the intervention arrangements and producer co-responsibility. On 25 April 1989 the Council adopted various socio-structural measures. They provide for the cessation of farming by farmers aged over 55 and the amendment of the regulation of 12 March 1985 on the set-aside of farmland. To qualify for aid the set-aside must equal at least 20 per cent on an individual holding over a period of five years.

The Guidance section of the European Agricultural Guidance and Guarantee Fund helps to finance Community policy on agricultural structures. Its aid covers between 25 and 60 per cent of the costs of a project, the remainder being funded by the national authorities. In 1989, its payments totalled 1 349 million ECU.

3. *Free movement of capital*

a. *Provisions*

Liberalization will enable capital to be employed where it will be of most use. Since the maintenance of external and internal monetary equilibrium requires some degree of caution, restrictions are to be removed only gradually during the transition period and only to the extent required for the proper functioning of the common market (Article 67,*1*).

Discrimination on grounds of nationality or the place of residence of the parties or the place where capital is invested must be abolished (Article 68,*2*). Current payments connected with capital movements are to be freed from restrictions by the end of the first stage (Article 67,*2*).

The Council issues the necessary directives for the implementation of these provisions (Article 69). The member states must endeavour to avoid introducing any new restrictions (Article 71) and to be as liberal as possible in granting exchange authorizations (Article 68,*1*). If capital movements disturb the operation of a capital market, the Commission can authorize protective measures (Article 73,*1*). The member country involved may take these measures on its own initiative if urgent decisions are needed or if secrecy is advisable. The Commission can then, after consulting the Monetary Committee, decide that the measures concerned should be altered or abolished (Article 73,*2*). Restrictions may be retained, however, in case of balance-of-payments difficulties (cf. Articles 108 and 109).

Loans for a member state or one of its territorial subdivisions must not be issued or placed in other EEC countries unless the states involved agree (Article 68,*3*).

Capital outflows from member states to non-EEC countries resulting from differences in exchange regulations of EEC countries are to be prevented by the gradual coordination of exchange policies. For this purpose the Council issues directives acting by qualified majority. It endeavours to attain the highest possible degree of liberalization. Unanimity is required for measures which constitute a step back as regards the liberalization of capital movements (Article 70,*1*). If this does not have the desired effect, any state whose interests are harmed may itself take appropriate measures after consulting the other EEC countries and the Commission. If the Council establishes that the movement of capital inside the EEC is restricted to a greater extent than is necessary, it may decide by qualified majority vote on a proposal from the Commission that the measure concerned should be altered or abolished (Article 70,*2*).

Member states are required to keep the Commission informed of any capital movements to or from non-member countries which they know about (Article 72).

b. *Operation*

In 1960 and 1962 the Council approved the first directives for the implementation of Article 67, but later proposals did not give rise to new Council decisions. After about twenty years of inactivity several communications and proposals led to the Council decision of 24 June 1988.

Under this directive — which went into force on 1 July 1990 — all restrictions on capital movements between residents of the member countries had to be removed. The deadline is the end of 1992 for Spain, Ireland, Greece and Portugal. For Greece and Portugal the time limit may even be extended for maximum three years.

A safeguard clause enables member countries to introduce restrictions on short-term capital movements for maximum six months should their monetary or exchange-rate policy be disrupted. An authorization by the Commission is required, although member countries may, in an emergency, take protective measures without authorization. Member countries must notify 'measures to regulate bank liquidity which have a specific impact on capital operations carried out by credit institutions with non-residents' (Article 2).

Member states must endeavour to achieve the same degree of liberalization with non-member countries as has been attained within the Community.

A joint statement issued by the Commission and the Council recognizes the need for a further progress on taxation. This concern has given rise to Article 6,5 of the directive instructing the Commission to submit by 31 December 1988 proposals "aimed at eliminating or reducing risks of distortion, tax evasion and tax avoidance linked to the diversity of national systems for the taxation of savings and for controlling the application of these systems". So far no agreement has been reached in this matter.

When the directive went into force member countries had complied to most provisions, with the exception of the four above-mentioned countries benefiting from derogations. A number of restrictions remained due to the incomplete liberalization of financial services.

C. *Monetary union*

At the Hague summit meeting in December 1969 it was formally decided to establish an economic and monetary union. On 9 February 1971 the Council again expressed its political resolve to achieve such a union before 1980. It was even provided that by 1980 definite exchange rates would be established (evidence either of admirable recklessness or of disarming *naiveté*). During a first three-year phase, ending at 31 December 1973 (which could be extended by two years) a series of measures had to be taken: the gradual coordination of monetary and financial policy, especially an approximation of tax systems, closer cooperation between central banks, a reduction in exchange-rate margins and a gradual liberalization of capital movements, medium-term economic assistance. It was agreed that even during the first phase the Parliament would be given limited control over Community Decisions.

On 14 and 15 December 1973 the Summit failed to agree on the adoption of measures for the transition to the second stage of the monetary and economic union. As is usual in such a situation, a commission was set up under the chairmanship of Professor R. Marjolin, a former vice-president of the Commission. According to the commission report of March 1975 the failures since 1969 are caused mainly by a "lack of political will" and "intellectual shortcomings, in that efforts had been started to move towards Economic and Monetary Union without any clear understanding of what was involved". Typical of the last-named phenomenon is the Tindemans report (29 December 1975) on European Union, which does not even give a definition of this 'union'.

Notwithstanding numerous reports and resolutions pleading for more coordination of economic policies, this objective has still to be achieved (on 15 October 1985, for example, the drachme was devalued without prior notification).

Once again, at its meeting in Hanover on 17 and 18 June 1988 the European Council instructed a Committee composed of central bank governors (in their personal capacity) and monetary experts, chaired by Commission President Delors, to study and propose concrete steps that would lead towards economic and monetary union. The resulting recommendations were accepted by the Madrid Council of June 1989: stage One of economic and monetary union would begin on 1 July 1990 and preparations would be started for stages Two and Three.

Stage One is to seek greater convergence of economic performance of member states; the EMS, the role of the ECU and of the Commission of Central Bank Governors has to be strengthened. Before the next stages can proceed, amendments to the Treaty of Rome are required to provide for the setting up of a new institution, the European System of Central Banks (ESCB or Eurofed).

During Stage Two the ESCB would be created and Stage Three would involve irrevocably locked exchange rates and the replacement of national currencies by a single Community currency.

In March 1990 the Commission published *Economic and monetary union: the economic rationale and design of the system*. Prepared by the Commission's own experts, it differs in important aspects from the Delors report. While this report admits that a monetary union does not necessarily require a single currency, the Commission makes it quite clear that monetary union must have eventually a single currency. Whereas the Committee favours binding rules and procedures for budgetary policy (implying upper limits on budget deficits), the Commission does not accept such an erosion of national sovereignty (although it admits that the monetary financing of budget deficits should be made illegal under Community law).

The EMS actually works as a DM bloc. The other member countries try to align their monetary policy with that of Germany. It was not Germany that decided the DM should be the dominant currency (it represents 21 per cent in the world's official holdings of foreign exchange). The market did that. The ECU's contribution to European unification has been marginal.

A central European bank runs the risk to be a politicized institution. Only two central banks in the Community are to a certain degree independent from their governments. The danger exists the Community could be sacrificing a stable and hard currency — the DM which is the anchor of the EMS — without knowing what it would be getting in return.

In December 1990 the European Council in Rome agreed that the above-mentioned amendments to the Treaty of Rome should be drafted: on the one hand a treaty of economic and monetary union, on the other hand a political treaty giving more power to the European Parliament and to the EC (in a number of areas such as culture, education, social law, energy, research). This seems in contradistinction with the subsidiarity principle.

D. *External relations*

1. *Provisions*

By unanimous vote the Council may, after receiving the assent of the Parliament, which acts by an absolute majority of its component members, conclude with a non-member country, a union of states or an international organization agreements creating an association with the Community. Where such agreements involve amendments to the Treaty, these amendments must be ratified by all member countries (Article 238).

The member states act in common in international economic organizations (Article 116).

In accordance with French wishes that the Community should provide financial assistance for her former overseas territories or associated states, there is a separate form of association, the basic principles of which are laid down in the Treaty (Articles 131—6), for the non-European countries and territories linked in one way or another with the EEC countries.

Products from the overseas territories are accorded the same treatment in the common market as products from the member countries (Article 133,*1*). These territories are required gradually to eliminate duties on imports from EEC states (Article 133,*2*). However, the associated countries may still impose duties intended to protect new industries or to provide revenue. These must gradually be reduced to the level of duties imposed on imports of the same products from the former mother country (Article 133,*3*). Discrimination is prohibited (Article 133,*5*). The Commission is empowered to recommend measures to prevent deflection of trade (Article 134), which might occur if customs duties on imports from non-member countries were lower than in the EEC.

Provision is made for a development fund for the overseas countries and territories, into which the member states are required to pay, over a period of five years, annual contributions. The Fund is administered by the Commission (Article 1 of the Implementing Convention).

The member states "shall endeavour jointly to formulate and implement a European foreign policy". They "undertake to inform and consult each other on any foreign policy matters of general interest" (Article 30,*1* and *2*).

2. *Operation*

Since the Community maintains relations with all other countries, it is impossible to pass relations with individual countries in review. There is, for example, a declaration (20 December 1990) on relations with Latin America (the Rio Group) and one on relations with the United States (23 November 1990); they provide respectively for annual and biannual high-level consultations.

In 1990 the EC issued its fifth report on US trade barriers and unfair practices. It deplores numerous elements of trade legislation which conflict with multilateral rules, illegal measures (e.g., the unilateral retaliation subsequent to the Community's banning the use of hormones for fattening livestock for human consumption) and the inordinate time taken to bring US legislation into conformity with the rulings of GATT panels. Similar complaints refer to Japan where progress still needs to be made towards opening up its market and adapting certain of its structures, including the distribution system.

Some special relations with groups of countries are dealt with below.

a. *EFTA Countries*

In the course of 1972 negotiations were opened with all member states of EFTA which had not applied for Community membership (Austria, Finland, Iceland, Portugal, Sweden and Switzerland). With the exception of the agreement with Iceland (1 April 1973) and Finland (1 January 1974) the industrial free trade agreements with these countries came into force on 1 January 1973. Norway, which initially applied for accession to the Community, withdrew after a referendum and negotiated an industrial free trade agreement which came into force on 1 July 1973.

The basis of the various agreement is similar: free trade in industrial products accompanied by safeguard measures. In principle, the dismantlement of customs duties and fiscal customs charges was to take place in five stages of 20 per cent between 1 April 1973 and 1 July 1977. For certain products the period was extended but at the end of 1983 all residual duties on the trade between the EFTA countries and the EC were abolished.

As to ECSC products, Austria, Finland, Portugal and Sweden committed themselves to apply the main provisions which were already in force in the Community (price lists and adequate publications of transport rates). As Switzerland does not practice these rules, the Community is allowed to apply a safeguard clause against that country (withdrawal of tariff concessions if competition is distorted in the Community).

A joint EFTA-EC ministerial declaration in Luxemburg (1984) aims at establishing 'a dynamic European Economic Area' (without defining this term). In 1989 decisions to embark on a structured partnership with common decision-making and administrative institutions were taken in Oslo and Brussels. EFTA ministers agreed that the structure of EFTA should be strengthened. Formal negotiations started in the first half of 1990. The following objectives should be fulfilled: ". . . the free movement of goods, services, capital and persons, on the basis of the relevant acquis communautaire, to be identified jointly; exceptions justified by considerations of fundamental interests, as well as transitional arrangements, would be matter for negotiation; equal conditions of competition should be ensured".

In 1989 two parallel negotiations were being held: the follow-up of the Luxemburg declaration of 1984 (the Luxemburg process) and the global approach initiated in 1989 (the Oslo-Brussels process). However, in 1990 the pace of the negotiations was slackening.

According to the EC there must be a balance of advantages and obligations and cooperation should not jeopardize the Community's autonomy. The poorer Southern EC countries want financial help from EFTA.

One of the most difficult problems is the kind of decision-making and supervisory bodies (for example, in the field of competition policy). The Community is against joint decision making and would only allow EFTA a say at all stages of the process of EC legislation. Some EFTA countries consider the European Economic Area as a temporary alternative to EC membership.

b.   *Former and present overseas territories of EC countries*

Most of the members' colonial territories have become independent since the Treaty of Rome was signed. This has not put an end to preferential treatment, since these countries, with the exception of Guinea, asked for it to be continued. The associated African states and the French overseas departments and territories, however, attach more importance to the operations of the European Development Fund than to the elimination of quantitative restrictions and customs duties.

As it took some time for proposals to be worked out for the allocation of grants by the Fund and the surveys involved proved to be time consuming, provisional approval had been given to projects totalling 440 million u.a. by the end of 1962, when the first five-year period of association expired. The bulk of the balance was allocated by the beginning of 1965.

The second Association Convention, which was signed in Yaoundé on 20 July 1963 and came into force on 1 June 1964, was no longer based on Articles 131 to 136 but on Article 238. This is why the contracting parties were under no obligations extending beyond the five years for which the Convention was to last. The third convention was signed in Yaoundé on 29 July 1969, and came into force on 1 January 1971.

The major products of the associated countries have been admitted into the Community duty free since 1 June 1964. In order to alleviate discrimination against producers in non-associated states, the customs duties concerned have been reduced by 15 to 40 per cent. Duties on some products, including tea and certain types of wood, have been suspended. The associated states enjoy EEC treatment as regards quantitative restrictions in the Common Market.

On 1 December 1964 the associated states were required to carry out the first reduction of customs duties on imports from EEC countries and also to abolish discrimination.

If required on grounds of their economic development (e.g., nascent industries, balance-of-payments disequilibrium), the associated states have the right, however, to reimpose customs duties and quantitative restrictions, and even to suspend imports of a particular product. Certain states have not applied the tariff cuts provided for in the Convention or have continued to levy charges for revenue purposes. A number of quantitative restrictions have been maintained in order to promote economic development or balance-of-payments equilibrium.

A provisional association agreement with the former British territories Kenya, Uganda and Tanzania was signed on 26 July 1968 and a definitive agreement on 24 September 1969; the latter (known as the Arusha Convention) expired on 31 January 1975, simultaneously with the new Yaoundé Convention. The agreement contains much the same principles as those adopted by the Community in its negotiations of the Yaoundé Convention, except financial aid. All exports, except for coffee, cloves and tinned pineapple, from these Eastern African countries were allowed into the Common Market free of duty, and in return tariff concessions were granted to nearly 15 per cent of the Six's exports.

Negotiations for the renewal of the above-mentioned association agreements (twenty-three states) and the inclusion of twenty independent Commonwealth countries in the new agreements started on 1 August 1973. In the course of the negotiations, the number of associates rose to 46; at present there are sixty-nine African, Caribbean and Pacific countries (the ACP states). Some states (e.g., Liberia) not had previous ties with the EEC members.

The first five-year ACP-Community Convention was signed in Lomé (Togo) on 28 February 1975, the second on 31 October 1979, the third on 8

December 1985 and the fourth on 15 December 1989. The fourth convention covers a ten-year period from 1 March 1990. A protocol with a fixed five-year duration covers the financial resources.

The ACP countries have full access to the Community (exemption from customs duties and quantitative restrictions) for all products, except those agricultural products for which the Community has worked out a common market regulation. The ACP countries undertake no corresponding obligation. They simply grant most-favoured-nation treatment on Community products.

The Lomé Convention includes a system for the stabilization of export earnings (Stabex), which applies as from 1975. This system provides — under certain conditions — for protection against losses of export earnings due to unfavourable economic conditions or natural disasters. The main products included are cocoa, coffee, leather and skins, wood. While the aim of Stabex is a relief to the sector where the shortfall occurred, the purpose of the IMF (see compensatory financing) is to assist members with an overall balance-of-payments deficit arising from the export shortfall. The second convention established another similar stabilization system (Sysmin) covering minerals such as copper, cobalt, aluminum, for which an amount of 280 million ECU is available.

Financial aid provided so far under the Association Conventions amounts to about 30 billion ECU.

The institutions of the Association consist of the ACP-Community Council of Ministers, which is the decision-making body, the Committee of Ambassadors, who manages ACP-EEC relations on a day-to-day basis, a Consultative Assembly (composed of two equal parts: members of the European Parliament and delegates from the ACP states) and a Joint Committee (composed of an equal number of ACP and EEC delegates) which prepares the meetings of the Consultative Assembly.

c. *Central and Eastern European countries*

After the peaceful revolution in central and eastern Europe (1989) the Group of Seven summit in 1989 (Paris) set up the Phare Programme. The summit charged the Commission with coordinating assistance from the Group of 24 western countries taking part in the programme. The so-called Group of 24 is created; it consists of the EC countries, the EFTA countries (except Liechtenstein) and a few non-European countries (Australia, Canada, Japan, New Zealand, Turkey and the United States).

The initial aim of the Phare Programme was to coordinate western aid to Hungary and Poland. But in 1990 its scope was extended to cover the other countries of central and eastern Europe.

The agreement between the Community and Comecon, signed in Luxemburg on 25 June 1988, opened a way for a negotiation of individual trade agreements with the Soviet Union and Central and Eastern European countries. These agreements will be the starting point for a second-generation of 'European agreements'. 'European agreements' would provide for statutory financial aid and would even go beyond the free-trade accords which the Community has concluded with the EFTA countries. Their implementation would be conditional on internal progress in the area of rule of law, the respect of human rights, the maintenance of the pluralistic democracy and the degree of economic liberalization. The size of the Soviet economy and its particular problems would require a different cooperation framework.

The Community is already committed to spending two billion ECU in assistance to Central and Eastern European countries in 1991—1992.

On 8—9 December 1989 the European Council in Strasburg agreed on the creation of a European Bank for Reconstruction and Development. The Bank's Articles of Agreement were signed in Paris on 29 May 1990. The capital of 10 billion ECU is provided by forty countries plus the Community and the European Investment Bank (together 51 per cent), by other European countries (9.57 per cent), the recipient countries (13.45 per cent; the U.S.S.R. 6 per cent) and non-European countries (including the United States 10 per cent and Japan 8.52 per cent). Thirty per cent of the capital has to be paid in; seventy per cent will take the form of callable capital.

The purpose of the bank is "... to foster the transition towards open market-oriented economies and to promote private and entrepreneurial initiative in the Central and Eastern European countries committed to and applying the principles of multi-party democracy, pluralism and market economics."

The Bank has a Board of Governors, a Board of Directors, a president and one or more vice-presidents. The Bank is located in London and will come into existence when two thirds of the members have ratified the Articles.

As a result of the Bank's purpose, the bulk of its lending will be to existing private-sector businesses or to the privatization of state-owned enterprises. However, some lending to the public sector (up to 40 per cent) will be needed to enable the private sector to develop (e.g., the construction of communications).

Due to its vast needs the Soviet Union might become the principal recipient of credits. This would reduce the Bank's capacity to help other Central and Eastern European countries. The Soviet Union has therefore agreed that, at least for the first three years, it should only be eligible for loans up to the capital that it pays in over the same period.

So far it has not been proved that the new bank alongside the European Investment Bank (see below) is necessary.

E. *Financing*

1. *The ECSC*

a. *Provisions*

The High Authority is empowered to raise the funds for its activities in two ways: by levies on coal and steel production and by borrowing; it is also allowed to receive grants (Article 49). The levy must not exceed 1 per cent of the assessed value of the production (Article 50,2).

ECSC borrowings are used solely for re-lending (Article 51,1). The High Authority is entitled to grant its loans and guarantees on such terms as will enable it to build up a reserve fund for the purpose of reducing the rate of the levy (Article 51,3).

The Merger Treaty of 8 April 1965, provides in Article 20,2 that 18 million dollars must be contributed from the levy towards the expenditure of the European Communities; this figure may be adjusted annually. From 1967 on, administrative expenditure by the ECSC is financed out of the general budget of the Community (see below). The Merger Treaty did not affect the provisions concerning the ECSC's operational expenditure but the powers of the ECSC institutions (Council and High Authority) are now exercised by the Council and the Commission of the European Communities.

b. *Operation*

The levy was gradually reduced from 0.9 per cent in July 1954 to 0.2 per cent in July 1962, but put up to 0.25 per cent in July 1965 and 0.3 per cent in July 1967 and changed to 0.29 per cent on 1 January 1972 and 0.31 per cent on 1 January 1980.

Since 1 January 1976 the EUA and since 1 January 1981 the ECU have been applied instead of the ECSC unit of account (equal to 0.88867088 g of fine gold) which in 1973 itself replaced the unit of account based on the gold parity of members' currencies.

The 1989 budget of the ECSC amounted to 435 million ECU, of which 184 million ECU for reemployment and 68 million ECU for aid to research.

Out of budget surpluses a guarantee fund of 420 million ECU (at 31 December 1984) has been built up. This is lodged in the form of time deposits with various banks in the member countries, which are thus enabled to advance medium-term loans to enterprises at reduced interest.

Since 1977 special amounts have been provided for interest subsidies on loans for conversion and investment in the steel industry (68 million ECU in the budget of 1989).

ECSC loans have also part-financed the building of numerous dwellings for miners and steelworkers.

2. *The general budget of the Communities*

a. *Provisions*

Revenue and expenditure are required to be balanced in the Community's budget (Article 199). Revenue includes contributions from the member states calculated on a given scale. The contributions to cover the expenditure of the European Social Fund are calculated on a different scale (Article 200,2). According to Article 200,3, this scale may be amended by the Council acting unanimously.

The Commission is to study how these contributions may be replaced by other resources — by revenue accruing from the common customs tariff, for instance — and to submit proposals to the Council (Article 201). The accounts of all revenue and expenditure are examined by a board of independent auditors (Article 206).

As was mentioned before (see above Parliament) the change-over to an own-resources system — outside the control of national parliaments — requires a strengthening of the Parliament's powers.

b. *Operation*

The problems arising from the financing of the common agricultural policy led to a serious crisis: discussions in the Council were broken off on 30 June 1965, and France refused to attend further Council sessions. France was unable to agree that revenue from the common external tariff should accrue to the Community and be allocated to the Agricultural Fund. She preferred direct contributions by the member states. The French also insisted that the agreement whereby intra-Community trade in farm products was to be liberalized by 1 July 1967 should be complied with.

Discussions were not resumed until 28 January 1966. Close attention was given to delimiting the functions of Council and Commission. It was agreed that the Commission should consult the Council when important matters are being dealt with. The members of the Council also agreed that in future decisions must be taken unanimously if they relate to the financial regulations concerning agriculture, the complementary measures necessary for the organization of sugar markets, the regulations relating to the market in oils and fats, and the fixing of common prices for milk, beef and veal, rice, sugar, olive oil and oilseeds.

On 16 July 1969 the Commission submitted to the Council a memorandum on replacing the financial contributions of the member countries by the Communities' own resources. An agreement in principle being reached on 21 December 1969, the Council signed a definitive text on 21 April 1970.

As from 1 January 1975 the Communities' own resources would cover revenue from levies and common customs tariffs, plus receipts corresponding to at most one percentage point on the basic rate of the VAT. This limit was raised to 1.4 per cent from 1 January 1986.

In point of fact, the payment of national VAT receipts to the Community budget was regularly deferred (see above: indirect taxation). Hence own resources out of customs duties and levies were not sufficient to cover all Community expenditure and consequently each year the remaining share had to be made up by national contributions based on the gross national products of the member countries. The 1979 budget was the first to be financed partly by VAT resources (0.74 per cent of the total VAT receipts).

In order to improve control of the Communities' finances, a Court of Auditors was set up in 1977 (Article 206), replacing the Audit Board.

On 29 and 30 May 1980 an agreement was reached on the contribution of the United Kingdom to the European budget, which was felt to be excessive, the British consumer being taxed for the benefit of the farmers in more prosperous countries. The temporary solution involves a reduction in the United Kingdom's net transfer by more than two-thirds.

The Council decision of 24 June 1988 on the own resources took retrospective effect on 1 January (after ratification by the member states). The new system differs from the previous one in that customs duties on ECSC products constitute Community own resources; that a new own resource, based on the sum of member states' GNP, is created; and that own resources assigned to the Communities for each of the years between 1988 and 1992 is limited to 1.15 per cent, 1.17 per cent, 1.18 per cent, 1.19 per cent and 1.20 per cent of Community GDP, respectively.

On 12 April 1988 the Commission proposed to harmonize definitions of GNP at market prices and to improve the statistics needed to estimate it.

The Communities payments made in 1989 totalled 41.131 million ECU, 63 per cent of which is for agriculture (12.3 per cent for milk products, 11.6 per cent for fats and 10.6 per cent for meat); 98.3 per cent is for the Commission, the rest for the other institutions. Revenue was provided by customs duties (11.5 billion ECU), sugar and isoglucose (1.4 billion ECU) and agricultural levies (1.3 billion ECU). VAT and GNP resources amounted to 31.6 billion ECU.

Germany became the greatest "net payer" in the Community (about 6 billion ECU). Estimates of costs and benefits can be criticized. Some "benefits" are not easily quantified. Customs tariffs and agricultural levies are not necessarily borne by the taxpayers in the countries concerned. This is the case when the imports are destined for third countries, such as part of the imports in Rotterdam and Antwerp that have Germany for destination. As a result the figures for Belgium and the Netherlands are over-estimated and the contribution of Germany is under-estimated. On the contrary the salaries of the EEC officials cannot be seen simply as a Belgian "benefit".

The Community budget is the result of a complex process, which involves the Commission, the European Parliament and the Council and extends over more than half of the previous year.

Financial operations by the European Development Fund are outside the budget. This is also the case for various borrowing and lending activities by the Commission and the European Investment Bank.

3. *The European Investment Bank*

a. *Provisions*

The European Investment Bank (EIB) is intended to facilitate the financing of projects:

1. for opening up less-developed regions;
2. for modernizing or converting enterprises or for setting up new undertakings called for by the gradual establishment of the common market;
3. of common interest to several member states.

Projects in the last two categories must be of such a size or nature as to put them beyond the financial means of the countries concerned (Article 130). The Board of Governors (see below) may decide by unanimous vote to increase the subscribed capital (originally 1 000 million u.a.). The admission of a new member entails an increase in the subscribed capital (Article 4,*1—3*, of the Protocol on the Statue of the EIB—PSEIB).

Originally 25 per cent of the capital had to be paid up. This percentage was altered by subsequent decisions of the Board of Governors to 20 per cent (1971), 15.7 per cent (1975), 12.86 per cent (1978), 10.17 per cent (1981) and 9.01 per cent (1986).

The rest of the capital constitutes a guarantee fund that is paid up as needed at the request of the Board of Directors (Article 5 of the PSEIB).

Unlike the European Social Fund, the Credit and Investment Directorate-General (ECSC), the European Development Fund and the Agricultural Fund (see above), the EIB is not managed by the Commission (it is independent from the Community administration proper), though the Commission is represented on the EIB Board of Directors and its approval is asked for each loan.

The Board of Governors, which is made up of ministers appointed by member states, lays down general directives for credit policy. It decides whether to increase the subscribed capital, authorizes special loans and approves the annual report, the balance sheet and the profit-and-loss account (Article 9,*1—3* of the PSEIB).

The Board of Directors of the EIB is composed of 27 directors and 16 alternates appointed by the Board of Governors for a term of five years. The Board of Directors decides on the granting of credits and guarantees and the raising of loans; it also fixes rates of interest and commission and supervises the administration of the Bank (Article 11,*1—2* of the PSEIB).

The Management Committee is composed of a president and six vice-presidents appointed for a term of six years by the Board of Governors on a proposal from the Board of Directors. It is responsible for day-to-day management, for preparing the decisions of the Board of Directors and for their implementation (Article 13,*1* and *3* of the PSEIB).

The Bank's operations cover loans, special loans, credits and guarantees.

1. The Bank may borrow the funds it needs on international capital markets. Borrowing on the capital market of a member state must be in accordance with that state's provisions applying to domestic issues. If there are no such provisions, the member country concerned and the Bank consult each other and reach agreement on the loan envisaged; a member state can refuse to give its assent only if there is reason to fear serious difficulties (Article 22 of the PSEIB).
2. On a proposal by the Board of Directors, the Board of Governors may (by qualified majority) oblige the member states to make special interest-bearing loans (from the fourth year after the Treaty comes into force). The Bank must show that it is unable to obtain money elsewhere.
3. Credits are granted to supplement other sources, and they must be for projects in the European territories of EEC countries (unless special authorization is given by the Board of Governors; this restriction applies only to the bank's "normal" activities, not to those it was subsequently empowered to engage in with regard to the associated countries) (Article 18,*1* of the PSEIB).
4. Loans contracted by public or private concerns can also be guaranteed by the Bank. The total outstanding loans and guarantees may not exceed 250 per cent of the subscribed capital (Article 18,*4—5* of the PSEIB).

The Bank does not finance projects opposed by the member state in which they are to be carried out (Article 20,*6*). Conditions are not imposed whereby money lent by the Bank must be spent in a specific country (Article 20,*4*); the Bank may even make the granting of loans conditional upon the call for tenders being international in scope (Article 20,*5* of the PSEIB). Interest and amortization payments have to be assured by earnings in the case of projects carried out by enterprises, or in other cases by an engagement undertaken by the government concerned (Article 20,*1* of the PSEIB).

b. *Operation*

The capital has been increased on several occasions; in 1971 (1 500 million u.a.) on the 1973 enlargement (2 025 million u.a.), in 1975 (3 543.75 million u.a.), in 1978 (7 087.5 million EUA) and twice in 1981: at the enlargement of the Community (7 200 million ECU), at the end of the year (14 400 million ECU), in 1985 (26 500 million ECU) and in 1986 (28 800 million ECU). From 1 January 1991 the capital amounts to 57 600 million ECU. It is subscribed on the following scale: 11 017 million each from Germany,

Italy, France and the United Kingdom, 4050 million from Spain, 3054 million each from Belgium and the Netherlands, 1546 million from Denmark, 828 million from Greece, 534 million from Portugal, 387 million from Ireland and 77 million from Luxemburg.

From the time it was set up (1958) until the end of 1989, the EIB financed projects totalling 83 million ECU. The bank itself borrowed 41324 million ECU.

Up to the end of 1989 the Bank financed projects totalling 75734 million ECU *inside* the Community. Italy received 43 per cent of the Bank's support. The sector receiving most was energy (35 per cent). The Bank financed projects *outside* the Community (Mediterranean and associated less-developed countries) totalling 5485 million ECU.

F. *Escape clauses*

1. *Provisions*

In addition to the safeguard clauses mentioned above (Articles 25, 73, 89, 107, 108, 109, 115, 235), the Treaty contains a general escape clause for the original transition period which expired on 31 December 1969. If there were serious and persistent difficulties in a given sector of the economy or a certain region (Article 226,*1*), the Commission could act without delay, at the request of the government concerned, to authorize derogations from the Treaty (Article 226,*2*).

When the Community was enlarged in 1973, in 1981 and in 1986, the Accession Treaties contained a similar escape clause for the transition periods.

2. *Operation*

Articles 46, 115 and 235 have already been dealt with. Article 226 has been invoked to facilitate the reorganization of industries such as sulphur, lead, zinc and silk (see above). It was also invoked for a number of finished products; here, however, the Commission was more strict and limited its application to only a few months in most cases (one of them for the protection of penicillin in the Benelux countries).

Following a Commission decision on 17 January 1963 authorizing France to apply safeguard measures against imports of refrigerators and components from Italy (until 31 July 1963), Italy filed proceedings in the Court of Justice. Italy's case was dismissed: a reduction of output coinciding with an increase in imports and falling prices in the industry concerned is evidence of serious difficulties within the meaning of Article 226.

Under Article 135 of the Accession Treaty, the Commission authorized the United Kingdom to introduce a system of licences limiting the export of certain steel products (14 February 1974) and Ireland to limit imports, in order to aid the ailing Irish footwear industry (10 July 1975—17 November 1976). The latter restrictions were extended until the end of the transitional period.

The problems of adapting the Greek, Spanish and Portuguese economies to the Community framework led to some measures, especially in favour of the Greek agricultural sector.

APPRAISAL

After more than thirty years' operation the major advantages and disadvantages of the European Communities are widely known.

The partial integration in the ECSC caused troubles: the High Authority had no jurisdiction over certain sectors of policy — notably social affairs, transport and foreign trade — while the necessary alignment by the governments has not been carried out. It has frequently proved impossible to reconcile the different national standpoints. The High Authority's supranational powers have not been popular, and its decisions and recommendations have often been obeyed grudgingly, tardily, or not at all. Hence the meagre results in maintaining or restoring competition and doing away with discrimination in transport.

The EAEC has not lived up to expectations; even attempts at updating its Articles of Agreement have met with opposition. (A proposal to amend the Chapter on the supply of nuclear products of the Euratom Treaty is in discussion since years.)

The creation of the larger EEC market has not given rise to more protectionism, considering the height and structure of the individual customs tariffs. The common customs tariff is on average similar to the United States tariff and has no peaks of high duties on some products.

The EEC has produced a change in the business climate. Businessmen's decisions are being taken with due regard to the Community that is being built. The number of mergers and agreements has grown appreciably, and this has brought about rationalization of production in many cases. Specialization seems to have occurred, but more at the intra-industry than at the inter-industry level, for example in the textile sector (Belgium for tapestry; Italy for blankets and silk textures), in the precision and office instruments sector (the Netherlands for typewriters, France for watches, Germany and Italy for calculating machines); in the electric machinery sector (Belgium and Germany for bulbs and tubular lamps, Italy for TV sets).

Outside the Community, too, the existence of the EEC is being taken into account. The increase in American and Japanese investment in Western Europe may be ascribed to this.

Achievements of the Community are the establishment of the common customs tariff and the elimination of customs duties between member countries eighteen months ahead of schedule.

As has already been pointed out in connection with the Benelux Union, the expansion of intra-Community trade — which rose (measured by imports) 408 per cent between 1957 and 1969 — is not necessarily a consequence of the reduction in customs duties. The impact of this factor cannot easily be distinguished from other influences such as scientific and technical advance and the increase in demand from outside the Community (imports from and exports to the rest of the world rose 121 and 157 per cent respectively over the same period). The rising trend of trade between Western European countries had in fact already made itself felt before 1958. On the other hand, the average annual growth rate in *per capita* gross national product was higher from 1950 to 1958 (5.8 per cent) than from 1958 to 1968 (4.9 per cent). Presently trade of each member country with other member countries represents at least half of total trade (Table 26).

As in the Benelux Union, agricultural policy has led to substantial production surpluses that cannot be marketed and must therefore be disposed of at a loss outside or inside the Community. The high prices have not been advantageous either to consumers or even to all producers. For all the billions that have been spent on the common agricultural policy, there is still no common agricultural market.

In the industrial sector many technical barriers (e.g., different requirements in respect of safety for electrical appliances) are sometimes more effective than quantitative restrictions. Free trade in goods from non-member countries is still not complete because a common commercial policy has yet not been fully worked out. It will therefore not come as a surprise to learn that the Community has just as many customs officials now as it did before 1958.

Competition policy

The Commission has adopted a case-by-case, legalistic approach, and little attention has been given to its repercussions on the level of prices.

Imported goods are sold at the same price as domestic products even if a lower price is possible. As a rule, importers with exclusive dealerships pay little attention to prices in the country of origin. Differences of 50 per cent and more are not unknown. It pays, for example, to buy electric appliances in Germany rather than elsewhere: in France these products often cost 50 per cent more, and in Belgium too they are much more expensive. As we have said, these facts are not related to competition policy. Since the Community's policy is less concerned with market performance, this is not surprising.

Moreover, cooperation from governments in applying Community competition legislation is very unequal. (Consequently, French and Italian firms are less "persecuted" than, for example, Benelux and German firms since their governments are more hostile to Community decisions.)

The Commission contributes towards the establishment of quota and price cartels, a clear infringement of Article 65 of the Paris Treaty.

Table 26. Selected economic data of the EEC countries, the USA and Japan, 1988.

Country or group of countries	Population (in million)	GDP (at market prices, in billion ECU)	GDP (at market prices, per head of total population; per cent of each country with respect to the Community)	Per cent of each country with respect to the Community GDP: (a) at current prices and current purchasing power parities	(b) at current prices and current exchange rate	Inflation rate[a]	Imports from member countries (in per cent)	Exports to member countries (in per cent)
B	9.9	127.0	100.9	3.1	3.2	3.4	70.4	74.2
DK	5.1	91.0	108.6	1.7	2.3	2.7	53.7	49.8
D	61.5	1017.6	113.1	21.4	25.2	2.7	53.3	54.1
GR	10.0	44.4	54.5	1.7	1.1	20.4	62.4	64.3
E	38.8	287.9	74.7	9.0	7.1	6.7	56.4	60.4
F	55.9	804.2	108.5	18.7	19.9	3.4	65.1	61.6
IRL	3.5	27.5	65.1	0.7	0.7	3.3	71.2	74.1
I	57.5	701.8	103.8	18.4	17.4	6.1	57.5	57.1
L	0.4	5.6	120.9	0.1	0.1	3.7	–	–
NL	14.8	193.2	102.6	4.7	4.8	2.5	61.6	74.7
P	10.3	35.3	54.0	1.6	0.9	13.4	66.4	71.5
UK	57.1	696.6	107.4	18.9	17.3	9.5	49.2	49.8
EUR 12	324.6	4032.2	100.0	100.0	100.0	5.7	58.1	59.6
USA	246.3	4076.0	156.2	118.7	101.1	5.4	19.3	23.7
JA	122.6	2403.6	114.2	43.2	59.7	3.1	12.9	17.7

[a] 1990.

Source: EEC.

If the Community is justified in protecting itself against dumping practices by non-EEC states, protectionism only serves to keep aging installations in business. Moreover, state aids are prejudicial to healthy firms. The authorities are required to account for the errors committed by the private sector. It would be better to use the sums involved to encourage growth industries.

A strengthening of competition policy "should be done in ways that focus more selectively on the cases of greatest importance to the Community market, with lesser intervention wherever only national or local markets are mainly affected" (T. Padoa-Schioppa).

The tentacles of the octopus

It is quite hard enough to carry through the aims of the Treaty: let that be task enough for now. And even then it is not always wise to do so: where the principle of equal pay for men and women *has* been applied it has often worked to the disadvantage of those concerned.

But I cannot understand why the Commission is writing papers and setting up committees on all possible aspects of general policy. The subsidiarity principle seems to be unknown. To take just a few examples: communications on education; papers on codetermination and work sharing; the creation of a European Centre for the Development of Vocational Training.

Typical of Community documents: mention is always made of greater social justice, better quality of life, but never of liberty or personal choice (which is impeded by increasing state intervention). To the intervention of the member states the Commission would like to add an even greater measure of intervention of its own. According to the Commission, a solution to difficulties lies in "le renforcement de son pouvoir de décision et par des moyens de gestion accrus *donc plus efficaces*"! ". . . the Community is a curious hybrid, charged with both drawing up policies and administering them. The danger is that as more common policies emerge, the spread of bureaucracy will produce an increasing bias to inertia" (*The Economist*, 21 August 1976). Former Federal Chancellor Schmidt considers 50 per cent of the Community employees to be superfluous.

At first, the Commission was obsessed by a veritable harmonization mania; this, however, entailed serious difficulties since it proved impossible to establish an acceptable average of the various provisions. In the event, the total harmonization method was abandoned in 1973 and other approaches were sought.

Is there any reason why the Community should pursue a regional and industrial policy (maintaining, for example, excess capacity, through regional policy, in the steel industry)? Can this not be left to the countries themselves? Why does Belgium need Community aid for the construction of a golf course near Malmédy? Also, what grounds are there fore "redistribution"? Is it not a fact that every member state seeks to apply the "juste retour" principle? If one member country contributes relatively more than another in order to maintain the agricultural policy, it will, for example, insist on obtaining relatively more from the regional fund.

The purpose of the Community

As Jean Monnet predicted, economic integration did not lead to political integration. Now efforts are being made to initiate the process of political integration. The objective of this integration, however, has never been defined. Even in the many reports on European Union it is impossible to find such a definition. I laid particular stress on this aspect in 1976 and recently, J. Lodge has pointed out that neither the national governments nor L. Tindemans had any precise conception of what they meant by the nebulous term "Union". If this denomination was finally adopted, it was only "because it was open to so many interpretations".

General statements on European solidarity are not very informative either. The basis for European Union is described by some EEC reports as being the Common "values" of the member states such as "democracy, free movement of persons and ideas, respect for human rights and maintaining a durable peace".

As regards democracy, one may well put the question why this principle has not been applied by the member states to date. Why are the Corsicans, Bretons, Basques and Alsatians banned from deciding on their own status? Here speed is of the essence, or the gallicizing process will be accomplished (see French Flanders). And is there any reasons for denying the German-speaking Belgians and Italians (South Tyrol) this right? The answers to these questions have closer links with the "maintenance of a durable peace" than one is at first disposed to imagine.

Democracy? Why then are association agreements concluded with states ruled by dictatorial regimes? Or does the status of former colony suffice to give all the required guarantees in this respect?

It would be of great assistance to the functioning of the Community if the latter confined its activity to the Treaty of Rome, which does not, for example, provide for either monetary union or the interventionist attitude adopted by the Commission. Greater importance should be attached to the motives for concluding the treaty in the first place, i.e. providing Europe with an improved defense system. Europe's "identity", the subject of so much discussion, would gain a great deal in clarity if Europe could be self-sufficient in terms of defence (which would not exclude an alliance with the United States).

"Integration" does not require a system of strict regulations in all fields. Moreover, cooperation on a less formal basis is preferable to an economic union which functions either erratically or not at all.

BIBLIOGRAPHY

A. *Publications of the Communities*

The Office for Official Publications of the European Communities in Luxemburg published in the nine official languages of the European Communities (Danish, Dutch, English, French, German, Italian, Greek, Portuguese and Spanish) the *Treaties establishing the European Communities. Treaties amending these treaties. Documents concerning the accession* (1978, also in Irish), *Amendments to the 1978 edition of the 'Treaties establishing the European Communities'* (1982) and the *Collection of the agreements concluded by the European Communities* (Vol. 1 to 5, 1958—1975, and annual supplement, 1976-). For the official texts of EC legislation and communications see the *Official Journal of the European Communities* (daily, in English since 1 January 1973; before 1958 there was a *Journal Officiel de la CECA*, with an English edition from 31 July 1954 to 27 December 1956, the *Official Gazette of ECSC*).

General information on Community policy is supplied by the Commission in its annual *General report on the activities of the Communities* (since 1967, combined for ECSC, EEC and Euratom) and in the *Bulletin of the European Communities* (monthly, with supplements on certain issues); before 1968 there was quarterly *Bulletin de la Communauté Européenne du Charbon et de l'Acier, Haute Autorité* and a monthly *Bulletin de la Communauté Européenne Economique* (since 1968 also in English), *Bulletin of the European Economic Community*. Published in conjunction with the General Report are the *Report on the agricultural situation in the Community*, the *Report on the development of the social situation in the Community* and the *Report on competition policy*. See also the annual *Review of the Council's work*.

Numerous reports and studies have been published on every aspect of integration. E.g., *Creation of a European financial area, European economy*, May 1988; *Community public finance. The European budget after the 1988 reform*, May 1989. For a detailed list see the annual *Publications of the European Communities. Catalogue 19-* and for up to date information on new publications the monthly list *Publication of the European Communities* (Also as annex to the *Bulletin of the European Communities*).

Statistical information by the Statistical Office of the European Communities is found in the annual *Basic Statistics of the Community* (for a general survey) and in the monthly *Eurostatistics. Data for short-term economic analysis*. In addition statistical series are published on agriculture, fisheries, industry, energy, social affairs, foreign trade, etc. See for up-to-date information on statistical publications the monthly *Eurostat news*. Since 1979 also *European economy* (3 issues per year) with its supplements *Series A. Recent economic trends, Series B. Economic prospects. Business survey results* (both 11 issues per year) and *Series C. Economic prospects. Consumer survey results* (3 issues per year).

Bibliography information on the European Communities is found in the *Documentation Bulletin*, which consist of four series. *Series A* gives weekly an analytical list of acts and documents of the European Community as well as articles from periodicals; *Series B* bibliographies on specified objects (irregular); *Series C* a cumulative list of the references of series A on single objects (irregular) and *Series D* periodicals containing information on the European Communities. For books see the *Systematic catalogue of books* (two-yearly) and the monthly *List of additions* which contains the acquisitions of the Commission Library.

In this connection: J. Jeffries, *A guide on the official publications of the European Communities* (2nd ed., London, Mansell, 1981). An extensive bibliography, also on other forms of European integration gives K. Kujath, *Bibliography on European integration. With annotations* (Bonn, Europa Union, 1977); for up-to-date information *Europäische Integration. Auswahlbibliographie* (8 numbers a year).

B. *Other publications*

1. *ECSC-Euratom*

W. Diebold, jr., *The Schuman plan. A study in economic cooperation 1950—1959* (New York, Praeger, 1959); *25 Years Common Coal Market* (Brussels, EC Commission, 1977) for an official review.

For a commentary on the Euratom Treaty: J. Errera *et al., Analyse et commentaire du Traité* (Brussels, Libraire encyclopédique, 1958). See further H. Krämer, Nuklearpolitik in Westeuropa und die Forschungspolitik der Euratom (Köln, Heymann, 1976) for the activities of Euratom and J.R. Lecerf and A. Turk, Le pari nucléaire des communautés est-il encore crédible? Essai de synthèse critique d'une "politique communautaire", *Revue du Marché Commun,* March 1978, April 1978 and May 1978.

2. *General publications*

Introductions: D. Swann, *The economics of the common market* (6th ed., Harmondsworth, Penguin, 1988); M. Calingaert, *The 1992 challenge from Europe. Development of the European Community's internal market* (Washington D.C., National Planning Association, 1988); T. Hitiris, *European Community economics. A modern introduction* (New York, Harvester/ Wheatsheaf, 1988); R. Tavitian, *Le système économique de la Communauté Européenne* (Paris, Dalloz, 1990); N. Colchester and D. Buchan, *Europe relaunched. Truths and illusions on the way to 1992* (London, Hutchinson Business Books, 1990); W. Nicoli and T. Salmon, *Understanding the European Communities* (Phillip Allan, 1990).

On certain aspects: Y. Fouéré, *L'Europe aux cent drapeaux. Essais pour servir à la construction de l'Europe,* 2nd ed., Paris, Presses d'Europe, 1976; J.F. Beseler and A.N. Williams, *Antidumping and anti-subsidy law. The European Communities,* London, Sweet and Maxwell, ICC, 1986; A. Mattera, *Le marché unique Européen* (2nd ed., Paris, Jupiter, 1990); I. Van Bael and J.-F. Bellis, *Anti-dumping and other trade protection laws of the EEC* (Bicester, Oxfordshire, Commerce Clearing House, 1990); The extract quoted is from *Efficiency, stability and equity. A strategy for the evolution of the economic system of the European Community.* Report of a study group appointed by the Commission of the European Communities and presided by T. Padoa-Schioppa, April 1987.

Other European organizations

1. *The Council of Europe*

The Council of Europe was set up on 5 May 1949, with headquarters in Strasbourg. Its aims are very general ("greater unity between its members for the purposes of safeguarding and realizing the ideals and principles which are their common heritage and facilitating their economic and social progress"). A Committee of Ministers may recommend matters to governments. The 340 members of the Consultative Assembly are elected by the Parliaments of member states. The Assembly may make recommendations to the Committee of Ministers. Initially there were ten member states; now they comprise the EC countries, most EFTA members (Austria, Iceland, Liechtenstein, Norway, Sweden and Switzerland), Cyprus, Malta, and Turkey. Finland, although not a member, participates in the Council's activities. Israel is an observer.

The Council has drawn up many conventions and agreements, including the European Convention for the Protection of Human Rights and Fundamental Freedoms, the Social Charter, the Cultural Convention.

2. *The Western European Union*

The Western European Union was set up 23 October 1954. It is an organization for collective self-defense, with seat in London. It consist now of the original EC countries, Portugal, Spain and the United Kingdom.

The Council consists of the foreign ministers of the member states. It meets at ambassador level under the chairmanship of the secretary-general (the permanent council). An Assembly is the only parliamentary body with power to discuss western European defense problems.

3. *Conference on Security and Cooperation in Europe*

The first conference was held in Paris in November 1990. Its 34 members exercise sovereignty on European territory; they include Monaco, San Marino and the Holy See. Albania only has an observer status. The Baltic states are not members and Turkey is a member since a minor part of its territory is in Europe. The United States and Canada are also members. A secretariat based in Prague prepares and services the regular follow-up meetings. An assembly of Europe is also planned; it will be composed of delegates from national parliaments and will use the facilities of the Council of Europe Assembly.

During the same conference the so-called Paris agreements were concluded between the NATO and Warsaw Pact members. A treaty on conventional forces in Europe places ceilings on numbers of tanks, artillery, armoured combat vehicles, helicopters and aircraft to be held by each side between Atlantic and Urals. There are no limits of manpower, but Germany will limit its forces to 275 000.

9. The European Free Trade Association

> *EFTA, by contrast [to the European Economic Community] — and largely because its objective was economic integration rather than political unification and its aims, in that respect, were pitched at the level of the currently and prospectively feasible — proceeded to the real nuts-and-bolts tasks of achieving effective integration free of the binding glare of political publicity.*
>
> H.G. JOHNSON

Still following the same pattern, this chapter will deal with the origins of the European Free Trade Association (EFTA), the most important provisions in its Convention and details of operation, concluding with a brief appraisal.

1. ORIGINS

While the negotiations for the establishment of the EEC were in progress, it was proposed in some quarters, notably the United Kingdom, that a free-trade area should be set up among the OEEC countries, with the EEC as such forming part of it. The non-EEC countries were apprehensive of the discrimination which was bound to result from developments in the EEC.

The EEC countries were of the opinion that attention needed to be focused not only on customs duties and quantitative restrictions but also on all other measures causing restraint of trade. They further considered that the United Kingdom was making relatively few concessions in exchange for compliance with its wishes regarding maintenance of Commonwealth tariff preferences and the exclusion of agricultural produce from the free-trade area.

Again, since a free-trade area does not comprise a common external tariff, they pointed to the unquestionable danger of trade deflection. It is in the interests of importers in countries with high tariff walls to obtain their supplies through low-tariff countries. This can, of course, be counteracted by

343

demanding certificates of origin, but this procedure seemed complicated and not to offer sufficient guarantees. In November 1958, moreover, France states that it could not concur in the idea of a free-trade area whose sole aim was the abolition of customs duties and quotas.

Since a large free-trade area was unacceptable for some members of the OEEC, it was decided by seven of the non-EEC countries to establish a "little" free-trade area. The countries in question were the United Kingdom, which had not joined the EEC on account of a fundamental aversion to any form of supranationality and had stubbornly adhered to imperial preference; Austria, Sweden and Switzerland, which either could not or would not depart from their policy of neutrality; Denmark, Norway and Portugal, much of whose trade is with the United Kingdom.

For Greece, Turkey and Iceland, the project had no appeal because their economic structure seemed to rule out any consideration of free trade in industrial products.

By 21 July 1959 a ministerial conference of the "Seven" had resolved upon the establishment of a European free-trade area, and less than six months later, on 4 January 1960, the EFTA Convention was signed. It came into force on 3 May 1960.

In view of its close ties with the Scandinavian countries, Finland could not remain indifferent to the establishment of EFTA. As soon as the EFTA Convention had been signed, negotiations for an association with Finland were put in hand. They culminated in an agreement which was signed on 27 March 1961 and came into force on 26 June 1961. A Joint Council of Finland and EFTA consisted of the representatives of the EFTA member states and of the Associate, Finland, each country having one vote. Its functions concerning the Association were almost identical to those of the Council concerning EFTA itself.

Until 1968 the two Councils met separately, the Joint Council much less frequently than the Council. However, this caused practical problems which led the two Councils to decide to hold their meetings simultaneously. Fundamentally, Finland had the same rights and obligations as the EFTA countries before it became a full member.

Through a special Protocol, the Convention also applies to the Principality of Liechtenstein, which has entered into a customs union with Switzerland. Liechtenstein takes part in EEA negotiations with a view of becoming a contracting party to a new EFTA-EC Treaty.

The rapidity with which the EFTA Convention went through is attributable, on the one hand, to the Anglo-Saxon distaste for large-scale codification, which would be far too binding on the governments, and, on the other hand, to the fact that the preparatory OEEC activities provided the necessary underpinning. Furthermore, the EFTA countries were anxious to make it clear as quickly as possible that the creation of a free-trade area would not encounter any insuperable obstacles and also to be in a stronger position in subsequent negotiations with the EEC.

The Convention also applied to the Faroe Islands, Greenland, Gibraltar and Malta once the country responsible for their international relations had made a declaration to that effect (Article 43,*1—2* and Annex F). Denmark did this in the case of Greenland (with effect from 1 July 1961) and the Faroes (1 January 1968). Later on, extension to the members' non-European territories may be considered (Article 43,*4*). Malta became independent in 1964.

Subject to the agreement of the Council, any state may accede to the Convention (Article 41,*1*). Iceland did so on 1 March 1970. Whereas there is no provision for withdrawal in the EEC Treaty, a member state can withdraw from EFTA if it gives one year's notice (Article 42). This clause was applied in the case of Denmark, the United Kingdom and Portugal. Once the negotiations with the European Communities had been brought to a successful conclusion, Denmark and the United Kingdom left EFTA on 31 December 1972 and Portugal on 31 December 1985. Finland became a full member on 1 January 1986.

Still subject to the agreement of all the member states, an association can be concluded with any other state, union of states or international organization (Article 41,*2*).

2. Objectives

In addition to general aims — to promote full employment, financial stability and a continuous improvement of living standards in the area of the Association and in each member state, and to contribute to the expansion of world trade (Article 2,*a*, and *d*) — the Convention aims at:

1. the securing of fair competition in trade between the member states (Article 2,*b*); the Preamble, too, states that the removal of trade barriers and closer economic cooperation between the OEEC countries, including the EEC countries, must be facilitated;
2. the avoidance of any appreciable disparity in the supply of raw materials produced in the territory covered by the Association (Article 2,*c*).

3. Organization

A. *The Council*

Every member state is represented in the Council and has one vote (Article 32,*2*). The Council supervises the application of the Convention and considers whether further action is required in order to fulfil the aims of the Association and to establish closer links with other states or international organizations (Article 32,*1b* and *c*). It further exercises the powers conferred upon it by the Convention (Article 32,*1a*).

Decisions and recommendations require unanimous vote. In certain cases, a simple majority is sufficient (Article 32,*5*). The use of majority voting is confined to the complaints procedure (see 4D below) and to matters involving derogations from a member country's obligations. Sometimes the Council has agreed in advance to accept a majority vote if unanimity should not be reached (see below: the rules on drawback).

The Council meets at Ministerial level, usually Ministers of Commerce or Foreign Affairs, twice a year. The permanent delegates meet every two weeks (there is no difference in the nature of the decisions taken). The chairmanship passes to another member every six months. The meetings of the permanent delegates are prepared by their deputies.

B.   *The Committees*

Up to the present, the Council, under the powers conferred upon it by the Convention (Article 32,*3*), has set up several standing committees, including:

1. the Committee of Trade Experts (1960) deals with matters related to the operation of the trade provisions covered by Articles 3 to 12 other than those dealt with by the Committee of Origin and Customs Experts, to questions relating to technical barriers to trade among member states and to the price compensation measures referred to in Article 21,*1*;
2. the Budget Committee (1960) advises the Council on financial affairs and assists it in establishing the annual budget and in determining the members' contributions;
3. the Economic Committee (1964) makes regular reviews of the economic situation in each member state (including all aspects of the economic and financial policies);
4. the Committee on Agriculture and Fisheries (1973) has replaced the Agricultural Review Committee (1963) after the departure from EFTA of Denmark and the United Kingdom. It assists the Council in questions concerning agriculture or fisheries;
5. the Committee of Origin and Customs Experts (1974) advises the Council on matters relating to the provisions on the Stockholm Convention and the Free Trade Agreements of the member countries with the EEC (see below). When establishing the new Committee the Council abolished the Customs Committee that had been set up in 1960;
6. the Steering Committee of the Portuguese Fund (1976) has the responsibility for the operation of the Fund;
7. the Committee of Members of Parliament of the EFTA countries (1977) is a consultative body created at the suggestion of members of Parliament of the EFTA countries;
8. the Committee on Technical Barriers to Trade (1984) examines how these barriers can be overcome;
9. the Group of Legal Experts (1987).

In addition, many *ad hoc* committees or working parties have been set up. Like the Committee of Members of Parliament (1977), the Consultative Committee (1961) is not made up of officials: each member state appoints five representatives from the business sector, the trade unions, etc. The Committee, which meets at least twice a year, is presided over by the chairman of the Council (at ministerial level). There is also an Economic and Social Subcommittee.

C. *The Secretariat*

The Secretariat is at Geneva and has a staff of less than seventy. Since 16 April 1988 it has been headed by G. Reisch. It has no executive power. The net annual budget is about 11 million Swiss francs. The size of the national contributions is determined by references to the gross national products at factor costs.

4. FUNCTIONS AND OPERATION

The main functions of EFTA are the liberalization of trade and the establishment of fair competition in trade between member countries. In order to retain the structure used in previous chapters, mention is also made of the provisions relating to freedom of establishment and the liberalization of services and capital, though EFTA only lately deals with the liberalization of services and capital. Finally, the complaints procedure and the escape clauses are discussed.

A. *Liberalization of Trade*

1. *Scope*

a. *Provisions*

The liberalization of trade in goods does not apply to agricultural products (Article 21) or to fish and other marine products (Article 26). The items concerned are listed in Parts II and III of Annex D and Annex E respectively.

On 14 June 1989 the Council decided that the Convention's provisions apply in relation to fish and marine products as from 1 July 1990. Any form of government aid is not compatible with Article 13 of the Convention and must be eliminated not later than 31 December 1993. Temporary exemptions for Sweden and Finland are possible.

When on 1 April 1973 free-trade agreements (see Chapter 8) between EFTA and the EEC came into operation, amendments were necessary to

Article 21 because of the differences between the provisions in the agricultural sector of these agreements and those previously in force in EFTA.

Annex D was divided into three parts. The prices of Part I goods (such as sugar confectionery, lemonade and biscuits) contain an agricultural element (the cost of the material used) and an industrial element (the value added in processing). Protection is allowed for the agricultural element only (e.g., by levies on the import of a variable component or fixed amount or by internal price compensation measures). Price compensation for the agricultural element in the price of processed foodstuffs should not exceed the differences between the domestic and the world market prices of the raw materials used (Article 21,*1c*).

The treatment given to imports of Part I products from another EFTA country may not be less favourable than that accorded to imports from the European Community. This is also the case with Part II products (e.g., macaroni, bread, some spirits), although they are basically treated as agricultural products falling outside the free-trade provisions (Article 21,*1d*).

Any price compensation measures for goods listed in Part I or Part II of Annex D must be notified in advance to the Council: a request for the examination of such measures can be made by any EFTA country (Article 21,*1e*).

No free-trade treatment is given to Part III products (such as live animals, dairy and vegetables). However, expansion of trade in agricultural goods should be aimed at. It should provide "reasonable reciprocity" to members whose economies depend mainly on agricultural exports (Article 22,*2*).

Existing and future agricultural agreements are notified to the other member states (Article 23,*1—2*). Any provisions relating to tariffs apply in favour of all other EFTA countries (Article 23,*3*).

The Council keeps Articles 21 to 25 under review and once a year examines the development of trade in agricultural products within the Association (Article 25).

b. *Operation*

After a first review in 1962, on trade in both agricultural and fish and other marine products, the procedure to be followed in respect of the former was laid down on 10 May 1963. As regards fish and other marine products, the annual review has been deferred, since many of the problems (e.g., the drying-up of fishing grounds) can only be studied in a wider context. On a number of occasions, Iceland, supported by Norway, has requested that Annex E be deleted and free trade treatment accorded to fisheries products. This was decided on 14 June 1989 (see above).

In an agreement of 24 October 1969 with Denmark, Norway and Sweden, the United Kingdom accepted the exclusion of quick-frozen fish fillets from Annex E and duty-free imports from the above-mentioned countries (Iceland became a party to the agreement upon its accession), provided they observe a minimum price scheme (to be established in three stages). The agreement came into force on 1 January 1970 and succeeded a similar agreement reached in 1960. The third stage came into effect on 1 September 1971. According to the 1970 agreement, any government may call for early consultations if imports cause disruption of the market situation (to the detriment of British producers or — in the case of imports from non-EFTA countries — of Nordic exporters), if British production develops in a manner that threatens normal EFTA trade, or if the minimum-price scheme is not observed.

The annual reviews on agricultural products led to a decision in 1966 to abolish tariffs or, in certain cases, to bind existing nil duties for some (but not always the same) products in most member countries. Since September 1971 certain agricultural products, although contained in Annex D, were given more liberal treatment in intra-EFTA trade.

As regards some processed foodstuffs (certain sugar confectionery, biscuits, chocolate), Austria and Switzerland were granted permission to maintain their duties at 40 per cent of the basic duties (until 31 December 1970), since the domestic producers of these products have to pay higher prices for their raw materials than other EFTA producers. From 1 January 1971 they were allowed to introduce variable import levies as a substitute for the previous system. (The levies being the difference between world market prices and domestic prices, taking into account the content of the raw materials in the processed product.)

In addition to the bilateral Article 23 agreements between the EFTA countries, certain EFTA countries have granted agricultural concessions to other member states. For example, in 1976 Portugal received further tariff concessions on exports of agricultural products to the EFTA partners.

2. *Elimination of custom duties*

a. *Provisions*

1. *Import duties*
Import duties and other duties with equivalent effect are to be gradually reduced and eliminated altogether by 1 January 1970. The reference import duties, called the "basic" duties, are those in operation on 1 January 1960 (Article 3,*1—3*).

Member states are permitted to carry out scheduled tariff reductions earlier than provided by the Convention (Article 3,*4*). The Council may decree earlier reduction, the possibility of which it must examine between 1 July 1960 and 31 December 1961. In the case of Portugal the pace of tariff dismantlement is slower (Annex G). These special arrangements are aimed at assisting Portugal's industrialization policy.

Iceland has a ten-year period in which gradually to dismantle protective duties on EFTA imports. In order to assist the development of new industries Iceland could, however, increase its basic duties before 31 January 1974. The other member states granted Iceland duty-free entry to industrial products on its accession.

2. *Export duties*
Duties on exports of goods to member countries may no longer be applied after 1 January 1962 (Article 8,*1*), unless used as a means of counteracting evasion on duties on exports to non-EFTA countries (Articles 8,*2*).

3. *Revenue duties*
Revenue duties or "customs duties and other similar charges applied primarily for the purpose of raising revenue" (Article 6) are not prohibited as such, but they must not have a protectionist aspect. The portion of the duty that is designed to afford protection of domestic producers of the same, similar or substitutable products has to be eliminated either on the dates laid down for ordinary customs duties or before 1 January 1965 (1 January 1975 for Iceland).

A list of the goods concerned and the abolition period selected must be notified to the Council (Article 6,*1—3* and *5*). At the request of another member state, information will be provided on the application of Article 6,*1—3* (Article 6,*4*).

b. *Operation*

1. *Import duties*
The timetable for the elimination of customs duties was drawn up in such a way as to ensure concurrence with the corresponding EEC timetable.

On 10 May 1963, after the collapse of Britain's first negotiations with the EEC, a final acceleration was agreed on so that tariff dismantlement came to an end on 31 December 1966 instead of 1 January 1970.

Norway was allowed to maintain the original timetable in the case of a small number of products accounting for approximately 3 per cent of that country's imports from the other member states.

The other EFTA countries pointed out that the United Kingdom's decision to impose, as from 26 October 1964, a surcharge of 15 per cent on imports of all goods, including those from EFTA countries, was inconsistent with Britain's obligations under the EFTA Convention. The surcharge was reduced to 10 per cent on 26 April 1965 and abolished altogether on 30 November 1966.

In September 1967 Portugal removed seventy items from Annex G. At the request of the Portuguese government Annex G was amended in 1975 and 1976 in order to extend the timetable to 1 January 1985 for particular products and to permit Portugal to introduce or increase duties on products of new industries, provided that the new duties are also abolished by 1

January 1985. The amendment came into force in September 1976 and in May 1978.

A new amendment to Annex G, adopted on 16 November 1976, allows the Councils to authorize Portugal, at its request, to introduce or increase import duties on certain industrial products of industries in a particularly difficult economic situation. It came into force on 2 May 1978.

2. *Export duties*

Export duties were eliminated in the three countries which applied them (Finland, Portugal, Switzerland) by 1 January 1962.

3. *Revenue duties*

Revenue duties relate mainly to tobacco manufacturers, alcoholic beverages, motor vehicles and confectionery; in some countries they were numerous (Portugal).

Determination of the protective element in such duties was usually difficult, unless there is no domestic production; an example of this was Norway's 20 to 30-per cent duty on motor vehicles.

The first method of elimination (see above) has been adopted by Sweden and, in the case of certain duties, Finland, Portugal and Switzerland; the second was favoured by Austria, Norway, the United Kingdom and, for their remaining duties, Finland, Portugal and Switzerland (Denmark had changed all its revenue duties into internal taxes before the first EFTA tariff reductions had come into effect). Many duties were entirely or partially abolished by 1 January 1965 (e.g., Portugal in 1960, the United Kingdom in 1962). The attention of certain governments was subsequently drawn to the fact that in some cases it was open to doubt whether obligations under Article 6 had been fully implemented. Finland agreed to remove the import levy on sugar confectionery and on certain chocolate and other food preparations.

In 1976 and in the 1982 the Committee of Trade Experts expressed the view that the relevant provisions were being complied with.

3. *Elimination of quantitative restrictions*

a. *Provisions*

As well as customs duties, quantitative import restrictions have to be eliminated before the end of 1969 (Article 10,*1—2*) in such a way that no "burdensome problems" are created (Article 10,*3*) and the member countries are treated on the same footing (Article 10,*4*).

The 1959 quotas had to be increased by at least 20 per cent on 1 July 1960 (Iceland: 1 March 1970). Global quotas, available to member and non-member states, must on 1 July 1960, be not less than total imports under quota from member states in 1959, plus 20 per cent of that total, plus total imports under quota from non-member states in that year (Article 10,*5*). In each subsequent year, they have to be raised by a further 20 per cent (Article 10,*7*). If there was an import ban or only a negligible quota in 1959, a quota of appropriate size must be fixed on 1 July 1960 (Iceland: 1 March 1970); any member state is free to enter into consultations on the subject with the country concerned (Article 10,*6*).

Should the gradual removal of quantitative restrictions cause serious difficulties, an alternative arrangement may be submitted to the Council in respect of a given product. The latter may authorize such an arrangement by majority vote (Article 10,*8*).

In the event of balance-of-payments difficulties, quantitative restrictions are permissible. These have to be notified, if possible in advance, to the Council, which may make recommendations aimed at mitigating the harmful effects and may render assistance. If such difficulties persist longer than eighteen months and the arrangements in question seriously hamper the operation of the Association, the Council may, by majority vote, propose suitable measures (Article 19,*1—2*). As soon as the balance-of-payments situation permits, the restrictions have to be removed (Article 19,*3*).

Export restrictions must be eliminated by 31 December 1961 (Article 11,*1*), save where they are designed to ensure compliance with quantitative restrictions on exports to non-member countries (Article 11,*2*; cf. Article 8,*2*).

Finland is also authorized to maintain quantitative restrictions on imports of a limited range of goods, notably fuels and fertilizers (Article 4 and Annex II of the Finland-EFTA Agreement). This is warranted by the fact that Finland has bilateral agreements with a great many countries, including the USSR, and has to fulfil its obligations under them. EFTA producers must nevertheless be afforded the opportunity of competing actively on the Finnish market.

Exceptions to Articles 10 and 11 are permitted in the case of measures for protection of health and law and order, monopolies operated by public enterprises or enterprises possessing exclusive or special rights, industrial property, national treasures of historic, artistic or archaeological value, and also in the case of measures for securing compliance with national laws on marketing of goods and relating to trade in gold and silver or goods produced in prison premises (Article 12).

b. *Operation*

Pursuant to the terms of the Convention, import quotas have been increased by 20 per cent each year. At the same time, the proposed measures have been studied jointly and frequently adjusted in consequence. In many cases, the minimum percentage has been exceeded.

On 10 May 1963 the time limit for complete abolition of quantitative import restrictions was brought forward to the end of 1966 (in the case of Finland, the end of 1967).

In mid-1965 an *ad hoc* working party reached the conclusion that — save in a small number of cases — the complete elimination of restriction would not give rise to any "burdensome problems". In fact, quantitative restrictions on industrial products have, with very few exceptions, been abolished.

Export restrictions have been abolished as scheduled; the EFTA states agreed, however, that they could maintain for the time being restrictions on the export of metal scrap. In 1969 the EC and EFTA countries signed supplementary protocols to the free-trade agreements to provide for the elimination of quantitative export restrictions as from 1 January 1991 (with transitional exceptions applicable to certain products until 1 January 1993).

In September 1965 a working group set up to examine exceptional measures applied under Article 12 recommended several changes in measures that were inconsistent with the provisions of the Article (e.g., the Norwegian import and export restrictions on platinum and chemical derivations of gold and silver, and the Portuguese export restrictions on some types of cork). The member countries concerned accepted these recommendations.

On its accession Iceland abolished quantitative import restrictions on a number of products. The remaining restrictions were, with a few exceptions (goods containing sugar), eliminated by the end of 1974.

A system of import licensing for a number of consumer durables was introduced in Finland on 29 August 1973, as a temporary measure to protect its balance of payments.

On 5 November 1975 Sweden introduced overall import quotas on leather shoes, plastic shoes and rubber boots, for reasons of defense policy. The leather and plastic shoes quotas were removed from 1 July 1977. The import quota on rubber boots was abolished on 7 December 1977 for imports from EFTA (and the European Community).

Since 1977 Portugal has applied several quantitative restrictions as a consequence of its economic difficulties.

4. *Goods from non-EFTA countries*

a. *Provisions*

Liberalization of trade within the Association applies only to goods which have been consigned to the territory of the importing member state from the territory of another member state and which may be considered to be of EFTA origin; imports from other countries are taxed in a different way by each member state, so free intra-EFTA trade in such goods is not permitted.

Since the proportion of goods from non-Association countries (especially basic materials) in the member states' production is in some cases very substantial and the EFTA origin of such products is questionable, it was necessary to lay down rules on the subject. In addition, a time-consuming and complicated supervisory procedure had as far as possible to be avoided.

Goods were deemed to be of EFTA origin if:

1. the value of the non-EFTA goods used in their manufacture did not exceed 50 per cent of their export price; or
2. a specific production process was carried out in the Association (former Article 4,*1*).

For all the products listed in the former Schedule II to Annex B (largely textile products), only the second of these criteria was applicable; for all other products, either could be employed. Basic materials, which appeared in Schedule III, were, however, considered to be of EFTA origin provided they were used in manufacturing process in the Association (former Article 4,*1—2*, and Annex B). Thus the aforementioned percentage was, in fact, frequently exceeded.

From time to time, the Council examines the origin rules with a view to simplifying them or applying them on a wider scale (Article 4,*4*).

Differences in tariffs or charges on imports from non-EFTA countries may cause trade deflection. The Convention assumes that such is the case when, as a result of internal tariff dismantlement and differing duties on imports of basic materials or semifinished products from non-member countries, imports of a particular item from another EFTA state increase and the importing country's production suffers appreciably (Articles 5,*1*). If trade deflection of a particularly urgent nature occurs, the matter can be brought before the Council. The latter must take a decision as quickly as possible, as a general rule within one month. Safeguard measures may be approved by majority vote, for a period of not more than four months (Article 5,*3*). Amendment of the rules of origin may prove necessary (Article 5,*2*).

The Council must, if possible, be given thirty days' notice of a reduction of duties on goods from non-member states (Article 5,*4*). Countries which feel that such a measure involves the risk of trade deflection can refer the matter to the Council (Article 5,*5*). In any alteration of a rate of duty, care must be taken to avoid trade deflection. Were appropriate, Article 31 (see 4D below) may be invoked (Article 5,*6*).

A difference in external tariffs is not regarded as giving grounds for complaint under Article 31 unless it entails trade deflection (Article 6).

Difficulties may sometimes be occasioned by full or partial refund or remission of duties on goods imported from non-EFTA countries and re-exported within the Association (i.e., drawback). On the one hand, exports are stimulated in comparison with home market sales and the structure of production is *ipso facto* influenced; on the other hand, an industrialist in a country with higher import duties is afforded compensation *vis-à-vis* his competitors in low-tariff EFTA countries.

Under both the EFTA Convention and the free-trade agreements with the

EEC and the ECSC countries, drawback is deemed to be irreconcilable with a free-trade area. The relevant provisions are not exactly comprehensive. From 31 December 1966, goods benefiting from drawback may be denied EFTA-origin status (Article 7,*1—2*). The Council may decide to amend the provisions of drawback and to apply further or different provisions either generally or to certain goods or in certain circumstances (Article 7,*3*).

b. *Operation*

There have been numerous amendments to the rules of origin. The main reason is that changes have been made in the Brussels Nomenclature of which EFTA has had to take account. Another reason is that when the origin rules were drawn up the processes listed for the purposes of the process criterion were those that were customary at the time in the manufacture of the various kinds of goods. As new processes have come into use the rules have had to be amended to allow them to be the basis for claims for EFTA treatment. As mentioned above, the most important changes were made after the conclusion of the free-trade agreements with the European Community.

So far the provisions of Article 5 have not given rise to major problems. Intended tariff changes have been notified to the Council with some frequency, but no member country has found it necessary to refer a case of consequential deflection of trade to the Council.

In November 1960 the Council authorized the granting of drawback during the transition period until such time as the import-duty reduction amounted to 50 per cent. Subsequently, however, it was decided to permit drawback up to the end of the transition period. Some countries, and in particular Switzerland, wanted drawback maintained after the transition period. In 1963 it was agreed to have the problem examined further, and there was a consensus that the matter should subsequently be settled by a majority vote. This vote was duly taken in October 1965, the majority (United Kingdom, Denmark, Norway, Sweden, and also Finland) pronouncing in favour of the abolition of drawback, so the no-drawback rule has been applied since 31 December 1966, that is to say, EFTA goods traded between the member countries may not benefit from both EFTA treatment and drawback.

After the free-trade agreements had been signed with the European Community in 1971—72 (see Chapter 8), free trade in most industrial products was in operation by mid-1977 in both the Community and EFTA. The Community proposed a system with two criteria, the "wholly-produced inside the group from materials indigenous to the group" and the "processing" (commodities which have undergone a given processing within the group). The processing criterion requires that products have to be sufficiently transformed to become products under another tariff heading. This criterion is the principal one since the "wholly produced" criterion only applies to basic materials and minerals.

The EFTA countries accepted these origin rules within EFTA also, in order to apply a uniform system. The new system of origin rules, referred to in Article 4, Annex B and Protocol 3 of the free-trade agreements, came into force on 1 April 1973 and a new text of Annex B on 1 January 1978. The new text involves no changes of substance and merely incorporates amendments made since 1 April 1973.

Under both the Stockholm Convention and the free-trade agreements, the basic rule is that, if finished products are to benefit from the free-trade rules of the treaties, duties on imported materials used shall not be refunded.

From 1 January 1988 rules for particular products were amended to take account of the introduction at the same date of the 'harmonized system' (the new nomenclature for the classification of traded goods).

Since 1973 the origin rules have become so complicated that they constitute a burden for the customs administrations and the exporters. Many exporters prefer to pay the third-country tariffs on their export (to other EFTA countries) instead of applying the time-consuming and more expensive origin rule procedures.

5. *Administrative and technical barriers to trade*

Administrative obstacles (e.g., charges of statistical services, as a contribution to port improvement, as payment for customs clearance) frequently hamper external trade as much as quantitative restrictions. The understanding in EFTA is that any such charge should not be permitted if it is at a level which accords effective protection to like domestic products, or acts so as to restrict imports or exceeds the amount of the approximate cost of services rendered.

Before the end of 1962 solutions had been found for several procedures which had been the subject of complaints. In 1965 Sweden drew attention to administrative regulations in other Scandinavian countries which obstructed trade. To some of these (e.g., Denmark's prohibition of the hawking of durable consumer goods) no EFTA objections were raised, provided foreigners were treated on the same footing as residents of the country concerned.

In July 1966 the Committee of Trade Experts reached the conclusion that origin marking should be compulsory only in exceptional circumstances. In April 1969 and again in December 1971 the Council urged member countries where such regulations were still in force to accelerate their removal. In October 1975, for example, the Committee of Trade Experts concluded that consumer protection in general was not sufficient justification for the introduction (by Finland) of compulsory origin-making regulations.

As early as 1964, the EFTA Councils agreed on a procedure whereby the participating governments were invited to notify each other through the EFTA Secretariat, in advance, of their intention to introduce new or amended statutory regulations enforcing technical requirements that could be of importance to trade within the Association. The purpose was to give the other governments time to consider the implication for their traders of the new regulations and to put forward their comments, in the hope that they could be taken into account in the text of the regulation finally published. In 1975 it was decided to improve the procedure and to widen its application.

In June 1988 a new procedure went into force. The product coverage is broader (agricultural and marine products are included), there is a commenting period of three months and a standstill obligation of six months.

Given the multiplicity of product standards in Europe and of regulations which may have a hampering effect on trade, the achievement of international harmonization is inevitably a long-term effort. However, arrangements short of harmonization can be made to overcome the trade barriers caused by the obligation to have products tested to differing standards in various countries. Such arrangements provide for the mutual recognition of tests and inspections.

The principle has been accepted in the EC since 1969 and in EFTA since 1988. Previously EFTA sponsored mutual recognition arrangements.

However, the Schemes and Conventions which have emerged from this work are not integral to EFTA itself, nor do they depend on the Stockholm Convention. Each is an international arrangement with an independent existence of its own, open to all countries which have comparable testing facilities. The link with EFTA is that the Association provides secretariat services for the arrangements. In fact, the wider the membership of arrangements for mutual recognition of tests and inspections, the better they serve the trading interests of all concerned.

Of these arrangements, seven take the form of international schemes which are intended to facilitate trade by making possible the reciprocal recognition of national tests and inspections of particular types of product. The participation in the schemes in some cases include a number of non-EFTA countries, some of which are members of the European Community.

The participants in the scheme relating to ships' equipment (introduced 1 January 1971) are the authorities responsible for approving any kind of ships' equipment in ten countries: Denmark, Finland, the Federal Republic of Germany, Iceland, the Netherlands, Norway, Portugal, Sweden, the United Kingdom and Yugoslavia.

Similar schemes exist, for example, for pressure vessels (1971), agricultural machines and tractors (1972), heating equipment using liquid fuel, lifting appliances (1978), gas appliances (1979).

In 1987 EFTA and EC signed two conventions in respect of a single administrative document and common transit procedure. By the end of 1988 the EFTA countries and the Community members had signed the Lugano Convention on the jurisdiction and enforcement of civil and commercial judgments.

B. *Establishment, liberalization of services and capital*

1. *Provisions*

The member states realize that restrictions on the establishment and operation of enterprises for the production of or trade in goods of EFTA origin must not "frustrate the benefits" of trade liberalization (Article 16,*1*). No elaboration of this general principle is contained in the Convention, though the Council must, for instance, consider before 31 December 1964 whether supplementary provisions are necessary (Article 16,*4*).

The EFTA countries are of the opinion that the obligations contracted by them in other international organizations in respect of the liberalization of services and capital are sufficient. If appropriate, additional measures may be taken (Article 29).

As regards invisible transactions and transfers, the EFTA countries undertook to treat Finland no less favourably than other member states, which, unlike Finland, at the time of the Association Agreement, were affiliated to the OECD and could therefore invoke the provisions of the relevant liberalization codes. Subject to a reservation concerning certain transactions (which are comprised in Annex III), Finland agreed to apply *vis-à-vis* EFTA countries no less favourable provisions than those which the member states were applying in the case of Finland at 1 May 1960 (Article 5 of the Finland-EFTA Agreement).

2. *Operation*

For the purpose of the review to be carried out under the terms of the Convention before the end of 1964, a working party on establishment met for the first time in January 1964. In its report, which was completed a year later, it leaves out of account, pursuant to Article 16, agricultural commodities, fish and other marine products and also services (e.g., in connection with transport, banking and insurance). In May 1966, on the basis of this report, the Council reached agreement on an interpretation of the provisions of Article 16 (the Bergen Agreement). Establishment by EFTA nationals in most branches of commerce must be treated on the same footing as establishment by nationals of the receiving country. As regards retail trade and handicrafts, however, some countries wished to maintain a certain measure of control and to examine each request closely. National treatment must also be accorded to "enterprises for production of goods which are of Area origin and of which a significant part is to be exported to other member states". Since this wording is somewhat vague, it was agreed that the relevant national provisions would be applied as broadly as possible. Top-ranking and other key personnel may also avail themselves of Article 16.

In 1968 the Council agreed that any less favourable treatment in practice as regards the establishment or operation of enterprises for commerce in or assembly of EFTA goods constituted "frustration" within the meaning of Article 16.

When Finland became an OECD member (in 1969), Article 5 of the Finland-EFTA Agreement was deleted.

The most important exceptions to the rule of immediate right to non-discrimination relate to the conditions for access to the capital market, investment in existing domestic enterprises and the ownership of national resources.

In a study completed in 1989 a working group of EFTA experts under-lines the benefits which may be expected from liberalizing capital movements and from financial integration.

C. *Approximation of market conditions*

EFTA does not aim explicitly at "approximation of market conditions". Its objective in this respect is "to secure that trade between member states takes place in conditions of fair competition" (Article 2,*b*). Of course the expres-sion "fair competition", is not a precise concept. According to an EFTA publication, the EFTA Convention "does not aim at harmonizing the condi-tions under which production takes place in member states, but only at abolishing distortion of competition brought about by protective measures, whatever form they take. It is the principle of non-discrimination which is the cornerstone in EFTA cooperation". EFTA sees Articles 16 (dealt with above), 13, 14, 15, and 17 (see below) as a group which it refers to as the "rules of competition". These rules, save those on dumping, do not apply to agricultural or fisheries products.

1. *Provisions*

a. *Economic and financial policy*

Member states recognize that the economic and financial policies of each of them have an effect on the economies of other EFTA countries. With the object of promoting the aims of the Association, views are exchanged at regular intervals on the various aspects of these policies. The Council may make recommendations to the member countries on such matters (Article 30).

b. *Tax policy*

Internal taxes and other charges on imported goods are subject to the same provisions as revenue duties (Article 6). The protectionist element in such taxes or charges must, however, be abolished earlier, namely before 1 January 1962 (Article 6,*3a*). If there is still any difference in treatment between domestic and imported goods, it has to be notified to the Council (Article 6,4).

c. Competition policy

1. Restrictive business practices

The following practices are deemed incompatible with the Convention in so far as they "frustrate the benefits expected from the removal or absence of duties and quantitative restrictions on trade between member states" (the "frustration clause", also to be found in Articles 13, 14 and 16):

a) agreements between enterprises, decisions by associations of enterprises and concerted practices aimed at or resulting in the prevention, restriction or distortion of competition within EFTA;
b) actions whereby one or more enterprises take unfair advantage of a dominant position within EFTA or a substantial part of it (Article 15,1).

Complaints concerning such practices are examined under Article 31 (see below) (Article 15,2). Before 31 December 1964 the Council must consider, in the light of experience, whether additional directives are called for (Article 15,3a).

2. Dumping

Anti-dumping action (extending to agricultural and fish and marine products) is permissible, with due regard to international obligations in this field (Article 17,1). The Convention also provides that goods which are exported to another member country may be returned to the country of exportation without being burdened by customs duties or quantitative restrictions (Article 17,2; the "boomerang clause"); producers have to contend with competition from their own products.

Since the dumping of non-EFTA goods in a member state may have an adverse influence on other EFTA countries' exports to that state, countries thus affected may request the government concerned to take anti-dumping measures (Article 17,3).

3. Government aids

Export aids which distort competition are prohibited (Article 13,1a). These include export bonuses, subsidies, remission of taxes or social security charges (in relation to exports), unduly low rates of interest in credit insurance and the delivery of raw materials by official agencies at prices below world prices (Annex C).

Any other type of assistance aimed principally at or resulting principally in neutralization of the liberalization measures introduced into intra-EFTA trade is likewise ruled out (Article 13,1b). As the Convention here refers to the "main" purpose or effect, numerous aids relating to the establishment of new industries and the combating of unemployment are not covered by this Article.

If any form of aid, while compatible with the provisions of Article 13, nevertheless thwarts the intention of the above-mentioned measures, the Council may, after applying the procedure laid down in Article 31,*1* (see below), authorize the member state adversely affected to take protective action (Article 13,*2*). The counterpart of Article 13 in respect of agricultural products is Article 24. The interests of other member countries must not be harmed by export subsidies which bring about an increase in exports of the products concerned in comparison with a recent representative period (Article 24,*1*). The Council is required to lay down before 1 January 1962 the procedure for gradually abolishing subsidies prejudicial to the interest of the member states (Article 24,*2*). Exemption of an exported product from internal duties is not regarded as a subsidy (Article 24,*3*).

Article 17,*1* and *3* makes express provision for measures against subsidized imports (including those of agricultural and fish and other marine products) to the extent that such action is consistent with international obligations.

4. *Public undertakings*
During the transition period member states have to bring about the progressive elimination by public undertakings of measures the effect of which is to give domestic producers protection which could be inconsistent with the Convention if achieved by duties, quotas or government aids. They also have to ensure that public undertakings do not discriminate on grounds of nationality in so far as each discrimination frustrates the benefits expected from the removal of tariffs and quotas on trade between the member states (Article 14,*1*). In addition, they have to ensure that no new practices of this kind are introduced (Article 14,*3*) either during or after the transition period.

2. *Operation*

a. *Economic and financial policy*

In the first years of the Association's life EFTA countries attached only minor importance to consultation on and coordination of economic and financial policies, even when EFTA trade was involved. Thus there was no prior consultation in the case of the introduction of Britain's 15 per cent import surcharge.

However, EFTA countries have on several occasions referred to the OECD's activity in this field. In so doing, they are prompted by the desire to avoid duplication. Even so, the criticism levelled at the unilateral measure taken by the United Kingdom on 26 October 1964 led to the creation of the Economic Committee, which met for the first time in July 1965.

Since then the Economic Committee, which consists of senior officials from the governments or the central banks, has met at least twice a year to review the economic and financial policies of the member states and their impact on their economies and the working of EFTA. The chairman reports on the meetings to the EFTA Council.

Development aid

After the events of April 1974 Portugal requested economic assistance: a longer period of protection for its industry, more outlets for its agriculture, technical and financial assistance. The first two aspects have already been dealt with. As regards financial aid, and EFTA Industrial Development Fund of 100 million dollars, was established on 7 April 1976. The contributions to be made available in five annual instalments are as follows: Sweden 30 per cent of the total; Switzerland 25.5 per cent; Austria 15 per cent; Norway 12 per cent; Finland 10.2 per cent; Portugal 6.1 per cent and Iceland 1 per cent. The Portuguese government undertook to guarantee the reimbursement of the contributions and the payment of interest. Reimbursement is to commence at the end of the eleventh year of operation and to be completed by the end of the twenty-fifth year. From 1 February 1983 contributions bear interest at the rate of 3 per cent per annum. In June 1988 the Council decided that the repayment should be postponed until 1998.

The Fund's objective was to provide finance for specific projects, particularly for the reconstruction or creation of small and medium-sized enterprises in both the public and the private sector. After Portugal's withdrawal from EFTA the EFTA Council decided to maintain the Fund into operation up to the year 2002 (the end of the twenty-five years originally foreseen).

Since the Fund first came into operation on 1 February 1977 up to 31 January 1989 it has granted loans totalling 42 billion escudos.

In 1967 EFTA initiated a privileged relationship with Yugoslavia. It was formalized in the Bergen declaration of 1983. In 1989 the EFTA ministers decided to establish an Industrial Development Fund for Yugoslavia with an initial capital equivalent of 100 million dollars in order to support reforms towards a market economy and to increase trade with the EFTA countries. Investments between 500.000 and 1 million dollars in specific regions and sectors creating job opportunities, will be encouraged. At least 25 per cent of the costs should be financed by the borrower and at least 33 per cent of the financing should come from other sources than the Fund.

b. *Tax Policy*

The measures taken in fulfilment of the obligation to remove the protective element in internal charges on imported goods before 1 January 1962 were examined by an *ad hoc* working party in March 1962. As this examination was not a full-scale review, the Council in 1966 instructed the Customs Committee to undertake such a review. This committee concluded that with few exceptions these charges were applied in accordance with the obligations of the Convention and that the few charges which contained protective elements were being adjusted. The exception cases were later brought into line.

Sweden submitted proposals for promoting competition by a certain harmonization of indirect taxes, but the idea did not appeal to any of the other EFTA countries. In May 1968 the Council asked the Secretariat to carry out an analysis of the impact on EFTA trade of changes in indirect taxation, such as the introduction of the value added tax in Sweden and later in Norway. Early in 1969 the conclusion was reached that this was not the case.

On the basis of a draft double taxation convention on income and capital adopted by the OECD Council, a working party set up in March 1964 was instructed to investigate whether a similar convention could be drawn up for EFTA. It reached the conclusion that a multilateral convention was feasible but that the degree of uniformity that could be achieved would be at most only insignificantly higher than that achieved in the existing system of bilateral conventions.

c. *Competition policy*

1. *Restrictive business practices*
Pursuant to the provisions that an inquiry into such practices had to be carried out by the end of 1964, a working group was duly set up and held its first meeting in April 1964. Its report, which was completed in June 1965, pointed out that the legislations of the member states are based on roughly the same principles. In a report of a second working party — accepted by the Council in September 1968 — a number of technical terms in Article 15 are clarified, partly on the basis of the corresponding provisions of the Rome Treaty. The Council has no power to compel firms to supply information, or to modify their practices, nor can it launch investigations on its own.

In October 1965 the EFTA countries agreed on a procedure for dealing with cases of apparent restrictive business practice. If a firm has drawn the attention of its authorities to such a practice in another state, the matter is taken up bilaterally (according to the consultation procedure of Article 31; see below). If there is agreement that the practice is incompatible with Article 15, the member states concerned take the appropriate measures. Reports on the case are circulated to the member states in order to promote the same interpretation of the Convention's provisions. If there is no agreement, the case can be discussed informally on a multilateral basis or brought formally to the Council (the complaints procedure).

A few cases have been dealt with according to this procedure. The bilateral contacts led to the removal of the practices concerned.

The cases concerned, for instance, a refusal by a manufacturer in one country to sell some special machinery, together with know-how, to a firm in another country because of an agreement between the manufacturer and some other firms; a system under which three companies gave a jointly-owned manufacturing subsidiary a proportion of the purchase price when they bought certain supplies — of the type which the subsidiary makes — from other suppliers; and a collective bonus given by an association of manufacturers to retailers on a scale related to their purchases of domestically-produced goods.

2. *Dumping*

The first case to have arisen was Portugal's complaint concerning the import of Austrian nitrogenous fertilizers. The matter was settled by mutual agreement.

In a study put in hand with the aim of determining whether measures were necessary to ensure the satisfactory operation of the provisions in Article 17 (including those relating to subsidized exports), a special working party found that this was not the case. The Council adopted its recommendation: notification and consultation between member states in the event of changes in legislation or the introduction of countervailing measures. In fact Article 17,*1* now refers to Article 6 of the GATT (Chapter 3). The "boomerang clause" (Article 17,*2*) has hardly been used in practice.

On 6 December 1975 Austria introduced reference prices for the import of tights made of synthetic fiber and imposed levies to compensate for the differences between the prices at the frontier and the minimum reference prices. The Committee of Trade Experts, however, observed that Austria had not carried out a detailed examination to establish that the prices of the imports were below the normal prices for the tights in the home market. This system was extended with some modifications until 31 October 1977.

3. *Government aids*

The problem of state aids came up for discussion in connection with the export rebate scheme introduced by the United Kingdom in October 1964, under which exporters were relieved from certain indirect taxes which enter into the cost of production of exported goods. In October 1965 EFTA decided that as from 31 December 1966 goods exported to EFTA would not be allowed to benefit from both EFTA tariff treatment and rebate of indirect taxes levied on auxiliary materials, capital equipment, services, etc., used in the process of production and marketing but not directly related to the goods produced. The British government has accordingly modified its export rebate scheme.

On the basis of a report by a group of experts set up to examine what new steps should be taken to ensure the satisfactory working of the provisions of Article 13, the Council of 3 July 1968 adopted a text setting out its interpretation of Article 13. This article does not "inhibit the freedom to introduce . . . aid measures as elements in the internal economic policies provided these measures neither fall under Annex C nor frustrate the benefits expected from the establishment of the Association". There is no obligation to harmonize state aids. Some examples are given of measures considered to be consistent with Article 13 (e.g., aids to rationalize the structure of industry, aids to industrial fairs, regional development aids) provided they do not give rise to discrimination.

Because negotiations were in progress at the time of Britain's first attempt to enter the EEC, the time limit for determining an arrangement for the gradual abolition of undesirable agricultural export subsidies was extended by eighteen months to 1 July 1963. It was not until 20 November 1964 that a decision to lay down rules on the subject was taken, and even then these rules were more in the nature of fresh exhortation to eliminate export subsidies.

A notification system was never applied. In November 1987 the Council introduced an obligation on member countries to notify each other of new or revised measures of government aid. The following categories have to be distinguished: grant, loans, guarantees, equity, export credits and guarantees, and tax concessions. In 1988 the EFTA Council and the EC Commission reached agreement that the notification required on each side should be exchanged between the EFTA secretariat and the EC Commission.

4. *Public undertakings*

On 10 May 1963, when the final date for the abolition of industrial tariffs was advanced to 31 December 1966, the final date for the abolition of undesirable practices by public undertakings was advanced to the same date.

In a first review by groups of experts of the implications and working of the provisions of Article 14 on public undertakings, completed in 1966, agreement was reached — and endorsed by the Council — that public undertakings were obliged to give equivalent treatment to domestic goods and to other goods of EFTA origin and to award contracts on the basis of commercial considerations. It was also agreed that in their trading activities public undertakings were obliged not to adopt practices which would lead to protection or discrimination between member states. Agreement was also reached on the interpretation of a number of the key terms in Article 14.

When the Council endorsed these views the EFTA governments agreed also to exchange lists of public agencies and enterprises responsible for major procurement and to give directives to these agencies and enterprises to the effect that all member countries should be afforded the same opportunities and be treated on the same footing as national suppliers in tendering for contracts. A list of the major public agencies and enterprises was published in March 1968 (and updated subsequently), together with an account of the provisions and implications of Article 14.

Since 1989 EFTA publishes tender notices for central government purchasing contracts through the Tenders Electronic Daily (TED) data base. Interested firms can obtain information about EC and EFTA contracts covered by the GATT Code on public procurement.

D. *Consultations and complaints procedure*

1. *Provisions*

If a member state believes its interests are (or will be) harmed by another EFTA country within the framework of the Convention, it may, after fruitless efforts to secure a settlement, refer the matter to the Council (Article 31,*1*). The latter must forthwith, by majority vote, arrange for the question to be studied. Any information required has to be supplied by the member states (Article 31,*2*). The Council must also, after the study has been concluded, make appropriate recommendations (Article 31,*3*). If the latter are not complied with, the Council may, by majority decision, authorize the injured parties to enact counter-measures (Article 31,*4*). Such authorization may even be given before the inquiry has been concluded (Article 31,*5*).

2. *Operation*

Article 31 has rarely been applied. In October 1962 there was one complaint, but the matter was settled before the Council needed to take action. In September 1963 there was another case, relating to classification of a product in the Customs Cooperation Council Nomenclature (which formed the basis of the member states' customs tariffs). This was disposed of after an opinion had been obtained from the Brussels Nomenclature Committee of the Customs Cooperation Council (in Brussels) and accepted by the country concerned, which duly reinstated the former classification. Subsequent matters, with two exceptions (1966), were also settled without the topic being brought before the Council for a formal decision.

Other measures by some EFTA Governments which were notified to the Council were subject to less formal methods of examination. They related, for example, to the Portuguese iron and steel industry, the aluminum smelters in the United Kingdom, imports of quick-frozen fish fillets into the United Kingdom, Finnish imports of certain consumer goods, the Norwegian quantitative restrictions on the export of wood and general measures such as the United Kingdom, Iceland and Finnish import deposit schemes and the Danish and Portuguese import surcharges.

E. *Escape clauses*

1. *Provisions*

Apart from Article 12 (exceptions) and 19 (balance-of-payments difficulties) referred to above, escape clauses are found in Articles 18 and 20. Article 18 lays down that the EFTA Convention constitutes no obstacle of national security measures (e.g., trade in arms, ammunition and war materials). Article

20 relates to difficulties in particular sectors. According to this article (as amended on 3 December 1970), if unforeseen and serious difficulties arise or threaten to arise in a particular sector of industry or region, and the situation necessitates the enforcement of measures which derogate from the EFTA Convention or from EFTA decisions or agreements, the country concerned may apply such measures under the conditions laid down in a prior authorization by the Council. The Council takes a decision as soon as possible (Article 20,*1*), and, in order to avoid a rapid deterioration of the situation, upon request of the member state concerned within fifteen days (Article 20,*3*).

The measures must not be applied for more than eighteen months unless the Council, by majority vote (Article 20,*7*), decides on an extension (Article 20,*2*). All member states must be treated on an equal footing (Article 20,*6*).

The Council may at any time make recommendations designed to moderate damaging effects of the measures or to assist the member state to overcome its difficulties (Article 20,*4*). Preference must be given to measures which will allow the maintenance of the trade benefits of other member states (Article 20,*5*).

2. *Operation*

On several occasions Article 20 was invoked, e.g., in November 1967 by Austria in respect of its match industry. The other member countries, however, considered that Article 20 could not be applied, since the Austrian match industry was not held to be "a sector of industry". Liberalization of trade in matches was restored as from 1 January 1968.

In December 1973 Norway referred to this Article in order to introduce a licensing system for the export of saw, sawn and planed wood on the grounds of a serious shortage of supply, but the system was abolished on 8 March 1974.

Emergency measures were taken by Portugal and notified to the Council in May 1974. After examination by the Economic Committee and the Committee of Trade Experts, the Portuguese measures were substantially modified in July 1974. Henceforward they are limited to the surveillance of certain imports and exports, with the exclusive aim of detecting attempts to transfer capital abroad illegally by means of incorrect invoicing. Iceland introduced a deposit scheme for imports of furniture as from 8 January 1979 till the end of 1980 in order to protect its industry.

APPRAISAL

EFTA owes its origin to the establishment of the EEC. Initially, it was to be viewed as a negotiating instrument in discussions with the latter, or as A.C.L. Day puts it: ". . . an interim arrangement pending some more satisfactory settlement with the EEC". After the accession of the United Kingdom and Denmark and later Portugal, which brought the population of the Association back to only 32 million (see Table 27), EFTA continued to develop as a successful free-trade area in industrial goods.

Table 27. Selected economic data of the EFTA countries, 1989.

	Austria	Finland	Iceland	Norway	Sweden	Switzerland
Population						
In millions	7.6	5.0	0.2	4.2	8.4	6.8
Gross domestic product (at current prices and exchange rates)						
In billion dollars	126.7	114.7	5.2	93.1	189.3	174.7
Per capita (dollars)	16632	23116	20553	22020	22432	25829
Inflation rate	2.5	6.6	20.7	4.6	6.4	3.2
Unemployment (percentage labour force)	3.4	3.5	1.7	4.9	1.4	0.6
Exports of goods and services (per cent of GDP, at constant prices)	44.0	27.8	33.7	52.8	36.9	41.5
Exports of goods (per cent of GDP)	25.6	20.3	27.1	28.9	27.2	29.5

Source: EFTA.

Whereas initially intra-EFTA trade increased faster than EFTA's trade with the rest of the world this is no longer the case since 1973.

Specialization has been promoted, although as in the case of trade expansion, it is difficult to determine the extent to which other factors have been responsible. Since the creation of the Association the Austrian tyre industry has narrowed the range of its output, exporting more of the types produced and importing more of the other types. The winter sports industry's production has increased substantially. Some enterprises have availed themselves of other opportunities offered by the larger market: Swedish firms, for example, have built factories in Portugal in order to export the latter's output to Scandinavia.

Most of the mergers and acquisitions have taken place in the Scandinavian countries — where, indeed, the trend towards greater economic cooperation had already found expression before the establishment of EFTA.

EFTA made it possible for the present member countries to enter into a new relationship with the enlarged European Communities through the free-trade agreements.

The functioning of the Association reveals a certain measure of realism — e.g., it is not obsessed with the idea of harmonizing everything in sight. As early as the period of its establishment, the member states of EFTA considered that enough was being done in the field of the free movement of services and capital by other institutions, such as OECD. Nor does the Association seek to focus its attention on every subject under the sun, as does the EC. This is borne out by a comparison between the number of civil servants employed by both institutions.

The functioning of EFTA may not be as spectacular, yet yields to nobody in terms of efficiency.

From 1960 to 1972 EFTA was "a sort of microcosm of Britain's vanished dream world, a planet surrounded by satellites" (U.W. Kitzinger). That Britain cared little about the reactions of its partners and regarded EFTA rather as a means of reinforcing its own negotiating position was evidenced by its decision on 26 October 1964 to introduce a 15 per cent surcharge on imports, including those from other EFTA countries. Some authors even urged Britain to "resist pressure for closer integration of EFTA, which can never be much better than a ramshackle make-shift" (A.C.L. Day). Indeed, EFTA is still a medley from both a geographic and an economic standpoint (cf. Table 27).

It is therefore not surprising that intra-EFTA trade is less developed than intra-EEC trade. Trade with the European Communities is for every country greater than intra-EFTA trade (Table 28). Austria's and Switzerland's trade is, indeed, mainly with the EEC (64 and 57 per cent respectively of their exports and 68 and 71 per cent respectively of their imports), and it is purely non-economic reasons that have caused them to stay out of the EEC.

Discussions about the European Economic Area (EEA; see Chapter 8) proved that EFTA countries have found the overwhelming part of Community rules acceptable. One of the EFTA reservations is that its member states want to maintain their autonomy vis-à-vis non-EEA countries. EFTA countries 'do not see the EEA as primarily a surveillance mechanism by which the EFTA countries enforce rules made by others'. They 'would find

Table 28. Percentage shares of EFTA and EC in EFTA countries total trade, 1989.

Country or region	EFTA		EC	
	Imports	Exports	Imports	Exports
Austria	7.1	10.7	67.9	63.8
Finland	18.8	20.0	44.3	42.8
Iceland	19.1	11.0	51.1	56.5
Norway	20.8	16.2	43.1	65.1
Sweden	17.0	19.0	54.9	53.2
Switzerland	7.3	6.6	70.8	56.6
Total EFTA	12.8	13.8	59.4	56.4

Source: EFTA.

membership with voting rights preferable to the "membership" without voting rights which the EEA is increasingly resembling' (P. Wijkman).

BIBLIOGRAPHY

A. *EFTA publications*

The European Free Trade Association (3rd ed., Geneva, 1987) and the *Update 1987—1989* (May 1990) give a good overall picture of the Convention's provisions and the organization's activities. The Association's *Annual reports* and the *EFTA Bulletin* may be usefully consulted.

See also *The Free Trade Agreements of the EFTA countries with the European Communities.* Occasional papers include N. Lundgren, *Government finance and foreign trade in the EFTA countries* (1986); P. Wijkman, *The effect of new free trade areas on EFTA* (1989); id., *Patterns of production and trade in Western Europe* (1990).

B. *Other publications*

F. V. Meyer, *The European Free Trade Association. An analysis of "The outer seven"* (New York, Praeger, 1960), and E. Benoit, *Europe at sixes and sevens. The Common Market, the Free Trade Association and the United States* (New York, Columbia University Press, 1961), Chapter 3, are useful works on the establishment of EFTA; V. Curzon, *The essentials of economic integration; lessons of EFTA experience* (London, Macmillan, 1974); R. Middleton, *Negotiating on non-tariff distortions of trade: the EFTA precedents* (London, Macmillan for Trade Policy Research Centre, 1975).

The extracts quoted are from U.W. Kitzinger, Britain and Europe: the multivalence of the British decision, in *European yearbook 1961* (The Hague 1962), p. 38; A.C.L. Day, EFTA and EEC — bridge-building on shifting sand, *British Industry*, 11 June 1965.

Nordic cooperation

A Nordic Council was set up in 1952, and various studies on the establishment of a Scandinavian customs union have been made since 1954. An agreement on Nordic cooperation was concluded in March 1962, and on 4 February 1970 a draft treaty to establish a customs union and to expand economic cooperation in many areas within an organization to be known as Nordek was agreed upon. In April 1970 Finland decided not to sign the treaty of economic union, probably owing to Soviet opposition. So far, no further negotiations have been instituted for the conclusion of an agreement between the remaining Nordic countries Sweden, Denmark and Norway, since Denmark became a member of the EEC. Since there is already free trade in goods (except agricultural products), a common labour market, similar commercial and social legislation, the economic arguments for and against a Scandinavian or Nordic common market are not very important. The problems remaining are mainly political.

Conclusion

In the years following World War II a large number of countries which had an interest in international trade being as free as possible proved to be ready to accept certain restrictions on their sovereign freedom of action. International trade became the "secteur privilégié" (J. P. Haesaert) as regards the international codification of rules and regulations, though the nations' willingness to band together was not wholly confined to trade in the strict sense but extended to the entire field of economic matters. This is presumably attributable to the fact that a "development in power is more easily brought about in organizations concerned with functional and economic activities than those that are concerned over the ultimate questions of peace and war" (E. Luard).

The number of international economic institutions consequently increased substantially during the postwar period. Some institution or other would be set up, and sooner or later its opposite number would put in an appearance (OEEC/CMEA, GATT/UNCTAD, EEC/EFTA, IBRD/ the regional development banks). Countless institutions are duplicating each other's work and coordination has not ever been envisaged (e.g., EAEC, the Nuclear Energy Agency of the OECD and the IAEA; on environment protection: EEC and OECD).

Efficient administration is the exception, waste the general rule. Some institutions are really no more than publishing houses (e.g., UNESCO, OECD). Parkinson's Law, alas, is amply demonstrated. Each institution invariably sets up a number of satellite agencies, mostly in order to improve opportunities for promotion for staff members (e.g., the European University Institute by the EEC, the International Institute for Educational Planning by the UNESCO). New departments are being established to "study" problems which have little or nothing to do with the aims of the institution concerned. Political considerations are a major factor in the way international economic institutions are operated. Staff appointments or promotions, for instance, are not necessarily decided on merit: there are national or regional quotas to be taken into account. Although staff members of international organizations are supposed to be loyal to these organizations "the international attitude of a United Nations official is directly related to the freedom of expression

371

which prevails in his country". This explains why the staff members of communist countries were in the first place representatives of their countries: "if, in taking their decisions, they gave precedence to the organization rather than to their country, they would in no time be accused of collaborating with the organization concerned against the interests of their country" (M. A. Bérard).

NEED FOR RATIONALIZATION AND ESCAPE CLAUSES

There is an obvious need for rationalization and for slowing down the proliferation of new institutions. Although the UNDP was supposed to finance and coordinate technical assistance, there are many other UN organs which supply a great deal of assistance while cooperation is found to be lacking. Development aid is another example of a field where amalgamation of institutions, or at least coordination between them, is necessary. But we should not entertain too many illusions on that score: after all, similar situations exist in many of the developed countries (with the multiplication of semi-governmental agencies) and the UN has not succeeded in putting its house in order either. As R. Blough has observed, "Throughout the history of the United Nations there has been substantial overlapping of functions among the various organs and agencies concerned with economic matters. Repeated efforts have been made with only limited success to reduce the duplication of studies and other activities toward the minimum that is inevitable and desirable because of differences in emphasis and viewpoint".

Moreover, the members of international organizations see to it that they themselves, rather than the institutions they have created, have the last word. What Jacob Viner said about some international charters in 1949 can now unfortunately be said about still more. "The preambles are magnificent examples of . . . wishful thinking. The rules which follow the preambles are for the most part ambiguous, elastic, or unimportant, or, if they are rigorous enough, are sapped of their coercive power by elaborate series of escape clauses . . ." And this is one of the reasons, as was pointed out in the Preface, why this book is confined to giving an account of only a few worldwide institutions.

Although the members of these institutions have undertaken to fulfil a considerable number of obligations — in respect of financing (e.g., in IBRD, IDA, IFC), exchange parities (IMF), tariffs (GATT), quantitative restrictions (IMF), elimination of discrimination (IMF, GATT) and subsidies (GATT) — the significance of their commitments is indeed emasculated by all manner of escape clauses. One relevant factor is that the organizations in question are not of the supranational type; another is that the countries involved have differing economic and social structures. The larger the number of participating countries, the vaguer on the whole their obligations and the greater the scope for evading them. The less-developed countries are anxious not to have their economic expansion hampered by international obligations. In order to stimulate their industrialization, they want to be able to rely on protectionism and discrimination. The different treatment accorded the industrialized and the less-developed countries is now the general rule in most international institutions.

VOTING POWER AND ECONOMIC ORDER

It is understandable that big and medium-sized countries, both in the United Nations and in its specialized agencies, cannot appreciate a situation whereby "countries representing less than 10 per cent of the population of the total membership and less than five per cent of the budget can make decisions by a two-thirds majority" (R. N. Gardner). It can therefore come as no surprise that UN-resolutions are not taken seriously and that important decisions are taken by the Group of Ten (instead of the IMF) and even by a Group of Five within the Ten (cf. Rambouillet November 1975). More realism in voting matters is required.

A great deal of support for international dirigiste measures has been received from international civil servants, who, like any type of civil servant, are concerned with extending their powers. Hence the enthusiasm they display in defending international commodity agreements (ICA). In this respect, A. R. Waters has rightly remarked "how permanent ... the Permanent Secretariats of ICA's (are), once they have been established. The tea council stood for a decade after its *raison d'être* had disappeared, and the magnificent building of the International Coffee Organization, beside the Thames in London, is still a bustle of activity despite the collapse of the ICA which created it in the first place".

"The strongest support for the NIEO (new international economic order) originates with the international bureaucracies of the United Nations ... staffed predominantly with people from developing nations who ... enjoy incomes ... many times above those they could earn in their native countries."

Since they mostly are writing reports for other UN agencies in order to keep "going a dialogue among countries of the world on a wide range of topics" they push the "new order" which "would provide them with increased power and status and ... lead to an expansion of bureaucracy, ... to greater demand and income for their services" (H. G. Grubel).

Nevertheless, we should not forget that more progress has been made in the field of international economic cooperation since World War II than ever before.

It is no wonder, however, that closer cooperation has been sought between countries with similar economic structures, nor that more attention has been focused on the need for coordinated economic policy. This is what has happened in Western Europe where Benelux set the example. That integration is no easy process can be seen from the EEC crisis of 1967, during which the rules of the game itself were flagrantly broken.

But, despite all this, there is no cause for pessimism. Slow progress, even if it is interrupted by periods of standstill or by retrograde steps, is better than no progress at all. Before there can be coordination of economic policies, there must be a change of heart, an awareness of the community of interests, and that will take at least a generation to come about.

The extracts quoted are from J. P. Haesaert, *Préalables de droit international public* (Brussels, s.n., 1950); E. Luard, Conclusions, in *The evolution of international organizations* (ed. E. Luard, New York, Praeger, 1966); M. A. Bérard, L'Onusien, cet homme du 3e type, *Le Figaro*, 27 April 1978; R. Blough, *International business, environment and adaptation* (New York, McGraw-Hill, 1966); J. Viner, *International economics* (Glencoe, Ill., The Free Press, 1951); R. N. Gardner, The hard road to world order, *Foreign Affairs*, April 1974; A. R. Waters, The economic reason for international commodity agreements, *Kyklos*, 1974, Fasc. 4; H. G. Grubel, The case against the New International Economic Order, *Weltwirtschaftliches Archiv*, Band 113, 1977, Heft 2.

List of Articles

BENELUX

Articles of the Treaty

Article	1	213, 219
	2	219, 220
	2,1	218
	2,2	219
	3,1	214
	3,2	214
	3,3	214
	4	218, 219
	5	216
	6	213
	7	214, 219
	8	220
	8,1	220
	8,2	220
	9	215, 225
	10	215
	11,1	225
	11,2	225
	12	223
	13	223
	14,1	226
	14,2	226
	16	212
	17,1	212
	18	212
	19	212
	28	212
	29	212
	33	212
	34	212
	40	212
	41	213
	42	213
	50	213
	52,1	213
	54	213
	55	219
	56	219
	57	219
	58	219
	59	219
	62	214
	63	214
	64	222
	65	221
	66,1	221
	66,2	221
	68	223
	69	223
	70	224
	71	223
	72	225
	75	225
	76,1	225
	77	223
	78,1	225
	79	224
	81,1	225
	85	216
	86,1	223
	90	220

Articles of the Transitional Convention (TC)

Article	3,6	215
	3,7	215
	4	214
	9	214
	10	214
	11	214, 215
	12	214
	13	214
	14	214
	15	214
	16	214
	17	214
	18	214
	19	214
	20	221
	21	214
	22,1	221
	23	214, 215
	26	225
	30,1	218
	32	224
	34	216
	35	217
	36	226
	37	226
	67	221
Schedule	A	214
Schedule	B	214

Articles of the implementing Protocol

Article	9,1	217
	9,2	217
	9,5	217
	11,1	220
	11,2	220
	11,3	220

THE EUROPEAN COAL AND STEEL COMMUNITY

THE EUROPEAN ECONOMIC COMMUNITY

THE EUROPEAN FREE TRADE ASSOCIATION

Index of Names

387

Index of Subjects